Herbert Eugene Bolton

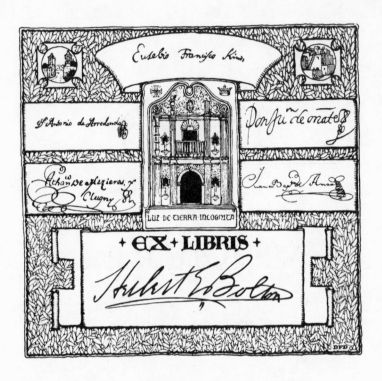

Bolton's bookplate was the product of his own design and artistry. In reply to a letter of inquiry from Elise Mannel, June 10, 1939, he described the plate in detail: "The figure in the upper left-hand corner is a representation of the old Spanish gate at St. Augustine, Florida, where Arredondo lived and worked. The figure in the upper right-hand corner represents one of the pueblos of New Mexico, which province was founded by Oñate. The facade in the middle of the plate is taken from one of the churches of Mexico City. . . . The five signatures are facsimiles of the signatures of historical characters about whom I have written [Kino, Arredondo, Athanase de Mézières, Anza, and Oñate]. The legend *Lux de Tierra Incognita* [Light on an Unknown Land] is the title of a book by Juan Bautista de Manje which I have translated."

Herbert Eugene Bolton

The Historian and the Man

1870–1953

John Francis Bannon

The University of Arizona Press

Tucson, Arizona

About the Author . . .

JOHN FRANCIS BANNON, S.J., has dedicated much of the past half
century to the study of colonial North and Latin America, in particular, the history of the Spanish Southwest. Since the middle
1960s he has been studying the life and works of Spanish borderlands historian Herbert Eugene Bolton with whom he first became
acquainted as a graduate student at the University of California,
Berkeley. He earned a Ph.D. under Bolton in 1939. He has edited
a volume of Bolton's works and is himself author of *The Spanish
Borderlands Frontier.* He was professor of history at Saint Louis
University from 1939 until his retirement in 1973. He is past president of the Western History Association and during the 1950s gave
more than 100 thirty-minute American history programs in four
different educational and commercial television series.

THE UNIVERSITY OF ARIZONA PRESS

Copyright © 1978
The Arizona Board of Regents
All Rights Reserved
Manufactured in the U.S.A.

Library of Congress Cataloging in Publication Data

Bannon, John Francis, 1905–
     Herbert Eugene Bolton: the historian and the man,
1870–1953.

     Bibliography: p.
     Includes index.
     1. Bolton, Herbert Eugene, 1870–1953.
     2. Historians — United States — Biography.
E175.B65B36   978'.007'2024 [B]   77-20951
ISBN 0-8165-0557-8
ISBN 0-8165-0644-2 pbk.

All the photographs which appear in this book are from the Bolton
Family Collection with the exception of the photograph of Fred-
erick Bolton used by courtesy of the Bancroft Library, Berkeley,
California.

Contents

Illustrations

Foreword

Herbert Eugene Bolton was a gigantic figure among American scholars. Explorer of archives and trails, cartographer, ethnographer, director of a great research library, teacher extraordinary, author of historical classics — he was the most innovative and versatile historian of America.

Early in his career he achieved fame by publication of the *Guide to Materials for the History of the United States in the Principal Archives of Mexico*. Although special attention was given to the Spanish Borderlands, the work was much broader than the title indicated and after sixty-eight years still remains the best volume available on Mexican archives as a whole. For many historians that monumental archival research project would have been a life's work. For Bolton it was just the beginning.

Throughout his career, Bolton's productive scholarship was tremendous. From his first visit to Mexican archives until his retirement from teaching, his thoroughly researched publications appeared each year for thirty-six years. Two great works were produced after retirement. Bolton's scholarly achievements were respected and highly rated by his distinguished contemporaries. Geographer Carl O. Sauer praised him for his work in cartography and historical geography. Ethnologist Frederick Webb Hodge and anthropologist A. L. Kroeber credited Bolton with making fundamental contributions to their fields of scholarship. The force of Bolton's historical work was thus evaluated by literary critic Lawrence Clark Powell in describing *Anza's California Expeditions*: "Everything about it is classic, epic, legendary; the venture and its leader, the chroniclers, and lastly the historian who, a century and a half later, discovered, translated and published the records of this great achievement." Historian Samuel Eliot Morison observed that Bolton's writing had emotional as well as intellectual appeal. He paid him the high compliment of ranking his literary style in the same category as that of Trevelyan.

Bolton's place in the hierarchy of great American historians is most clearly discerned by comparing his achievements with those of Frederick

Jackson Turner and Francis Parkman. Bolton admired both scholars and sought to emulate them by making a lasting contribution to American history. In many respects he surpassed them both. His monumental publications, based on archival research, were beyond the range of Turner. His broad knowledge of many subjects, extensive field work, and impressive teaching record differentiated him from Parkman. As a teacher of graduate students he was unequaled. With one hundred successful candidates for the Ph.D. degree and more than three hundred for the M.A., his influence on the teaching of history in universities, colleges, and high schools was greater than that of any other historian on record.

In teaching at the undergraduate level Bolton was uniquely successful. His famous course, "History of the Americas," was an innovation. It was based on his idea of broadening the teaching of American history by including in one survey course all the Western Hemisphere nations. This original concept so challenged the history profession that, twelve years after his death, a book was published with the title, *Do the Americas Have a Common History? A Critique of the Bolton Theory.* More than a dozen historians contributed, although no one seemed to understand that Bolton's primary motive had been simply to decrease provincialism among his students by showing that there was more to American history than the history of the United States. If Bolton had any theory, perhaps it was that history is universal and loses validity when strictly confined by narrow political boundaries and ideas. Over the years, students, more interested in substance than theories, jammed the thousand-seat auditorium where he lectured. They loved both Bolton and his "History of the Americas" course.

In 1917, Bolton delivered a remarkable research lecture at the University of California entitled "The Mission as a Frontier Institution in the Spanish American Colonies." At the time of presentation and publication only a historian of rare foresight could have predicted that the influence of the Spanish mission system would be strongly felt in the United States a century and a half after Spain withdrew from North America. Yet few scholarly contributions have had more prophetic implications. As we reread the essay, we are made acutely aware of its relationship to our national emergency in dealing with vast numbers of immigrants from the region once known as New Spain.

Realistically, as well as figuratively, the millions of Mexicans now entering the United States are "children of the Spanish mission system." As Bolton explained, Spanish missionaries accomplished the tremendous task of unifying diverse Mexican Indian tribes by giving them the Spanish language, the Christian religion, and the rudiments of European civilization. Thus they laid the basis of modern Mexican nationality. Within a few years the Spanish-speaking population of the United States will become its largest minority. The "children of the Spanish mission system" have come to stay and are spreading across the nation with an increasing impact on its life and culture. Thus the significance of Bolton's essay increases in proportion to that rising tide of immigrants from the old mission areas south of the border.

"The Mission as a Frontier Institution in the Spanish American Colonies" by Bolton and "The Significance of the Frontier in American History" by Turner were landmark historical essays. Turner's theory created a veritable revolution in the writing of United States history, yet it was oriented toward the past. Bolton presented no theory, but the importance of his essay has grown with the passage of time. Present developments reveal his genius for recognizing what was vital and enduring in the stream of American history. His book, *The Spanish Borderlands*, likewise demonstrated this rare quality which set him apart from many historians. Turner's frontier has disappeared. Its influences have faded. By contrast, the Spanish borderlands, with their increasing millions of Spanish-speaking people, every year become a more permanent part of United States history.

Because of our many discussions during my twenty-eight years of association with Bolton, I was as much impressed by what he said as by what he wrote. His conversations were fact and idea laden and, sparked by a sense of humor, always interesting. Obvious was the wide range of Bolton's thinking and his profound knowledge of what was fundamentally important in history. In his research, he specialized in the colonial period, in the beginnings of significant movements. In our conversations, he demonstrated a remarkable understanding of modern trends and where they were leading. After the passage of more than a quarter century since his death, the accuracy of his historical judgment becomes more evident. In his writings, his vivid imagination was limited by strict adherence to thorough documentation. Yet it was there. He had a brilliant mind and, even in old age, could be described as an "idea man." Hundreds of students received their initial inspiration to engage in historical research from challenging ideas thrown out by Bolton in conversation or lecture.

Only a Bolton student could adequately describe those qualities which contributed to Bolton's greatness as teacher and historian. It is appropriate, therefore, that his biography should have been written by one of his most distinguished students. John Francis Bannon, in his widely used *History of the Americas* text in two volumes, has followed the Bolton tradition in his broad approach to the study of history. Furthermore, Bannon has demonstrated his thorough understanding of Bolton's major field of research in his magnificent works, *Bolton and the Spanish Borderlands* and *The Spanish Borderlands Frontier, 1513–1821*.

LAWRENCE KINNAIRD

Preface

The writing of biography is fascinating but can also be a dangerous business. This is particularly true, when the subject has been dead for just a short quarter-century. Contemporaries in age will hardly be around to pass judgment. But there were many others who knew the subject well — family, younger colleagues, former students, and acquaintances; these rightfully will demand the man whom they knew and admired. Others not that close will be looking for information on a man of whom they have heard much, with whose works they have become acquainted, whose name they have been taught to revere; they will be anxious to learn more about him, how he came to be what he was, and all sorts of other how's, why's, what's.

Herbert Eugene Bolton made the task of telling his story considerably easier by the very sizable file of papers which he left behind, especially the hundreds of letters which came to him from many sources, as well as copies of letters which he sent out over a span of forty-odd years, not infrequently preserved with the handwritten draft which went to his secretary for copying. He did not know that the several hundred letters which he sent to his brother Frederick over the years, beginning in 1885, would be preserved by the same Frederick and would be added to the Bolton Papers. These valuable bits, warm, intimate, frank, and revealing, have been a very special boon to the biographer — actually, they have made the early chapters of this book more an autobiography than a simple narration of data culled from less personal sources. First-rate raw materials certainly were not lacking.

The great bulk of the Bolton Papers is in the Bancroft Library, University of California, Berkeley. These papers, with permission of the Bancroft, have provided the backbone of this study. Initially George P. Hammond, then director, opened the Bolton Papers to this writer and for several years reserved them for his exclusive use. In succeeding years, Director

James D. Harte was most generous in approving continued and unrestricted access thereto. To both, many thanks. The Bancroft staff through the years, especially Vivian Fisher and John Barr Tompkins, were regularly more than simply properly cooperative. Chester Kielman and the staff of the Eugene C. Barker History Center, University of Texas, Austin, were helpful. A word of thanks is in order to others, too many to name, who gave permission to quote from letters to Bolton found in his in-coming file; these pieces have added much flavor to this study. Through the preparation years a number of Bolton's former students responded to the appeal for "Memories of HEB;" to them sincere thanks for taking the time, and the same to others who passed on "Memories" orally. Noted with gratitude is the fact that the Social Science Research Council made summer grants, in 1966 and 1967, to help get this project off the ground.

Warm appreciation to Bolton's surviving daughters and their brother for sharing recollections of their father, and particularly to Jane Bolton Adams for furnishing a cross-section of photos from the family collection. A very special word of gratitude goes to Lawrence Kinnaird, possibly closest to the master of all Bolton's students, for the Foreword and for constant encouragement; he and his wife, Lucia, painstakingly read the next-to-last draft and offered important suggestions and insights. Not to be overlooked in this thank-you action is the University of Arizona Press for effecting publication of this book, and to its editor assigned thereto, Pat Shelton.

One final note. The original manuscript was much fuller and longer than the story here presented. As happens so frequently, author and editor pruning was necessary. The editor has kept the author judicious in choice of data to be included, has prevented him from being boringly repetitious, and has helped him to maintain sound reader perspective, which in his enthusiasm over the wealth of accumulated detail tended to be overlooked. As a result not a few of the possibly well-remembered bits of Bolton lore, events, anecdotes, and the like, interesting but not truly essential, have, so to speak, been left on the cutting-room floor. The Chronology device may preserve some of these seemingly undiscovered or not recorded aspects of Bolton's life. What I have attempted to present here is the uncluttered picture of the great man whom I knew, admired, and by whom I was inspired. Him I share with you, the reader — may he and his charisma thus be perpetuated.

J.F.B.

Chronology of Bolton's Life

1870   Born July 20.

1873   Boltons move to Nebraska; return to Wisconsin before the year is out.

1885   Death of father; begins high school.

1889   Graduates, Tomah High School; rural schoolmaster, York, Wis.

1890   Enrolls, Milwaukee State Normal.

1892   Receives State teacher's certificate, Milwaukee State Normal; principal at Fairchild, Wis.

1893   Enrolls, University of Wisconsin.

1895   Awarded Bachelor of Letters degree, University of Wisconsin; marries Gertrude Janes; principal, Kaukauna, Wis.

1896   Returns to University of Wisconsin, graduate work.

1897   Enrolls, University of Pennsylvania.

1899   Receives Doctor of Philosophy degree; instructorship, Milwaukee State Normal.

1901   Teaching position, University of Texas, in medieval and European history.

1902   First summer's research in archives of Mexico; first articles published.

1903   Second summer's research in archives of Mexico.

1904   First book published — *With the Makers of Texas*.

1905   Third summer's research in archives of Mexico.

1906   Contracts to prepare *Guide to Materials for the History of the United States in the Principal Archives of Mexico;* fourth summer's research in archives of Mexico.

1907   Spends year's leave in Mexico preparing *Guide to the Mexican Archives* (June 1907 to September 1908).

1908   Contracts with Arthur H. Clark for Anthanase de Mézières and Kino translations, and "Documentary Sources of American History in the Spanish and Mexican Archives" series; accepts position in Department of History, Stanford University for 1909.

1909   Elected honorary Phi Beta Kappa (Texas); August: to Stanford University.

1910   Accepts professorship, University of California, Berkeley; Christmastide field trip into Kino country.

1911   August: Tenure at Berkeley begins; Spaniards in America proposal to University of California President Benjamin Ide Wheeler.

1912   Proposal for documents series to Edward L. Doheny; helps bring about expansion of Texas State Historical Society *Quarterly* to *Southwestern Historical Quarterly*.

1913   Birth of first son, seventh and last child.

1914   Directs first Ph.D. dissertation, for Thomas Maitland Marshall; publication of *Guide to Materials for the History of the United States in the Principal Archives of Mexico* and *Anthanase de Mézières*.

1915   Participates in Panama Pacific International Exposition; negotiates with Macmillan for American history text; publication of *Texas in the Middle Eighteenth Century*.

1916   Negotiates with Denoyer-Geppert for publication of history maps; curator of Bancroft Library; publication of *Spanish Exploration in the Southwest*.

1917   March: Gives Faculty Research Lecture, "The Mission as a Frontier Institution"; acting chairman of the Department of History; elected to the Council of the American Historical Association.

1919   Assumes full chairmanship of Department of History, University of California; inauguration of History 8 (History of the Americas) undergraduate class; publication of *Kino's Historical Memoir of Pimería Alta* volumes.

1920   Appointed director of Bancroft Library; gives Lowell Institute lecture series, Boston; publication of *The Colonization of North America*.

1921   Publication of *The Spanish Borderlands*.

1922   Contracts to coauthor *California's Story;* summer field trip through New Mexico and Arizona; early contacts with the National Park Service (NPS); hospitalized with an infected tooth.

1923   Field trip through Georgia and Florida in preparation for publication of Arredondo document; Bolton's Scenic Avenue home leveled in Berkeley fire, September 17; Sidney Ehrman looms as his "angel."

1924 Offered presidency of University of Texas.

1925 Founder's Day address at Brigham Young University, "The Mormons in the Opening of the West"; Christmastide field trip on Anza trail; publication of *Arredondo's Historical Proof of Spain's Title to Georgia.*

1926 Field trip on Escalante trail; made Knight Commander of the Order of Isabela la Católica; publication of Palóu *Memoirs of New California.*

1927 Summer field trip in Utah and Arizona; Christmastide field trip to cover "Camino del Diablo" stretch of Anza trail; publication of *Fray Juan Crespi, Missionary Explorer on the Pacific Coast 1769–1774.*

1928 Publication of *History of the Americas — A Syllabus.*

1929 Awarded first honorary degree, St. Mary's College, Moraga; speaks at Trans-Mississippi West conference, University of Colorado, "Defensive Spanish Expansion and the Significance of the Borderlands."

1930 Field trip into Mexico along Western Slope of Sierra Madre Mountains; second honorary degree, St. Ignatius College (University of San Francisco); publication of five Anza volumes.

1931 Intersemester trip through Central America; vice president of the American Historical Association (AHA); Sidney Hellman Ehrman Chair of European History established, Department of History; named Sather Professor of History; summer trip to Europe (May to August) as Native Sons Traveling Fellow — visits Spain, Rome, the Tyrol, Bavaria, and Jesuit archive in Holland; Margaret Byrne Professorship of American History established, Department of History; made Knight of the Order of the Crown by the King of Italy; publication of *Outpost of Empire* and *Font's Complete Diary.*

1932 President, American Historical Association; speaks at Kino monument dedication, Tucson (published as *The Padre on Horseback*); summer field trip into Kino country; *Outpost of Empire* gold-medaled by Commonwealth Club of San Francisco; honorary degree, University of Toronto; presentation of first Festschrift, *New Spain and the Anglo-American West.*

1933 First trip by airplane, to New York, to preside as chairman of Committee on Latin American Research; appointed to Historic American Buildings Survey (HABS), National Park Service.

1934 Field trip into northern Mexico; speaks to American Catholic Historical Association, "The Black Robes of New Spain."

1935   Helps Bancroft Library obtain a valuable collection of Jesuit documents; publication of revised edition of *History of the Americas*.

1936   Helps inaugurate Jesuit Historical Institute of Loyola University; named to NPS Advisory Board; publication of *Rim of Christendom*.

1937   Initiates investigation of authenticity of Drake Plate; honorary degrees, Marquette University, Milwaukee, and University of New Mexico; *Rim of Christendom* gold-medaled by Commonwealth Club of San Francisco; advises NPS on restoration of Mission La Purísima and on Jefferson National Expansion Memorial project, St. Louis.

1938   Raises funds for purchase of Venegas manuscript; field trip on Escalante trail; appointed University of California's representative at Seventh Pan American Conference, Lima.

1939   January: Tours Latin America — made honorary member of faculty, University of Chile, Santiago; Pan American Day speaker, UCLA; speaker at dedication of a Garcés monument, Bakersfield, Calif.; speaker at National Education Association convention — "Cultural Cooperation with Latin America" — at Treasure Island, Calif.; addresses American Planning and Civic Association, Santa Fe; field trip on Escalante trail; verbal agreement with University of New Mexico to write biography of Coronado for Cuatro-Centennial Series; publication of *Wider Horizons of American History*.

1940   Field trip into Mexico on Coronado trail; Research Associate of Laboratory of Anthropology, Santa Fe; named to Heraldic Order of Cristóbal Colon by Dominican Republic; honorary degree, University of Pennsylvania; retires from University of California July 31; tours northern New Mexico and Texas Panhandle with NPS; field trip on Coronado trail, U.S. section.

1941   Speaking tour in Colorado, Wyoming, and Utah; speaking engagements in Ohio and western Pennsylvania; gives fourth Bernard Moses Memorial Lecture; editor-in-chief of Centennial History of California series; represents University of Wisconsin at Stanford's fiftieth anniversary; Escalante field trip down the San Juan River into the Colorado, with NPS.

1942   Rehired by University of California as lecturer in history and director of Bancroft Library; contracts with Denoyer-Geppert for Latin American maps; honorary degree, University of California; trip to Mexico City with NPS to plan Coronado International Monument on the border; appointed University of California's representative to receive and entertain Latin American visitors.

1943   Reworks Centennial History of California Series into "Chronicles of California" series; helps plan U.S. assistance to national library of Peru.

1944   March: Re-retired from University of California; helps NPS survey Big Bend country of Texas; second field trip to Texas Panhandle canyon country.

1945   Collaborator-at-large for NPS; honorary degree, University of Wisconsin; conducts seminar, University of Mexico, Mexico City, for Department of State; August 20: fiftieth wedding anniversary; presentation of second Festschrift, *Greater America*.

1946   Teaches summer field session of University of Texas Institute of Latin American Studies, Mexico City.

1947   Coordinator of university's efforts for California centennial; presents "The West Coast Corridor" before American Philosophical Society; submits Coronado biography manuscript to Whittlesey House, McGraw-Hill, instead of University of New Mexico — compromise effected; begins teaching at San Francisco State College.

1948   Consults with Paramount Studio, Hollywood, on California Centennial film; Coronado manuscript wins Whittlesey House Southwestern Fellowship Award.

1949   Fifth Serra Award of the Academy of American Franciscan History; publication of *Coronado, Knight of Pueblos and Plains*.

1950   *Coronado* awarded George Bancroft Prize.

1951   Publication of Escalante story, *Pageant in the Wilderness*.

1952   Suffers several strokes.

1953   Dies January 30.

1

Boyhood and
Early Education

RURAL AMERICA, which through the nineteenth century had developed the habit of furnishing the nation with a very sizable share of great men and women, in 1870 saw another son on his way to join that company. Herbert Eugene Bolton, the fourth child born to Edwin and Rosaline Bolton on a woodland Wisconsin farm "on the ridge" between Tomah and Wilton, was destined to become one of America's ranking historians. During the next eighty-odd years he would uncover a rich new field of historical research, and as a teacher and writer would come to be spoken of as the man who, in the words of Samuel Eliot Morison, produced "history that sings to the heart while it informs the understanding."

Edwin Latham Bolton was born in Leeds, England, on May 18, 1835. His father, John, from Manchester, was one of twelve brothers, all of whom were employed in the woolen industry. John Bolton, with his wife Harriet Latham and son Edwin, came to the United States in about 1850 and initially settled in New York. Whether John was able to find work there as a woolen finisher is not clear, but the John Boltons subsequently moved to Wisconsin, where in 1856 they bought a farm near Wilton. About that same time son Edwin, now twenty-one, purchased eighty acres of land also on the ridge, where a few years later he brought his young wife Rosaline Cady to begin their own family.[1]

Edwin Bolton had met Rosaline when he attended the Methodist church in Tomah where her father was pastor. James Cady and his wife Mary Dolbear and daughter had come to Wisconsin from Vermont, but the ancestry of the Cady family could be traced to the Mayflower family of Richard Warren. Sometime in the early 1860s Edwin and Rosaline were married by her father at New Richmond.

The first child of Edwin and Rosaline Bolton was stillborn. In 1863 son Wesley was born shortly before his father went off to war. In a Wisconsin regiment, because of his skill as a penman, Edwin Bolton was charged with much of the paperwork for his unit and rose to the rank of sergeant major. His campaigning took him to the sea with Sherman.

After Appomattox Edwin Bolton returned to his wife and son, and the farm. In the next year, which was 1866, Frederick was born, and two years later Alvin James. Herbert Eugene Bolton was born on July 20, 1870.

Edwin was an adequate farmer, but seemingly not enthusiastic. The Boltons enjoyed a measure of prosperity, however, because their eighty acres were fertile and well wooded. Cattle and horses could range the woods; the pigs had plentiful food in the abundant acorns and hickory nuts; potatoes, squash, and pumpkins flourished with little tending; in season there were berries, currants and grapes growing wild on their property. When Herbert was three years old, Edwin Bolton decided in the spring of that year to sell the farm and head for the grandly touted lands along the right-of-way of the recently completed Union Pacific Railroad. The Panic of 1873 was weighing heavily on the farmer folk of the Old Northwest and making them highly sensitive to the railroad's persuasive promises of utopia on the plentiful, rich, and cheap lands of Nebraska. They knew well that the first years would bring problems, but soon saw that these were of a kind not exactly anticipated. It was a shock to former woodlanders to be in a land without timber. Water had never been a worry, nor had fuel, but with summer came the grasshoppers in particular force that year. Later Frederick Bolton would describe it like this:

> When we reached Nebraska late in May, the prairie was beautiful, and on the cultivated home-steads the wheat was a few inches high. Early in June the grasshoppers came in such clouds as to obscure the sun. They ate all the grass and the wheat down to the roots; gnawed the wooden spokes of the wagon wheels, the wood parts of the farm plows, the wooden shovel handles, cleaned every bush of leaves, leaving a barren waste.

Before summer was out, recognizing the move to Nebraska had been a mistake, the Boltons were en route back to Wisconsin and more familiar and hospitable woodland surroundings. This time Edwin Bolton settled with his family on a piece of land near Tomah, the "La Grange farm." On this farm near Tomah in western Wisconsin, Herbert Bolton spent his boyhood years; growing up as a woodlander, early opportunities for Herbert would be great.

Edwin and Rosaline Bolton had eight children, five boys and three girls, who survived to maturity. Their hand in helping shape the destinies of their children was making itself evident all through the growing years. Their attitude toward education manifested itself many times. Although

Edwin Bolton's formal education had ended shortly after his arrival in America, at about fifteen years of age, his intellectual curiosity continued throughout his life as reflected again in the words of son Frederick:

> Although meagerly "schooled," I am sure that he was as well-founded as the average college graduate, and had much more accurate knowledge of reading, spelling, grammar, history, algebra, geometry, bookkeeping, world events than most college graduates at the time of their graduation. . . . By private study and contact with German neighbors he could read, understand and speak everyday German. He knew a great deal of law through reading and also was well in touch with applied sciences as related to agriculture. . . . He possessed the instincts and studious habits of the genuine scholar. Many times I have seen him take to the wood-lot, along with axe and saw, his algebra or his geometry, and when tired would sit on a log and study his mathematics.

Rosaline Bolton had grown up in an educated family and herself enjoyed the opportunity of several years at the Female Academy at Fox Lake, Wisconsin, which later became Downer College. Thus she fully shared her husband's devotion to and respect for education; she wanted the best opportunities possible for her children.

Edwin Bolton set patterns for his children in other ways. One way was his public-mindedness and interest in community affairs. He held many town offices, such as clerk and treasurer. He was long-time secretary of the County Fair Association, was named to various posts in the Grand Army of the Republic, and was licensed by the church to preach, and did so on occasion.

BECOMING A HARDY HUMAN

In addition to the guidance and support of his parents, life on a farm in those days could and did in the case of Herbert Bolton help build a hardy human. As the family grew in numbers, the four older boys found themselves sleeping in a lean-to built onto the farmhouse. It was not of sturdiest construction with the result that not infrequently on winter mornings the boys awoke to find a light covering of snow atop their blankets. Warmer weather was welcome because it allowed the young Boltons to save on shoe bills; it also made possible a more varied diet, supplemented with the bounty of fruits and berries waiting to be gathered. Hand-me-downs and homemade clothes were standard wardrobe. The boys often did chores for a neighbor woman who paid them in knitted socks and mittens. A Singer sewing machine made Rosaline Bolton's task of clothing her family a bit easier, and the Butterick patterns, new at the time, added somewhat more stylish lines to the girls' dresses.

Wesley and Alvin regularly helped their father with the heavier work of the farm. Herbert and Frederick teamed together and hired out to neighbors — planting, haying, harvesting, threshing. The two of them also cut much firewood, both for family use and for selling; they even developed a small-scale business of cutting railroad ties. In season berry-picking, especially cranberries, was another profit-making enterprise; for picking, raking, and drying the fruit the brothers netted two dollars a day. Marketing was generally done in nearby Tomah, or in Tunnel City, four miles farther north on the railway.

All was not work. Both Herbert and Frederick long remembered some of their neighbors, an encampment of Winnebago Indians. Frederick later wrote: "[We] played with Indian boys, got bows and arrows from them, rode Indian ponies, laughed at big Indians riding little ponies, while the squaws walked. . . . We knew Chief Artichoke and many others by name. . . . We saw them on the roads and in their camp. . . . We could hear the tom-toms on clear summer evenings." Herbert was thus getting his first acquaintance with some of those native Americans who later would be so prominent in his historical studies of farther frontiers.

To be sure, there was school. Until his boys were old enough to go to Tomah High School, Edwin Bolton drilled the elements of the three R's into his own and some of the neighbors' children. He had set up a little log schoolhouse on the La Grange farm. Herbert and Frederick were among his more eager pupils. The schoolmaster did not limit instruction to the simple basics; he opened young minds to history, telling them of "his" war, acquainting them with the heroes of the American Revolution and with great world figures, past and contemporary.

Sensing the special promise of Herbert and Frederick, Bolton provided his sons with some challenging reading. He subscribed to the weekly edition of the *Chicago Inter-Ocean* and to *The Youth's Journal,* which, to the boys was much more exciting, with its adventure stories running through several issues. The two of them thought nothing of tramping to the Tunnel City post office to pick up the latest number, which they regularly devoured long before they got back to the farm. The stories of the West were fascinating to them. In those days Herbert could hardly have guessed how many "westerns" he would write in the years ahead about the real, not simply fictitious, makers of the West, but a seed of interest had been planted.

Rosaline Bolton was expecting another child when on March 30, 1885, Edwin Bolton died of what was probably pneumonia. His premature death saddled her with heavy responsibilities. Wesley was twenty-two and overnight became head of the family. He immediately took charge of the farm, and Alvin was willing to work with him. Frederick, not quite twenty, had nearly completed high school, done in piecemeal fashion, and was teaching in a village school. He already envisioned teaching as a profession. Herbert was ready to begin high school at Tomah. He would have to begin to think more seriously about his future. The next four children ranged from ages eleven to three. Rosaline Bolton, with great hopes for her children, faced the future with confidence although with meager means to ensure the realization of her dreams.

TRAINING OF A RURAL SCHOOLMASTER

In the fall of 1885 Herbert Bolton began his formal education at Tomah High School about five miles from the family's La Grange farm. With Frederick schoolmaster at Glendale, Wisconsin, by this time, Herbert, who had a great love and admiration for his brother, missed him greatly, and sought to keep close by letter.[2]

In the first letter which has survived Herbert told of initial experiences at Tomah High School. On December 13, 1885, he assured his brother that he was getting along well in his studies, "all except English and I detest that." Since he was a bit older than his fellows, he had been asked to substitute one day for a sick teacher. This first turn in professorial role left him cold. "I do not think that I would like it first rate."

After the holiday break he confided on January 15, 1886:

> I like school very well, very much better than I had expected. I think it is just O.K. I don't like the Prof too much, but he is a good teacher, so that's all right. . . . Miss Rual is a splendid teacher, I think. I study Grammar, History, Book Keeping, and Algebra. I like Book Keeping very much but get it pretty well mixed up. . . . Don't have much time for mischief for I have to walk from Wesley's place.

A short time later he was able to eliminate the five-mile daily walk into Tomah and back by making arrangements to live with the family doctor in town. In return for room and board Herbert took care of the doctor's two horses and did odd jobs around the house. There was one drawback, however—his room was in the loft of the barn; in warmer weather it was fine, but when the season changed, was much too cold.

Before another winter came, the housing problem had been solved. The family of one of Herbert's classmates and good friends, Will Naylor, operated Tomah's hotel. Will persuaded his father to allow young Bolton to live at the hotel in return for the odd jobs he would perform. This living arrangement continued until Herbert's senior year, when his mother and the younger children left the farm and moved into Tomah.[3] A lasting friendship developed between Herbert and Will Naylor.

The summer before Herbert's senior year in high school he had a job as printer's devil on the weekly *Tomah Journal*. This first association with the publishing business continued through the next school year and netted him six dollars a week. In a letter September 9, 1888, Herbert wrote to Frederick: "I will send a V for you must be pretty short of cash at this time." Frederick, recognizing that, if he wanted to make teaching a career, he needed more than his mere high school background, had gone over to State Normal School at Milwaukee for the two-year teacher-training course. Herbert, well aware that Frederick would have to do this on the proverbial "shoestring," wanted to help. This started a most interesting and truly edifying pattern of fraternal cooperation. Soon Frederick, having finished at State Normal School and in a teaching position, would be assisting Herbert in his Normal School years, and so the pattern of mutual help would continue until each had earned his bachelor's degree. Herbert's senior year at Tomah High School opened toward the end of September 1888. He was one of a student body of seventy, and one of the five who were seniors — four boys and a girl. After school began, Herbert reported to his brother that there were a number of new girls enrolled, "three dandies" among them. One of the last group was Gertrude Janes from Tunnel City, a "commuter" who arrived each morning on the 8:20 A.M. train and returned home on the 4:20 P.M. In the same letter Herbert added: "I don't suppose that this interests you, but it does me, but not as much as it used to." What happened to provoke the following remark in his October 26 letter is not clear, but he confided to his brother: "I for one won't have anything to do with girls, bad medicine." This was evidently not to be taken too seriously since his letter of February 28, 1889, had quite a change in tone, with a bit of boyish braggadocio thrown in; he told his brother that he had been home with a bad throat and that within forty-eight hours no fewer than eight solicitous females had been by the Bolton residence to check on the state of his health.

In November of his senior year Herbert announced that he and two classmates had decided that they would all go to the University of Wisconsin. "However," he added, "Ed [Cassels] and I will have to work for a while." On January 22 he wrote: "The more I study Pedagogy, the more I like it and the more I think I would like to be a teacher. That is what I shall be for a time at least." As the year rolled along, he became more serious about this newly developed ambition and put in long hours diligently preparing for the April examinations required in order to earn the elementary teaching certificate. On May 1 Herbert proudly announced his scores: On a base of 10 — orthography, 10; geography, 8; physical geography, 9½; constitution, 8½; penmanship, 7½; arithmetic, 7½; mental, 9; grammar, 8½; physical, 8; algebra, 10; geometry, 7½; physics, 9.

As graduation day approached, excitement mounted and preparations for end-of-year festivities and entertainment were stepped up. Sometime in the spring Herbert "made the mistake" of writing the best oration which carried with it the responsibility of delivering it at June graduation exercises.

As a high school graduate Herbert immediately began to shop for summer work and, more importantly, for a teaching job for the coming year. He sent out a number of feelers while doing some farm work for Uncle Sam Griswold. Later in the summer he was taken on at a logging camp at Granite, Wisconsin, as bookkeeper, and enjoyed several weeks with his older brother, who was also working there for the summer. Herbert stayed on at the camp until a teaching job at York opened in mid-October.

York was hardly a metropolis, with its one general store, two blacksmith shops, one shoe shop, one gristmill, one "elegant skating pond," and about a dozen residences. Mail came in and went out twice a week, by stage.[4] The school was ungraded, enrolling tots and mustachioed men. "I do not have a large number of scholars, but they are, most of them, large." At York Herbert had ample time to keep up correspondence with Gertrude Janes, the young lady he had met in high school.

During the long evenings at York, Herbert Bolton began to think and plan for the years ahead at State Normal; like Frederick, he recognized that if he intended to stay in teaching, even for a time, he, too, needed further work and study. He asked his brother to send him books and examination questions so that he might use his leisure hours to prepare for the equivalency examinations, a number of which he hoped to pass and thus write off requirements without having to sit through classes.

By early February 1890 he had served the term of his contract at York and decided not to renew. He wanted time to study for the tests and felt that he could do so more effectively without distractions. He recognized that the ideal place for such study would be in Milwaukee, but at the moment this seemed a financial impossibility. Very much of his York income had gone to his mother and to Frederick for school expenses. Once back in Tomah, however, he must have found the means (it is likely that his brother Wesley supplied the help, at least in part), for on March 1 he was able to inform Frederick, by card, that he would join him the following Monday in Milwaukee.

The brothers were together from March until the end of the term in 1890.[5] Herbert passed the equivalency tests and was able to write off many requirements as he had hoped. These months were one of the last times the two brothers would be together for an extended period. After Frederick's graduation, in June 1890, and before he left to become principal at Fairchild in Wisconsin, the two worked together for another summer at a logging camp, each earning funds for the year ahead. Frederick wrote of those summer weeks:

> Herbert and I worked in a logging camp one summer when we were both in Milwaukee Normal School. . . . I was manager of the company store, book keeper, timekeeper, and U.S. postmaster for 10 weeks. H. worked at manual labor, loading lumber, etc. Evenings and Sundays he helped me. Then every day we ate at the company boarding house and we both slept in the store. Incidentally, we had many wrestling bouts with some of the big loggers who thought college boys were softies. We gained their respect for H. was such a superb all round athlete and I held my own in a wrestling match with the "champee." H. and I had a most wonderful summer together.[6]

After this work-vacation Herbert said good-bye to Frederick again and returned to State Normal for his second or senior year.*

The first letter from Milwaukee on September 4, 1890, was a newsy one.[7] Herbert reported that he and two companions had two fine rooms at the corner of 21st and Wells, "with board, heat, light and everything for $3.75 a week." A little later, "My studies for the present will be Math and Lang Teaching, Rhet, Music, Phys and Latin. Pedagogy will come when Gillen gets back." Toward the end of September Will Thomson from Tomah came to Normal, and he and Herbert moved around the corner to 2023 Wells; Herbert continued to take his meals at the old house (Robinson's) for $2.75 a week. The shift added up to a savings of $.50 a month, which he considered worthwhile—he paid $.87½ a week for lodging.

During 1890-91 correspondence shows that Frederick was working and sending money to Herbert to meet expenses at State Normal School. In December Herbert wrote that "The V [five dollars] was very opportune" and later in that month noted that he was in Frederick's debt to the extent of $80. On March 20, 1891, he tried to be poetic in his thanks:

---

*The letters of the next few years offer a quite unusual opportunity to see Herbert maturing and finding himself.

> To you from whom my banknotes flow
> Whom I can't repay the debt I owe
> I'll write a line of humble verse
> To thank you for replenished purse.
> The cash came yesterday to hand,
> When when when
> (What a language with no good rhyme
>   for *hand*).

At the end of the school year, when Herbert drew up a formal financial report, he set down that, besides the funds from Frederick, he had received $20 a month from Wesley, his oldest brother, that his mother had sent $20 in two installments, and that his brother Alvin had given him $10.

As end-of-year graduation loomed Frederick evidently wanted to do a bit of budget planning. He wrote to Herbert, who answered on April 14:

> You ask how much I shall need in the way of "cash-ualities" to pull through. Well, it will cost me a little over $40 for the necessities of life, eat and sleep, besides the trimmings for the "beginment." I do not want to go so very heavy on these. I suppose that I will have to get a suit of "close," but I think that I won't get quite as costly a suit as yours, if I can do anything otherwise. By Caesar: it costs lots and yet I am careful.

Later in that month he wrote in a humorous vein:

> I must stop now to go to work at "breeches carpentering." I have been meaner to my pants than Miss Romaine used to be to Arnold. Have "sat down on them" till they have become exhausted. I can get a very good suit for $28.50 at Browning, K[ing] & Co. and one not quite so good for $23 at another place. I think that it will be good policy to get the better one.

As May ran into June the tempo of things at State Normal stepped up. There was Senior Oration Day; Herbert reported that his presentation was well received and drew quite favorable comment from the faculty, and also that a judge in the audience praised him for his forceful delivery but hinted that he did not agree with all the views presented.

Commencement exercises were held on June 19, 1891, and Herbert Bolton was qualified and certified as a State teacher. As of that date he had no position for the coming year; however, with Frederick definitely leaving Fairchild and heading for the University of Wisconsin in the fall to complete his bachelor's degree, Herbert hoped that he might be able to fill that vacancy.

While working at a summer job in northwestern Iowa selling subscriptions for a Chicago-based mail-order house with the impressive name, The National Library Association, Herbert received word that he was being seriously considered for the post.[8] "Yes," he wrote his brother July 9, "I will *willingly* accept $70 per month from Fairchild. But *wring* for more." If Frederick tried a pressure tactic, he was unsuccessful. Herbert signed to go to Fairchild at $700 for the year 1891–92.

He arrived at his new post in early August and, as top man, had all responsibility for the school which included both the primary and secondary grades.[9] Once again he was in a position to help Frederick with school expenses.

Shortly after getting settled at Fairfield, Herbert began his long-range preparations for his years at the University of Wisconsin. He turned back to the study of German, devoting to it an hour and a half of "hard work" most every day. Here he began seriously to dream of his academic future and to let his thoughts range beyond a first college degree to graduate work and possibly even a doctorate, even though he was far from settled on what field. During this time his attitude toward choir practice is perhaps indicative of the life-style he was adopting. He wrote that it "takes more time than I can afford."

In March 1892 the school board at Fairchild signed him for the coming year and in May raised his salary for 1892–93 to $900. Meanwhile, he was looking for a summer teaching spot which might net him some extra money. Ultimately he signed to go to Black River Falls and added $100 to his bank account.

In the second year at Fairchild Herbert teamed with one of his new teachers and took quarters in the hotel, two rooms—one for study and the other for sleeping—at four dollars a week. They were soon reading William H. Prescott's three-volume *History of the Conquest of Mexico* "a few minutes each day," and Herbert's reading program went even farther afield to Egyptian history, but with much American history on the side. With a bit of money finally available he could begin to build his personal library, and he acquired some books on the history of "ancient peoples, Persia, Medea, Assyria, China, etc."

In November and December he set for himself a program of intensive reading, about 350 pages a week. He was still not sure of his future direction. "I think that I will work in mathematics and history a good deal, but cannot say." A bit later he was wondering if, perhaps, a civics-history combination might not be sounder preparation for law, for during this time he gave a lot of thought to the possibility of studying law.

On the first Tuesday of November 1892 he had his first opportunity to vote in a presidential election. As a Republican, his ballot was for Harrison, who failed in his bid for a second term. His November 11 letter found him philosophizing on politics. He was in a serious mood this November — on the twenty-second he wrote of love, women, and marriage: "I have come to the conclusion, that when I know what I want and need a woman as a partner in my life, I shall look around me, decide 'whom I shall devour,' and then fall in love with her." Like thoughts ran through several of early December letters; Frederick's announced plan to marry Olive Foster possibly triggered these musings. His December 4 letter had the curious observation that, when Frederick would get married, Herbert had better follow suit, for otherwise it would be like a "divorce," with the younger brother left without his constant listener and advisor.

The new year arrived, and Herbert, after Christmas vacation at Tomah, went back to Fairchild. As university days edged closer, his thoughts became more and more Madison-oriented. He read and studied and, most of all continued to ponder the future:

> I hope I shall tumble into something I like and make a success of it. I am getting very eager to get at something which will *lead me to something* soon. I have my mind quite strongly fixed on law, but I do not know enough to decide as yet. I suppose that to make anything at law I must study about six years. That means ten more years of waiting.

It was in this frame of mind that Herbert Bolton enrolled that fall as a junior at the University of Wisconsin, Madison, and set into play another, and a very important, phase of his life.

2

The Historian
in the Making

T HE TIMING OF Herbert Bolton's arrival at the University of Wisconsin in 1893 could hardly have been more propitious.[1] During the 1890s the faculty nearly tripled in size. Between 1887 and 1903 the student body enrollment grew from 700 to better than 2000. Most important for Herbert Bolton would be the fact that history was emerging as one of the more forward-looking of the departments in the College of Letters and Sciences.

As he had planned, Herbert enrolled that fall in a pre-law program. His range of classes included elementary law, Roman law, French, and English constitutional, the last course putting him in contact with Charles Homer Haskins. After his first weeks at the university he wrote to Frederick that Haskins "will be good and 'awfully tough.' "[2] Haskins had joined the faculty two years before. His interest was in European history, and it was in early contacts with Haskins that Herbert Bolton first began to recognize that history could be a fascinating field of study. By second semester at Wisconsin he had completely changed his mind about studying law and was manifesting interest in other directions as reflected in this letter to Frederick of February 19, 1894:

> As to what I shall do after graduation I cannot say as yet. I do *not* think that I shall study law; I think I shall teach, but *what* I do not know. I know so little about everything that I am not fit to decide what I am good for. I think that it will be history or mathematics, tho I should like economics very much. I am afraid that I haven't an "economics" head. Of course I shall have to follow high school work for a time at least, unless I should pull for a fellowship here, which I *might* do in history; however, there are better men whom I could not compete with in case they should try. I stand in with Haskins pretty well, and I am all right with Coffin. A Normal man don't have time to read much history in two years, besides doing his work in languages . . .

[12]

With the direction of his professional life just beginning to take shape, Herbert Bolton made another important decision during his second semester at Wisconsin — this one relating to his personal life. He had been writing to Gertrude Janes for some time; she then had taken a job in Madison which enabled them to see one another often. The following excerpt from a letter of January 28, 1894, indicates that they had arrived at a mutual understanding regarding marriage:

> I have sworn off studying on Sunday: Don't you think that a good move? I did this not through religious scruples, but because I think that I can do as much work in six days as by less concentration I will do in seven. Gertie and I swore together; or, I told her I would, if she would, and rather than stand in my way, she agreed. I see Gertie quite often, of course, but work keeps me from seeing her as often as I would like to — I have tried not to interfere with her working hours, and I know that my work has not been neglected at all because of her being here; on the contrary I think that I can work more earnestly because of her presence in the city; every time I see her I receive anew the strongest inspiration and incentive to work. I would like to achieve something for her sake, and be somebody of whom she can be proud, and her nearness keeps the motive more vividly before me. Fred, you do not know how happy I've been of late; I feel more like a man than I ever did before, and I believe that Gertie is happy too. I think we should have been, in a way, foolish if we had not come to an understanding when we did. Gertie has told her nearest friends how things stand between us, and no one seems displeased, and this is a great deal of satisfaction to me, both the fact that she is happy to tell her friends and the knowledge that there is no dissenting to make it unpleasant for Gertie. And of course the greatest source of happiness to me is Gertie herself and the knowledge that other's opinions would not affect her love for me or mine for her. I wish you were better acquainted with her and knew her worth better than I can tell you of it; and I shall look forward to the time when Olive and she may become acquainted.

As that second semester moved along, the perennial problem of finances became a worrisome and nagging constant in his life. He more than once debated the advisability of leaving at the end of the junior year, in order to take a job for a year or two. He did not particularly relish such a prospect, but neither did he like to live on the charity of those who could hardly afford to be charitable. He was able to get a summer school teaching position at Neillsville, Wisconsin, however, with seventy-four students enrolled. He had to carry six branches of instruction; his arithmetic class drove him more or less crazy, but there was a bright side in that he earned $120 for his efforts. Still, in the August 4 letter, he commented: "I do not think that summer schools are a very good thing for teacher or student, but they keep a man at work, if so he must." During the summer Gertrude was assured a teaching position for the next year at Farmington, Minnesota. Herbert was unhappy over the prospect of the separation, but both agreed that it was an economic necessity. As a result of the summer work he was able to return to the University of Wisconsin that fall for his senior year.

When school started Herbert got additional work as overseer of his fraternity house. (He had joined the Theta Delta Chi fraternity the year before.) That job gave him his room free, and reduced regular living expenses to $3.00 a week for his board. He pieced together a number of odd jobs to further supplement his needs. He did some teaching at the Boys' Academy and part-time work at the Capitol Library.

Leaning still harder in the direction of history as his major field of study, he enrolled that fall in two American history courses. One of these was under the direction of young Frederick Jackson Turner, who would eventually distinguish himself as one of America's great frontier historians.[3] Just a short time before Herbert Bolton arrived on the University of Wisconsin campus, Turner had returned from a meeting in Chicago where he had sounded the challenge for the study of the frontier in his subsequently famous paper, "The Significance of the Frontier in American History." It was at this very propitious time that Bolton came under Turner's influence, which would be one of the final determining factors in his ultimate choice of a career. Of him Herbert wrote at this time: "My work under Turner is fine. He and Haskins are ahead of all others I have had."

Herbert graduated from Wisconsin the following June with a bachelor of letters degree. He was just a few weeks short of his twenty-fifth birthday. Late June brought word to him in Tomah that he was assured a job teaching at Kaukauna for fall. He would for a second time be his brother's successor and would once again take a turn helping Frederick with expenses — this time for graduate school at the university. Roy was also enrolled there in undergraduate school, but Laura, oldest of the Bolton girls, had become an earner, and some of the financial pressure from home was relieved.

Meanwhile, in late summer, 1895, Herbert Bolton and Gertrude Janes were married in Tunnel City. The wedding took place "at the bride's parental residence in Tunnel City under a beautiful canopy of ferns," at six in the evening of August 20; Reverend W. O. Nuzum, of Tomah, performed the ceremony.

It was a gala affair according to the reports from the two local journals of Tunnel City and Tomah; the Tomah *Journal,* on which Herbert had worked during his high-school days, devoted a third of a column to reporting the event:

Promptly at six o'clock the wedding march, one from Lohengrin, played by Miss Una Richardson, announced the coming of the bride and groom, attended by Miss Lulu Janes as bridesmaid and Mr. Isaac Witter, of Grand Rapids, as groomsman. Their pathway was thickly strewn with ferns, golden-rod and marguerites.

After the ceremony the guests, about a hundred in number, partook of a most bountiful repast, served upon the spacious lawn. At the supper the company listened to numerous college and fraternity songs excellently rendered by members of the Theta Delta Chi fraternity of which Mr. Bolton is a member . . .

At 9:30 o'clock the happy couple, amid showers of congratulations and rice and attended by the Theta Delta Chi yell, departed for Milwaukee, where they will visit for a few days before going to Kaukauna where they will reside during the next year.

In Kaukauna Herbert Bolton once again joined company with a small local school system, this time as principal. In addition to his work at the school, he began to hold himself rigidly to a self-imposed regime of reading and study. During this year he appears to have acquired a great deal more self-confidence. He became much more definite about what he wanted to do. For example, he definitely opted for history as a major field. He aspired first for a master's degree from the University of Wisconsin, and his plans included finally a doctor's degree. The change was reflected also in his relationship to Frederick. A shifting of roles seems to have taken place with Herbert assuming a more dominant position. For the first time Frederick began to appeal to Herbert for advice concerning the direction of his life — should he proceed in philosophy-pedagogy or mathematics? From this time, Herbert is seen frequently giving advice, encouragement, and seeking to build Frederick's morale.

That year at Kaukauna Herbert started a master's degree program *in absentia* working through Victor Coffin, now chairman of the Department of History at the university. Periodically he was ready to send for an examination. In late February 1896 he could report that Turner had returned a very favorable verdict on his test covering the Jeffersonian period. In April he was ready for another examination, and again Turner's report came back indicating that his performance had been satisfactory. At some point during the year he saw his way clear to be able to spend the next year in residence, for in an August 9, 1896, letter to Frederick, who is about to sail for a graduate year in Europe, he comments:

I hope to leave for Madison about Sept. 20 to begin a steady year's profitable work, in which I wish to accomplish enough work to do one of two things, secure me a fellowship and 2nd year, or in case that fails, to enable me to get a Ph.D. the second year. If I should get a fellowship I'd not try to hurry so much, I think.[4]

THE GRADUATE YEAR AT WISCONSIN

Herbert's master's program at the university included courses under Turner, Haskins, and the economist Richard T. Ely. In December 10 and 13 letters to Frederick he revealed that he was still not definitely decided on a particular field of emphasis in history, but remarked that if the choice turned out to be European history reading German for Haskins' course would be invaluable practice.

Hesitation about what direction was right for him, however, is recorded one more time in a letter to Frederick January 16, 1897. Having just returned from the annual meeting of the Federation of Graduate Clubs at Baltimore where he was a Wisconsin delegate, he was feeling somewhat depressed about the accumulated backlog of obligations, which probably accounts in part for his introspective mood. "Do you, Frederick," he wrote, "ever get troubled with mental ennui, a feeling that you don't care to see a book, or that, perhaps, you aren't cut out for books anyway?" Even though he admitted he was depressed and was sure the feeling would pass, he wondered if he were pointing in the right direction after all:

> I would never be satisfied going into anything but college work . . . so I guess the best way is to keep in the right direction — if one makes slow progress, but faces the right way, he will surely accomplish something in time. And so with me; I may not get a professorship or even an instructorship, nor a degree right away, but I shall hang around some institution until out of pity or necessity something comes my way.

He concluded this letter with the note that he would need a fellowship in order to continue the next year.

Exciting news went out in the January 27 letter: the Herbert Boltons, as of the day before, were the proud parents of a baby girl — this was Frances. Herbert wrote the letter on the date noted, but did not remember to mail it until February 8. Frances had arrived a bit ahead of schedule; hence, the unexpected and added new duties, and not necessarily premature absentmindedness, could account for the delay.

By March Herbert Bolton was once again deeply involved in planning for the future, giving a great deal of thought to the possibility of winning a fellowship in order to continue in graduate school the next year. His first choice was Wisconsin, where he would be able to continue his graduate work under Turner's direction and, possibly, expand his abolition topic into a doctoral dissertation. It was Turner who had alerted him early to the fact that there were new fields to be opened for research and interpretation; he had given him something of a pioneering outlook.[5] Turner had

FAMILY
ALBUM

Rosaline Abigail Cady Bolton, Herbert's mother, at about the time of her husband's death in 1885.

Herbert Eugene Bolton at age ten.

Edwin Latham Bolton, Herbert's father, a Wisconsin farmer.

Gertrude Janes in 1893, two years before her marriage to Herbert Bolton.

Herbert Bolton in 1893 while studying at the University of Wisconsin.

Frederick Elmer Bolton, Herbert's favorite brother and frequent correspondent from his boyhood through early adult years. Photograph taken about 1915.

Gertrude Bolton in 1905.   Herbert Bolton in 1910.

The Bolton clan in 1915 across the street from their home
on Scenic Avenue. Left to right: Helen, Laura, Eugenie,
Mrs. Bolton, Herbert, Jr., Gertrude, Frances, and Jane.

also assured Bolton when he began graduate study that he could finish a doctor's degree in two years, but fellowships at Wisconsin were distressingly few — only ten for the entire university. And more than that, in history, he would be in competition with another crack student, Carl Lotus Becker.* So considering his chances and at Turner's suggestion, he wrote about possibilities at Harvard and Columbia.

May came and disappointment tagged along. Only half of the university fellowships went to hometowners, and historians were not among the lucky five. Turner was upset; he promised Bolton a spot as his assistant and also proposed that he might do some work with the Extension Division. From the standpoint of continued close association with Turner this offer was very attractive, but it would pay very little, and if the extension work were added, the setup would be very time-consuming. So Turner also began to put pressure on the University of Pennsylvania in Bolton's favor.

Faced now with the likely need of changing graduate schools, Bolton regretted that he had not taken the time necessary to write his master's thesis. He did intend to take all the requisite examinations and at least have that fact on his record. Then in late May came the news that he had been named to an Alumni Fellowship at Wisconsin. While it was not a large stipend, it would help. By this time he and Gertrude had decided to make ends meet as best they could, so that he might remain at Wisconsin. Then, in early June, came word that he had been named to a fellowship at the University of Pennsylvania; the Harrison Fellowship carried an award of $600. The summer of 1897 was spent with relatives, and the Herbert Boltons made ready for the one-thousand-mile move to Pennsylvania.

❧ ❧

Another phase of Herbert Bolton's career ended in that summer of 1897. He was on the history road. Turner and Haskins had given him his first initiation. In later years he would be proud to be a "Turner man," a relatively early one. And Turner, as the sequel will show, considered him one of his "boys." The Turner example of pioneering a new field Bolton would put to use, and in exemplary fashion. He would have his own West and, although he would never surpass the master in national ratings, his name would often be bracketed with Turner's among Western historians of first rank.

---

* Carl Lotus Becker was a colonial and Revolution historian and a predecessor of Bolton as president of the AHA.

TO PENNSYLVANIA AND THE DOCTORATE

The Herbert Boltons arrived in the City of Brotherly Love in mid-September 1897. After a bit of searching they found a large room (16'x20') on the second floor at 3715 Lancaster which rented for ten dollars a month and was only six blocks from the University of Pennsylvania. The transition from the open university town — with its wide streets, green lawns, plentiful trees, and picturesque lake, its state capitol and its university set in spacious and beauteous surroundings — into the heart of one of the nation's older cities was a bit of a shock to the farm-town couple. The narrow streets and darkish lanes, the impersonal bustle of a metropolis, and most of all its university sandwiched between buildings of all sorts and gasping, so to speak, for air — these things despite all their historic memories left them unimpressed and more than just a little depressed. The Pennsylvania years, although rewarding, were not always the happiest or the most comfortable.[6]

Bolton had little time for depression, however, when the school year opened, and he was quickly caught up in the busy existence of a graduate student. John Bach McMaster accepted him among his doctoral students and agreed to be his dissertation director; also, Bolton would take his seminar. There was another seminar under Edward Potts Cheyney. At Wisconsin he had known Turner and Haskins, younger men on their way up; now he would be exposed to two men already at the top of their profession. He would also work with Herman Vandenburg Ames and Dana Carleton Munro, men also well established in their fields. At Wisconsin Carl Lotus Becker and Guy Stanton Ford were fellow students; at Pennsylvania there were, among others, William Lingelbach and Frederic Logan Paxson.

In several fall letters he outlined his plans for the Pennsylvania period:

> I have not decided whether to lay out a two-year course or to try for a degree in one year. If that everlasting thesis were only done, I could make a bluff. They tell me that I would not be required to take more than one more Economics for a minor; that would enable me to take one extra course in European history; and McMaster seems to think my American history is all right. So if I had time to "plug" for exams, I could possibly make it. . . .
> The Library building is fine but the Library itself is not as good as I am used to — I won't find a place as the Wisconsin Historical for privileges. . . .

By mid-October he had already begun work on the dissertation. His subject was broad and he recognized that in time he might have to trim it.

He had not gotten far, in fact, before he felt that possibly his single pro-posed first chapter might be enough; he had initially set himself to study the status of the Negro as slave, changes effected in his status by emanci-pation and reconstruction, attempts by the South to make these legislated changes less imperative, and a few other aspects besides. A month later his topic was simply "The Status of the Negro in 1860"; and it was to shrink still smaller.

He explained the process which he proposed to follow. He wrote that he would try to "clean up" a section in each of the following six months and get each section approved in order to be "kept on the right track and be pretty confident of approval in the end." In a December 22 letter he announced that he had about forty pages ready to be read; these he hoped to present to McMaster and to the seminar right after the vacation. He worked steadily. From the time of Bolton's first acquaintance with the typewriter, he much preferred pen or pencil. He admitted that the type-writer made reports more presentable, but apart from that, it had little to recommend its existence. Throughout life he was never an enthusiast for this product of the machine age. By early March, as the work of the year developed, Herbert gave up any ideas he might have had for finishing in one year. He applied for a renewal of his fellowship.

On the national scene in these early months of 1898, the Cuban situ-ation was the hot issue, as the United States and Spain moved toward ultimate belligerency. Throughout his life Herbert was constantly and keenly interested in national and international affairs; he talked of them often, but rarely put his thoughts and views on paper. Frederick had evi-dently shared his views and in April 1898 Herbert responded:

> I have great respect for your opinion in all matters; but I do not quite agree with you on the Cuban question. I deplore war as you do. And I think that when war comes, it will prove no "thirty minutes to thirty days" job. I think that the ultimate result, however, is cer-tain. But I do not think that the United States is wholly to be con-demned for interfering in Cuban affairs. The disorder at our doors has not only been one of long standing and accompanied by un-Chris-tian barbarities, but it has directly involved American interests. The War of 1812 was fought on commercial grounds altogether. The commercial interests of the United States are more deeply involved in the Cuban question than most like to admit, because they put humanitarian motives to the fore-front. McKinley desires peace, but I believe he is the most determined man in America on the question of war, if war is necessary to stop the barbarities in Cuba. And if you have noticed it, *he* bases the right and duty on commercial as well as humanitarian grounds. I think history will justify him. I do not concur altogether with what you say about charity beginning at home. It does, or should; but it should not *end* there. I think we will

be no less able and no less likely to take care of our problems by going outside and helping others.

I do not know what the outcome of the war will be, surely one of three things: Spain will be left in possession, Cubans will be left in possession, or the United States will be charged with the care of the island. The second result seems to be the desirable one. Spain has proved entirely unable to care for colonial interests. At the opening of the century she was in possession of the whole American continent from the headwaters of the Missouri to Tierra del Fuego. Today she possesses nominally Cuba and Porto Rico [sic].

Most of her possessions have been lost by revolution, all through incompetency. This seems to be her last stand in which she is using unheard of methods to maintain her hold. Why prolong the struggle, when the end is certain? I am no jingo. You are a conservative. I think I am. I have expressed few opinions on the Cuban question, because I have not been certain that I had any. I have read the papers (which are a nuisance generally) and have talked with men of opinions. McMaster thinks that with no Cuban question there would have to be war now, on the ground of the Maine disaster. That of course is suppressed, as it is really the result of the Cuban question.

I am no less "patriotic" than some others but I do not want to go to war until they need me. I am glad that my time in the organized militia is out, and that Roy's is.

Well, there may be no war. I hope there may not; but if there is I think it will be well fought.

These and some other views of Spain as a colonial power are interesting as those of the man who later was to become so fair and balanced an interpreter of Spain in the Americas. One can only say that, as of 1898, Herbert Bolton was still an "unreconstructed" Black Legend man, the traditional American who found little, if any, good to say of the Spaniards, past or present, in their relations with the Americas.

Herbert Bolton toward the end of April had to face one of those temptations which seem to be perennial in the lives of doctoral students of every age. An old professor friend from Milwaukee Normal with whom he must have maintained contact through the years and who was following his academic progress with interest, wrote that the position of head of the history department at South Side High School, Milwaukee, was open. Herbert gave the matter more than just passing thought — "it would be a fill-in for a year, and there would be a chance of permanence." He debated, talked with Gertrude, and then, even though he did not know what the summer might bring, decided to bypass the opportunity in order to complete his degree program, knowing well that the coming year would be in straitened circumstances. As usual his wife was willing to struggle in order to see him to his goal — the doctor's degree in hand.

Summer 1898 was one of very few summers spent more or less leisurely for the Boltons. Jobs were scarce. Gertrude was homesick for Wisconsin, so with a small amount of money they had managed to keep in reserve, Herbert decided to pass up a job he could have had as cashier in a resort town near Philadelphia, and head for Tunnel City. During the long summer weeks of quasi-inactivity Herbert Bolton may have redreamed a dream which he had shared with his brother in late spring. He wanted desperately to take a quick turn in Europe, to see the Old World, but more particularly to perfect command of another foreign language which he felt would be one of the valuable by-products of his weeks abroad. But it was a financial impossibility. He even went so far in his dreaming as to choose Italian as the language he would most like to practice. It could be most useful, was his reasoning, if he were to pursue further his interest in the Renaissance period (Cheyney, obviously, was leaving his mark, and he was being abetted by Dana Carleton Munro). Ironically, in view of the future, when Bolton was weighing the pros-and-cons of several languages, Spanish was the first one he ruled out.

The Boltons went back to Philadelphia in early September, to have time to do a bit of house hunting. With daughter Frances growing and becoming loquacious, Herbert had found it more and more difficult to study and write at home. Since this was to be a year of writing, with the doctoral dissertation at the top of the agenda, a change was imperative. After much tramping around in the university neighborhood they came up with a third-floor apartment with three rooms and their own bathroom, but the bathroom was one flight down, and so was the water supply; the place was only partially furnished, which meant an outlay for some furniture; but Herbert would have his own study. He was going to need that, not only for the dissertation, but for his round of course work which included a bibliography-sources course from Dana Munro, "England and the Continent, 1400-1700" from Edward Cheyney, "American Constitutional" from Herman Ames, and an economics course from Simon W. Patten — all this besides reporting to McMaster for the dissertation.

From late October through November and into December the recurring theme in his letters was the dissertation, and the constant tune "The Dissertation Blues." There was some consolation in the fact that McMaster seemed well pleased with the developing product. On December 2 he reported that "McMaster accepted my last batch . . . with the comment 'Very good.' "

Christmas came, and the new year, 1899. Things seemed to be moving along nicely and the end of dissertation work was nearing. Then in late January daughter Frances became seriously ill. Her condition baffled the doctors, and for several days she was on the critical list. Everything was disrupted; worries piled up; so did doctor bills and medical expenses. Herbert was getting little done beyond attending classes, and it was well into February before he could get back to the dissertation.

Even with the delay, on April 22 Bolton could report with some exultation that the bulk of the dissertation was in McMaster's hands. He wrote on May 2 that the thesis was "OK," and that the major examination had been passed, with the second and the third imminent.

Herbert Bolton appeared for his final oral on May 23, 1899. Sitting in judgment were McMaster for American history, Cheyney for European history, and Patten for economics. The thesis Bolton was defending was entitled: "The Free Negro in the South before the Civil War." The next day he wrote to Frederick:

> Well, I got through yesterday with no great honor and no great scars or scares. I might as well have passed the exam a year ago as now. It had no relation to what I have done here . . . I am glad that I am no longer a school boy. That gives me more satisfaction than the degree (which has depreciated much with 24 hours) . . .

Herbert Bolton was just about two months short of his twenty-ninth birthday and, finally, ready to move into the career he had chosen. At Pennsylvania, McMaster had deepened Bolton's Turner-given awareness of social factors in history. Haskins, Cheyney, and Munro had kept him mindful that American history, to be sound and truly understandable, must have many Old World roots; in their own several ways they trained him to be an expert American colonialist. Few men of Bolton's generation, or any other for that matter, were as fortunate as he had been in being exposed to such a galaxy of "greats."

There were days of packing and goodbyes, and by early June the Boltons were back in Tunnel City. Dr. Bolton began to comb the area for an opening, sometimes by letter and occasionally by interview. Letters to Stevens Point got no reply; a trip to Waupaca was unrewarding — the position there had been filled ten days earlier. He was, understandably, more than a bit discouraged.[7]

He taught summer school at Appleton, which he described as a "baneful experience"; time had not changed his opinion of summer school. Four weeks work netted him $129. But he still did not have a job for the coming year. He heard there was an opening at little Albion College in Michigan and asked Ely for a recommendation, since economics was involved, only to learn that Ely had already sponsored another for the spot. He turned to Turner. Turner told him of a one-year opening at the University of Missouri. The position would carry the rank of assistant professor but would pay only $500. Although he admitted that Missouri "might be a good place to jump from" after a year, the figure, the temporary nature of the position, and the expense of moving to Columbia did not appeal to him.

Just about the time that prospects for the year seemed one or several degrees below nil, there was an offer from one of his former schools, Milwaukee Normal. Frederick had been teaching there the past year and may have had a hand in the offer. At any rate, Herbert Bolton's first postdoctoral job would be at State Normal, Milwaukee. He would begin as instructor in economics and civics.

3

Texas and a
Field of His Own

EIGHT YEARS BEFORE, Herbert Bolton had come to State Normal as a student for the spring term, in March 1891, a farm lad going on twenty-one. The intervening years of the 1890s had seen changes in Bolton, the school, and Milwaukee, but in Bolton, possibly, most of all. In September, 1899, he was returning to his alma mater as a member of the faculty, a full-fledged doctor of philosophy, after several exciting years at the developing University of Wisconsin and a couple at the old, staid, and prestigious University of Pennsylvania. Through those eight years were interludes as teacher and principal in three schools of rural Wisconsin, which, along with his formal training in history, gave him firsthand experience which he could now pass on to his students at Normal.

When he had finished his degree work in May, he recognized that, most probably, the first several years of his college-university career might have to be spent at the normal-school level. Most of his job-hunting of the summer had been among the Wisconsin teacher-training colleges. Although his ultimate ambition soared much higher, he was realist enough to know that he had to start somewhere and was not at all averse to beginning in such a position, although he hoped it would be temporary. He was not too unhappy that his own Milwaukee State Normal was welcoming him back, and the fact that his brother Frederick was also on the faculty put another check in the plus column. He was not enthusiastic about his first teaching assignment, economics and civics; naturally he would have preferred history. The promise was that he would have some history classes in his schedule the following year. At this particular point in time, he was grateful that he had a job, one which would give him his first respectable salary.

Of Herbert's two years at Normal as a teacher his brother could recall:

[28]

At Milwaukee Normal School Herbert made a hit with the students. They regarded him as a superior teacher, no matter what the subject. Normal school presidents and faculties had not reached the stage where they realized the value of specialization; and therefore, during his two years at Milwaukee, Herb was never allowed to teach American history. He had to accept what was handed to him at the opening of each term; he taught mathematics, economics, ancient history, etc. The young men in the debating society soon discovered his merits and versatility and selected him as their coach; he led them to the championship in their joint debate with the other normal schools.[1]

In mid-January 1900, getting a bit restless at Normal, Herbert went down to Chicago to talk with Ginn and Company about the possibility of joining their staff as a "traveler" to the high-school and normal-school trade. The salary was attractive, $1500 and expenses; he had little hope of reaching that figure at Normal for at least another year or possibly two. But, again, as in an earlier flirtation with such a publishing-house connection, the problem of the great amount of time to be spent on the road made the prospect much less attractive. He resisted the temptation and went back to Milwaukee and Normal for the new term.

As the school year closed Herbert's brother Frederick went off to a post in the Department of Education, State University of Iowa, Iowa City; the separation was painful to Herbert, and once again regular letter-writing resumed.[2] Herbert's letter to Frederick of August 12, 1900, was from Appleton, Wisconsin, where he was teaching summer school, still not liking it but accepting it as a necessary evil, in order to fill the salary-less months. This letter was penned on stationery with the impressive letterhead "H. E. Bolton, Ph.D. – Professor of Economics and Civics." As of September the letterhead had changed to "H. E. Bolton – Professor of History and English." The history did not stand for American history, but he was getting closer. His schedule, however, was no lighter, three courses and two "library reading periods" daily. Such a load left little, if any, time for productive scholarship, and this upset ambitious Herbert Bolton.

As winter loomed in Wisconsin, Herbert's spirits reflected the gloom of the impending season. He complained that he was tired of "teaching everything" and remarked that debate was taking much too much of his time. He was not particularly thrilled over having to detour to Oshkosh for a teachers' meeting en route to Tunnel City for the Christmas holidays. He knew that attendance at such meetings was *de rigueur* for the normal-school professor, but this did not make them any less boring to him.

He had taken sections of his doctoral dissertation and worked them into an article, "The Free Negro," and submitted it for publication to the *Atlantic Monthly;* a pink slip came back in January 1901. As the new term ran along, he became more and more restive. A friend at Pennsylvania wrote him that there was an opening in economics at Brown University. He was more interested in the rumor that there might be an opening in history at Dartmouth College and actually went down to Chicago for an interview with President William Jewett Tucker. This Dartmouth matter hung in the balance until late May; then word came that the position was his for the signing but that the appointment would be for one year only. He had, meanwhile, written to his trusted old masters at Madison, Turner and Haskins. The former advised him to stay at Normal for at least another year, or until he had the security of something more permanent. By early June he had decided to follow this advice.

A month later he rather regretted this decision. The 1901–02 contracts came out; he had hoped for $1500 but was pegged at $1450. He admitted to his brother that he was "down," and the prospect of an impending teachers' institute at Appleton did nothing to raise his spirits. There would be another at Waukesha, preceded by a two-week summer session at Port Washington. When the Waukesha institute was cancelled, he was distressed to find himself with several income-free weeks before the opening of the new semester. Even though summer work had already netted $245, he disliked this non-productive period. The prospect of out-of-the ordinary medical expenses, and soon, was a bit frightening. Gertrude was expecting their third child imminently — Helen was the second daughter, born in November of the first year at Normal. Accordingly, Herbert was working in the office at Normal, handling the day-to-day business during the absence of the president and the secretary. The situation seemed to be under control.

Then in early September things began to explode. Word came over from Tunnel City that Helen, already there with Grandmother Janes, was quite seriously ill with an intestinal upset. Gertrude was in no condition to travel, so Herbert prepared to go, hoping to be able to bring Helen back to Milwaukee and to better medical care. At this juncture, on September 10, he received a letter which, literally and in every sense, was to change his life.[3]

The letter was from Professor George P. Garrison, Chairman of the Department of History at the University of Texas. The message: one of the senior professors (Lester Bugbee), ill with consumption, would certainly be unable to teach the coming year; it was even possible that the position might open permanently; the field was European history, the salary $1500, and the rank instructor; was Bolton interested? Ill-timed though it was, Bolton recognized that this might well be his first real chance. He sent off a quick letter to Garrison, requesting more details, and then hurried over to Tunnel City. He found Helen sufficiently improved that he could safely bring her back to Milwaukee. During the next anxious days his prime preoccupation was with his sick child, but he still had the energy to fret over the slowness of Garrison's answer to his letter.

It finally came: the position was still open; filling in for Bugbee would put the new appointee into two sections of medieval history and one of modern European; classes would open in early October. He had already thought and rethought, weighed and pondered; he had thoroughly discussed the matter with Gertrude; he had written to Frederick. He wired his acceptance. On September 25 he wrote to Frederick: "The die is cast. They offered the Texas place to me and I accepted."

Without fully recognizing it at the moment, as September 1901 merged into October, Herbert Bolton was moving toward his destiny. They were hectic days. He had already told the officials at Normal of the feeler; now he had to inform them that they must definitely find a replacement. They were generously cooperative and understanding. He had to do all the heavy packing, since it was decided that the family would stay in Wisconsin until he found suitable housing in Austin. Helen was much improved, but she was still a care. Frederick was urging that he swing over to Iowa City en route south. He wrote a letter on October 6 to say that time was too short for that luxury. Before he mailed his note the following morning, he had a postscript to add. At 3:00 A.M. on October 7 the third Bolton daughter, Laura, was born just in time to greet her father before he left the next day for the University of Texas.

THE UNIVERSITY OF TEXAS

Bolton's first report from Austin on October 16 told that classes had begun a few days before and that, as Garrison had indicated, he was teaching two sections of medieval history and one modern European history course. He also enclosed a clipping from the Austin *Daily Statesman,* announcing the new addition to the Department of History and sketching his academic background. He already was developing a warm rapport with one of his younger colleagues, Eugene C. Barker.

Garrison had, in the letter in answer to Bolton's inquiry about the Texas position, spoken of "odds and ends" among the duties expected of him beyond his classes. The chairman clarified this vague phrase on Bolton's arrival. Whether it was one of the "odds" or one of the "ends," Herbert found himelf as editorial assistant on the Texas State Historical Association *Quarterly,* then in its fifth year of publication. Very quickly he saw that, for time being at least, this editorial work would give him some contact with American history even though it might have a rather heavy Texas flavor. He had learned even more quickly that American history at Texas was Garrison's preserve, jealously guarded and carefully fenced off and posted. Thanks to his fine training with Haskins and more with Cheyney and Munro at Pennsylvania, Herbert Bolton felt himself reasonably at home in his medieval history course, but he still yearned for an opportunity to interpret the United States story to young Americans, to put some of the Turner ideas and insights to work, and his own as well.

By late October Bolton was getting settled and endeavoring to fit into the Texas routine. The university was still in its initial growing stage in 1901. Founded in 1883, Texas like so many of the state institutions which opened in the later years of the nineteenth century was developing slowly. In Bolton's first year there (1901–02) enrollment reached only 1300 including 191 summer students. The academic or non-professional department during the regular year had an enrollment of only 436. Bolton did not have large numbers in his classes, but he soon found his students eager and interested.

After much shopping around, Bolton rented a house at 1408 Colorado Street and began to ready it for the coming of Gertrude and the girls. This was a slow process, since university duties took much of his time. Then in December a smallpox scare in Tunnel City sent the four Bolton females scurrying southward ahead of schedule. The sudden "invasion" was bad enough, but almost as soon as they arrived Helen had a recurrence of the intestinal upset; Herbert got little done in the next weeks and through the holiday season.

Toward the end of the first semester, in January, Garrison began to plot out the departmental schedule for the coming year. He asked Bolton if he would be interested in giving a course which might be labeled "European Expansion: Commercial and Colonial Activities, Sixteenth and Seventeenth Centuries." Bolton was delighted; while he would not be teaching his favorite United States history, he would be getting closer, at least into the western hemisphere; besides, such a course fitted into some of his most recent planning for his own future. He had given up hope that Garrison would be likely to share the U.S. story with any one of his colleagues, and he soon saw that American history at Texas was heavily Texas-oriented; in fact, as he told Frederick, Texans were interested primarily in two areas of history, that of Texas and that of the Holy Land; all else was more or less inconsequential, and they rather demanded that their university's Department of History share the same vision. In this framework Garrison had already preempted the American segment. He had likewise learned that his friend Barker, with Garrison's blessing and urging, was becoming interested and laying claim to the Mexican and

short-lived independent period, 1836–1845. (Barker was already beginning his long-range preparation for becoming the authority on Stephen
Fuller Austin and his contemporaries.) This left only one part of the
Texas story still free, namely, the Spanish or colonial segment. Bolton
felt that it could be his for the asking and was inclining in that direction.
Early in 1902 he had confided to his brother: "I think in time that I shall
be able to block out a field of *my own* here." Now Garrison's proposed
course for 1902–03 was playing into his hands.

As the early weeks of 1902 went by, Herbert reported that he was
spending a good deal of time on tasks connected with the *Quarterly;* he
had done several book reviews, which would appear, unsigned, in the
current number. And his new thinking about future orientation was beginning to be more clearly defined.

> As to the place, I believe that Texas is preferable for History to
> any place outside the Northwest [the Old Northwest] or the far west.
> ... Texas has the key to Spanish American history. I am grubbing
> Spanish, so that I may be able to turn the lock. My new course is a
> triumph for me, for it is Garrison's permission to tramp on his
> ground.

He was serious about his Spanish study — "I want to handle it well by
fall." He was taking lessons from Bill Buckley and then added still another
tutor, as we learn from an interesting sidelight in Louis H. Hubbard's
privately printed volume, *Recollections of a Texas Educator.* Hubbard,
one-time Dean of Students at the University of Texas and subsequently
president of Texas State College for Women at Denton, in recalling his
undergraduate days wrote:

> In order to augment our income Mama continued her teaching of
> Spanish in Austin though in a private capacity. Several members of
> the faculty were among her students, and I remember particularly
> Dr. Herbert E. Bolton. He had come to the University, while yet a
> young man upon completion of his doctorate at the University of
> Pennsylvania, and was interested in carrying on a program of
> research. He soon learned of the University's connection with the
> García Collection of historical materials, and saw in those docu-
> ments his opportunity. But since they were all in Spanish, he could
> not read them. Thus he began his lessons with Mama and applied
> himself so assiduously that within six months he acquired a reading
> knowledge of Spanish and was digging into the Collection.[4]

Hubbard was a bit premature in getting the García Collection to Texas
in 1902 — it was not acquired until several years later — but Bolton did
know of much material in Spanish which might serve his research dreams.

Garrison had been to the Archivo General de la Nación in Mexico City for materials to supplement his study of American Texas; he very probably told his ambitious young colleague of the wealth of almost unused Spanish documents in the Archivo which could support his developing interest. At any rate, Herbert Bolton was studying Spanish, and diligently.

His March 3 letter gave some idea of cost-of-living figures in Austin. Rent for their Colorado Street house was $25 a month; utilities ran to $5; food and household necessities averaged around $40; there was a $9 item for servant help. All of this left only around $25 per month, out of a salary check of $125, to pay off debts, to make insurance payments, and to meet other such regularly recurring demands; obviously, this did not allow Herbert Bolton much of an opportunity to build a contingency reserve. In fact, the next month, when the insurance premium came due, he had to ask Frederick for the loan of $20 to $25 for a few weeks in order to meet the $121 payment — "I have always been your debtor, and still am." That first year at Texas Bolton's salary was $1500; two years later he was only getting $1600. These were days when all academic salaries were low — even the president of the university received only $3333.34 per annum, but did have some other perquisites.[5] It was almost imperative in this situation that Bolton accept the opportunity to teach in the summer session for the supplement to his income.

The Texas commencement, on June 11, was followed immediately by the summer school session. Bolton welcomed the $175 which it would bring, but was not wholly enthusiastic about his assignment. He had to pick up the two courses which Lester Bugbee had long before been scheduled to teach, Greek history and general European history. With a June 17 letter he returned his brother's recent loan and announced that he had twenty students in his Greek history class and eighty in the other course; he related, with a touch of disappointment, that the regents, who regularly met around commencement time on matters academic, had made no promotions. Then he came back to what was very much in his thoughts at the moment:

> If it were not for leaving the family alone I should go to Mexico to spend the rest of the vacation, for the purpose of getting a speaking knowledge. I would like to conquer Spanish now that I am at it. It is the key to Southwestern history, in which I must work as long as I am here.

He was back to the same theme in a July 8 letter: "I am making hard efforts to get the Spanish language now, and want to get into the heart of Southwestern history by getting familiar with Spanish civilization and the mine of sources that lie in Mexico."

Later in the month, with razor-edge budget planning, he saw how he could realize this visit-to-Mexico dream. Mrs. Bolton and the three girls would go back to Wisconsin for the weeks of his absence from Austin. Perhaps those August weeks would open for him that "field of his own"; he would now be able to test the possibility firsthand.

SOUTH OF THE BORDER

Mid-summer 1902 was the time of Herbert Bolton's first excursion into Mexico. With the summer session over and Gertrude and the girls bound for Wisconsin, he went over to El Paso to catch the southbound train. He was feeling his way into a new area of study — Spanish Texas — which he had determined to make "his field" at least as long as he was at the University of Texas. Actually this first foray into Mexico would prove to be more a beginning than he could have visualized as he set out to explore in this third summer of the new century.

A postcard to Frederick dated August 8 told of the beginnings of his research. "This morning," he wrote, "I am going to venture into the Archivo General to begin work. It is a bold venture but I have the nerve."[6] One Sunday when the Archivo General de México was closed, he went off on his first field trip to retrace a part of the "Cortes trail." Years before, on long winter evenings at Fairchild, he and his roommate had, bit by bit, read Prescott's fascinating tale of the conquest of Mexico; now he could relive it on the spot. That Sunday he discovered the thrill of "trailing," and he had set still another pattern for the future.

He returned to Austin on September 6, his suitcases bulging with document copies. He himself was bubbling with enthusiasm and convinced that he had uncovered "a field of his own." Of his six weeks in Mexico he wrote to Frederick: "I think that my summer has been profitable. It will keep me in powder for shooting off historical fireworks most of the year. I shall get one or two articles in the October publications." He now had something to write about. The first part of "Some Materials for Southwestern History in the Archivo General de México" appeared in the October number of the *Quarterly*; it attracted some attention and good comments, and he reported in a January 1903 letter: "I opened a relatively unexplored field there — I hope to exploit part of it myself." In those days history-minded Texans, proud of the new *Quarterly,* read it eagerly and cheered new insights such as young Bolton was now offering. The January 1903 number carried his second literary effort, "Tienda de Cuervo's Ynspección of Laredo."

The University of Texas, just in its second decade, was growing slowly. Enrollment for 1902–03 showed an increase of only fifty-seven over the previous year, to bring the total to 1348. At the beginning of the year Herbert Bolton had forty-three students in his medieval history course; there were fifty in modern European, and his new European expansion course drew eight. But Texas was growing and Bolton was growing with it. During this year he was also doing some translating for the Blair-Robertson series of documentary volumes on the Philippines.[7] The recompense was not too generous, but he welcomed the opportunity to work on his Spanish and recognized that this "exposure" was quite good for a developing young scholar. He was anxious to move into prominence as quickly as possible and was willing to expend the effort required.

In February 1903 a theme, which was repeated more than once in the next few years, began to appear in his letters to Frederick. He assured his brother that he would welcome a job offer from another university, which he might use as a "lever" in bargaining with Texas. Promotions at Texas did not come easily or frequently; actually no one likely to stay had been promoted lately. "I'd consider most anything with a good salary attached, for I have good reason to think that they would not let me go."

The regents met at the end of the year, right after commencement ceremonies. Bolton received no promotion, but there was some consolation in that they showed recognition of the work he was doing by decreeing him a salary raise of $100 for the next year. This may have been just as well for Texas, since Bolton in the next month turned down a chance to "be considered" for an assistant professor position at the University of Washington. At the time he was, however, deeply involved in a project with colleague Eugene Barker, and might not have been swayed to make the change even if he had not received a raise. He and Barker were busily gathering documents for *With the Makers of Texas: A Source Reader in Texas History,* geared to the high school market. The two young instructors had pooled meager resources to subsidize the small volume, hoping that the venture might turn into a gold mine, but the book, published in 1904, was only moderately successful.[8] It put neither of the authors among the expanding class of Texas millionaires. Even though a few years later American Book Company bought out their publication rights (it seemed promising at first to have a national house as distributor), Bolton and Barker lived to regret this seeming good fortune. Within a short time American Book Company fell into disfavor with the State textbook selection committee — this was deadly in a state where the textbook jury practically dictated choice of all elementary and secondary books. *With the Makers of Texas* did serve, at least, to put Bolton's name on a first book.

Teaching in the summer session of 1903 was less a chore since both of his classes were "repeats" of courses taught during the year and demanded less day-to-day preparation. This gave him more time for research and planning for another post-summer-session trip to Mexico. This year his expenses were paid since, besides doing his own investigations, he would be directing the University-State Library joint project of manuscript copying which Chairman Garrison had set up a few years before to bring materials on American Texas to Austin. The student copyists were experienced, so Bolton had relatively little supervising to do; this left much time for his own archive-grubbing. The fruits of this summer began to show in a spate of articles on colonial Texas which in the next years would appear in the *Quarterly* — one in 1905 and three in 1906.

Much of his spare time in 1903, even after returning from Mexico, went into more work on documents for the Blair-Robertson collection; six pieces, some of them sizable, appeared in the volumes of the series published in 1904. Then, shortly before Christmas Bolton and Barker were named associate editors of the *Quarterly*.[9]

The work on the *Quarterly* was just part of the increasing load of responsibility outside his teaching and personal study that Herbert Bolton was assuming in these early years at Texas. In a March 18, 1905, letter to his brother he said he had recently been appointed an associate member of the Public Archives Commission. President William L. Prather was drawing upon his abilities and calling upon him to do a considerable number of odd jobs around the university; he was flattered by Prather's confidence in him but unhappy about the time being taken from his writing and research, for this was where his greatest interest and enthusiasm lay. With the progress he had made in his first two summers in Mexico, he was anxious to return. He was not able to do so in the summer of 1904.

The next year he arranged to return to Mexico for a few weeks in the latter part of the summer. The first part of the summer he did not teach, but instead, allowed himself a vacation through most of July. He, his wife, and now four daughters (Eugenie was born in September 1904) went North. He could leave on July 1 with a certain exhilaration; shortly before, the regents had given him an advancement in rank to adjunct professor and raised his salary for the coming year to $1800. He returned to Austin later in the month to make preparations for his upcoming excursion to Mexico. He left on August 2. By this third summer he knew what he was about and was able to put his seven weeks stay to fullest advantage. "By this means of grubbing summers," he wrote Frederick, "I hope to retain my right to a place in university circles, if nothing more."

If Herbert Bolton was in a musing and reflective mood as the last hours of 1905 melted into the first minutes of the new year, his thoughts might have run something like this. Four years and four months before Texas would simply have been one of the forty-six states, largest of them all, a place on the map, the state in which he had found some of his subjects, the "Free Negroes," for his doctoral dissertation. Then, all of a sudden, as of September 1901, Texas began to have a very real pertinence in his life, when that letter postmarked Texas arrived in Milwaukee. Within a few weeks he was in Texas, a faculty member of its university. Thanks to work with Haskins at Wisconsin and with Cheyney and Munro at Pennsylvania, the assignment to medieval history was no problem, but he had no desire to turn into a medievalist. American history was his field. Irked at the time that Garrison had not been a bit more generous in sharing the American load, Bolton could be most thankful that Garrison was so jealously possessive. Not that he could not have brought to American history the freshness of the Turner approach or the socioeconomic outlook of McMaster, but he still would have been one among many Americanists. What a stroke of fortune, as he now saw it by hindsight, that he had been forced into North America, so to speak, by the backdoor, with his European expansion course! The situation at Texas had compelled him to find something new. He had done just that in Spanish Texas; what he now considered "his field" was just waiting to be discovered and worked. For his purpose, the Mexican archives were a virtually untapped resource. The challenge of uncovering the entire Spanish effort in both the Americas lay before him; there were almost no limits for new research and writing, and at Texas the *Quarterly* was a ready outlet for his scholarly production. He was rapidly gaining at least a local reputation; Texans were appreciative of being told about their "ancient" history — it was a source of pride to them to be able to proclaim that their history went back farther than that of some of the Atlantic seaboard and all the rest of the American states.

Texas had been good to him and for him. Above all, Texas had given him "a field of his own." The new year was going to bless him even more. He could hardly have guessed just how abundantly.

4

Early Recognition

THE YEAR 1906 put Herbert Bolton on his way to prominence among American historians. In a very real sense it was the year he was "discovered." He had probably wondered more than once if anyone outside of Texas read the *Quarterly*. A few days after New Year's a letter reached him to prove that he had been writing for more than just a Texas audience.

In those early years of the century J. Franklin Jameson, commissioned by the Department of Historical Research of the Carnegie Institution of Washington, was contacting scholars and researchers and sending them off to survey and record the riches in foreign archives which had bearing on United States history. Charles M. Andrews was already in England; William R. Shepherd was in Spain; others were under contract to calendar various other national depositories. Jameson had seen Bolton's two articles in the *Quarterly* (October 1902 and January 1904) on "Some Materials for Southwestern History in the Archivo General de México," as well as several of his other articles. This was enough to convince him that Herbert Bolton would be the man to do the calendaring job in the Mexican depositories, which were evidently rich in materials pertaining to United States history. Accordingly, on January 4, 1906, he wrote: "As I am writing to Dr. Garrison, I have concluded to ask you to undertake for us the important task of making a comprehensive guide to materials for the United States which may be found in the Mexican archives."[1]

Garrison was jubilant; recognition such as this did not come often to the young Department of History at Texas. He informed new President David F. Houston* and immediately called the Austin *Statesman*. The

---

*Houston became president of the University of Texas after Prather's death in 1905.

[39]

news notice, which appeared and which Herbert sent to his brother (January 14) with the terse comment that Garrison "claims everything in sight," spent more space telling of Garrison's 1900 visit to the Mexican archives and the document-copying project being carried out by the university, than it did in lauding the young professor to whom the important invitation had been tendered. Bolton admired and respected Garrison but was not blind to the driving pride of his chief and his desire to be considered *the* historian at Texas.

Bolton consulted Garrison and Houston, pondered the proposal for a few days more, and then on January 18 sent off a long reply to Jameson's equally long initial letter. Besides making the invitation, Jameson had asked how soon Bolton would be able to start the work, what archives outside of Mexico City would merit investigation, what the expenses would be, what compensation would be expected, and, finally, when in the near future Bolton could come to Washington to talk over and lay out the project in greater detail. Bolton replied that he would be free to devote the coming summer to the project, but that he must return to Austin for the 1906–07 school year. Barker was to be on leave 1906–07 in order to go to Pennsylvania to complete his doctoral studies (Barker, like Bolton before him, was to have a Harrison Fellowship). Bolton told Jameson that the department could hardly be without its two junior members nor could the *Quarterly* be left without either of its associate editors. He would not be able to return to Mexico until he summer of 1907. Then, however, there was the likelihood that he might be granted leave of absence, so as to remain through the whole year 1907–08 and into the summer following.

He professed firsthand knowledge of the Archivo General y Público de la Nación (AGN) but admitted that he knew little of the holdings of the provincial depositories. He warned that hearsay evidence in Mexico on such matters could be highly untrustworthy and affirmed that on-the-spot investigation was absolutely necessary. He listed a number of provincial archives whose manuscript treasures he felt would bear inspection, regularly adding enough historical information on each to justify its inclusion. For example, he cited Querétaro and Zacatecas, noting that he would expect the archives there to be rich in materials concerning the missionary effort since each was the home base for Franciscan friars who had worked in the United States — in Texas, New Mexico, or Arizona. He had often run into the Querétarans and Zacatecans while working the Texas story. He was giving all of this data to lay groundwork for his estimate of costs which Jameson had specifically requested.

In answer to that matter, he listed his current university salary at $1900 for two semesters with an additional $300 for a summer session.

He warned that living expenses in Mexico he had found higher than in Austin; however, he had no way of estimating such costs for his family, who had not been with him on his previous summer excursions.

Within a week there was another letter from Jameson. The director of the Department of Historical Research had, it seems, talked out of turn. The Mexican project, although definitely planned for inclusion in the guide series, might have to be postponed, at least for another year. There was some slight chance, Jameson assured Bolton, that the trustees in their February meeting might vote the necessary funds, but he was not sanguine; maybe it was not so unfortunate that Bolton would hardly be able to begin in 1906. In that same January 22 letter Jameson strongly urged Bolton to lay a broad base for the work ahead, extending his knowledge of the United States-Mexican story to areas beyond Texas, so that New Mexico, Arizona, and California materials might not be overlooked. Jameson also asked his opinion as to whether there should be two guides, one for the civil and a second for ecclesiastical archives. If two, would a man like Adolph Bandelier, a Catholic, be likely to have easier access to church records.

Bolton replied on January 28, expressing the hope that the shelving of the Mexican guide project would be distinctly temporary. He confessed that to date his preoccupation in research and writing had been Texas-oriented but assured Jameson that his interests and acquaintance extended much farther afield through the Greater Southwest. On the matter of two guides, he felt that it would be difficult, if not impossible, to separate the church and the state stories in the colonial period; in the national period, perhaps this might be possible. In conclusion he informed Jameson that, with no Carnegie moneys available, he would have to teach summer session but assured him that he intended to go to Mexico at its close.

Jameson had read the signs correctly; the Carnegie trustees did not approve funds for the Mexico guide in 1906. He so informed Bolton in mid-February. Bolton settled down to a more or less normal routine — his classes, his administrative duties, editorial commitments, the family, and a tennis-bowling program. He had, however, developed a new academic distraction.

As far back as a year before, Bolton had read a notice to the effect that the Bureau of American Ethnology (BAE) was contemplating a handbook on the American Indian and had written a letter asking for more information and noting that he had much manuscript material, in Spanish, which might be of interest to the editors.[2] There does not seem to have been a reply for many months. January 20, 1906, he wrote a second letter, with the same message. Penned at the bottom of this letter by someone at the bureau was the notation that "a reply to a letter from the same writer, covering the same material" had been drafted "a few days ago." Evidently the experts at the BAE had done some checking on this "same writer" because W. H. Holmes, chief of the bureau, sent Bolton the following message on January 18, 1906:

> With your knowledge of the Texas and Mexican archives, I have no doubt that you possess much information that would be of value to us in the preparation of the *Handbook of American Indians North of Mexico*. If I may take such a liberty, I shall be glad to send you from time to time proofs of brief articles on Texas tribes, missions, and settlements, in the hope that you may find time to call attention to any radical change that might be necessary to ensure accuracy. . . .

Bolton had replied quickly, offering notes and observations on the proofs submitted, several suggesting extensive changes "to ensure accuracy." Holmes, evidently sensing that "he had a tiger by the tail," thanked him but expressed regret that the work had progressed too far at that time to permit some of the corrections and additions which Bolton submitted — maybe in the next edition there could be substantial rewriting of the Texas articles. Then, recognizing that the "next edition" might be long in coming and interested in tapping Bolton's obvious extensive knowledge, Holmes in a letter of February 12 asked Bolton to consider "a proposal to prepare for this Bureau a memoir on the history of the tribes of Texas with a view to its publication." It was in this way that the idea of a book on the Texas Indians was conceived. (Unfortunately, it would never be completed.)

Bolton answered this letter February 16, promising "careful consideration of your proposal." He informed Holmes that the business of the guide to the Mexican archives was pending; he did not wish to get himself overextended. Curiously, on the day he was writing to Holmes, Jameson was writing him to say that the guide project would have to be postponed. After receiving this last letter from Jameson, Bolton was free to give "careful consideration" to the Holmes suggestion. Actually, he already had a study on the Hasinai Indians of Texas in process; he would be able to return to that and expand coverage to all of Texas. Accordingly, on March 1, he wrote Holmes:

> I have decided to undertake the work of preparing for the Bureau a Memoir on the history of the Texas Indian tribes, providing satisfactory arrangements can be made, which I trust can be the case. . . . I think that it would make a fairly large volume — perhaps, 150,000 words.

To do the job he indicated that he would need help in working the Bexar archives, already at the University of Texas; further, he felt that two trips to Mexico would be necessary and also a trip to Washington in order to confer with the men in the bureau and also to see what materials were available there.

Holmes, undaunted by Bolton's conditions, wrote back March 20 that he was "greatly pleased" by Bolton's willingness to undertake the commission but vowed that he was at a loss to know what the remuneration should be. He asked for a dollars-and-cents estimate. In reply on March 28 Bolton, skirting any mention of possible personal remuneration, confined himself to matters of "clerical assistance and travel": two trips to Mexico, $100; copying assistance in Mexico, $100; copying assistance at Austin (The Bexar archives), $50. Holmes's answer of acceptance was followed April 18 by the reply: "I wish . . . to say that after deliberate consideration I have decided to offer my services to the Bureau under the conditions you state. I shall push the work vigorously from now on . . ."

Things had been happening so fast since early in 1906 that Herbert had allowed his correspondence with Frederick to lapse for several weeks.[3] On April 18 he brought him up to date:

> Things have opened up for me since I last wrote you. I had a talk with the president [Houston] about the advisability of engaging to do the work proposed in the enclosed letter [Holmes to Bolton, February 12], since it bears upon the whole question of the direction of my energies. The question has been to what extent it was wise to get into the field of Spanish American and Southwestern history, when Professor Garrrison is the teacher of American history, and (let me whisper it) very sensitive to competition, if only apparent rather than real.
>
> My talk with the president resulted in his telling me to go ahead and create the field and the chair will be made in due time. This is what he wished me to do. Of course, it will be much more to my taste to feel that I can have a swing in Spanish-American history, than to make medieval my major work. With the recognition that is coming to me now in one way or another, I have hopes now of being able to get in the van of Spanish-American history students. I might be a full professor of medieval history sooner than there will be a demand for a chair in Spanish-American history, but I feel that the ultimate chance for standing is much greater in the latter field, and I would prefer to wait.

In his next letter (May 25) he reported that work on the Texas Indians was progressing, that he was planning something of a general article for the *Quarterly,* that he would definitely teach in summer session, before going to Mexico for August and much of September.

Bolton spent many of his free hours during the summer teaching session listing materials available at the university for his Texas Indians project in order to avoid duplication and loss of time in Mexico. He was able to tell Holmes July 23 that he had found that the university holdings were quite full after the 1788 date, but contained much less prior to that year. He had asked the week before what financial arrangements, if any, he might count on in connection with his forthcoming trip to Mexico. Holmes came back, July 25:

> I take pleasure in saying that the sum of one thousand dollars has been allotted to your work for the current fiscal year [July through June]. This amount will be paid you by check on completion and receipt by the Bureau of the first half of your proposed manuscript on the Tribes of Texas, the total manuscript to consist of two parts, aggregating 150,000 words. Under the necessary regulations it is not possible for the Bureau to reimburse you for any of your expenses for travel, subsistence, and copying, but it can purchase your manuscript when it is submitted.

This is the first mention of what recompense he might expect for doing this piece of work. In reply he told Holmes July 28 that in line with the letter of July 25 he felt justified in making certain expenditures and then went on to ask for suggestions as to the possible organization of the study.

Bolton went to Mexico on August 1. This was his fourth summer research jaunt beyond the border. A day or two after arrival in Mexico City and after he had had a little time to think and plan, he wrote to Holmes (August 6) that he had concluded that, possibly, the most workable approach to internal organization of the Texas Indians book would be to open with a general history of the tribes and then take the nations alphabetically; he also noted that he would have a series of maps to show location and distribution at various periods and he promised to be on the alert for linguistic data and affinity of the tribes. (This last area would be of interest to John R. Swanton of the bureau.)

On this trip Bolton had his own helper. This was one of his graduate students, William Edward (Eddie) Dunn, whom he was introducing to the Mexican archives. The exposure "took," for in time Eddie Dunn became one of his most regular, efficient, and productive archive-searchers. He was able to pay him $60 for his summer's work.

Even though these summer months were his own time, Bolton kept an eye, and sometimes an ear, open for the guide project. He sent a long letter to Jameson September 3 before he left Mexico detailing some of his newest finds in the archives. He mentioned that he had picked up valuable information concerning the provincial archives. Further, he had done quite a bit of foraging in the Sección de Cartografía of the AGN and had come up with some highly significant map discoveries. For example, he had turned up the Pichardo maps bearing on the Louisiana-Texas boundary dispute which had followed the American acquisition of Louisiana Territory; he had found the Lafora maps of northern New Spain, made during the inspection tour of the Marqués de Rubí in 1760; there was a map of the Jesuit missions in the north, and he had also seen the 1829 sketch of Texas done by Stephen Austin.

There was a letter from Jameson waiting for him when he returned to Austin, and with good news, for Jameson was reasonably confident that the necessary funds would be allocated by the trustees in 1907's budget; therefore, he asked when Bolton would be able to come to Washington for a conference. Before he could get to his correspondence, Bolton had to turn attention to problems and demands of the new school year. Barker had gone to Pennsylvania; Charles W. Ramsdell had been added to the staff to take over some of Barker's load, but departmental and *Quarterly* duties were heavy. Bolton's growing reputation on campus as a colorful and interesting teacher had attracted two hundred students to his medieval history course.

It was not until October that he could begin catching up. First, there was a letter to Holmes October 4, which gave a run-down on his weeks in Mexico and passed on the information that he had found much data on the Karankawa tribes, up to that time not well known or documented. Finally, on October 22, he suggested in a letter to Jameson that he would be free for the proposed conference in Washington during the Christmas vacation.

After the exchange of several letters he and Jameson worked out the time problems connected with the proposed conference. Christmastide would find Jameson busy with the affairs of the annual meeting of the American Historical Association of which he was the executive secretary. He suggested that Bolton meet him in Washington and then go on to Providence with him, doing their conferring on the train. Bolton jumped with enthusiasm at this proposal, for it would give him at long last a chance to attend his first AHA meeting.

Bolton obviously kept busy during the fall, for there are several letters from Holmes thanking him for short articles done for the *Handbook*. Before he finished he had prepared over a hundred short articles on Texas tribes and places for this reference work. These writings brought in a trickle of extra income. In early December he had to turn down a very tempting invitation to teach the summer session at Iowa, but the work on the guide project precluded acceptance.

Two postcards to his brother and a long letter told of developments during the 1906 Christmas season. He wrote a postcard from New Orleans, on Christmas Eve, that he was en route to Washington; a second card, from Houston January 6, announced: "On my way home from Boston, Providence, Philadelphia, Washington." The letter January 22, 1907, reported what had transpired in the Bolton-Jameson conferences. There was a point of divergence in the area of finances: Jameson suggested $150 a month plus travel; Bolton countered that he could not possibly go at that figure and set $225 a month plus travel funds and a subsidy for clerical assistance. A compromise was effected: the monthly check through 1907 would be $175, and after the new year it would be increased to $225. Bolton also indicated that he wished to take his family; Jameson was not prepared for this, but later he informed Bolton that the Carnegie Institution would pick up this travel bill, too.

In this same letter Bolton told his brother that there was talk in Washington of a possible series of Spanish *monumenta* for Southwestern history, a collection on the order of the "Jesuit Relations" which Reuben Gold Thwaites had edited. He confided that he might draw the assignment of editing ten or so volumes on Texas. He pointed out that he was already moving in select company with the men who were working on the Carnegie archival guides; if this new venture developed, he would be working with other scholars of like stature.

The late winter and spring months of 1907 flew by. There was much to be done as he prepared for the year's leave of absence from the University of Texas. In all the bustle he had to pause to welcome a fifth addition to the family — Gertrude was born on March 2. About that time a second summer session invitation came in, this one from the University of Colorado. Again, he had to decline, with regrets; but there was real satisfaction in feeling that his reputation was spreading.

It was in that same spring, 1907, that Bolton shared his knowledge of Texas colonial sites and history with a group of business adventurers and put them on the trail of the famous Los Almagres mine, uncovered in colonial days, never extensively worked because of the Indian danger on the far frontier, then "lost" but living in myth and legend. Bolton was contacted and he led the hopeful millionaires to the spot. In the company which was formed to exploit the supposedly fabulous silver lode Bolton was given a ninth interest, with no investment demanded and the assurance that he would not have to share in possible losses. Perhaps, there might be a payoff for the scholar, but he was not so sanguine as to change his life-style or neglect his work. The future proved him right, for the venture never made any of the partners rich; it simply gave Bolton a chance now and then to joke about his "mining interests."[4]

While Bolton was making preparations in Texas for the year to be spent in Mexico, Jameson was giving some time and thought to "greasing the diplomatic rails" in order to ensure smooth operation for the guide project. He promised to contact the American ambassador in Mexico and his counterpart in Washington to explain the nature and importance of Bolton's work. He also sought to enlist the interest of Secretary of State Elihu Root. Then on occasion he suggested that Bolton might help him to repay "debts" while in the Mexican archives. For example, Jameson suggested that if Bolton found materials which might be of interest to Arthur C. Doughty, archivist for the Dominion of Canada, he might note these; again, if he found pertinent Oregon materials, Jameson could use these to repay a favor to the Oregon Historical Society. Before Bolton finished in Mexico, he would be besieged by requests from individual scholars, especially after his paper before the American Historical Association at the Madison meeting of December, 1907, wherein he sketched some of the remarkable things which he was uncovering.

There was never a formal contract between Bolton and the Carnegie Institution; however, the Jameson letter of June 6 came close to that. It outlined what was expected by the institution in conformity with the patterns being followed by the other guide-makers. On June 24 Jameson added a point: the suggestion that Bolton send back a monthly report. Waldo G. Leland, at work in Paris, was doing this, and the device was proving very helpful to Jameson. It not only kept him informed, but gave him something to present periodically to the Carnegie trustees.

In the June 6 letter Jameson forwarded a document which could serve as formal introduction to the various archivists, librarians, and assorted officials whose cooperation Bolton would need:

> This letter is to certify that the bearer, Professor Herbert E. Bolton of the University of Texas, visits Mexico with the interests of the Department of Historical Research in the Carnegie Institution of Washington for the purpose of preparing a guide to the materials for United States History contained in the various Mexican archives. This book will be published by the Carnegie Institution for the benefit of historical scholars of the United States. In view of the benefits to scholarship which will ensue from this work, and of the aid which such studies may be expected to give toward the promotion of mutual understanding between the citizens of Mexico and the United States, I beg leave to bespeak for Professor Bolton all assistance from officials and others as may be possible for them to render consistently with due regard to the public interest of their own country.

With the groundwork completed, Herbert Bolton's monumental task lay before him. A few days before his departure for Mexico, he met with President Houston, who assured him that were he on campus the next year, it would be with the rank of associate professor and at a salary of $2,250. Perhaps Houston, recognizing the stature of the man, wished to provide the added incentive to draw Bolton back to the University of Texas after his leave in Mexico. In a short half dozen years he had come far, and the future seemed to hold ever greater promise and prominence for Herbert Bolton.

THE GUIDE IN THE MAKING

Of the dozens of books and articles which Bolton produced in his long life of scholarship possibly no other was quite as important as his first major work, the famous *Guide to Materials for the History of the United States in the Principal Archives of Mexico,* researched in 1907–08 and published finally in 1913.[5] This firmly established him as master in "his field," the Southwest, or as the area would be known in time, "The Spanish Borderlands." The *Guide* put hundreds of American scholars in his debt. The experience and the knowledge acquired in putting it together confirmed Bolton's already existing orientation toward writing history from documents. The Mexican months also gave him materials to put at the disposal of the dozens of graduate students whom he would train. From every point of view these were highly important months in his life as an American historian.

On June 20, 1907, Bolton left Austin on this exciting adventure for which he had so carefully planned in the preceding year. This sojourn would last for fifteen months. En route to Mexico City, he made stops at Matamoros, Reynosa, and Camargo for a quick look at their archives. On learning that a series of documentary volumes was being prepared by the State of Tamaulipas, he did not tarry long. He next paused at Querétaro for a first glance at archives which he suspected might turn out to be very valuable for his purposes, given the fact that so much of the Franciscan missionary effort in Texas and elsewhere in the North had stemmed out of the Colegio de Propaganda Fide de Santa Cruz, located there. The church records were in much better order and more accessible than were those of the state. Here, as elsewhere, he quickly found that being a Protestant was no handicap. However, looking into the future and wishing to be prepared for all contingencies, he suggested that Jameson obtain for him a letter from Cardinal James Gibbons of Baltimore to the archbishop of Mexico City which might forestall any possible blockage at that higher level. Actually, he never had to use it, either in the capital or in the provinces.

A first letter went to Jameson on July 18. For the early weeks Bolton had confined his attention to the AGN, but he informed Jameson that he would soon be ready to branch out to other archives in the capital, those particularly of the various departments of the government. Elise D. Brown, a graduate student and candidate for the master's degree at the University of Texas, was assisting him. She was working for the experience and asked nothing more, by way of compensation, than living expenses. When a little later she went off to the country to live on a hacienda, Bolton found himself seriously handicapped; Miss Brown had developed into an expert copyist. In time he gathered a corps of Mexican assistants, one of whom, Dolores Hurtado, remained his trusted contact with the archives through the years. Very often in later times, relying on his *Guide*, he would send off a "cry for help" to Señorita Hurtado, asking for a transcript of this or that *legajo* or *expediente* needed for his own work or that of one of his graduate students, and she quickly had the desired material on his desk.

Jameson again suggested periodic, preferably monthly, reports on the progress. The first such official report was sent July 24. In his "July Report" Bolton asked Jameson if the *American Historical Review* (*AHR*) might be interested in some documentary finds which he had turned up in the sections Historia and Provincias Internas. There were Vancouver materials regarding the Nootka Sound controversy; many pieces on Philip Nolan; the Miró correspondence concerning Thomas Green and the establishment of Bourbon County along the Mississippi by the Georgians. In those years the *AHR* quite regularly had a documentary section in each issue. Ultimately, Jameson, the editor, did request the Bourbon County materials, which he matched with complementary sources from other archives.

Bolton boarded the train for Austin July 24 to bring his family south and was back in Mexico City on August 3. The seven Boltons lived for the next several months in a house Bolton had rented on Calle Venecia. He returned to work and in the "August Report" indicated that he had spent that month in the sections on the Californias, the Missions, and that he was well into the Correspondencia de los Virreyes. He wrote to his brother August 18 that he regularly spent his mornings at the AGN and then transferred to Museo Nacional or the Biblioteca Nacional in the afternoons; the Archivo General was open on a rather restricted schedule:

> I am over my ears in work. I get to the Archivo General at 7:30 A.M. and leave at 1:30 P.M. Every other afternoon I go either to the Museo Nacional or the Biblioteca Nacional to work in the MS [manuscript] collections there. In the former I can remain until 6, in the latter until 8 P.M. The other afternoons I remain at home to

arrange my notes and to catch up with myself generally. Whatever
time I have, which is found mainly on Sundays and nights, which are
short after long days, I spend on the *Handbook of the Indians* or my
Indian history. My correspondence with the Carnegie and the Smithsonian is considerable — besides I have to keep preparing the way
for future work in the archives.

The materials in the Biblioteca were valuable but in such disarray that not
even the Mexicans seemed to know precisely what they had. He could tell
Jameson that he had turned up such California pieces of importance as
original letters of Serra, Palóu, Crespi, and Garcés. However, his prize
discovery was the lost account of Padre Eusebio Kino, the "Favores Celestiales," often referred to and quoted by eighteenth-century Jesuit writers
but judged by moderns to have been lost or destroyed. This find introduced Bolton to the man who in time became his "favorite Black Robe."
He ended this report with the estimate that he would have completed his
major work in the AGN by the end of September. It should be recalled
that he had become reasonably familiar with that archive during his four
previous summers in Mexico.

The next was a very busy month, if one can judge by the "September
Report." He worked through fifteen *secciones,* sometimes with great
profit and in other instances finding little or nothing bearing on the history
of the United States. In the draft of this September report Bolton set down
the following two not untypical experiences:

> To illustrate the necessity of a personal examination of every-
> thing, I may state my experience with the section Reales Cédulas y
> Ordenes. I worked most of the time for several days, perhaps ten, on
> the series downstairs — the only one I had seen or heard of — when
> I discovered another on the second floor. I then made inquiry as to
> its nature and its relation to the other, and was told that it consisted
> of registers or copies of the others. An examination of each volume
> showed me that this was only partly true, and resulted in my dis-
> covery of what could have saved me most of the ten days spent on
> the other series — namely, an admirable five volume collection of
> selected duplicate cédulas, dealing with the Provincias Internas, well
> indexed and classified by province. It was just what I needed, giving
> me in five volumes what I had sought in 150, but none of the officials
> had known of its existence, nor were the volumes so labelled or
> placed that one would know of its existence without opening every
> one of the 176 volumes of the series they were in. The collection
> was made a century ago.

The next experience set down was even more frustrating:

> To illustrate the scattered condition of things I may tell you
> another experience. Mixed with volumes on the correspondence of
> the viceroys I found a valuable volume of collected cédulas on the

expulsion of the Jesuits, made by the collector of the Provincias Internas documents. I noted it in my notes as a stray volume, and called the director's attention to it. Later, when at the Biblioteca Nacional one day, I dug out of the dust a companion to it. On my showing it to the librarian, Mr. Vigil, he told me that they had three volumes — the series "complete" — and had just entered it in their new printed catalogue. But an examination of the catalogue and the volumes catalogued showed me that the three were distinct, and were shelved on a different side of the room from the other. This accounted for five volumes. A little research and inquiry revealed another volume in the Biblioteca, while I found a seventh in this unknown section of Cédulas Reales. All but one of the eight volumes highly valuable, indispensible volumes have now been accounted for. But no one knows how the five volumes got out of the Archivo General.

Such things went into the making of the *Guide*. For years after publication, it would not only be an aid to the United States scholar proposing to work in the Mexican archives, but also something of a bible for the Mexicans themselves.

Despite the almost total absorption in his work, Bolton did look beyond the guide-to-be, as was evidenced by his letter to President Houston of Texas, August 11, 1907.[6] He told of finding masses of Texas history "in the raw," which could so admirably supplement the university's Bexar archives and other collections, all of which would be valuable for his own research and that of graduate students working in Texas history. He needed funds and begged Houston to supply them. In October he came back to the same theme and presented a formal and quite extensive proposal, showing how for as little as $1000 he could assemble ten to a dozen volumes of transcripts, each bulking to around five-hundred typed pages. His estimate was that the work could be done for about sixteen cents per page — transcribing, typing, and verifying each document with the original.[7] Houston was interested and two appropriations were allocated, each of $500 — the first for January 1908 and the second for February.

Secretary of State Elihu Root visited Mexico in October 1907. Bolton managed to talk with him, to explain what he was doing, and to enlist a promise of his assistance, if and when needed. Jameson was pleased; he was enough of a politician to recognize the importance of having the United States government properly apprised of what the Carnegie Institution was contributing to the cause of cordial relations with the neighboring republic.

In a letter of October 21 Jameson seconded Bolton's recent suggestion that he report to the profession during the Madison meeting of the American Historical Association in December. Jameson admitted that similar reports by Andrews and Shepherd at previous AHA meetings had been helpful and well received. Accordingly, Bolton began to plan for a quick trip to the North during the coming Christmas season.

In the "October Report" Bolton gave enlightening instances of the continual problem which he faced:

> During the month I examined thirty additional volumes of the California section which were covered up by a stack of papers, and whose existence was known to no one until by chance the papers were removed.
>
> There is a great stack of material that is utterly impossible, and will be until the archive is transferred to larger quarters. Some of the material is in bound volumes, much more in *legajos*. When this transfer is made, which I predict will not be soon, the guide will need revision.

At the Archivo de la Secretaría de Relaciones, to which he moved in November, Bolton made one of his more exciting discoveries. There was much in that archive which merited notice in the guide-to-be, but nothing quite as interesting as the packets of papers which had been taken from Zebulon Montgomery Pike at the time of his 1807 arrest and detention by the Spanish officials of New Mexico. It was well known to historians that Pike had had more papers than he was able to smuggle out in the gun barrels of several of his men. Now here they were! Jameson was intrigued and asked for copies, to be published in the *AHR*. Bolton sent a listing of the papers; Jameson checked and found that several had been published by Elliott Coues, but allowed that the bulk of the lot would be new to United States historians.[8] News of this discovery aroused a flurry of interest in Pike and awakened the hope that, perhaps, at long last, some key information might come to light on several unsolved mysteries — for example, what Wilkinson's instructions to Pike were when he sent him westward from Saint Louis in 1806.[9]

At the end of this "November Report" Bolton asked Jameson to do a bit of detective work for him — to find out what he could from the Mexican Embassy in Washington concerning the archives of Chihuahua where Bolton hoped to find a great body of material on the Provincias Internas, more even than in the large store of documents which he had already seen in the capital. Inquiries at the Mexican Embassy brought only a little, and that rather discouraging, information. The Chihuahua papers had been moved to Santa Bárbara in the days of governor E. C. Creel; they had, supposedly, been locked up there for safe keeping; however, when the Chihuahua Historical Commission had later opened them up, many of the older pieces were missing. Sr. Salado Alvarez of the Embassy volunteered the guess that some of the missing documents might have found their way into Hubert Howe Bancroft's collection — Mexicans, at the time resentful of some of Bancroft's gathering, had accused him of indulging in a bit of piracy. No proof exists that this was true, but with this information Bolton changed his initial plan to return from Madison via the northern capital.

Bolton went to Madison in December and delivered his paper. It was published in the April 1908 number of the *AHR* under the title "Materials for Southwestern History in the Central Archives of Mexico." The Madison appearance definitely established Herbert Bolton as *the* man in the new field which was opening to American historians and gave him excellent exposure.

Even before he left for the North, a December letter from Jameson had brought a sort of early Christmas present. The Carnegie trustees had voted funds to see the Mexican project through to completion, and in addition they had raised the December monthly payment from $175 to $200 — after the first of the year it had already been agreed that the monthly stipend would be $225.

Herbert's letters to Frederick during these Mexican months (actually only a bare dozen) do give some interesting sidelights, along with information pertinent to the guide project. His letter of March 6, 1908, was not only long and newsy, it was typed. He reported in some detail on his trip to Madison in late December; told of the article, his Madison paper, which he was readying for the *AHR;* called attention to his new address, 716 Avenida Tabasco; and also recounted some of the details of his visit with President Houston, when he dropped off in Austin en route back to Mexico City in early January. Houston had indicated both promotion and substantial salary increase for 1908–09. In June 1908 the Texas regents promoted Bolton to the rank of associate professor and upped his salary to $2400, which was even better than they had promised.

In this same letter he included a most interesting note which would have an important connection with his future. He told his brother: "Turner writes me that he has advised the University of California to look me up, to develop their field there. If they do, it may serve as a lever." Herbert returned to the Turner suggestion in a letter of March 17; evidently it intrigued him: "Turner has written to California to tell them to look out for me there. I do not care particularly to leave Texas, a fact which is going to militate against my promotion here I fear." Even though he talked of the possible California offer as a "lever," he was not at this time really serious about bargaining. Texas had been good to him; he was appreciated at the university and was becoming well known around the state. And there was also that chair of Southwestern history which President Houston had predicted could be a reality in the not too distant future.

For the first six months of 1908 Bolton was busy in the various archives of the capital. The work on the Texas Indians handbook for Holmes, therefore, had gotten more or less pushed aside. In a report to Holmes in June, 1907, before he went to Mexico, Bolton had indicated that he was interested in the handbook and was involved in background work at the university. He had combed all available printed sources in French, the Bexar archives at the University of Texas, the Nacogdoches archive, the Lamar Papers, the mission records at the residence of the bishop of San Antonio, and the growing accumulation of transcripts from Mexican and Spanish archives in the University of Texas library. Besides, he had developed a card index which was growing to sizable proportions. He reminded Holmes that he had prepared a number of short articles for the *Handbook,* and once more wrote at length of his developing study of the Hasinai. He expressed the hope that the bureau might be interested in publishing that piece separately.

The proportions of the work, as Bolton conceived it, began to dawn on Holmes, and in a June 10 letter he came back with a possible new format. Instead of a monumental work, it might be more feasible to break the study down into a series of shorter papers, "each to consist of either an ethnic or a geographic group." Obviously anxious to have something from Bolton, Holmes hinted that he might send the Hasinai paper as a starter.

During late 1907 and the early months of 1908, however, Holmes had written Bolton several times in Mexico. On October 25, 1907, he wrote requesting some indication of Bolton's plans, in order to know how to handle his work in the 1907–08 budget. He still left Bolton with the option of a single monograph to be delivered in two installments, at $13.30 per thousand words, or the proposed series of shorter studies. Bolton did not seemingly reply to this letter, for on December 13 Holmes tried again. "If we receive your introduction to the history of the Hasinai by July first 1908, I shall be well satisfied." When he had heard nothing by April 15, 1908, he wrote to ask if he would be able to divert the funds appropriated for the Texas Indians work to some other project prior to the close of the fiscal year. Bolton replied on June 8, 1908, regretting that he had nothing ready to submit. Holmes answered that he was disappointed but was certain that the arrangement could be extended into 1909. That was, however, the end of the Holmes file in the Bolton Papers, and also the end of the Texas Indians project. Increasingly distracted by and absorbed in other interests and commitments, Bolton never completed that study.

WINDING UP WORK ON THE GUIDE

If Bolton fell short in his commitment to the Texas Indians project, the same could not be said for his work on the *Guide*. In mid-April 1908 Bolton received a letter from Jameson in which he praised Bolton at length:

> The fact is that you are turning up so many remarkable things in this virgin field that the "Reviews" cannot attempt to deal with more than a small fraction of them. Indeed, you will be giving work, for a long period, to all available agencies. Your Guide is more likely than any other so far constructed to give a great impulse to historical production in the United States. . . .
> I am afraid that in answering your letters one by one, as they come, I never rise above details enough to express my general sense of admiration for the manner in which you are preparing the Guide and my appreciation of the excellent and helpful quality of your reports, which I feel enable me to always know pretty well what you are doing. . . .

Such commendation probably provided a boost for Bolton during more frustrating periods in his work. April 1908 was one of those periods. Holy Week intervened, and there were days when archives and libraries were not open. Then at the Secretaría de Gobernacíon Bolton experienced less than a cordial reception — really very rare in his Mexican experience. However, he kept on, despite minor obstructions, because here was an archive which had a great deal of material for United States-Mexican dealings through the nineteenth century and into the twentieth. This archive also had much on California prior to 1848; and more things besides. He finished Gobernacíon in May, "finding valuable materials right down to the last legajo."

The Secretaría de Hacienda, next on his list of archives, proved, in the main, disappointing. First, the recent files contained little that was pertinent to the United States. Then, while the older papers were numerous and probably valuable, they were in such complete disorder that it would not have paid to take the time to turn them over one by one to ascertain precisely what they contained. One reason for this disorder was that, mixed up with the old Hacienda records proper, were quantities of documents from the archive of the archbishopric of Mexico City. During the nineteenth-century revolutions, the old archiepiscopal palace had been confiscated and turned into the headquarters of the Secretaría de Hacienda, and many of the church records had not been transferred. Bolton listed the materials in broad categories and went on to the secretariat of the archdiocese, which he found very unproductive, at least for United

States history. He reported to Jameson that he would be able to get into the old Colegio de San Fernando, home base in the eighteenth century for the Franciscans who had established the California missions. However, he predicted that this would be for little more than to satisfy his curiosity, since the Franciscan historian Engelhardt had not listed the San Fernando archive as one of importance for the California story.[10]

In July he made ready to move out into the provinces. Querétaro was the first stop, and he stayed eleven days. The Franciscan archive was particularly rich. Thence he went to San Luis Potosí, where he ran into difficulty. First, he lost several days, having arrived on the anniversary of the death of Benito Juárez, which was a holiday, and the next day was Sunday. Next, he encountered one of the relatively few instances of something less than open-handed cooperation. Later he asked Jameson just how he should warn future researchers against this problem, so as to save them the time and trouble of going to San Luis.

From Querétaro he went on to Guadalajara, Chihuahua, Parral, and Santa Bárbara. Although forewarned, he now had to face the reality of disappointment of not finding the original archive of the Comandancia General de las Provincias Internas. He reported to Jameson from another important northern center, Saltillo, on September 22:

> I continued my work in Chihuahua until the 12th of this month, going thence to Parral and Santa Bárbara. Though there is good material at Chihuahua, I did not find the archive of the Comandancia General, and the question of its whereabouts remains to me a puzzle.
>
> At Santa Bárbara and Parral I found almost nothing, as I expected would be the case, after having worked at Chihuahua. I have in my possession a letter, from an American in Parral, which I have treasured four or five years, waiting for an opportunity to visit the place. In it he tells me that he examined the archive there and concludes that there is no other archive in existence so rich for early Texas history. But I found nothing. My conclusion is that he had heard that Parral was once a "capital" for the north country and having seen in the archives numerous bundles of old papers bearing dates to him fabulously old, he concluded that they must be important for early Texas history. I cite this incidentally as an example of the value of a layman's opinion in matter of archives. The opinions of Mexican officials generally and of archive custodians in particular are just as worthless, and anyone who relies upon them will make no progress. I suspect that the same would be true in the United States and elsewhere.

Doubling back from Parral, he passed through Zacatecas and then went on to Durango. He arrived there to find things closed tight during the Independence Day fiestas. Here, again, a well-intentioned "helper" raised his hopes — this time an American lady. According to her the cathedral had a fantastic archive, but he found nothing of value to him, "ni un papel." Durango had other depositories, however, which proved definitely rewarding. This experience led him in a September 17 letter to Frederick to comment rather trenchantly on archivists:

> In this I was not disappointed, for I had long since learned not to place confidence in such reports. On the contrary, neither do I pay any attention, as a rule, to archive keepers and other officials when they tell me that they have nothing. I humor them by saying "Of course not, but I'd like to look around a little," and generally I find what I expect to find. Sometimes the negative assertion of the official is due to ignorance — usually so.

On his return to the United States, Bolton would give the *Guide* what time he could. Even so, it would not be until mid-September 1910 that he would be able to bundle his hundreds of pages and thousands of notations into an express package and send the same off to Jameson at Washington. The end of the story was still three years into the future. The fresh delays, however, were not of Bolton's making. Publication would not come until November 1913.

Meanwhile Bolton's family caught up with him in Saltillo in mid-September, and together they left for Austin. The long fifteen months were over, and everyone was glad to be heading home. The time had been immensely valuable to Herbert Bolton; Mrs. Bolton had not always found life in a foreign land easy or thrilling. The girls had lost a year of schooling but had gained in many other ways; the older ones had quickly become bilingual. All in all, it was wonderful to be returning home.

5

The Stanford Calling

WHILE TRAVELING BACK to the United States Gertrude Bolton put in her husband's hands a letter, now almost a month old, from E. D. Adams, chairman of the Department of History at Stanford University, California.[1] It had come to their home in Mexico City while Herbert was making the rounds of the provincial archives, and Gertrude, for fear it would not catch up to him, had felt it unwise to mail it while he was on the move. She probably sensed its possible significance since Herbert had been in touch earlier in the summer with John M. Stillman of Stanford who had telegraphed Bolton, asking tersely if he would be interested in a one-year appointment to the Department of History at Palo Alto. Bolton had replied that he could not consider such an appointment unless it carried reasonable assurance of permanency. "I suspect," he wrote to Frederick July 18, 1908, "that the interim proviso is intended as a means of giving me a trial." He had figured, at the moment, that this answer would put an end to the matter.

Now came this letter from Adams, and it was a lengthy one. In it Adams explained that he had just returned from Europe; during his absence several unexpected resignations had panicked the folk on the campus; he apologized for the "temporary" idea which Stillman had put in his telegram. "In this connection, permit me to say that if I had been on the ground, I should not have thought of proposing to a man in your position and of your reputation a temporary appointment." He assured Bolton that no permanent appointments had been made for the year about to open but that two such would be likely for the following year. Stanford would be looking for a United States political-constitutional man and another "to take up, more particularly, aspects of western history." Adams concluded: "I should like very much to hear from you in detail of the type and character of work in which you are interested as a teacher and a student."

Adams, probably not aware that Bolton was on the move, trying desperately to finish his Mexican work and be back in Austin for the opening of the new school year, became somewhat impatient and on September 30 sent off a note to Bolton at Austin and enclosed a copy of his August 31 letter. Bolton had written on September 28. He explained the reasons for his tardiness in replying, thanked Adams for continued interest, then added: "If, after you have read the statement given below, you are still interested in my work and my plans, I shall be glad to furnish any additional information you may desire."

In the statement mentioned Bolton gave some enlightening information about himself. He affirmed that as a graduate student, first under Turner at Wisconsin and then under McMaster at Pennsylvania, his special orientation had been toward western and socioeconomic history. Since coming to Texas his interest had shifted to Southwestern history. In this area his prime emphasis had been on the Texas story, but he noted that his recent work in the Mexican archives had definitely broadened his perspective to include New Mexico, Arizona, and California; he added that on all these regions he had sizable packets of transcripts which he planned to exploit in his subsequent writing. He emphasized the fact that his teaching assignments at Texas, medieval and early modern European history, did not reflect his research interests, but he noted that he did give a course on "Spain in America" and that he was directing several research theses in "his" field. As to teaching ambitions for the future, he listed in order of preference the undergraduate courses he would like to be able to teach: the history of the West, the history of the Spanish Southwest, and social and economic history of the United States. As for graduate work, he would like to offer seminars on the Spanish Southwest and the Anglo-American West, in that order. He sent off the letter, at the moment not really imagining that anything would come of it.

In a letter September 6 to his brother, in which he had told of plans for the immediate future, he had mentioned this Stanford feeler and remarked:

> What I have outlined above discloses a reason why I am not anxious to move. To do so would distract my attention to the work of giving new courses, and I would lose much time and momentum in that way. I feel that academically I may lose opportunities by being thus tied down, but I hope that I will not be too old or too narrow after I get through the present cycle to be wanted somewhere.

However, the Stanford overture could not help but cause him to do a bit of thinking, which is reflected in his next letter to Frederick on October 1:

> To my surprise the California [Stanford] people have written me again, this time regarding a permanent place there. I have just answered them what I want to do, which is all they asked of me. Maybe they will think I can be useful there, and maybe not. I do not care to move unless I can do what I want, or unless there are considerable inducements. If anything better than a full professorship at $2700 or $3000 were offered, they could not equal it here, even if they were so inclined. I think, however, that they would come to the lower figure at once, and to the other in a short time.

Bolton had a chance to be surprised, for Adams wrote back almost immediately (October 3) and at some length:

> Your letter is inspiring in the thought that there is so great a field for work in Western and Southwestern history. . . .
> But without further comment upon this at this time, I am going to ask still another favor of you. Will you kindly indicate for me where I am able to find the principal contributions made by you to historical study and knowledge, and to which you refer indirectly in your letter . . . I am getting information from various sources and about various men to lay before the Department and ultimately before the President. I shall say also, that in my opinion, the field of Western and Southwestern History, particularly with reference to Mexico, is the most logical field for special development by our Pacific Coast universities, and that it seems to offer the greatest opportunities for new and original work.

Adams was also intrigued by Bolton's mention of transcripts of archive documents, but he remarked that this sort of operation could become very expensive. Still, he wondered what Bolton might consider as an annual appropriation necessary "to do really creditable work." Adams could not have known it at the moment, but with that last remark he was lifting the lid from Pandora's fabled box. Before negotiations with Bolton were concluded, Adams probably wished more than once that he had never heard of transcripts from the Mexican and other archives. The matter was very much in the Bolton-Adams exchanges of the next months. Adams quickly learned that Bolton not only wanted his transcripts but was going to have them, come what might. Bolton at this point saw his whole research future intimately bound up with this sort of continuing contact with the archives.

Bolton was prompt in furnishing Adams with reprint samples of his published articles. In the October 11 letter which accompanied the reprints he outlined in a general way his plans for translating and editing some of the archival treasures he had discovered, in order to indicate what use could be made of the transcripts obtained and, hopefully, to be acquired. He also promised cost estimates in a next letter. He did not, however, warn Adams to brace himself!

This next letter, October 13, gave a plan as to how one should proceed with a transcript-copying project. He gave around twenty cents per page as a reasonable cost estimate. He insisted that a trained American be sent as the supervising copyist and, more importantly, as verifying agent; the rest of the copying force could readily be recruited in Mexico. He listed some of the materials which might be transcribed immediately and which would furnish the raw materials for excellent research theses. He suggested, among other examples, the California documents for the years 1768 to 1790. He felt that the average thesis would require around 1000 pages of transcripts, with the overall cost running to about $200. He said that a fund of at least $3000 would be necessary to launch the project, but then there would have to be an annual budget of from $500 to $1000 to keep it going. In this letter he also remarked that the library would have to have ample resources for the building of a collection of indispensable printed works. It was quite evident from this letter that Bolton, if he came, would "come high." And still there was no mention of possible salary.

Adams was not scared off. He wrote November 2 to explain at length the appointment process at Stanford, and he asked if he might submit Bolton's name:

> What I propose then to you is this: To name you for an Associate Professorship of American History, at a salary of $3000, with the understanding that your work is to be primarily in the control and development of studies in American history connected with the West and the Southwest. By American history here I do not mean to limit the field to United States history at all, but rather to emphasize Spanish American history. In short, I should hope that you would continue the work you have begun so excellently and really develop this field.

Adams went on to observe that the rank of associate professor was normal for a man coming in, save with a top reputation or from "one of the greater universities." He was apologetic that he was not at the moment able to assure a manuscript fund, but he promised to try to obtain one. He called attention to the fact that Stanford was in its final stage of "earthquake reconstruction" — the university had suffered considerable damage in the famous quake of 1906 — which, along wtih the disastrous fire, had put San Francisco on the front pages of newspapers around the nation and the world. Adams asked for a quick answer to this letter and hinted strongly that he had little doubt that the trustees would approve an appointment for August 1909. Adams closed with the invitation to Bolton to send on any questions which he might have.

Bolton's reply was quite prompt, drafted on November 16 and sent several days later. He accepted the invitation to present his questions, which came in two categories. Were he to get the transcript appropriation, how would this affect his share of the general library budget? Just how well stocked was the Stanford library in the area of Spanish-American history? Would a Stanford man be welcome and have access to the Bancroft Library at neighboring University of California? What about living costs at Palo Alto, and what about housing? Then there was the much more touchy matter concerning academic rank. He told Adams that he had been treated well at Texas and confessed that he must have a compelling reason to move. A full professorship might add up to such a reason. Without saying it in so many words, he insinuated that, promised a professorship, he would be willing to move, even though the salary might be pegged at the quoted $3000 figure.

Adams answered on November 24. This letter, if one reads between the lines, showed that Bolton's demands were making life a mite difficult for the Stanford chairman. Adams stated that he was in no position to give firm assurance of the transcript fund; further, under no condition, would it be over and above the ordinary library budget — that year (1908–09) the Department of History's share of the annual budget of $25,000 was $1146. He did admit that he might be able to assist Bolton in his work with some other departmental money, accruing in small quantity from other sources. Adams had to hedge on the question of the full professorship. He guessed that the living costs in Palo Alto were considerably higher than in Austin, maybe even as much as twenty percent. He concluded with the hope that Bolton would come, even though he could not give a definite yes or no to all his demands.

Bolton now had a major decision to make. On December 3 he drafted an answer. He asked for definite commitments in regard to the appropriation for transcripts and on the matter of rank, warning that he could not decide without clarification on these two points. Adams replied December 13 that, even though Bolton's letter had arrived late, he would make every effort to have the matter on the agenda for the meeting of the trustees, which was imminent. He obviously succeeded, for on December 19 he could write:

> At the meeting of the University Trustees, yesterday afternoon, President Jordan was authorized to offer you a Full Professorship in American History, at a salary of $3500.00. On the other hand, the Trustees refused to make any appropriation for next year for transcripts or to promise such appropriations in the future.

Adams noted that the last matter was presented somewhat hurriedly and ventured to suggest that, possibly, for that reason was not thoroughly discussed. He added that "the Trustees were favorable to the development

of a field of Southwestern and Spanish-American history, and to my idea
of placing a special emphasis on it in the future development of the
Department of History." He tried to reassure Bolton that President Jordan
had the feeling that the trustees in time would come around to the transcript appropriation, and Adams pledged himself to continue to work to
that end. Next, there followed an outline of the regular salary increments
and the suggestion that Bolton might share in the current library budget
of the department by setting down book needs for his work. Finally he
came to the matter of courses, proposing a possible two-hour course on
the West, a graduate course on the Southwest, and a three-hour undergraduate course on Spain in America, or, possibly, a second graduate
course — "a seminary."* He mentioned that the normal teaching load
was three courses, totaling to seven hours. Again, Adams closed with the
hope that Bolton would opt for Palo Alto and asked, "May I hear from
you soon?"

By the morning after Christmas Herbert Bolton had made up his
mind; he telegraphed his acceptance and later in the day penned Adams
a long letter:

> I assume that you received in due time my telegram informing
> you of my decision to accept the offer made me there, and to cast
> my lot with Stanford University. The decision was most difficult for
> me to make but I am going to trust that it was wisely made, and to
> look forward, not back. The most unsatisfactory feature of the
> arrangement, as you will understand, is the lack of definite provision
> for the securing of manuscripts, but, knowing that your chief reason
> for desiring my services is my fitness to direct work in Southwestern
> History, with special reference to the Mexican archives, and con-
> sidering all your statements, my judgment tells me that provision is
> bound to be made; hence, my decision. Before proceeding to the
> matter of courses, which is the main point of this letter, let me express
> my appreciation for your efforts to arrange everything to my satis-
> faction and for your patience with my delays. . . .

Bolton was busy that day, for a long letter to his brother also bears the
December 26 date:

> The deed is done. I this morning telegraphed my acceptance of
> the place at Stanford. My decision came after a long, hard struggle.
> You may wonder why it was hard for me to decide, but I can explain.
> The president here [Mezes†] came up with a full professorship at
> $3000.00 and an appropriation of $500.00 a year to work with. At

*The word "seminary" means the same as seminar.

†Sidney E. Mezes succeeded Houston who resigned in the summer of 1908.

that time all they had offered me at Stanford was an associate professorship at $3000.00 with the prospect of coming up to $4000.00
and a good appropriation. I wrote them that unless they could tell
me just when I might expect to advance and guarantee me what I
considered a fair appropriation, I could not go. In reply they offered
me a full professorship immediately at $3500.00 and a promise of a
raise of $250.00 for the third and fourth years, respectively, in case
I make good, as they expect me to, thus putting me on the $4000.00
basis. The trustees would make no advance promise in regard to
appropriations for transcripts until they see me, and . . . in this
Adams was disappointed, but he assures me that this action is only
to preserve a ruling the trustees have made, as a result of some embarrassing experiences, and that I will get what I want. . . . Common
sense tells me that I shall, because this work is the very thing and
the only thing they cared to get me for. . . . And this gives me confidence, since Adams seemed very anxious to get me for this work,
that I will be liberally treated.

I shall be the first man in the department of American History,
with the special field of Southwestern and Spanish-American History
in my charge. . . . With all the advantages of Stanford over Texas,
there are many reasons why I should like to remain here. They have
treated me well lately, and I could work undisturbed more at my
writing here than there, because demands of courses would be only
what I might choose to make them. But there are probably higher
standards, and more demands for lecture courses for large advanced
classes there. But I shall look forward, not back, and try to make
good there, as I managed to do here.

Delighted to have corralled one of the rising men in the field of American history, Adams replied on December 31:

> I was delighted to get your telegram of acceptance a few days
> ago, and at once notified President Jordan, requesting him to send
> you formal notice of appointment. Your letter came today, but I
> am not going to answer your questions about courses, for I want a
> little while to think that over.

Bolton had also inquired about the rest of the American history teaching
staff, hoping for a possible opening for Barker, although without mentioning his name at that point. Adams did touch the question of another
man or men in American history, telling Bolton that he himself might take
over the general political history course on the United States. He justified
this quasi trespass by indicating his interest and research in the area of
Anglo-American relations which had forced him to acquire a sound general acquaintance with the American story. (By training, Adams was
really an English history specialist.)

Adams, after some thought, wrote concerning courses on January
7, 1909. He suggested that the course on Western America might well be

scheduled for two hours a week and run for both semesters as a general offering in American history and might pick up a broad freshman-sophomore enrollment. As for advanced offerings, there might be a course on the Spanish Southwest and another on the Anglo-American Southwest and West. The seminar offerings could build on these. He informed Bolton that there would be $377 available to him from the current library budget, which he might spend immediately and should spend before August 1, the date on which unexpended moneys would go back to the general university fund. Bolton in his next letters suggested materials which might be copied in view of possible seminar work in 1909–10.

With all this excitement stretching over several months it is easy to guess that Bolton did not have much time for the *Guide*. Already a marked characteristic of his scholarly life was beginning to show — a tendency to allow his dreams and ambitions to overextend themselves unrealistically.

Still another commitment was getting shortchanged during the time Bolton was trying to make a decision about the Stanford offer. This involvement was with another publisher, the Arthur H. Clark Company of Cleveland, and it had begun while Bolton was in Mexico in 1908. He had first contracted to deliver to Clark a translation of materials on Athanase de Mézières which he had found in the Mexican archives. The story was of a Frenchman "turned Spaniard" on the Louisiana-Texas frontier following the cession of the Trans-Mississippi to Spain in 1762. Bolton considered it one of his major finds, and he determined to keep the information for himself rather than to pass it along to other scholars. The De Mézières story would be a splendid example of how Spain had to shift her Indian policies after acquiring so many Indians who had not been and were not likely to be subjected to the mission pattern of control. He had told Clark that the translation would be in his hands by December 1, 1908;[2] he had then agreed to begin a translation of the "Favores Celestiales" of Padre Kino for Clark also — this Bolton considered to be his greatest find. Finally Clark had pegged Bolton for involvement in a series called "Documentary Sources of American History from the Spanish and Mexican Archives." Clark considered Bolton the logical choice to do the Mexican volumes, and Bolton had reacted to the proposal with enthusiasm since this would help fulfill a dream long cherished — to make the sources of Texas history more easily available to researchers and students. When he learned, however, that Clark envisioned a series broad enough to include California, he was more than a bit chagrined, and for a reason.

In November 1907 Jameson had encouraged Bolton to be helpful to a certain Iowa lawyer and history buff, Irving B. Richman, who was interested in collecting materials for a history of California during Spanish and Mexican days.[3] Bolton, without too much enthusiasm, had gone along with the idea and had begun to furnish Richman with what he considered to be prime materials. Jameson had written on November 25, 1907: "He [Richman] is an excellent scholar and a man of means. What he will produce will be so worthwhile that I should be tempted to comply with his request, even if it meant some hindrance to the work of this department." It is not clear just how Richman had this much influence with Jameson, but the fact remains that he seems to have had.

Richman was not slow to take advantage of an on-the-spot researcher and immediately letters were traveling southward. Bolton was irked, but one thing which lessened this somewhat was the fact that in mid-December Richman forwarded a New York draft for $100, authorizing Bolton to engage a typist for an amount "not to exceed $100 a month." By early 1908 a long list of pertinent California documents was Iowa-bound, and soon thereafter the first batch of transcripts went to Richman. Richman, however, soon got on Bolton's nerves with his persistence and increasing demands.

When the Clark proposal came, therefore, Bolton realized that the best of "his" California finds were about to be lost. Bolton's reaction? He wanted "his" documents back. There was an exchange of letters, with Richman being quite completely taken aback by Bolton's attitude. Because he seemed to recognize the ill-concealed resentment of the young man, Richman agreed that the California volumes of the projected Clark series might be coedited — he would have his documents, and Bolton could have the glory of being "kingpin" in the series.

Satisfied that "his rights by reason of discovery" would be protected, Bolton sent Clark a long letter July 24, outlining under this arrangement general plans for the series. It should be broken into two parts, the first to run to 1763. This would mean that his own volumes on Texas, or several of them at least, would be out and the series linked with his name before publication moved into the California materials. This was agreeable to Clark, and he said so in a long letter of August 15. This same letter went into considerable detail concerning the series; the division of the Spanish and the Mexican documents with Robertson was sketched; Bolton was told to deal with Richman, since "our arrangement is with you"; Clark asked for a list of documents to be included in the first series, which was to run to ten volumes, the last being an index. Then Clark added: "Now we must define your field and mine — you are a specialist in your field of American history, I in my field of publishing"; the implication clearly was: you do your job and do not try to interfere in mine.

This letter was followed August 13 by a contract to be signed and a suggested timetable for the series. Clark proposed that the first volume running to 1763 be published by May 1, 1910, and that each of the next eight appear in succeeding months, with Volume Ten, the index, scheduled for July 1, 1911. Bolton, feeling that this was a manageable timetable, signed the contract. Almost immediately he began to talk of "my series."

As hinted earlier, "my series," along with other projects, tended to get lost as the first months of 1909 ran off the calendar. Clark was concerned, but he was even more upset by Bolton's failure to deliver his De Mézières manuscript. He nudged him, gently at first, but then a little less gently. Clark did not know it, but he was already on one end of what would develop into a real tug-of-war with Bolton during the years ahead.

On April 13 Adams had good news for Bolton. The Department of History at Stanford had voted him a student assistant at a salary of $800 for the year. Bolton had already written about his prize student, Eddie Dunn. Adams informed Bolton that "he [Dunn] would be assigned you as your student assistant and his work would be such as you choose to arrange with him, with the general proviso that it should not occupy more than 15 hours per week of his time." Bolton was delighted and in a later letter to his brother (June 1) paid Eddie Dunn this glowing compliment:

> By the way I am to take with me my most valuable assistant, Mr. Dunn, who has worked with me and worked for me in Mexico several times. He will go as my assistant in the Department, and will study for his Doctorate. He is a senior this year and has been helping me since he was a sophomore. He is regarded as the best modern linguist in the University.

As the last of Bolton's days at Texas drew near, his thoughts turned more and more to the upcoming move to Stanford. In a letter to Frederick June 4 he reflected:

> One of the features at Stanford is that I may expect a half year every three, or a full year every six, or rather, at the end of every six. I shall probably take the half years as they come. In that way, by combining the half years with vacations, one can be about three fourths of a year off every three years. I shall probably put my first one in in Spain. . . .
> I can't say when I can get away. I have much work here before I go, on the other hand I need considerable time to prepare for my work there. I shall have a big course, all lecturing, for which there are few books of direct and continuous usefulness. I have never given it, and I do not know what the library there contains. I am glad that it comes only twice a week. It is the Westward Movement in American History. One of my seminary courses will be new to me also. The

extra demands of teaching for the first time is one of the strong reasons why I hated to move. I am very sorry at times that I decided to
do so, and yet, I guess I should have to make the same decision again,
if the question were to come up.

I am pegging away seven or eight hours a day on my Guide to
the Mexican archives, in addition to my other work. This comes hard,
but I must stand it for a while. . . .

I am at present in the History Vault, where I spend most of my
time. I never take much of my stuff home, for fear of fire. I have
worlds of stuff that cannot be duplicated in the United States, and it
would cost much money to get it again in Mexico. I personally have
twenty or thirty volumes of transcripts, transcripts from the Mexican
archives. Each one of these costs $100 or more, not counting the
time. There is where my money goes, you see.

I have two Master's candidates this year, and they have made a
real contribution to Southwestern history. . . .

I hear that I am to be elected an honorary Phi Beta Kappa at
Commencement for "distinction etc" as the constitution prescribes.
Well, it costs nothing. I shall appreciate the honor, whether I merit
it or not.

At the end of this letter he noted, "I am my own stenographer." In late
years he had become somewhat more expert on the typewriter — the
demands of editorial work on the *Quarterly,* he said, and particularly the
need for preparing clear copy for the *Guide*. At Stanford he would know
one of the luxuries of the academic man, the assistance of an expert typist;
hence, his "feud" with the typewriter was just about at an end.

On that same day, June 4, 1909, Bolton was obviously a busy man at
the typewriter. He typed a long letter to President Mezes:

Before severing my connection with the University of Texas I
wish the privilege of again expressing to you my great regret therefor,
and of making it known through you to the Honorable Board of
Regents, if you will be so kind as to convey my brief message.

My relations with the University of Texas have been from first to
last of the very pleasant kind. I have received just and generous treatment from the Board of Regents, Presidents, and faculty, and I feel
certain that it would be hard to find a more satisfactory student body
to work with anywhere in the United States. Besides these highly
satisfactory conditions, I have found here a very interesting and
profitable field of historical work; as you know, ever since coming
here I have made the special object of my research the Spanish Southwest, and especially Texas. Besides the fact that it is an undeveloped
field, and therefore attractive to a student, it is intrinsically of great
interest. Moreover the authorities of the University and the community at large have shown an inspiring appreciation of my efforts
in this particular work.

It is not surprising, therefore, that when the opportunity came
to go to another university, I was extremely reluctant to leave the

University of Texas, and I wish you to know that the decision came only as the result of the victory of reason over inclination, and does not involve the abandonment of my work on the Southwest, but, rather, seems to offer an opportunity to prosecute it with greater advantages. My interest is in the whole Southwest, and residence in California offers the opportunity to make the intimate personal acquaintance with that extremity of the field that residence in Texas has given me of this. California has valuable collections of historical materials which I wait the opportunity to study. Since my work and that of Professor Garrison have a tendency to overlap at certain points, I shall feel freer in some respects there to follow where my interests lead than might be the case here. Stanford University has shown not only a special interest in the kind of work in which I am engaged, but also a disposition to provide more means to foster it than the University of Texas seems at present able to provide or than it seems to be able to provide in the near future. Finally, out of duty to my family I have been forced to consider advantages of climate and salary which are offered at Stanford.

This is a frank and correct statement of the reasons for my resignation. I believe that the University of Texas has a bright future, and should be proud to have a part in its development, which I shall watch with a warm personal interest and sympathy.

A few weeks after commencement Bolton said his adieus and was on his way. His eight years in Texas were ended. Important years they were; he had found himself and his field; he had gained recognition; he was on his way to the top of his profession. Another phase of his life, "the Pacific Coast years" or "the California years," was opening. If there was ever any validity in the old expression that "life begins at forty," he was on the threshold — he had just celebrated his thirty-ninth birthday when he arrived in Palo Alto. The next forty-odd years in this other of his Borderlands were destined to be very full years. Alta California would treat him well, but he left a part of his heart in Texas.

6

The Stanford Years, 1909-1911

WHEN HERBERT BOLTON ARRIVED at Stanford in August 1909, the university was just beginning its eighteenth year. Its generous founder, Leland Stanford, Sr., had died shortly after its opening, but with the help of his widow and its remarkably capable president, David Starr Jordan, Stanford had gotten through an "iron age of austerity" in the late 1890s; more recently it had survived, but with much damage, the jolt of April 1906 which the shifting San Andreas Fault had dealt the western side of the Bay Area and the Peninsula. Enrollment was just short of 1,800, the large proportion of whom were undergraduates, since dreams of graduate work were being realized only slowly.[1]

Bolton was and wasn't happy at Stanford. His students were receptive and cooperative, more sophisticated than his rough-hewn Texans, but not quite the eager geniuses which the administration hoped they would be. The fact that at last he was teaching exclusively in his field of interest and research was a definite positive value. The administration, both at the top and the departmental levels, tried to be cooperative. Even so, Bolton was unsettled. Some of his disillusionment showed in a January 27, 1910, letter to Frederick:

> Now for my idea of the place... Stanford seems to have very little hold on the schools of the State. The State University has that, naturally. Stanford is a good college, but there is little advanced work here, and very little evidence that it will be developed in the near future. The History Department, for example, has not as good a spirit in this respect as that of the University of Texas. Thus, except for climate, which has many good features, Stanford is not the most desirable place in the world. . . . I have lost no less than a solid year of actual investigation, and am no better off otherwise than I should have been at Texas.

Perhaps a key to this restlessness is to be found in the postscript to this letter. It would seem that his brother in a recent letter mentioned having run into Henry Morse Stephens of California at a meeting, for Herbert queried: "Was there any indication that Morse Stephens was thinking of me for a place? Berkeley is where I belong, and some of them up there have already recognized it."

Now that he was so close to the University of California, he was very likely letting his dreams of the future run toward Berkeley. He had not forgotten, as he had reported in a letter to Frederick from Mexico on March 8, 1908, that Turner had written to say that he had advised the University of California to keep an eye on Bolton as one who might very well help them "to develop their field there." Several times since arriving at Stanford, Bolton had gone up to Berkeley to see firsthand the great wealth of the Bancroft Collection which California had lately acquired. The sight had made him drool, and dream — what a boon it would be to have such California, Southwestern, Mexican riches within ready reach!

In his first year at Stanford Bolton faced a new school situation involving new courses, new colleagues, and a new library, and he and his family were confronted with new living quarters, too far from campus to suit him. All these things called for readjustment. Besides, he had many personal projects to which he was able to give much too little time and attention. He still had to finish the *Guide,* and Jameson was needling him gently but enough to make him somewhat uncomfortable. Arthur Clark was pushing for the Athanase de Mézières volume, and reminded him of his other commitment to the "Documentary Sources" series. He was getting along well at Stanford; Adams and history colleagues were cordial and the students enthusiastically cooperative. Days when he felt particularly harried, however, he often wondered if he should have left Austin. As spring ran toward summer, he planned for those free weeks and filled the days with much hard work.

Those weeks turned out to be anything but free; a rugged several months lay ahead.[2]

THE TORTURED SUMMER OF 1910

When Bolton heard of George Pierce Garrison's death, he at once realized that this meant the chairmanship of the Department of History at the University of Texas was vacant. Actually Bolton had never quite put Texas behind him, despite his periodic affirmations of being satisfied at Stanford. All his early research and writing had been on Spanish Texas, and he still had much work he wanted to do in that field. This interest would continue to surface throughout his career from time to time as it did even some twenty years later when Bolton wrote to a friend (February 19, 1929):

I have never given up my interest in Texas under Spain. I have been drawn away from it, as you know, by a variety of circumstances. Other persons, dear friends of mine, have gone into the field. I have a strong inclination to write a general sketch, perhaps a little book of three hundred pages under that title [Texas under Spain]. . . . I am foolish enough to think that I might write a worth while sketch, if I would devote a year to it.[3]

He knew the California story, had seen thousands of California documents and planned to exploit them, but the Texas story continued to fascinate him to the extent that he could not feel altogether happy in his latest position.

He pondered the situation and on July 30 sent off a long letter to President Sidney Mezes in Lake Placid, New York, where he was vacationing. A telegram had preceded the letter which read:

You doubtless received in due time the telegram signifying my interest in the place left vacant by the unfortunate death of Professor Garrison. In view of the very generous treatment which you accorded me last year, I felt that I could with propriety open the subject, and my failure to do so sooner has been due not to indifference, but to the conflict of motives which has kept me undecided. I wrote a part of this letter two weeks ago, but decided not to send it without further consideration. One strong reason for refraining from writing has been my unwillingness to injure any prospect for advancement which Dr. Barker might have as a result of changed conditions; but he, without my suggestion, has more than once assured me that I need not hold back on that account.

I have not for a moment been uncertain of my personal inclination in the matter, for I have from the first been desirous of returning to Texas in case you should regard it with favor. I feel that viewed from the standpoint of what I wish to do, Texas is where I belong. Though I am interested in developing the whole field of Southwestern and Spanish-American history, I approached it from the Texas side, and in my personal work am in the midst of tasks of which Texas is the center, and which, because of local collections, and especially because of a sympathetic atmosphere, can be done better there than elsewhere.

My work here has been very pleasant, and has met with gratifying appreciation. But I feel the danger that the same local patriotism that gives Texans such an enthusiasm for their own history will force me more and more, and indirectly my students, into the study of Pacific Coast problems, and away from the tasks which through years of work I have well under way. Personally, as to scholarship, if my work is worth while, this would mean a loss.

Moreover, I look with enthusiasm on the prospect for and covet the opportunity to take part in the development in Texas of a really distinctive and distinguished School of History, as, indeed, it has in no small measure already become. As I see it, the most promising fields for historical work in this country for the next twenty-five years are Western and Spanish-American history. For the development of Western history three universities are at strategic points and already bear the stamp of leadership. These are Wisconsin for the Old Northwest and the Mississippi Valley; the University of California for the Far West and the Pacific Coast (this rather than Stanford because of the great handicap of the Bancroft Collection and the enthusiasm of the people of the state for a state institution); and the University of Texas for Southwestern history, in both the narrower and the broader sense. Texas can not only best exploit the history of the great region of which she is the center, but she also stands at the gateway to the Mexican archives and to Spanish America. With the patriotic interest in history that is so strong in Texas, the growing financial strength of the University, the scholarly traditions already established in the School of History, and a proper organization and utilization of the working force, nothing can keep the University of Texas from taking a prominent place for historical work.

It is unnecessary for me to add to this explanation of my inclination, my fondness for Texas and Texas people. To go back would be like going home, and if you desire my services I should consider it not only a great honor but also a great opportunity to be able to return.

Perhaps it will be improper for me to raise the question of terms before hearing from you on the main question, but knowing what you were willing to do for me had I remained, and knowing the importance also of saving time if any change is to be made this fall, possibly I may venture a remark in this connection without danger of impropriety, under the circumstances.

If I felt that I could in justice to my family, I should offer to come back at the terms as to salary and appropriations proposed last year, but I hardly see how I can afford to do precisely that. I do not know what the prospects are in Texas for a general raise in the salary of head professors, but I have wondered if that would not come of necessity soon, and, in that event, if I might not possibly take advantage of the advance at this time or at some stated time in the future. If that is out of the question, but you would like to have me return at the terms proposed last year, kindly let me know.

In view of my sincere desire to work in Texas, and of the generous treatment which I received there, I would not wish to ask the University to bid against an institution with more means, any farther than business prudence require it. I have good reason to expect that Stanford will give me better terms this coming year than I am getting now, and I have just been asked if I would consider a more attractive place in a large institution, although no formal offer has been made as yet, and it may not be made. [This may have been a hope; there is no evidence of such an offer in the Bolton Papers.] But my preference is for Texas if the place is open for me, even if I were to have to take it at some pecuniary disadvantage, because I feel that there I could be most useful and do my work under the most propitious conditions.

If it were so arranged, I should bring to Texas the benefit of a year's very valuable experience in a portion of the Southwestern field, and where I have been in touch with forces with which Texas will expect to compete and to cooperate in the development of her School of History. I should expect to settle down to my life-work there, barring unforeseen circumstances. If I were to make the change, I think there are many reasons why it should be better to make it this fall rather than later.

This letter has been very difficult to write, for, in view of the fact that no offer has been made me I have found it hard to say what I wanted to say without running the risk of violating proprieties. I hope that I have not committed that error. The essense of what I have wished to say is that I should like very much to return to Texas, and that I should be very strongly disposed to accept such terms as you might offer, feeling assured that they would be as good as the circumstances there would permit.

With these two communications at hand, the telegram and now this long letter, Sidney Mezes sent off a night letter the evening of August 6:

Your telegram and letter received. I am glad to hear that you would like to return. I wish that we could increase last year's offer but present resources and conditions do not permit that. I hope, however, that our bright prospects especially in history will decide you to accept for this fall.

This seemed practically the equivalent of an offer of the position. And Bolton with this assurance from Mezes entered on a period which was to add up to several tortured weeks of indecision.

He had to weigh a number of factors: in the first place there was the matter of the very definite gap between the Stanford and the Texas salaries; secondly, there was the matter of Gertrude's wishes; then quite unexpectedly, to add to the inner turmoil and further complicate the decision-making process, came an invitation from Henry Morse Stephens, Chairman of the Department of History at California, to join him at lunch in Berkeley on August 12. The long letter of Stephens, written the next day, gives an account of what happened at the luncheon table that Friday afternoon on the Berkeley campus:

Private and Confidential

I am very grateful to you for coming over at such short notice to take luncheon with me and thoroughly enjoyed our talk together; and I was particularly glad that you had the opportunity to meet President [Benjamin Ide] Wheeler.

Professor Stillman [Stanford] told me in camp [at the Bohemian Grove, most probably] that he feared you were going to leave Stanford for Texas, which made me resolve to see whether, if you are leaving Stanford, you might not be willing to come to California rather than to return to Texas. On this point I desired to be assured before I make a recommendation to President Wheeler. You know the situation here; you know that we hoped to get Turner; and you know the nature of the position which would be offered to you. You would be practically my second in command with the entire charge of American History and with Dr. MacCormac as your assistant professor. You would have your own seminary room with Mac-Cormac in the new library building and I should never dream of interfering with your management of everything pertaining to American History. If we cannot have Turner, let us have Turner's most promising pupil.

Now with regard to terms and this must be confidential between us at present, in order that we can freely discuss matters, I am prepared to recommend to President Wheeler your appointment as full professor of American History at $3,500.00 a year, your term to begin either January 1911 or next August as you should prefer. It seems to me too late to ask you here at once, since our term begins this week and it should be hard to modify our announcement of courses. Also it seems a little hard on Adams, if you resolve to come to us, not to give him time to get your successor. I fancied from what you said that, even if Adams were ready to release you at once, you wanted to go to Mexico again upon your Source work and would not be sorry to have a term off. Let me know how you regard this proposition.

If — and so far this is strictly confidential between us — you would prefer coming here on those terms to going to Texas, will you let me know and I will lay the matter in the form of a formal recommendation before President Wheeler. What he will do, of course, I cannot say; it is custom here to lay such matters as the appointment of a full professor before the committee of professors in allied departments; and I suppose the custom will be followed. But I am, above all things, glad that you had the opportunity of meeting President Wheeler yesterday, so that he can speak to the committee with personal knowledge of you. I need hardly add that I hope we shall be able to come to terms, for, with Turner lost, I know of no one whom I would rather have by my side as my special colleague to handle American History than yourself.

P.S. On re-reading this letter I am inclined to think that I have not made one point sufficiently clear. I have no desire to entice you away from Stanford. That would not be fair to Adams. It is well understood further between the two universities in California that they should not compete for each other's professors. Lapsley, for instance, did not receive an invitation to join our history department, until he had definitely resigned from Stanford. Indeed, I should not have thought of asking you, if I might suggest your name to President Wheeler, had I not been informed already that you had virtually decided to leave Stanford for the University of Texas.

This postscript serves in consigning to the category of mythology one of the stories connected with Bolton's transfer from Palo Alto to Berkeley — that it was his case which gave rise to the "no piracy" agreement between Stanford and California. Quite obviously, a gentleman's agreement was in force prior to the Bolton case. Further, the story of these weeks of 1910 puts another Bolton myth to rest, namely, that he looked upon Stanford as a mere stepping-stone to California. Without question, once Bolton was at Stanford, he dreamed of a possible move to California, but the facts show that he could hardly have engineered it.

Bolton's life had become very complicated by mid-August: he was signed for the coming year at Stanford; the door at Texas was open; now the possibility of moving instead to California had become a major part of the decision he would have to make.

On Thursday, August 18, Bolton went back to Berkeley for another conference with Morse Stephens. And again, a Stephens letter of August 19 gives the details of what happened:

> Our talk of yesterday cleared up many things and I am much obliged to you for coming over from Palo Alto to see me. It is clearly understood that you will have resigned from Stanford to accept the call from the University of Texas, before any call can come to you from the University of California. It is clearly understood that Professor Adams is not to be put to any inconvenience and that any call that may be extended to you from here would be from 1 January 1911 — or if Adams felt that he could not get a successor to you in time, from 1 July 1911.
>
> The question of a specific grant for books in Western history — or indeed in American history in general, in which the Library is woefully deficient — is left to me to deal with as best I can, and you make no condition about it.
>
> The last and most difficult question is that of salary. You tell me that President Mezes has raised his offer to you, since we met last Friday, to $3500 a year with promise of $4000 in the near future,* and that your arrangement with Stanford, if you had resolved to stay there, would have given you $3,750 for 1911–1912, and $4000 for 1912–1913 onwards. Under these circumstances I shall be glad to recommend your appointment to President Wheeler at $4,000 a year, the amount set down in our budget for a professor of American history, from January 1, 1911 — and if you approve of this, he will open formal negotiations with you. The nomination of a full professor, as I wrote you before, is a matter submitted to a committee of professors, and this will be the next step to be taken, if formal negotiations between President Wheeler and yourself authorize it.
>
> Hoping to have you as a colleague. . .

---

*Written in the margin of this letter in Bolton's hand is the following statement: "This part denied in my reply of August 24, 1910, of which a copy is attached."

Stephens obviously was in close contact with Wheeler during these days, for there is the following postscript added to this letter in Wheeler's hand:

My dear Mr. Bolton:

I have just read this and in order to make things as definite as possible and to hasten a settlement, I will say that the salary of $4000 will be available for you from July 1, 1911, and that during such part of this acad. year as you may spend with us, say from Jan. 1 the salary will be $3500, i.e. at that rate if you come.

The copy of Bolton's reply of August 24 has not survived, but typed onto the end of the handwritten letter from Stephens, and below the Wheeler postscript is the following:

Extract from reply of August 24:

Before closing I wish to correct in slight measure the promise, as stated in your letter to me, on which your recommendation to President Wheeler is based. What you say of my Stanford arrangements is correct. It is also true that I was on the point of resigning to accept a call to Texas when the California matter opened up, and this of course is the essential point — in fact I had gotten to the point of going to the telegraph office and writing out a message of acceptance, but decided that I would wait until they could offer me a salary. No specific sum has been offered me subsequently, though Professor Barker informs me that no permanent appointment will be made so long as I am considering the place.* This is the way the matter stands, and I wish you to know it.[4]

August merged into September and, when Stephens had heard nothing further from Bolton, he became a little anxious and wrote on September 6:

---

*There is only one August letter from Barker in the Bolton Correspondence; it is dated August 4 and must be the communication referred to by Bolton in his August 24 letter to Stephens. Barker writes: "Just once more; you can't come for 1910–1911 anyway; they won't take another man as long as you dicker with them — couldn't get one before next winter, if then; uncertainty may help me get out of the rank of Adj. Prof. into Assoc. class; so, if my logic seems good to you, hang on without giving a definite answer. I write because Mathews tells me that Mezes is in correspondence with you." This Barker letter most certainly reached Bolton before the California offer was made; it may have been one of the reasons Bolton hesitated to send the telegram of acceptance to Texas. Bolton was not above a bit of conniving to assist the cause of his friend Barker. In the Bolton-Barker relations, if there was collusion, as was suspected at Texas, it cannot be proved. Not necessarily on this point, but on Barker's career, see William C. Pool, *Eugene C. Barker: Historian* (Austin: Texas State Historical Association, 1971).

While I do not wish to hurry your decision or to hamper Adams' arrangements in any way, I am naturally anxious to hear from you as soon as possible. The salary question I cannot touch further, as this is President Wheeler's business. The book and MSS business you must leave to me. The conduct of American history is left entirely to you. The reappointment or not of MacCormac is specifically left to you by President Wheeler's wish. It is for you to settle in committee with MacCormac, Don Smith, and Teggart, what work is to be offered next year in American history. You have first say in all matters of American history, seminars, graduate work, undergraduate classes, etc. American history includes Latin American history. . . . For my part I shall be glad to be quit of all responsibility for American history. . . .

Stephens ended this letter with the note that the pressure for a decision was made necessary by the fact that he would soon have to present his departmental requests for 1911–12 to the Library Committee. The next day Stephens telegraphed Bolton, perhaps to hasten a reply by resort to what in those days was not the most usual means of communication: "Please telegraph reply before noon tomorrow after receiving my last letter."

At this point on September 10 Bolton sent off to his brother a definitely agonized letter:

I have been badly disturbed during the past two months by reason of opportunities to move: Professor Garrison died on July 3 and the headship [Department of History at Texas] was offered to me. The temptation was great, because the field is dear to my heart, and the people generous in their attitude toward me. I received numerous letters from all over the State, from business men and educators, urging me to return "to the State where I belong," as they put it. But the salary is only $3000, Gertrude does not like the climate and is contented here, and I could not afford to bear the expense of moving. On the other hand, when they heard of the possibility, the Trustees here voted me $4000.00 cash to spend on my work, and in other ways showed reluctance to let me go. Almost before the Texas deal fell through, the University of California offered the headship of American history at $4000.00 a year, and I am still undecided. They will raise to $4000.00 a year here to meet it, and I like the surroundings here better, but the great Bancroft Collection, the greatest in my field, is there, while I feel that UC is forging ahead of Stanford in reputation, and I am afraid that I shall have to go. Thus you can easily see that I am somewhat unsettled.

Along with the business of making these decisions Bolton during these late summer weeks was working furiously to complete the manuscript of his *Guide*. Whether this involvement was the reason for his delay in replying to Stephens one cannot say. There seems to have been no reply to the telegram of September 7. On September 21 Stephens tried again:

> I have managed to put off allotment requests for books until next Monday, but I cannot do so any longer. I do not wish to press you for an immediate answer, but, if I cannot get it by Monday, the special grant for books on Western History must go over for a year. I ought also to begin search for another man, if you cannot come at once.

Stephens was shrewd enough to recognize the tremendous importance which Bolton put on a well-stocked library; hence, he pulled out that stop in the drive to get his answer. And it is clear that his patience was wearing a bit thin, with the talk about search for another man.

It was probably this last ploy which worked. He got his reply "by Monday," since on September 21 Bolton wrote:

> I have decided to cast my lot with you and to accept your very much esteemed invitation to join your faculty. I am sorry that I could not give my decision sooner, and thus help free your mind of the matter. There has been no new element in the situation since our last conversations, but I have not been able until now to make the final decision. . . . Now that the decision has been made, however, I am for California and I shall not look back.

The next day Bolton drafted a letter to Mezes of Texas and then spent some time in reworking one of the copies. Earlier he had sent Mezes a telegram, declining the Texas offer (it is not easy to determine just when this wire was dispatched). Now at greater length he detailed the reasons for his final decision:

> I owe you an apology for not having written sooner to give a fuller explanation of my answer, sent by telegram. The essence of my not accepting your very much appreciated offer at this time, however, was contained in the telegram itself. My inclination was exceedingly strong to go to Texas. When I opened the correspondence I really hoped that I should be able to go, and it was a great disappointment when I found that I was in duty bound to say that I could not come. I even went to the telegraph office and wrote out a message saying that I would come, and then reversed my decision. . . .
> I reiterate what I wrote you in regard to my inclinations. I believe that I should be more useful in Texas than anywhere else. But having left there for better or for worse, it has not seemed possible for me to return under present circumstances.

He went on to indicate some of the principal reasons, most of them financial. Moving expenses would have run to around $400; he would have lost a month's salary at Stanford, another $700; the Texas offer was only $3500. There was still one other very telling consideration which greatly influenced the final decision: this was California's Bancroft Library. During his remaining months at Stanford, he would mention this last point a number of times in letters to various friends and associates, in order to explain his decision to move from Stanford.

And so ends the story of how Herbert Bolton was engaged to move from Stanford to the University of California, as of the summer of 1911. These summer weeks of 1910 formed one of the most important time spans in his long life; they show a very human Bolton. The man whom colleagues, associates, and the profession generally, would come to see as a self-assured person, self-confident, at times almost to the point of arrogance, on occasion domineering, was not always so: this was not the last time he would struggle for direction in his life; as strong and assertive as he certainly was most of the time, he, too, had periods of self-doubt, indecision, and conflict.

THE SECOND YEAR AT STANFORD

With the decision made to go to the University of California the next school year (1911–12) and the manuscript for the *Guide* finally in the mail to Jameson, Bolton was able by late September 1910 to go back to being a Stanford professor full-time. Those summer weeks had been hard from every point of view — physically, psychologically, emotionally. His teaching schedule was substantially the same as that of the previous year, history of the West and of the Southwest. Besides a large undergraduate class, he had a little circle of graduate students working under his direction and moving toward their master's degrees. Some of these had followed him from Texas; others were new. Bolton had known the satisfaction of directing advanced students at Texas; now at Stanford this pleasant duty continued.

Even though engrossed in work at hand — he was still working diligently on his Western history course, which he had taught for the first time the previous year — he allowed himself to dream of the future. The visions of the University of California at times showed in his letters. For example, on November 30 he wrote to Jameson:

> With regard to the California matter I say, since you are glad to get news, and since I am interested in having you hear it, that I have accepted the professorship of American History at Berkeley, my appointment to take effect July 1st. I shall be expected to devote the greater portion of my time to graduate work, which is much to my

satisfaction. I shall be glad indeed to have my work and my office across the hall from the great Bancroft Collection. That collection, indeed, was the real factor in inducing me to leave Stanford, where I have been very happy and which I like very much.

A December 27 letter to his old master, Frederick Jackson Turner, had a similar theme with something of a view of what he hoped to be able to do in the future:

> I tried to look at the matter in an objective way and concluded that, had the two places opened up on the same basis when I was at Texas, I should not have considered coming to Stanford. My present liking for this place and the fine crowd of men here made it hard for me to take this view, but I finally was able to do so. The Bancroft Collection is a magnificent one and I could not have collected it better myself from the standpoint of my own purposes. I hope that we shall be able to build a strong department in Western and Spanish-American history, for both of these are in the center of the stage. My own personal interest lies on the border between the two and I expect plenty of help on the two flanks.

This last sentence is revealing in regard to what Bolton was beginning to consider himself — neither straight Western man nor full Spanish-American man but someone "on the border between the two."

Although Bolton was sincere in making such statements regarding Stanford and its men, they were, in a sense, the "party line" or the proper thing to say. Often a better mirror of his inner thoughts and opinions can be found in his letters to his brother. A January 30, 1911, letter is probably the most straightforward and honest reflection on the decision he had made:

> I have decided to go to the University of California, beginning in July. I am sorry to make the move for many reasons, but the great collection of materials in my field (the Bancroft Collection) will put me in command of the best plant for western and southwestern history in the world. Indeed, I think that there is no question but that the Professorship of American History at California is the academic position in history of most influence west of the Mississippi. Stanford is a comfortable place, but Stanford has no policy, and no one knows today what will be done tomorrow. It is a big college, and most of the authorities wish to keep it such. California is becoming an important graduate center, and I shall be expected to devote most of my time to graduate work. Taking everything into consideration, I felt that I could not afford to refuse the place. I shall go at $4000.00 and was told that I could soon be advanced to $5000.00, but this is no promise. . . .

I shall teach in the summer session there, in order to get myself oriented and to learn the conditions of living. . . . As I said, I hate to move, and would prefer to go back to Texas, personally, but it seemed the thing to do, and here goes.

Even so there were reasons why Bolton hated to leave Stanford which he put into a letter of November 11, 1910 to his mother: "I like this place, and the family likes it very much. Besides, this is a nicer place to bring up children than Berkeley. Berkeley is a suburb of San Francisco, and has many of the objectionable features of a city, as well as some of the advantages."

During Christmas vacation, 1910, Bolton did a quick turn in Arizona and Sonora. He had thought for a time of going to the annual meeting of the American Historical Association, at Indianapolis, but, as would happen so often in later years, the prospect of a week or so "in the field" proved much more alluring. Even this early in his career he was fully convinced that to have been "on the ground" was important for sound historical writing. Arizona-Sonora was the "ground" on which Padre Kino had worked, and he was still working on the edition of the Jesuit's "Favores Celestiales." This matching of desk work with field work would be one of the hallmarks of Bolton's scholarly writing and editing.

A TIFF WITH RICHMAN

During this last year at Stanford, after having delivered the manuscript for the *Guide* to Jameson, he was free to turn to his commitment to Arthur H. Clark — the Athanase de Mézières and the Kino books. Dealings with Clark during this 1910–11 year were more or less amicable. The publisher, probably despairing for the moment of an early realization of the scheme for the "Documentary Sources" series, concentrated most of his drive toward getting the long overdue De Mézières manuscript. He did nudge Bolton now and then about the series, as in a letter of November 11, 1910:

> What is the status of the Mexican series, and when will we receive the manuscript? This, as you know, has been greatly delayed beyond the contract, and, as I already have a number of orders for the set, I am anxious to get the work out as early as possible. Let me hear from you.

Whether Bolton reported is not evident.

Relations with Irving B. Richman, the man to whom Bolton had supplied resource material while in Mexico and then had wanted it back, were spotty at best and toward the end of this second Stanford year became definitely strained.[5] As his work on California's early history moved toward completion, Richman was anxious to have a look at the Kino material which Bolton had promised but was exasperatingly slow in sending. One wonders whether Bolton was forgetful, was simply procrastinating or, possibly, just being difficult. He had become very possessive of this one of his prize discoveries, the padre's "Favores," and did not seem overly anxious to risk being scooped by his Iowa-businessman rival. Bolton, however, needed a favor from Richman in the summer of 1910 — the loan of the index cards on the California materials which had been made years before for Richman; he wanted to make a double check for the *Guide*. Therefore, the two men made the exchange. Richman returned the Kino translation in good time; Bolton was not so considerate in regard to the California cards, despite frequent requests by Richman for their return. When he finally did send them back, it is likely that he did not do so with grace.

In early spring of 1911 Richman's *California under Spain and Mexico* came off the press. Bolton's first sight of it came in E. D. Adams' office; Richman had sent him a copy. A quick glance at the volume raised Bolton's blood pressure. He drafted a quite bitter letter; his secretary put the typed copy on his desk for signature; but it was not sent. The master copy is still in the Bolton file, marked in pencil and possibly at a later date, with the notation "Never sent." There is no copy of the revised version of what actually went off to Richman, but from the latter's immediate reply one can surmise that even this revised letter was somewhat strong. From the "Never sent" letter one can gather the focal point of Bolton's pique:

> . . . I cannot refrain from saying that I am sorry that you did not give me due credit for my work on the *Favores Celestiales,* in connection with Chapter IV. It is left, or put, in about the same light as the rest of the MSS, which I helped you secure, as though you had secured and interpreted it yourself, whereas you not only used my manuscript, but even my translation, without the least intimation that such was the case. . . .
>
> Missionary work and the necessity of earning my living has forced me to give away most of my discoveries — and now I find that I need expect little acknowledgement — but I had hoped to save one find for my own exploitation. But now the edge is gone, and I must make the best of it. . . .
>
> This letter is the product of two days' reflection, and I send it to you feeling that it is justified by the facts. If I am wrong, please inform me.

Evidently Bolton reflected into a third or a fourth day before sending a letter to Richman. What he sent brought the following on June 12:

>   If I have failed to meet your ideas regarding proper credit for
> material used in the "California" I sincerely regret the fact. It was
> in no way my intention to subtract from what was due you. . . . I
> have connected your name prominently with every document which
> I was enabled to use through you. . . . It seemed to me that, beginning
> with the Preface mention, and throughout, I was making it evident
> to whom I was indebted for my Mexican sources. . . .

The business of the index cards for the California sources had rankled
Richman quite obviously, for he went on to chide Bolton for his unco-
operativeness in returning them promptly on request and of the "curt way"
in which he finally did send them back. Richman closed with a parting
thrust: " . . . and when I wrote you regarding the fact that my book was
soon to appear . . . , I got no response. I have, therefore, not felt free to
send you a copy, although I wished to do so, and should be glad to do so
yet." The record does not show how this scholars' fight ended. It does,
however, seem to prove the dictum of Charles F. Lummis made later
to Bolton and often quoted by him, that "scholarship can be hell on
manners."

A CAMPAIGN FOR HIS SPANIARDS

Herbert Bolton's last months at Stanford were by no means idle. On
the contrary, they were fairly typical of the kinds of activities he would
be involved in at Berkeley. February 13, 1911, Bolton sent a feeler to
his friend Jameson, who was, along with his many other commitments,
editing a series of volumes known as the "Original Narratives of Early
American History." Hodge and Lewis had written a volume, out in
1907, entitled *Spanish Explorers in the Southern United States, 1528–
1543.* The publication of the Cabeza de Vaca, De Soto, and Coronado
narratives, by Bolton's reckoning, told only a very small segment of the
story of the Spaniards in the United States. He wondered if there might not
be a place in the series for a companion volume which would make available some of the source materials on the many later Spanish explorers
of Southwestern United States. Jameson thought well of the idea. Bolton
was opening a campaign to bring "his" Spaniards to the notice of American scholars and students; ultimately he would add a volume of his own
to the narratives series.

Another idea for his campaign led him to write on May 24 to Charles
R. Hull, of Cornell, program chairman for the coming AHA meeting,
asking if there might be a spot on the 1911 program for a session on the
Southwest. Among other observations, he told Hull that there was thought

and talk of organizing a Southwestern Historical Association. Again, he was successful. When the occasion demanded, Bolton could be quite a lobbyist!

The *Quarterly,* too, continued to be a medium through which Bolton could communicate the story of his Spaniards. Even though Barker had become editor after Garrison's death, Bolton had maintained his active interest in the *Quarterly* after leaving Austin, continuing, at Barker's request, as associate editor. A letter written by Bolton to Barker on June 8, 1911, reflects that they were contemplating broadening the scope of the journal and changing the title. On coming to Stanford Bolton had written to potentially interested Southwestern scholars and to the presidents of the universities in the area to ascertain if they would not be interested in seeing the *Quarterly* expand its base and interest; to the administrators he raised the question of whether their institutions might be willing to give some financial assistance in the event of such a change. He obtained approving replies, but no promise of funded help. Even so, he and Barker moved optimistically ahead, and with the July 1912 number, the *Quarterly* of the Texas State Historical Association would become the *Southwestern Historical Quarterly (SWHQ).* Bolton's "The Spanish Occupation of Texas, 1519-1690" was the lead article.

Herbert Bolton left Stanford to go to the University of California in August 1911, intending to continue his emphasis on colonial Texas, but local circumstances would soon have him broadening his own horizons.

7

Settling Down
at California

D URING THE SUMMER SESSION, when Herbert Bolton was com-
muting to Berkeley to teach classes, he managed to find a large
house to rent on Spring Street,* north of the campus, to accommo-
date himself, his wife, and now six daughters.† The house was described
in a letter from Gertrude's mother to Rosaline Bolton in Tomah, Wisconsin:

> They have a ten room house and that does not include the small
> rooms. They have a living room, Herbert's study, dining room,
> kitchen, children's study room; that makes five large rooms. Then
> there is a reception hall with a great wide stairway, . . . a pantry,
> laundry, back screened-in porch, a side porch from the children's
> study room and a big basement, besides any amount of cupboards.
> The second floor has a long wide hall with 5 bedrooms, each with
> a large closet. . . . Besides all that they have an immense sleeping
> porch which would make four good-sized bedrooms; then a large
> attic the size of the whole house all fitted with gas, electric lights,
> etc. — a fine place for the children to play rainy days.[1]

The Bolton daughters many years later would recall the good times
enjoyed during growing-up days in this house, the cheery living room,
their Dad's study with its shelves lined with books and according to them
— "a wonderful, wonderful house in which to grow up!" In this home in
Berkeley, halfway up a hill overlooking the Bay, Herbert Bolton and his
family lived, grew and worked for the next dozen years.

---

*This was the house on 1526 Scenic, Spring Street having been renamed a few
years later.

†The Boltons' sixth daughter, Jane, was born during the Palo Alto years. The
last child, Herbert, Jr., was born in November, 1913.

THE UNIVERSITY OF CALIFORNIA IN 1911

When Herbert Bolton came to Berkeley, he was a few weeks short of his forty-first birthday. The University of California was only two years older than he, having been founded in 1868. In 1911 the university was far from being the multiversity which it later became.[2] Enrollment on the Berkeley campus was 4,112 — 2,250 undergraduate men and 1,133 undergraduate women — while in the graduate division there were 311 men and 207 women. Davis was still the "College Farm," the San Francisco professional complex was just being born, and there was as yet no "Southern Branch," as UCLA would be called in its early years. Bolton joined a faculty which numbered, on the Berkeley campus, 245.

Only within the most recent years had the first of the grander buildings envisioned in the Benard Plan been rising up to join already venerable North and South Halls, Bacon Art and Library Building, Harmon Gymnasium, and Hearst Hall, the women's physical-education building. The new library, named for Charles Franklin Doe, was near enough to completion to be put to use for the 1911 fall opening. Bolton's office was here on the first floor of the new library, and the Bancroft Collection would soon be moved from the attic of California Hall to space in the new library conveniently close for Bolton.

Benjamin Ide Wheeler, eighth in the line of presidents, was in his second decade of leadership.[3] Bolton had met Wheeler the previous summer, when at Berkeley conferring with Stephens. A quite warm relationship of mutual esteem developed between the two men; Bolton respected Wheeler, and the president quickly recognized the promise of his new professor.

Not only was the University of California growing in those early years of the century's second decade, but so was the Department of History.[4] It had come a long way since those years in the 1880s when Bernard Moses, personally and single-handedly, was the department. Toward the end of that decade he had picked up some help from colleagues in the Department of Classics in an effort to expand the offerings. In 1902 the remarkable Henry Morse Stephens, English by birth, had been enticed away from Cornell and added to the California faculty.[5] That same year instruction in economics had been divorced from history's responsibility, and the next year the Department of Political Science had been organized. History then was free to develop unencumbered.

History's emphasis at first was heavily European. That was Stephen's field, and his famous "History 1," an early version of the Western Civilization survey of a later time, was one of the most exciting and popular courses on campus. The wily Britisher was not unaware, however, that the rebelling thirteen former colonies and their progeny of thirty-three states had a history of their own. He set out to build the "trans-Atlantic" side of his department. He tried to bring Frederick Jackson Turner out from Wisconsin but found, to his chagrin, that Harvard had signed him. Young Eugene MacCormac was brought in as of 1910. But even then Stephens was looking for a man to interpret the West, and very particularly the West of which California was a part; he also wanted someone who would put to use the Bancroft Collection, which he had had a large hand in pushing the regents to acquire in 1905.[6] Stephens found this man in Herbert Bolton. Under the aegis of this quite remarkable man Bolton began his California years, and from the first, as at Stanford, his assignment of courses was in his favorite areas of study — the West and the Southwest. Very soon he would begin to gather around him a little band of enthusiastic graduate students.

A DREAM OF THE FUTURE

By December 1911 he was ready to make his first major move toward building his new university into *the* center for Southwestern history, and once again he would be campaigning indirectly for his Spaniards. In a long and carefully detailed memorandum he informed President Wheeler that "one of the greatest needs in the field of American history is the publication of a comprehensive body of historical materials relating to Spanish activities within the present limits of the United States."[7] Here was the dream of a "documentary series" once more coming to life; Bolton's own work plan for himself and his graduate students was beginning to take form.

He pointed out to Wheeler that for nearly three centuries the southwestern quarter of the United States "constituted a portion of the Spanish possessions in North America, while for nearly half a century Spain possessed the whole Trans-Mississippi West." He went on to underline the importance in United States history of the impact of the Spaniards on so large a segment of the continent; he wrote of the significance of the half century of conflict between the Spanish- and the Anglo-American frontiers. All this history "cannot be properly interpreted without first devoting to these antecedents a complete and thorough study." Such a study, he reminded Wheeler, had not yet been made. He noted that because of rather extensive study of French activities in North America "it is . . . assumed that the French influence was the more important of the two" — "France in America had a Parkman, while Spanish America had none." He expressed his belief that some of this neglect of the Spanish period and of the West generally was due to the fact that for a long time "the history of the United States has been written almost solely from the standpoint of the East and of the English colonies"; even Turner's West "has not thus far reached beyond the Mississippi Valley." He insisted to Wheeler that the lead in investigation of the history of the Southwest and Far West "must be taken by us here in the West," and specifically by the University of California. He then went on to detail some of the vast materials in the archives of Mexico and Spain bearing on the history of the Southwest and the West and pleaded for the publication of the more vital of them — "the number of these of fundamental value and great human interest is immense." Then came the punch line on this publication project: "a beginning on a large scale is imperative, and I have proposed undertaking a twenty-five volume collection, if funds can be found to make it possible." Wheeler could see that he had hired a man of vision, and he liked such men around him. He also may have been a bit worried, however, for Bolton promised to be an expensive acquisition.

Wheeler could do nothing right then, or at least did nothing; he appreciated Bolton's proposal enough to keep it in mind. A dozen or so months later he thought he had a possible "angel" for the project in Edward L. Doheny. The oil man asked to see the proposal spelled out in detail; accordingly, at Wheeler's urging, on February 1, 1913, Bolton presented an elaborate plan for the twenty-five volumes of source materials. His hopes soared as he suggested "Original Sources of Southwestern History" as a possible title for the series. Following the pattern set by Thwaites in the *Jesuit Relations*, he proposed that both the Spanish original and the English translation be published. Further, he felt that the whole series might be divided into four sub-series: (1) New Mexico and Arizona; (2) California; (3) Texas; and (4) the northern provinces of Mexico.

A year later, when nothing had been heard from Doheny, Bolton sent a memorandum to him (April 14, 1914), hoping to jog his memory to the effect that he had promised to talk to Wheeler about a possible $50,000 subsidy for the publication project. Recognizing that he was talking to a businessman, Bolton even offered a monthly budget plan: the first monthly installment would be $2000, observing that it would be a bit expensive to get the business off the ground; this could be followed with $1000 monthly through 1914; then from January 1915 through the succeeding four years and four months the monthly allotment would drop to $833.33. Bolton proposed that the total grant be made to the university, to be administered by the regents, who in turn would put him in charge of expending the monthly sums. The University of California Press would do the printing, publishing, and distribution. The income accruing from sales could be deposited in a "Doheny Fund" to subsidize even more volumes than the original twenty-five. The professor hinted, rather strongly, that a May check would be most timely. He knew that Eddie Dunn was planning to go to Spain that summer, and with funds available this old-time gatherer could pick up many valuable pieces in the Spanish archives. Bolton explained that, while he planned to begin the series with documents already at hand, ultimately he would want many things from the Archivo de Indias at Seville.

Doheny, disappointingly, did not rise to the bait. Commencement Day of 1914 came and Wheeler had no Doheny bequest to announce. But Bolton did not give up. In late August he once more wrote Doheny, quietly suggesting that with Dunn currently in Spain a few hundred dollars would be most timely. Bolton did, however, note that with affairs in Mexico in turmoil (knowing that Doheny had heavy oil interests there) and with the European situation worsening day by day his prospective benefactor might not feel that he could act at the moment. He evidently read the situation correctly; Doheny did nothing in connection with this particular project. Some years later Bolton had contact with the magnate on another project, which was more of Doheny's than Bolton's making and which was much more trouble and many more headaches than it was worth. Late summer 1914, however, was the end of "Empresa Doheny," much to Bolton's disappointment.

In those early California years Bolton tried to interest other possible sponsors in his pet project — sometimes proposed as the "Spain in the United States" series if he felt that this angle might be more attractive. As far back as August 2, 1912, he had written to Edward E. Ayer of Chicago, whose enthusiasm for things Hispanic was well known. He tried to show the Chicago railroad man what could be done with $25,000. Admitting the importance of manuscript collections, Bolton argued that these alone were not enough; series of printed and translated documents, widely available, would be the surest method of stimulating interest and research among scholars and students, since only an occasional fortunate one was likely to be able to use the great library holdings. In this letter he pointed out that "the manuscripts in the Bancroft Collection at the University of California were not accessible even to all members of the History Department." Ayer was sympathetic and in basic agreement with Bolton, but he pledged no immediate assistance. Bolton would keep after him through the years, politely but persistently; the two men became good friends, but the Newberry Library continued to be Ayer's "love," and the collection there which he helped to build became one of the country's most notable for materials Hispanic and Luso-Brazilian.

While realization of his dream was slow in coming, the 1911 AHA meeting at Buffalo saw the fulfillment of at least one of Bolton's less dramatic, but still worthwhile, efforts. While at Stanford he had managed to have a Southwestern history session put on the program, and he had organized it. It was so well received that there were requests for a similar session the following year. This favorable reaction of his colleagues was heartening, as was the warm commendation of his chairman, Stephens.

A RIGOROUS SCHEDULE

In all of these areas of involvement with their accompanying responsibilities Herbert Bolton was more than capable, and he was certainly enthusiastic, but he was not always as free as he would have liked to devote time to tasks of his own choosing which is reflected in a letter March 7, 1912, to Frederick.[8] He assured his brother that he was very happy in his new post but very busy. His class schedule was light, one three-hour lecture course on the West and a pair of seminars; but "I am on the run every minute from the time I get up till I retire. I am pretty regular in regard to the latter, as I work in my office in the Library for the most part, and the doors are closed at ten P.M., but I am put out by the janitor, as well as Sunday afternoon at four o'clock." He continued: "I am happy in my work especially when they let me work at my work. . . ." He complained of the inevitable committee assignments, the theses which needed "doctoring," manuscripts for the University Press demanding editorial attention. Then there were the perennial time-takers: "The thing that makes me maddest is to have some person come in to 'talk' an hour or so, just because he has nothing in particular to do and assumes that the same is the case with everybody else."

Within a short time after coming to Berkeley, Bolton had developed a personal schedule so exacting that his hours regularly extended beyond the established hours of others. Once securely rooted in his own field, he was almost completely absorbed in it. His work was his play, and at it he played long and hard. Physically he was a big man, just short of six feet tall, and he was blessed with exceptionally good health throughout most of his life. His strength combined with his having been conditioned early to the hard work of life on a farm enabled him to maintain an exacting schedule — six and most often seven days a week. His basic routine for the next thirty plus years was close to the following account.

He would arrive at his office about eight o'clock; then there was desk work, or class, or other business until noon. He would, on days it was open, lunch at the Faculty Club, conveniently close by — across campus. Then he would be back in his office or in the classroom until around six. About that time he would call home and announce that he would be at North Gate awaiting "taxi service" by someone of the family. Many stories are connected with this part of his daily ritual. He had most often simply left the physical trappings of his work on his office desk; he would inadvertently carry his work home in his head and could be very distracted therewith. One of his daughters tells of driving up and calling out "Dr. Bolton, can I give you a lift?" She was greeted with the answer, "Thank you, no — one of the girls is coming to pick me up." Or again, there was the evening, a rather darkish one, when, on arriving at North Gate, he saw a car waiting and a white-haired lady driving. Paying very little attention and thinking that it was Mrs. Bolton, he climbed into the car. The lady, a neighbor who actually was waiting for her own professor husband but who knew Dr. Bolton well, drove off after a quiet greeting. They were well on their way up the hill before Bolton discovered that he was an intruder. He was embarrassed but his neighbor, chuckling inwardly all the while, delivered him. They both told the story, for Bolton could always laugh at himself. His family subjected him to kidding about allowing himself to be "picked up."⁹

At dinner he was expansive, full of good humor, hungry. He was hardly a gourmet and never a gourmand; food was fundamentally fuel. His historical heroes often came home to dinner with him. All the Boltons were quite familiar with the goings and comings, deeds and achievements of padre, conquistador, and friar alike. When the Bolton children were younger, Sunday afternoons were often spent in the Hupmobile with the entire family on their trails around the Bay Area, with Dad as driver, commentator, and voluble tour guide. Full of his work and interests, he talked history almost constantly during his waking hours at home. Herbert, Jr. tells the story of one of his university chums who through one whole night listened, with no objection and sincerely fascinated, to sizable segments of *Outpost of Empire,* when Bolton was proofing the manuscript and had it home for polishing. This may have heightened the young man's already developing interest in history; subsequently he went on and took his doctorate in American Studies at the University of Minnesota.

As a rule, after dinner each evening Mr. and Mrs. Bolton would retire to the study for a short time of quiet and conversation, often a radio newscast. By eight o'clock Bolton was ready to go back to work, at the university. Those undisturbed night hours he loved.

Sometimes in the evenings when he went back to work with the car, he found a parking place remarkably convenient to the library — in those days few people parked in crosswalks! Congratulating himself on his good fortune, he parked in the open spot and blithely went up to his fourth-floor office. A day came, however, when a vexed university policeman appeared at the door of Library 426 with a handful of violation stubs. Bolton professed surprise that he had been parking in the crosswalk but said that on occasion he had noted the movement of something across the windshield as he drove off. He had been wondering why the birds kept selecting his car as a spot on which to perch. Whether it was innocence or a topnotch acting performance, the officer issued a warning for the future, tore up the tickets, and went off.

Midnight was very often his cut-off hour. Of course, as mentioned earlier, this was long after regular closing hours of the library. Several more stories are connected with his being "swept out" by the janitors. On occasion a new janitor might not know that one of his duties was to flush Bolton out of his office; in such instances he found himself locked in, in days before doors were fitted with panic bars. Once he went around lighting lights, hoping thus to attract attention; on another he was too tired to resort to this stratagem and searched until he found a spot where he could pass the night with a modicum of comfort. He had to vacate the chaise longue in the women's restroom early enough the next morning to avoid being unexpectedly found, but he had gotten several hours of rest.

The Bolton familiar to fellow historians, university colleagues, and students was not as much a stranger at home perhaps as Bolton, the family man, was a stranger to them. As one of Bolton's daughters has put it, "Dad moved in two orbits, his University life and his home life." Few persons from his professional life ever saw him in home surroundings — the Bolton daughters do remember evenings when Dad and Mama enjoyed the company of a group of faculty friends who called themselves the "Dippy Hops." But for the most part Bolton's homelife has been recreated here from stories told by members of his family.

Hardy though he was, Bolton was sensitive to cold. Several of the stories center around this fact. Fortunately, he was able to live two-thirds of his eighty-two-plus years in a moderate climate, Texas and then California. Even so, it was his wont to bundle up well as he went to bed. Sometimes he awakened during the night and read or wrote, which happened not infrequently as the family attests. They noted that his light burned much of the night and that light bulbs in his bedroom needed more than just ordinary replacement service.

This need to keep warm inspired a clever poem by daughter Eugenie, whose Muse often was at its best for festive family gatherings. Genie wrote:

> When Dr. Bolton goes to bed
>   He has two pillows at his head,
> Six blankets piled up to his throat
>   A sweater and an overcoat.
>
> The register is opened wide,
>   The windows shut the cold outside.
> I wonder what would Palóu say
>   Who slept upon a pile of hay?

Fray Serra, Font, and Crespi, tòo,
  Would rise in horror, if they knew.
Such luxury is a sin — unlawful —
  A martyr's life must be quite awful.

All reverence due to true ascetics
  Who punish self in strange athletics
That sleeping cold was Kino's forte
  And keeping warm was very naughty.

Sir Herbert needn't emulate
  The padres of an early date;
Those wooly pants, if naught else will,
  May help to keep away the chill.

One of the gifts for Dad that Christmas was a pair of heavy pajamas.

On one rare occasion, when Mrs. Bolton went out of town for a few autumn days, the weather turned warm; the thermostat was set for the anticipated cooler Berkeley days of that season. The house became unbearably warm, even for Herbert, but the mechanics of the thermostat baffled him, so he solved the problem by opening all the windows before going off to his library office on campus. This account points to two other Bolton characteristics — his low aptitude for things mechanical and his often comical lack of domesticity.

One of the daughters could recall his total contribution to the morning hassle of getting everyone ready to go off to school was to button the top button on "Brother's" shoes and then get down to his simple breakfast. Herbert Jr., in his notes has a priceless paragraph on this matter:

> Dad's domesticity was limited to dressing himself, save on special occasions when he needed Mama's help to put in his shirt studs or tie his tie, and to putting his dirty clothes down the laundry chute. He seemed to think that this last operation was all there was to the laundering process; put them in dirty; then by some magic they appeared in his drawer, bright and shiny, smelling clean as spring air, and pressed neat as a pin. I guess he thought Olga, our most faithful cleaning lady, was there to entertain Mama. I doubt if he could boil water, let alone an egg. Shopping was something that the womenfolk did quite satisfactorily, so he needn't bother about that. Though I suppose that from time to time he bought himself a pocket comb or some such article.

Herbert, Jr., did not speculate as to how his father may have paid for that comb or what-have-you. Bolton never carried much money with him when in Berkeley; it was much easier to write checks, sometimes for as small an amount as fifty cents. This was one reason why he found the Faculty Club so convenient a place for lunch; all he had to do was to sign the chit and then know that Gertrude would settle accounts at the end of the month. It is said that she not only had to send a monthly check but periodically had to return a neat package of Faculty Club napkins collected by Herbert when he would absent-mindedly jam one into his pocket after lunch and go off to his absorbing work in the library.

Herbert, Jr., relates another story pertaining to his father's shopping competence:

> One day Mama had some ladies in for tea. It being nearly time for Dad to come home, she called him at the University and asked him to bring home some rolls for her party. When Dad arrived, he was laden down with bags full of things. The things were thirteen dozen rolls — he bought all the store had.

Perhaps some of the best stories belong under the heading "Bolton versus the Automobile." The first family car was the Hupmobile touring car fitted with wide jump seats to make it a conveyance for the family of nine. Young Herbert tells of those Sunday afternoon tours into the country. "The ride was more bumpy than blissful, on those rough roads, with Dad at the helm of the old Hup." He was better as tour guide than driver.

> The old Hup served well, chugging and boiling at its top speed of 35 miles an hour, as Dad followed the trails of the Spanish pioneers. The Hup, perhaps, was responsible for giving him a zest for field research. . . . On one of the trips the battery shorted out, giving Mama the hot-seat, as Dad clung stubbornly to the wheel and drove on with a heavy foot on the throttle. With her frantic pleading, he finally stopped, just in time. She hopped out as the seat burst into flame.

Bolton was no mechanic. If the car was running, he drove it. There were family cars other than the famous Hupmobile but, says Herbert, Jr., "Dad never learned to drive any of them worth a damn." Let mechanical trouble develop and he was lost, as the following attests:

> One morning my mother looked out and saw that the car wasn't there. When Dad came down to breakfast, she asked where the car was. He said that he had had trouble with it and had left it down on Oxford Street. "What kind of trouble?" Mama asked. "Oh, I think there's something the matter with the exhaust," Dad replied, quickly dismissing the subject. My mother was no mechanic, but she had the

car serviced regularly. It had been behaving pretty well, and she had never heard of a car having exhaust trouble. But she smiled and said nothing. Dad walked to work that morning, and she called the service station to have them pick up the car and find out what was wrong with it. An hour or so later, the man called back, hardly able to talk, he was laughing so hard. It seems that Dad had had a flat tire. Completely oblivious, he had driven on for a mile or so, until the tire wrapped itself around the rear axle housing. The poor car just couldn't go any farther.

The automobile, when operated by someone else, was hero rather than villain. It made possible through the years his coverage of thousands of miles throughout the Southwest and northern Mexico, trailing his Spanish pioneers. It had its place, so long as he did not have to wrestle with its intricacies or cater to idiosyncrasies. Those things simply took too much time away from scholarly production. He was equally intolerant of other types of regular time-takers such as professional meetings about which he developed his own philosophy shortly after coming to California. This philosophy surfaces in a letter to Isaac Joslin Cox (January 14, 1914) who had written to say that Bolton was missed at the Christmastide meeting of the AHA. Bolton responded:

> I am sorry that I could not be with you at Charleston. It is too far and costs too much time and money. Unless I use my vacations for work I shall never get anything done. The whole profession makes a great mistake by too much "associating," thinking that somebody will remember them, having seen them. This is one of the reasons why American scholars do not produce more work.

Bolton's intense devotion, heightened by his ability to keep long hours, made it possible for him to turn out an amazing amount of scholarly production. Beginning in 1915 and for a half dozen years thereafter, he would very nearly let his enthusiasm and desire to achieve run away with good sense; he would learn the painful and often discouraging meaning of being overextended. He simply had too many projects.

8

Into High Gear

THE LONG-STANDING COMMITMENT to Arthur H. Clark to deliver the edition of Kino's "Favores Celestiales," was already long overdue by early 1915. The publisher would have an even longer wait for this translation than for the two volumes of *Athanase de Meziérès and the Louisiana-Texas Frontier, 1768–1780,* but that story will be told in full in the next chapter. Meanwhile, that work would be pushed aside by other commitments such as the one to his friend, J. Franklin Jameson, with whom he had worked while preparing the *Guide.* Bolton had convinced Jameson that "Original Narratives of Early American History" should have another volume on the Spaniards to complement that of Lewis and Hodge, and therefore, one of his activities in this year 1915 was choosing a number of selections for translation from Spaniards still quite unfamiliar to most American historians — Juan de Oñate, Alonso de León, Sebastián Vizcaíno, Padre Kino, and others. These he translated, edited, and introduced in *Spanish Explorations in the Southwest, 1543–1706;* the volume bore a 1916 imprint. Reviews were encouraging.* In fact, although books of selected readings ordinarily do not get "rave" reviews, *Spanish Exploration in the Southwest* proved an exception to this pattern. Clarence W. Alford, in the *MVHR* (December 1917), credited it with a new kind of historical scholarship:

> In Dr. Bolton's volume a more startling and unexpected innovation is noticeable; instead of confining himself to material in English already printed, one-third of the volume is composed of documents never before printed in English translation, and *mirabile dictu* another third contains documents never before printed in any language.

---

*For the purposes of this study note will be taken only of the reviews appearing in the *American Historical Review* (*AHR*) and the *Mississippi Valley Historical Review* (*MVHR*); these were the most prestigious of the journals during most of Bolton's career. In time book review policies of the state journals and others became higher and more demanding, but to cover even a few of these would take this survey much too far afield.

[97]

Alvord went on to regret that the scope of the "Original Narratives" had not initially been broadened to make sure of the volumes like the Bolton contribution. Frederick W. Hodge commented on the inclusion of new materials and remarked, in the *AHR* (October 1917) that "Professor Bolton's book is of such importance and usefulness to students of the Southwest and the Pacific Slope as to be indispensable."

Before the end of 1915, Bolton would pull together a number of his Texas studies for yet another volume, this one to be published by the University of California Publications in History and entitled *Texas in the Middle Eighteenth Century.* Claude H. Van Tyne in his review of the book in the *AHR* (July 1916), wrote: "In this, as in other printed works, Dr. Bolton has shown himself the pathfinder . . . a leader in the younger school of historical writers and students in this field." This work was really the first that was Bolton's from start to finish, evidencing his ability to build a story from the mass of data which he had extracted.

Then in the summer of 1915 when San Francisco played host to the Panama Pacific International Exposition (P.P.I.E.) — its first venture into the world's fair business — once again Bolton was called upon to exercise his developing skill as a writer. Following the pattern set at Chicago in 1893, the historians of the Bay Area, principally Morse Stephens, had persuaded the American Historical Association to advance the date of its annual meeting and to participate in the gala academic fête, along with other associations and disciplines. "The Pacific Ocean in History" was the central theme; a book consisting of the papers which were read ultimately bore that title.[1] Besides coediting the book with Stephens, Bolton read two papers of his own during the course of the sessions — "The Early Explorations of Father Garcés on the Pacific Slope" and "French Intrusions into New Mexico, 1749-52," both based on his pioneer digging in the Mexican archives.

HIS CONTINENTAL APPROACH

Again, in 1915 there were negotiations with Macmillan for a multivolume history of the United States. Even though he had many pet ideas which he wanted to incorporate into such a textbook, he had professed himself hesitant to undertake so large and predictably time-consuming a project by himself. When Macmillan publishers let him know that they would not shy away from a collaborative work, Bolton approached Thomas Maitland Marshall and found his former pupil both interested and willing. Actually, only the first volume, the quite revolutionary Bolton-and-Marshall, saw publication. (A number of chapters of the proposed Volume Two are untouched in the Bolton Papers.)

What appeared in October 1920, *The Colonization of North America,* 1492–1783, was really Bolton's first major opportunity to put between two covers many of the ideas and much of the data which he had been using in his several classes on the West and the Southwest in late years. He had put in a letter to his brother (June 2, 1912) what would be the basic idea of the text:

> Of most general importance, perhaps, is my general course in Western history. I have established a point of view which will cause a rewriting of text books, much as Turner's work did. I approach American history from a continental and European standpoint, instead of from the standpoint of England alone. This gives the West its due prominence in the colonial period as well as in the national period.

In his lectures he had given increasing emphasis in the colonial story to his favored Spaniards and also to the French. Telling these aspects of the colonial centuries he reserved for himself, leaving to Marshall the task of preparing those chapters which were primarily English in content. A key to respective responsibilities comes from a letter of Bolton to Marshall (March 16, 1920), saying that he would prepare the index slips for "Chapters 1, 2, 3, 4 (pp. 1–104), 13, 14, 15, 16 (pp. 233–308), 20, 21, 22 (pp. 359–424). These are the parts of the book which I had most to do with." Marshall, having done most of the Anglo chapters, assumed much of the drudge work, but the "senior partner" still did his share, thus complicating his increasingly busy life. By 1919–20 Bolton's multiple commitments were catching up with him in fullest force.

The Colonization of North America was more than a little revolutionary in its approach to the colonial period, so much so that it had profoundly shocked the editorial readers at Macmillan, when they went through pages and pages, almost one-fourth of the manuscript before coming upon the traditional "first Americans" at Jamestown. Equanimity was not exactly restored when they later found the Anglos sharing the remaining three-fourths with the same strangers to the American story — 140 pages out of 430 told of seventeenth- and eighteenth-century activities of Spaniards and Frenchmen, Dutchmen and Swedes, as well as a few Russians. The work caused a bit of a ripple in historical circles and received a number of interesting reviews. Verner W. Crane, in the *AHR* (April 1921), caught the message; commenting on the non-Anglo sections of the book Crane wrote: "Indeed these chapters give the book its real distinction." O. G. Libby likewise recognized the novelty of the approach in the *MVHR* (March 1921), and noted that "altogether this venture is well adapted at every point to convince and persuade a large

and influential constituency of scholars and general readers that . . . a
new field for scholarship has definitely been opened for future work."
With this book Bolton served notice on the profession that his concept of
"American" was continental in its scope. About the same time, in his
History of the Americas course on the Berkeley campus, he was beginning
to make it hemispheric.

Nineteen fifteen was only the first of several hectic, overcrowded
years to come. A similar theme would run through each year until 1921
and the publication of *The Spanish Borderlands*. In late 1916 Bolton
wormed his way into the "Chronicles of America" series of which *The
Spanish Borderlands* was to become a part. This involvement, like that
with Arthur H. Clark, both of which will be detailed in a later chapter,
would plague Bolton for several years to come.

THE FIRSTS AMONG HIS DOCTORS

No matter how busy he was, Bolton's graduate students were always
of concern to him. He was ever on the lookout for funds with which to
assist young men and women who came to Berkeley to study under his
direction. In the very early 1900s a hundred dollars or so a year often
meant academic survival. As associate editor of the *Quarterly* he could
feed much of the research production of many of his students into its
pages. His connection with the *SWHQ* as a sort of West Coast representative made it possible for him to pay one or other of his students for
keeping the books. He was reaching the age when he could adopt a
fatherly attitude toward them; they were his "boys" and his "girls."

Eddie Dunn had been one of Bolton's first students, studying under
him first at Texas, and later following him to Stanford. Dunn's own
description of their meeting at Texas is characteristic of the Bolton
approach in the classroom and of his attitude toward his students:

> A tall and handsome young instructor was about to lecture to
> his medieval history class at the University of Texas back in 1905.
> "Is there anyone present," he asked, "who knows some Spanish and
> would like to work in the history of the Spanish Southwest? If so,
> please see me after class."
> A verdant freshman myself, with more interest in Spanish than
> in history at that time, I responded to his call. The instructor's con-
> tagious enthusiasm — his offer to pay me twenty cents per hour —
> induced me to take a part-time job working in the State Capitol in
> Austin indexing and copying old manuscripts inherited from the
> Spanish and Mexican regimes. I gradually learned to read the ancient
> Spanish orthography, and the next summer vacation my teacher

and employer took me to Mexico City to do similar work in the Mexican National Archives. Thus began my long and intimate association with the most indefatigable, prolific and inspiring historian that this country has produced in many a decade.

The young instructor . . . accorded me the privilege and honor of becoming his first graduate student. . . . A native of Wisconsin, he began his teaching career at the University of Texas in 1901. . . . He immediately perceived a great opportunity to pioneer in an almost virgin field — the history of the Spanish Southwest, where legend and tradition rather than historical research still ruled. Very little use had then been made of original documents in the Bexar Archives at Austin and much less of those in the archives of Spain and Mexico. . . . Each summer until the Madero revolution in 1911, Dr. Bolton would he himself go to Mexico to delve into the national and provincial archives. . . . I had the good fortune to accompany him on all of these trips after 1905. . . . At all times I found him a delightful and inspiring companion despite the difference in our ages. He had a remarkably keen sense of humor, despite his extreme industriousness, and never tired of poking fun at himself. . . .[2]

Bolton once wrote to Dunn: "You are my first and most promising foster child and your long association with me and the family causes me to regard you as one of the family. . . . One of the finest things about my work with you, Hackett, and Martin, is that I hardly realize that I am not one of the boys with you."[3] Bolton was influential in getting a $650 fellowship for Dunn to Columbia where he studied under William R. Shepherd. Dunn would eventually work in a field of more contemporary Latin American history.

Charles Wilson Hackett likewise had followed Bolton from Texas to Stanford. He then transferred to University of California and was an early favorite. Bolton had been truly grieved when, in 1912, young Hackett had to drop out temporarily. He had arranged with Stephens to award him a fellowship at Berkeley. Hackett would come back after a short interlude, complete his doctorate in 1917, and go on to a brilliant career at the University of Texas, in a real sense carrying on the work there which Bolton himself might have done had he chosen Texas over California in that summer of 1910. He maintained close contact with Hackett over the years and as late as the summer of 1946 was invited by Hackett to lecture in the off-campus session of the University of Texas' Institute of Latin American Studies, held in Mexico City.[4]

Thomas Powderly Martin, the third name mentioned in Bolton's letter to Dunn, completed his master's work with Bolton in 1914 and later went to Harvard for his doctorate (1922). He ultimately became assistant chief, Manuscript Division, Library of Congress, after holding similar but not such prestigious positions in the Harvard library system. He was often able to repay Bolton's kindnesses with favors and services from his Library of Congress post.

At Stanford Bolton had picked up Thomas Maitland Marshall and put him to work on a segment of his transcripts from the Mexican archives. Marshall also transferred to California with him and in 1914 had become Bolton's first Ph.D. Bolton was also able to place his doctoral dissertation in the University of California Publications in History series, *A History of the Western Boundary of the Louisiana Purchase, 1819–1841*, and as mentioned earlier Marshall coauthored *The Colonization of North America* with the master.

Shortly after moving to California Bolton had attracted one of his most productive students and most loyal and ardent admirers. Charles Edward Chapman came to the University of California with an interestingly varied background.[5] A Yankee, graduate of Harvard, with a law degree from Tufts, and a fine collegiate athlete, Chapman first thought of carving out a career for himself in professional baseball. An injury dissipated that dream and sent him into business, but the desire to work with young people soon had him in a high school classroom. The step to graduate school in history at California was a natural one. Chapman won his master's degree in 1909 and was one of the "old" graduate students on campus when Bolton arrived from Stanford. Not quite "comfortable" with his earlier director, Chapman soon found in Bolton a mentor whom he could admire and also one who knew a great deal about the dissertation topic he had chosen for himself, "The Preliminaries of the Spanish Advance from Sonora to California, 1687–1773." This study was "right down Bolton's alley," beginning as it did with the exploits of Padre Kino in Sonora. He enthusiastically adopted Chapman, who in 1915 became his second Ph.D., and then his colleague in the Department of History at California.

Hackett, Marshall and Chapman would be among the graduates from 1914 to 1919 who came to be known in later years as the "firsts," the first of many who having studied under Bolton would graduate with doctor's degrees. Also in 1916 were Gordon C. Davidson, a Canadian who was attracted to Berkeley, Bolton, the Bancroft Collection, and became an authority on the North West Company; Roy Gittinger who did not have much time to publish extensively before the University of Oklahoma pulled him into administration; and Cardinal Leonidas Goodwin who later wrote extensively on the Trans-Mississippi West. In 1916 Bolton saw Herbert Ingram Priestley doctored, and he recommended to Stephens that he be added to the growing history department at California. Owen Cochran Coy, who became well respected in later years for his many writings on the history of California, and Andrew Love Neff, one of the first of a long line of young men of the Mormon faith who came to Berkeley to work with Bolton, made up the 1918 doctors. Rounding out the "firsts" was William Henry Ellison, long History chairman at Santa Barbara State College; his Ph.D. was conferred in 1919. These first doctors became convincing advertisements for Bolton, his seminar, and the brand of graduate training which he was establishing at California.[6]

❦❦

Bolton was consistently a super-salesman of history. Always warm and charming, he was particularly so in welcoming a new graduate student, and there were times when he sowed seeds of interest early. The following account falls into this last category; it is from the son of a man who was studying for his doctorate under Bolton and had his family in Berkeley with him:

> My father first went to Berkeley in 1936. During that year Dr. Bolton several times asked him to bring me to see him. Father put it off, thinking that the interest was part of the friendly Bolton interest in the whole man, not just the student. In the summer of 1937 he made it an order so father took me (just 14 years old) to see Dr. Bolton. After I was introduced, Dr. Bolton looked at father and said, "You have a lot of work to do and this young man and I have a lot of talking to do, so you run along."
>
> Dr. Bolton asked me about my reading in history and shortly we were discussing the Northmen's discoveries. He questioned me and listened with intense interest to what little I knew and then sought my opinions and why I had them, as though it were most important to him to learn them. Then we got into a discussion of his trip to Spain and the huge collection of documents he had acquired at the Casa de Contratación. He had already learned that I was taking Spanish and asked if I would like to see them.... Bolton handed me a document and asked me to read it. To my own amazement I was able to read it with an occasional help on an unfamiliar word. Bolton darted back and forth, rummaging in the stacks and handing me other documents to read and then we would discuss the contents. ... Father returned for me about four — he had returned earlier and Bolton told him we were busy.

The reporter tells of his return to Berkeley later as a student and of his visits to Bolton. After graduating from California, he went to another university for his doctorate and subsequently established himself in the profession. He concluded his letter: "I never saw Dr. Bolton again [after graduating from California] but he has always lived in my memory as the great man who spent a whole afternoon talking as a colleague with a fourteen year old boy." Bolton probably knew that he was doing a bit of missionary work for history that afternoon.[7]

First meetings with Bolton left living marks on many memories and here are several examples to prove the point:

> I was very fortunate in that Dr. Bolton received me as a friend the first time I walked into his office. I must have seemed a rather unusual specimen — a chemistry major ten years out of the University of Michigan with only three units of lower-division credit in history, who wanted to take advanced history courses. When he asked why I wanted to study history, I said that I could probably think up a lot of plausible reasons, but the simple truth was that I wanted to study history for fun. He looked me over for a minute and then gave what for me seems a prophetic answer. "I have been looking for someone who wants to study history for fun." His exact words have always stuck in my memory.

The next man's introduction to Bolton has its own familiar yet distinctive turn:

> His name first came to me through one of his alumni, Arthur Scott Aiton, whose Latin American courses I took at Michigan. Another former student, John Lloyd Mecham, made my interest more direct by advising me to come to California to study under Dr. Bolton when I decided to leave newspaper work and take up graduate study. This was based on his preeminence in the newly popular field of Latin American history. I came without knowledge of his personality, or of the University — even its location.
>
> He impressed me at once, when I came out in August 19 . . . , by his geniality, his candor, and his facility at making people feel at ease. He made me feel promptly that I had a friend in a strange place. He apologized for the fact that my letter of application had had for reply only two telegrams, the decisive one three weeks before school opened, saying that he had not known how many of the previous teaching fellows would return. He took a long chance in giving me a teaching fellowship, since I had had no graduate work, no teaching, not even quite an undergraduate major in history by California standards. He later told me that he banked on a letter from his one-time classmate Professor Claude H. Van Tyne, and on the eagerness expressed in my own letter. This was typical. He was always willing to accept a student's interest and confidence as evidence that the person was worth spending time on.

Not only Bolton's doctors were recruiters, but so were some of his masters, who were liberally scattered through California high schools:

> I first heard Bolton's name through a teacher at Pasadena High School who had taken her M.A. with him, and who was full of enthusiasm for him. When I went to Berkeley for summer session in 1930, she gave me a letter of introduction to him, and the result was that I took his History of the West. . . . The course was delightful

and an exciting experience for me. Although the freshest of undergraduates, Bolton was generous of his time and encouragement with
me. I was an undergraduate at Stanford in 1931–1933, but during
those years I called on Bolton occasionally in Berkeley, and he
encouraged me to come there for graduate work. . . .

Another one of his "boys" tells us his first meeting with Bolton, and his
experience conforms to the pattern:

> I met Dr. Bolton first about May 19 . . . , when I was at Stanford
> finishing up for an M.A., under the late Ephraim D. Adams, himself
> a figure of note in the historical world. Stanford had little in the way
> of fellowships then, and Professor Adams advised me to go up and
> see Bolton. I did and got in to see him; he was busy and I knew he
> would rather be at work and I was a damned nuisance, but he was
> most affable and put me at ease. I recall his desk, about the longest
> I had ever seen, piled with papers, books, and manuscripts in the
> same disarray as mine later was, and is to this day. . . . He said he
> would see what he could do for me. The next fall I was a teaching
> assistant under Paul B. Schaefer [medievalist]; the following year
> I was with Bolton in History 8.

Bolton was not above doing a bit of pirating when he found a student
in one of his classes in whom he recognized real potential. One of his
"prizes" was a young man who thought he was heading to a law degree.
He had taken a couple of Bolton's courses during his program in juris-
prudence. The young man had developed a strong secondary interest in
history but still was bent on law. He ran into Bolton commencement day
right after the graduation ceremony, and when asked what he intended,
he affirmed his intention of becoming a barrister. "Bolton snorted and
said 'Why don't you come over to history, we have a fellowship waiting
for you.' " The reporter laughs as he tells the sequel. His wife had not
stayed for graduation but had chosen that time to visit her parents, to
whom she had proudly announced that she would soon be the wife of a
great lawyer. By the time she returned to Berkeley, she found that she
was the wife of an aspiring historian.

Such examples would be multiplied, but enough has been recalled to
show Bolton the salesman, in a one-on-one situation. His effectiveness in
classes helped to inspire many an undergraduate to choose history as a
major, and no inconsiderable number of these went on to graduate work.

There were times when Bolton's women students felt that he was
anti-feminist. Bolton's feeling was that a woman's place is primarily in the
home, but he was also realistic, for in his day the profession was anti-
feminist, being not particularly favorable to women historians. He was
perfectly willing to see endowed girls go on to the master's degree, which

could be valuable to them as teachers, both personally and financially, but he encouraged few to go on beyond to the doctorate. In his day history was a field almost universally considered to be a man's profession with the positions in women's colleges somewhat limited. More than once Bolton told aspiring young women that he was dead set against accepting a graduate student in a doctoral program unless he felt that he had a reasonable chance of placing that student in a position properly commensurate with his/her training.

During his years of study of the American West, Bolton had come into frequent book contact with the Mormons of the nineteenth century. About 1916 or a little earlier a number of young Mormon students began to come to Berkeley for graduate studies and to regularly choose to work with Bolton. By 1929 his so-called "Utah gang" would number half a dozen doctors or near-doctors, including Andrew Neff, Joseph Hill, William Snow, LeRoy Hafen, Thomas Romney and Leland Creer. In 1925 as a token of appreciation to Bolton for the help he had given these students, Brigham Young University invited him to give the Founder's Day address. "The Mormons in the Opening of the West" turned out to be one of his more notable studies. The *Deseret News* published it serially in October and November; the following January it was reprinted in the *Utah Genealogical and Historical Magazine* (XVI, 40–72).

ADDED RESPONSIBILITY

All Bolton's involvements were not of his own making; for some he was not personally responsible, such as his late fall 1916 appointment as curator of the Bancroft Library. Stephens in his annual report to the president on the department succinctly recorded this development:

> The chief event in the history of the Department was the transference of the Curatorship of Bancroft Library. . . . The special devotion of Professor Bolton to Spanish-American history and the history of the old Spanish territory now within the limits of the United States make him particularly fit for administering the Bancroft Library, and he has been ably helped by Professor C. E. Chapman and Professor H. I. Priestley.

Thus began an involvement of a quarter-century and more. Bolton shared the chores of leadership with Priestley (not always to the complete satisfaction of the latter). Together they would build this already magnificent collection into one that was even greater and more extensive. Bolton was delighted with this new charge, but it would crowd even more his already full-to-capacity schedule.

This appointment further widened the gap between himself and J. Frederick Teggart, in charge of the Bancroft up until that time. For several years Teggart and some of his associates and students had exploited the California-history riches of the collection and published several valuable and useful works. The coming of Bolton to the campus Teggart viewed as a distinct threat to his position and a potential dimmer on the fame which he was acquiring. Bolton had brought to Berkeley with him a number of his own packets of transcripts from the Mexican archives and for space and safety reasons had stored them in the Bancroft Collection. Teggart tended to be possessive of these materials and often made it difficult for Bolton to consult and use his own transcripts. This was the basis of the "feud" which had developed over the years. Teggart was not precisely happy at being replaced. A few years later when Teggart was up for advancement to the rank of professor in political science, his field of prime competence, rather than history, Bolton wrote to President Barrows (December 6, 1921), asking that he not be on the committee to pass on the nomination, lest, if the decision were unfavorable to Teggart, he be accused of prejudice. A tough in-fighter when his students or a pet project of his own were involved, he was not interested in personal feuding — actually, he had much respect for Teggart as an academe, although he may not have liked the man personally.

That Christmastide, 1916, Bolton stayed close to his desk, for he had a very important immediate job to do — a job which again would challenge his creativity as a writer. He was preparing for the evening of March 23, 1917. Several years before, in early 1912, he had been part of a committee, appointed by President Wheeler, to consider the inauguration of an annual series of faculty lectures, one each year, which might give an outstanding faculty member the opportunity to share the fruits of his research with the university community. The committee reported back to Wheeler, April 29, 1912, highly recommending such a series. It was provided that the professor be chosen by his colleagues of the Academic Senate, and the lecture would be one of the features of the annual Charter Day commemoration. The first was given in 1913; William Wallace Campbell, future president of the University but at that time director of Link Observatory, was the lecturer. John Campbell Merriam, Armin Otto Leuschner, Charles Mills Gayley had followed in the next years. Late in 1916 the university's Academic Senate named Bolton as the fifth in the distinguished series. He was pleased to the point of being positively thrilled, for this was high recognition by his peers. He later described the distinction to his brother (March 31, 1917): "It will not mean much to you, till I tell you that it is equivalent to an honorary LL.D."

The auditorium in the recently completed Wheeler Hall was the place; the date, the evening of March 23, 1917; the topic, "The Mission as a Frontier Institution in the Spanish-American Colonies." This was one of Bolton's finest and most enduring studies, the quintessence of fifteen years of study. He showed how by late in the sixteenth century the Spaniards were beginning to count more and more on the missionaries as agents, not only in the Christianization of the native Americans, but also as agents of control in preparing the frontiers for peaceful exploitation and settlement. It was one of those seed studies which inspired much subsequent research and writing on the mission phenomenon, not only in the colonial Hispanic world, but in other American empires as well. This was the sort of thing which Bolton planned to do often, namely, to sit back and isolate a theme running through his pioneering factual researchings and highlight the institution. But as time passed, he found so many basic Southwestern stories untold and in need of telling that he never quite had time for that job.* This lecture of 1917 was first printed by Jameson in the October 1917 number of the *American Historical Review* XXII.†

Bolton could not tarry long to savour the exhilaration of that evening of March 23, for another involvement not of his making was demanding much of his time and energy. Chairman Morse Stephens had been stricken in New York during the inter-semester break and was critically ill; Bolton had been asked to take over as acting department chairman. This made for a heavier than usual semester. Besides his new charge as curator of the Bancroft, there were his classes and an increasing load of students

---

*A dozen years later Bolton did develop his study of the defensive character of the Borderlands to set beside this mission piece. See "Defensive Spanish Expansion and the Significance of the Borderlands" in *The Trans-Mississippi West: Papers,* edited by James Field Willard and Colin Brummit Goodykoontz (Boulder: University of Colorado, 1930, pp. 1–42; also reprinted in Herbert Eugene Bolton, *Wider Horizons of American History* (New York: Appleton-Century, 1939) and in *Bolton and the Spanish Borderlands,* edited by John Francis Bannon (Norman: University of Oklahoma Press, 1964).

†A year or two later, when Jameson and a jury of advisors were combing through the back numbers of the *AHR* to select the best articles for an anniversary volume, "The Mission as a Frontier Institution in the Spanish-American Colonies" was one of their choices. It has been reprinted singly and in collections a number of times since then and can be conveniently found in Herbert Eugene Bolton, *Wider Horizons of American History* (New York: Appleton-Century, 1939) and in *Bolton and the Spanish Borderlands,* edited by John Francis Bannon (Norman: University of Oklahoma Press, 1964).

requiring research direction, his own varied commitments with publishers, and a number of committee assignments in the university. The entry of the United States into World War I, in April, further complicated matters. Since the summer of 1914 Bolton had been acutely aware of and vitally interested in what was going on in Europe and elsewhere in the world touched by the hostilities, but like most Americans the war touched his life very indirectly.

With the United States now a belligerent, he was anxious to be as vital a part as possible of the war effort. He was well beyond service age, but he made time to participate in the university's "war aims" course and was named a member of the State of California committee which had the task of gathering materials concerning the role of California and Californians in the conflict.

As acting chairman of the department it became his duty, in late spring, to make the annual report to the History Committee of the Native Sons of the Golden West on the fellowship program that organization had been supporting for the past half-dozen years. He had spoken to the Native Sons on several previous occasions; now, however, he was acting in official capacity. This 1917 appearance was the beginning of an important relationship which was to endure for years to come.

Back in 1910 Morse Stephens, promoter par excellence, had talked the Native Sons into establishing a fellowship at the University to sponsor the study of the history of California and of the Pacific West in general.[8] He had convinced them that they might thus realize an optimum return on the funds invested. The Native Sons adopted the idea and established first one fellowship, and then in 1913, two annual fellowships, to be administered by the university's Department of History. These fellowships carried a quite generous stipend of $1500 — in those days enough to allow the recipient to carry on research in foreign archives. With the advent of Bolton to the department, Stephens knew that he had a man on hand who could direct the work of these Native Sons fellows to great advantage.

It was with a large measure of pride that Bolton made the 1917 report. He told the Grand Parlor of the Native Sons that Charles Edward Chapman's *Founding of Spanish California* was already in print — he had been one of the first young scholars whom they had backed; so, too, was William L. Schurz's *Manila Galleon;* in press was Gordon Davidson's *History of the North West Company,* built in large measure on materials which he had been able to gather in England, thanks to the Native Sons; Herbert I. Priestley had not been a NSGW fellow, but his forthcoming *José de Gálvez* was made possible by archive copies which earlier fellows had accumulated for the Bancroft Collection. Over the years such source transcripts from Spain and elsewhere would accumulate in the Bancroft Library, and so would the list of publications of the Native Sons fellows. The continuing support of the Native Sons would be a vital factor in the telling of the fuller story of California and the Greater Southwest, and most of this work was done under Bolton's direction. The Native Sons might be said to have been his first "angels," — the name he gave to various benefactors over the years.

During this year, too, Bolton was very much a part of the drive which ultimately brought two new scholarly journals into being. He put his influence and prestige behind colleague Charles Chapman, who had already been promoting what soon was to be the *Hispanic American Historical Review*.[9] Bolton had been elected to the Council of the American Historical Association on the 1917 slate; hence, he felt obligated to attend the late December annual meeting of the association at Philadelphia. Being on the ground, he was able to give Chapman and partner, James Alexander Robertson, a powerful assist in finally selling the *HAHR* idea to the profession. His support continued as one of the first advisory editors of the journal. Friend Aurelio Espinosa of Stanford also leaned on Bolton for suggestions and support as he schemed to realize the dream which became *Hispania*.[10]

Second semester of 1917–18 was relatively uneventful, and he could be thankful for that since he had many things to do. At the 1918 commencement he was one of the academically best dressed men at the ceremony. His doctors had gotten together and presented him with a new academic outfit — cap, gown, hood. They were nine by that date: Chapman, Coy, W. Ellison, Gittinger, Goodwin, Hackett, Marshall, Neff, and Priestley. This thoughtful manifestation of esteem and affection touched him deeply. Such little acts made a devoted mentor forget the long hours spent in advising and encouraging, and the even longer ones given to reading and correcting dissertations. Periodically he might complain that the load of graduate work was deadening; but then there would be a student's book or article, or something like this token, to thrill him and give him the warm feeling that it was all worthwhile.

The summer of 1918 Bolton stayed on campus, taught summer session, and worked on several of his many projects. In September a letter to Frederick summarized in a few lines the restlessness he was feeling, occasioned he felt by the war and his minimum involvement in his country's effort. His work, too, was getting to be a major problem:

> One of my difficulties has been my enslavement to three or four tasks of writing which have insidiously developed separately in their infancy but in their matured force have combined simultaneously to chain me to my desk and to harry me, waking and sleeping. Several years ago I began the editing of the famous Kino Memoirs

which I discovered. While they were in the publisher's hand, or at some other stage of quietus, I jointly with Dr. Marshall wrote a college text book on *European Expansion in North America* [*The Colonization of North America*]. In an interval last summer when Kino was being set up and the text book was being considered by the publishers, I wrote in a Yale series a popular sketch called *The Spanish Borderlands.* . . . In the course of the year these all have come tumbling back upon me for various kinds of attention. The Kino to be proof-read, the text book to be shortened and provided with maps, the *Borderlands* to be revised in the direction of levity.

Meanwhile a pestiferous map publishing company (Denoyer and Geppert) got a hold on me. Some two years ago they made proposals that I prepare some school maps for them, and I told them that when I got free I would do so. As you can guess they have been dogging my tracks ever since. I am vowing to slay these hounds one at a time and be a free agent a day or two before I start anything new.

Here in a nutshell is a large story, or better several stories. By fall 1918 the "hounds" were snapping at Bolton's heels, sometimes rather viciously.

First in line was Arthur H. Clark, and not far behind were Editor Allen Johnson and Publisher Robert Glasgow of the "Chronicles of America" series. He was going to have to do some first-rate killing to be a "free agent for a day or two."

9

The Tug-of-War
With Two Publishers

FOR A MAN who accomplished in the area of scholarly output as much in a lifetime as did Herbert Bolton, it is not surprising that at times throughout his career he had serious problems getting done everything which he wanted to do, or even everything he was committed to do. Often he missed deadlines, especially where book publishers were concerned, but there was a period in his life when this was more obviously true, when his failure to deliver manuscripts on time had serious, unpleasant and in one instance, far-reaching consequences. This was early in his career, when he still gave full vent to his own enthusiasm, believing that he could, indeed, accomplish the overwhelming goals he set for himself. While he did have the physical capacity for working tirelessly, he regularly required more of himself than was either wise or reasonable, and herein lies the story of his relationship to publishers Arthur H. Clark and Robert Glasgow and editor Allen Johnson. The confrontations between Clark and Bolton, and to a lesser degree between Bolton and Glasgow, reveal several facets of Bolton's character, not all completely edifying.

Contacts with Arthur H. Clark had begun as far back as 1908, when Bolton was still in Mexico developing the *Guide*.[1] Clark, then based in Cleveland, had been the successful publisher of two large series of historical sources materials and was projecting still others. The "Great Western Travels" series, with Reuben Gold Thwaites as editor, had done well and Clark was just completing the even larger "The Philippine Islands," with the assistance of Emma Helen Blair and James Alexander Robertson. The reception in the historical profession of the monumental edition of "Jesuit Relations" seemed to suggest a possible like interest in a documentary series dealing with the Spaniards in North America. Clark was minded to try. He could envision a dual series, one making available materials from the Spanish archives; for this he thought of Robertson as editor. He was aware of the documentary riches which Bolton was uncovering in the Mexican archives and felt that a selection therefrom could well constitute a second series. Not only was Bolton the logical man to edit such a series, but Clark found the young professor from the University of Texas definitely interested. After several exchanges the two men entered into a contract: Bolton would prepare ten volumes of "Documentary Sources of American History from the Spanish and Mexican Archives" and would begin to dispatch the materials to Clark beginning in January 1910, at latest, and keep them flowing so as to allow publication of a volume a month between May 1910 and January 1911. Clark was pleased; Bolton was delighted. Clark got his announcements of the new series ready; Bolton began to plan and to line up translators as soon as he returned to his Texas post. His assistant was Edith Z. Rather. Not only had Bolton arranged for what he was quickly calling "my series," but he had also in the course of the exchanges sold Clark on two projected works of his own and had signed contracts in April and in August 1908 for the Athanase de Mézières and Kino translations, respectively. When he first stumbled on the Athanase de Mézières materials, he recognized their potential importance and determined to exploit the story of this man who had been so influential on the Texas-Louisiana frontier in the later eighteenth century, but who was so unknown to his American colleagues. The uncovering of the Kino manuscript, "Favores Celestiales," long thought to have perished, he regarded as one of his prize finds and immediately planned to translate and edit the same.

After his return to Austin, however, his university classes and other duties consumed a great portion of his time. Pressures to finish the *Guide* were both self-imposed and external. Negotiations with Stanford had taken many other hours. The result: little was accomplished on the documentary series, on Athanase de Mézières, or on Kino. In July 1909 Clark wrote asking for "some reasonable assurance as to progress of the work and the time of its delivery in satisfactory form to me." He went on to note that "we were to advance $50.00 per month, beginning May 1st, 1909, on receipt of your report each month, as to the work of translation and transcription done upon the series. So far we have received no report from you." Clark also took this occasion to remind Bolton that he did not like the delay with the two other manuscripts (De Mézières and Kino). A few weeks later (August 3) publisher Clark was asking for some idea of when the first volumes of the series would be in his hands in order that he might plan his manufacturing schedules.

Bolton wrote apologetically October 16, alleging the great pressures which he was encountering at his new post (Stanford) and warning that he would be tardy in submitting the manuscripts. Clark came back: "Yes, indeed, your letter of October 16th is a bitter disappointment to me; first, because it gives me not even an idea of when the manufacture of the series can be started; second, because it is evident that you cannot fulfill the dates of delivery provided for in our agreement, or anything reasonably near them." He suggested that a new contract, with revised dates, would be needed. More or less reconciling himself to delays with the series, Clark shifted his drive to obtaining the De Mézières volumes.

Months stretched into a year and Clark still had nothing. A November 26, 1910, letter showed a certain exasperation: "What is the status of the Mexican Series, and when will we receive the manuscript? This, as you know, has been greatly delayed beyond the contract, and, as I have a number of orders for this set, I am anxious to get the work out as early as possible." Nothing was forthcoming.

When Bolton moved over to the University of California, he was still in Clark's debt for the two contract promises, the De Mézières and the Kino volumes. Clark had ceased to talk of the "Documentary Sources" series and was trying to pry at least the De Mézières manuscript out of his delinquent author-editor. It was more than two years later, in early 1913, before Bolton did deliver the 1400-page manuscript on that fascinating actor on the Louisiana-Texas frontier of the later eighteenth century.

When at long last Clark did have the copy, his real problems began. Bolton was not overly prompt in returning the galleys, which Clark had produced very quickly; there was haggling over the title and the maps; worst of all, from Clark's point of view, Bolton too often wished to substitute "better documents," after those originally submitted had been put into type. The two volumes appeared in early 1914. In the summer of 1913, hoping to keep the documentary series idea alive, Bolton suggested in a letter to Clark that these two might constitute Volumes 1 and 2 in a series to be titled "Spain in the West";[2] further the Kino volumes could be the third and the fourth, and a translation of Morfi's History of Texas the fifth. Although Clark made no commitment, he did not dismiss the idea completely. Bolton came back to this in a letter of December 18, 1913: "Kino, Morfi, and de León would make good volumes to follow up in this series, and I am perfectly willing to start one or two of them next Fall"; however, the possibility of doing more business with Bolton, after the De Mézières experience, forced Clark to issue a fervent plea: "I want to ask a special favor for you, as well as for ourselves, that you will spend what time is necessary on the manuscript and endeavor to get it to us in as near final shape as possible, so that it can be produced rapidly and without so much expense to either of us." If Clark considered that he had had trouble with Bolton over the De Mézières volumes, fortunately he was not clairvoyant and could not foresee the headaches which would be in store for him when the Kino manuscript went onto the presses.

The reviews of *Athanase de Mézières* were laudatory. The volumes gave critics a first chance to evaluate Bolton as editor-author. Isaac Joslin Cox in the *American Historical Review* (October 1914) highlighted two points, the "Historical Introduction" of over a hundred pages which preceded the documents, "that for the casual reader will constitute the most valuable feature of the work," and the use which Bolton had made of his multiple contributions on the Texas Indians which had already appeared in the *Handbook of American Indians*. Eugene C. Barker, drawing the assignment for the *Mississippi Valley Historical Review* (September 1914), spoke in glowing terms of Bolton's acquaintance with both archives and bibliography — not really surprising since, as his colleague at Texas, he had watched Bolton begin his intensive digging south of the border and through the years had followed his friend's continuing work therein. But after a promising start, sales dropped off quickly and to Clark, almost frighteningly. Of course, there was the outbreak of the war in late summer which upset business and was destined to have its influence for several years to come. Reporting to Bolton December 15, 1914, Clark advised him that the publication of the Kino volumes might have to wait until the conclusion of hostilities. This information upset Bolton and he came back several weeks later (January 21, 1915) with a long letter. He told Clark that he would not like to see the Kino delayed and assured him that 1915 should be a good year for a book connected, even though a bit indirectly, with the California history (reference was to the coming meeting of the American Historical Association on the West Coast in connection with the P.P.I.E.). He further assured the publisher: "I have another volume all translated and ready for editing ["Morfi's History of Texas"], besides two or three more volumes collected and largely translated. If the series is to count as it ought, it should move along, even though slowly. But on this I defer to your judgment." Clark (January 26, 1915) was not convinced that a chance occurrence such as the gathering of historians in San Francisco would have any notable effect on the sales of such a work as the Kino. And he added: "Regarding the continuation of the series, I do not know just exactly, at present, what to say." During much of 1915 Bolton was almost too busy to pursue the matter.

After another year, however, he began to be concerned for the Kino volumes. Feeling that the slow movement of De Mézières on the market might make Clark very chary about a similar work, in mid-January 1916 he came up with what might be styled a save-the-Kino proposal. The University of California was approaching its semi-centennial year (1868–

1918); Bolton suggested that an effort might be made to have the university contract in advance of publication to take 250 sets of the Kino off Clarks' hands, to be used as anniversary gifts to individuals and/or other universities. This would mean that Clark could be certain of unloading one-third of his projected printing. He was not overly enthusiastic about the idea; however, he was willing to furnish Bolton with quotations and to set conditions under which he would consider proceeding, so that Bolton might have something concrete to present to the university. Clark closed this letter of January 25, 1916, on a rather pessimistic note: "I am going to speak frankly . . . . The facts are that I am very skeptical of our being able to make a financial success of this *Spain in the West* series. . . . We put forth considerable effort, and some of it very special effort, to push the sale of De Mézières, but it has not been, I am sorry to say, a success, and we are still at a very considerable loss on its publication."

With the Clark figures in hand, Bolton was in a position to approach the university's Semi-Centennial Committee with his proposition. On February 24, 1916, Bolton regretfully had to report that the committee, on the advice of the manager of the university press, had turned down Clark's condition for a joint publication: "It is not a good one from the University standpoint." Bolton asked Clark to consider a revision of his proposal, but Clark was adamant in his refusal. Things seemed at an impasse; however, Clark did leave Bolton with a ray of hope when he mentioned that he might consider an early publication of the Kino, if Bolton could assure him of a sizable Catholic market for the work.

With this Bolton got to work; he also enlisted the help of several of his Catholic graduate students, especially that of Jesuit Theodore Pockstaller, who circularized most of the Jesuit colleges and universities in the country to test interest in the story of one of their earlier brethren. Besides this Bolton evidently did a certain amount of politicking in the right places on campus, for on April 1 he was able to write Clark that the Semi-Centennial Committee had reconsidered its decision and would accept the publisher's conditions provided he gave assurance that the work would be completed and the 250 books delivered by May 1, 1918. The Kino contract was redrawn in those terms. Optimistic as usual, Bolton promised to deliver the Kino manuscript by the end of the summer and felt that he could do the same with the Morfi history of Texas, which had also been included in the deal, by November 1.

Bolton was sincere, but again he overestimated his ability to meet these deadlines. He was committed to teach the summer session at the University of Michigan and was confident that, being away from his home campus, he would have much time to ready the Kino manuscript for submission to Clark. The end of summer came, but Clark had no manuscript.

He waited a few weeks and then nudged Bolton (October 18), gently, but with the reminder that if contract deadlines with the university were to be met, he must have the manuscript quickly. Bolton promised (November 1) to have it in Clark's hands right after the first of the year; Clark set the date — January 15, 1917 — agreeing that this would still be adequate time.

Mid-January came and went. Ten days later, January 25, G. M. Robertson, Clark's editor, reminded Bolton that the manuscript was overdue. There was a February exchange concerning several technical points in connection with the manuscript; Bolton, too, was insisting that the Spanish original be included along with the translation. He was influenced in this demand by the format which Thwaites had used in his edition of the "Jesuit Relations." He promised delivery by April 1. He told Clark that Stephens's illness had put a number of unforeseen administrative burdens on him; also mentioned was the fact that the curatorship of the Bancroft Library was taking more of his time than he had anticipated. He did not, however, breathe a word of his recent involvement with Allen Johnson and the volume for the "Chronicles of America" series, which, as time passed, would increasingly complicate the problem of meeting a deadline.

This latter involvement had begun one October day in 1916 when Bolton was working through the pile of mail on his desk and came upon an intriguing advertising piece, issued by the Yale University Press and announcing a series of several dozen volumes which promised to constitute "a consecutive history of the United States." Inspired by the success of the thirty-two-volume "Chronicles of Canada," issued by the Edinburgh University Press and published by Glasgow, Brooks and Company of Toronto, Yale Press agreed to cooperate with Robert Glasgow on a similar series for United States history, to be known as the "Chronicles of America." Allen Johnson of Yale had been signed as general editor. Popularly written history by top American scholars was promised — as readable, intriguing, exciting as the United States story could be made. Without naming names, the sponsors indicated that they were carefully selecting experts to do each projected volume. Bolton read the blurb. The general approach promised interested him greatly, since this was precisely the sort of history which he dreamed of writing about "his Spaniards," whose exploits in North America he hoped to "Parkmanize." He checked the listing of the proposed volumes and found to his dismay that only two promised any notice of the Spaniards and their contributions to American history.

Applying the age-old theory "nothing ventured, nothing gained," he sent off a letter October 16, 1916, to Editor Allen Johnson:

My purpose in writing you is to inquire if perhaps you might find it desirable to fit me into your scheme. I have been preparing to write a popular scholarly sketch of the expansion of New Spain, with special reference to the northern frontier (i.e., the United States Southwest, from Louisiana to California).[3]

Johnson did find it "desirable" and came back with a telegram on November 1: "Thank you for your letter - would have sought you out before if I had known your desire to write in a popular way - will be glad to have a volume from you on Spain in the Southwest - letter with details follows."

This letter, a long one, was on its way two days later. Johnson had talked with Robert Glasgow, the publisher, and with Professor William Shepherd of Columbia; both men were in agreement. Johnson explained that it was necessary to check with Shepherd, because "the only way by which we could make provision in the series for a volume by you was to ask Professor Shepherd to yield a portion of the field which his volume proposed to occupy." Shepherd would treat Spanish colonization and Irving B. Richman (the other author with a Spanish theme and the Iowa businessman Bolton had dealt with in earlier years) would stop at the sixteenth century, with the conquest and early exploration story. Shepherd would leave the Southwest to Bolton. "I do not quite know what to entitle your volume but would like your suggestions." Johnson then summed up: "Stated broadly this is the proposal which I should lay before you. I hope that it is one which you can accept." Johnson had mentioned that the series was not to operate on the normal author-royalty basis; rather, on completion of the manuscript each author would receive $750.00. He asked when the manuscript could be ready but then gave a deadline: "I think that I must insist that it be in my hands not later than June 1st, 1917." Bolton solemnly assured Johnson that his story of the Spaniards in the Southwest would be in by that date; this work had quickly assumed top spot in his priorities, and further delayed him in fulfilling his commitment to Arthur H. Clark.

By April 1917 the pressure on Bolton was tremendous. The Kino manuscript was due Clark on the first. Within less than two months, he was committed to the completion of the manuscript for editor Johnson. On April 9, when Clark still had not received the Kino from Bolton, he was greatly provoked and wrote an ultimatum to Bolton:

> I am sorry to have to write you in regard to the manuscript for *Kino,* but the facts are that unless we have it immediately, it will be impossible to get the work out in time for delivery to the University of California by the date set [May 1, 1918]; and unless we can be absolutely sure of completing it, I simply cannot start on it.

This warning jolted out of Bolton the first part of the manuscript three weeks later. By June 13 the rest of it was in Clark's hands, enough for three volumes in all, much more than Clark had expected.

By this time, however, Bolton was two weeks past due the deadline set for delivery to Johnson of the Spain in the Southwest volume. Bolton could breathe a little easier with the Kino off his desk, but that would not last for long, and meanwhile, he was faced with the displeasure of his other anxious publisher.

The working relationship with Johnson up until this time had been mutually satisfying. Bolton had sketched in a letter to Johnson November 16, 1916, what he envisioned for his proposed volume on Spain in the Southwest:

> For a brief account, of 40,000 words, it would seem wise to sketch the foundation and development of New Mexico, Texas, Pimería Alta (Southern Arizona) and California, with their appropriate backgrounds, down to the end of the eighteenth century. . . . The book might be entitled *The Spanish Colonies in the Southwest,* or *The Southwest under Spain,* or *The Spanish Pioneers,* or some equivalent title which may occur to you and seem more suitable to your series.

He added an outline, with the dates 1580 and 1800 as the termini. Then he noted the possibility of including the story of Louisiana under Spain, and even of having the New Mexico story preceded by a chapter on Florida, "but it would have some disadvantages."

Richman, far from being upset by the prospect of sharing his immense subject with Bolton, was overjoyed to be rid of the explorers who were threatening to take too many of his precious 40,000 words. Johnson informed Bolton November 22 that Richman would

> confine himself to the conquistadores south of the Rio Grande and leave you free to narrate the exploits of De Leon and Narvaez as well as of the explorers of the southwest within the limits of the present United States. In view of this, then, you will need to revise your outline. Florida and Louisiana as well as New Mexico and Alta California will come within your purview, and I would like you to carry your narrative down to the Anglo-American advance in the southwest.

Johnson hardly realized how vast a subject he was dumping into Bolton's lap, since he could hardly have been aware how much new history Bolton had been unearthing since 1902 and his first sally into the archives of Mexico.

In this same letter, Johnson offered some advice on "popularization," the guiding principle of the series. He reminded Bolton that one cannot tell everything in 40,000 words and warned that the editors did not want a text, "but a live, vivid, gripping story," which will emphasize "the biographical rather than the institutional." He told him that Richman had been accorded the title "The Spanish Conquerors"; he asked about using "The Spanish Explorers," with appropriate subtitle.

With the scope of his study thus broadened, Bolton submitted December 5 a new outline. As to title, he noted that he had suggested earlier "The Spanish Pioneers," but warned that Charles Lummis had already preempted that title; hence, he wondered if "The Spanish Frontiersmen" might not be better. In the same letter he expressed the hope that his volume might be good enough to warrant translation into Spanish.

The formal contract came and Bolton returned it on the day after Christmas 1916. When Johnson sent back Bolton's copy, he told him that his was to be Volume 23 of the series and that they had decided on the following title, "Frontiersmen of New Spain: A Chronicle of Colonial Adventure in California, the Southwest and the Gulf Lands." Again Johnson emphasized the kind of writing expected:

> I trust that you will attack the problems connected with the writing, bearing in mind that the volumes are not to contain discussions or expositions, but the story element. They should deal with character, incident, personality, and life in its entertaining and dramatic aspects as far as possible.

Bolton in a reply of January 8, 1917, approved the new title.

Glasgow knew from experience that titles were very important in a series such as this one. He and Johnson, and possibly others, kept working on that angle, not only for the Bolton volume but for others as well — some of them went through several changes. On January 15 they submitted several alternates: "Old Florida and the Southwest," "Frontiersmen of New Spain," and "Old California and the Spanish Gulf Lands." Not until later (April 18) in a general letter to all the authors committed to the series, did the "Borderlands" tag appear; there is no clue to whose idea it was, but it was not Bolton's.

Johnson apologized to his authors for seeming to be something of an omniscient and dictatorial editor. He noted, among other things, the pressures he was under to extend the series beyond the originally determined four dozen volumes. Had he yielded, he confessed, the figure soon would have topped seventy or better — evidently others besides Bolton felt that their subjects deserved treatment. He did admit that he had succumbed to pressure in two instances, after having done some juggling to open up two new volumes; one of these was "The Southwest under Spain: A Chronicle of Old California and the Spanish Borderlands." Here for the first time is the "magic" word, in a subtitle.

Johnson wrote February 10, 1917 that he had showed Bolton's second outline to Shepherd who had made some observations: the term New Spain might be confusing to readers, the section on the Manila Galleon might be eliminated, and a few other minor points. Johnson enclosed Shepherd's outline for Bolton's observations. "In a cooperative history of this sort," affirmed Johnson, "we can accomplish our task only by give and take." Bolton replied March 3, shooting down several of Shepherd's criticisms, especially the non-inclusion of the Manila Galleon story, which Bolton claimed was matter essential as background for California. He told Johnson that a copy of Richman's outline would be much more helpful to him, and this was sent March 12. Johnson called attention to the fact that Richman was staying "on his side of the Rio Grande." Several days previously Johnson had written that the Chambers manuscript was in, that he had covered the story of the Spaniards in Louisiana from the 1760s forward, and thus Bolton would not have to worry about treating that area. Bolton was happy to have that windfall in matter of wordage, for he was having much trouble in getting his story into the word limit.

It was at this point in June 1917 that just at the moment Bolton finally managed to complete the Kino manuscript for Clark, Johnson, who was thoroughly put out at the deadline just missed, really began to pressure Bolton. Bolton sought to ward off Johnson's wrath with a lengthy letter of June 16, detailing a long list of involvements which he had not anticipated back in the previous autumn: Stephens' illness, the curatorship of the Bancroft Library, his designation as Faculty Research Lecturer for March 1917. He carefully avoided mentioning that during those same months he had been trying desperately to quiet Arthur H. Clark who was pressing simultaneously for the delivery of the long overdue Kino manuscript.

Bolton quickly found that Johnson's response was somewhat the same as he was getting from Clark, only perhaps more severe. Unimpressed by the reasons which Bolton gave for failing to meet the June 1 deadline, Johnson sent a stinging letter June 26:

> You can hardly expect a gracious letter in reply to yours of the sixteenth. Considering that at your solicitation I made place for you in the series and named a date for the completion of your manuscript, I do not see why you can expect me to take account of the engagements which you have made. If I should allow authors to consult their own inclinations, the manuscripts would never be completed.

The series will not be delayed. Manuscripts are now in the printers' hands. If you cannot complete your manuscript at once, in all fairness you ought to say so — so that I may take steps at once to secure a substitute.

Bolton had finally gotten the Kino manuscript off to Clark a day or two before this letter of June 16 to Johnson and was devoting most of his time to this "Chronicles" book. On July 13, he wrote that he was

pushing ahead with the manuscript as fast as I can. When I wrote you before I already had a draft, in type, covering the entire field. But this draft was written to block out the period as a whole, and more in the nature of a summary than of personal sketches, such as are desirable for the finished work. I am now recasting to bring out the personalities and subordinating the summaries which will serve as connecting paragraphs.

It will be September by the time I finish the MS but I have every reason to think that I can deliver it by then. This is the best that I can promise.

Back in New York after his vacation and evidently more relaxed, Johnson answered, somewhat softened but still stern:

I am grievously disappointed at the delay in completing your manuscript, but I suppose that I must adjust myself to the inevitable. There is no one whom I would rather have write the volume of our series. So then, if you will give me the manuscript by September first, I will try to possess my soul in patience, hoping and believing that the manuscript, when it comes, will be of exceptional excellence.

Bolton could not, however, stop pushing, for a week after Johnson's letter, on July 21, the first part of the galleys of the Kino volumes from Clark were moving toward Berkeley. By August 13, they were all in Bolton's hands. Ten days earlier, hoping that now that the Kino materials were well on their way to completion, the others projected for the series might be along in a reasonably short time, Clark had written Bolton that he was planning a large mailing to Catholic institutions and libraries and sent him a draft of the proposed circular concerning not only the two Kino volumes but the series as a whole. Bolton acknowledged receipt of the first batch of galleys in an August 8 letter, but he informed Clark that he could not possibly get them back before the end of the month. He told Clark that he did not like the proposed circular since, in announcing the series, it was practically committing him to deadlines, and these he could not promise to meet. He closed expressing once again his unhappiness over the exclusion of the Spanish text.

This was the beginning of a lengthy slugfest by mail. Bolton's letter rubbed Clark the wrong way and he blasted back August 13: "Your letter of August 8 received. It is unsatisfactory and a disappointment to me." He reminded Bolton that the series had been carefully planned on a financial basis: "If the plan is not satisfactory, then let us drop the whole thing with the completion of the Kino and cancel the contract for the series." He reiterated that he had to have the proofs back before the end of August. Further, he informed Bolton that the proposed circular was his own personal brainchild and that it must stand substantially as written, or "we drop the series." He affirmed that it would be impossible to advertise each publication separately, since the cost would be prohibitive. Again he warned that, if there were a series, publication would have to be on schedule — the "Jesuit Relations" series had come out at the rate of one volume per month and only once was Editor Thwaites late. Clark was obviously provoked, ending with the tart question: "Do you wish us to go ahead with the series or do you wish to cancel the contract with the publication of *Kino?*"

This letter got a reply from Bolton August 24, but no proofs. More than a little chastened, Bolton wrote:

> Much as I regret to have to say it, I find it impossible to make any promises for the delivery of other volumes of the series in the immediate future. This is why I object to issuing a circular making time promises, or even specifying the contents of the volumes. It is quite within my hopes, plans, and expectations to go on with the series next year, or as soon as possible. . . . If this means the series is to be closed, I shall have to abide by that decision.

The next communication was from Clark's editor, Robertson, who reminded Bolton September 8 that no proofs had come back as yet. A week later Clark was less polite when he detailed for Bolton the dates on which galleys had been sent and noted further that type was being tied up by Bolton's tardiness in returning the galley proofs. He went on: "In view of what you say [August 24] we must decide to drop the series after the publication of the present two volumes of *Kino.*"

The next weeks and months were tense. Both men exchanged letters with more than a little exasperation, and at times they were almost childish. Bolton answered this letter of September 15. Clark came back September 21 to remind him that the contract with the University of California was only one consideration, noting that type was being held and that this was costing the house money. On October 16 Clark reminded Bolton that not a single galley had been returned and added that, as a result, sixty pages had to be pulled down in order to release the lead for another work. Bolton came back October 22 to assure Clark that his assistant, Charles Hackett, was working on the proofs, added that other very important and pressing business had intervened, and then, as a parting shot, recalled that the University of California contract had put $1,700 into his hands even before the book was manufactured. Clark, cooled a bit by this reminder, was slightly less gruff in his next, but called for the proofs at the earliest possible date, "as justly due us."

November ran into its later weeks, and still there was no proof out of Berkeley. On November 23 Clark wrote that he had received a bill for $150 from his printer, to cover rental of type which had been tied up for six months; he noted that "this bill I shall have to charge to you, as I feel that you have worked me a great injustice in this matter." He also observed that he would need a formal extension of the delivery date agreed on with the university, initially May 1, 1918.

There was a strain of sarcasm from Clark on December 5, thanking Bolton for two "undated letters." He did admit that they brought good news and that it was "nice" of Bolton to offer to "help"; however, he insisted that the greatest possible contribution which Bolton could make would be to return the galley proofs — "nothing could help quite as much." A week later Clark told Bolton that it would not be possible to conform to his request that a Table of Contents be included in each volume; the volumes were already well beyond the number of pages originally planned. Bolton next expressed himself as greatly disturbed by the fact that sixty pages had been torn down and then reset; he asked for galley proofs of these pages. Clark (December 17) refused, claiming that he could not afford the expense of such an additional run. Meanwhile, Bolton wrote that he was going to the meeting of the American Historical Association in Philadelphia during Christmastide and promised that he would work on the proofs during the long hours on the train.

By January 23, 1918, when the proofs were not forthcoming, Clark was vexed and chided his delinquent author:

> The proofs which you had with you at Philadelphia, and which you had solemnly promised me would be sent immediately on your return to California, have not arrived, and I am disappointed. Will you kindly send these at once and cooperate with us for the completion of this long delayed work?

Bolton really had done his homework and by the end of January 1918 the galleys were on their way to Cleveland — by any form of reckoning the time span from late July to late January was rather considerable.

Clark was relieved to have the proofs but on paging through them was more than a little dismayed to note the amount of internal changes. Some footnotes had been dropped and others substituted. The eliminations and additions were so scattered that he could foresee the need for a large amount of resetting, all of which would be time-consuming, not to say expensive.

Then a new battle was joined. Hoping to avoid future delays, Clark (February 6) thought to outmaneuver Bolton: "To save delays, especially as this type must be released for other work I am under contract upon, I am going to ask that you permit the page proofs to be read here." The ploy did not work, for Bolton telegraphed immediately, insisting on seeing the page proofs personally. Clark reluctantly conceded February 13 but demanded that each batch be returned within two weeks after receipt. He was to learn to his sorrow and dismay that "two weeks" meant something quite other to Bolton than the ordinary understanding of a fortnight or fourteen days. The page-proof tug-of-war was to last through much of 1918.

The first batch of page proofs went off to Berkeley on March 26. Four weeks later, and still without proofs, Clark wrote April 24 asking for some of them at least. A week later Editor Robertson reported that nothing had shown as yet. Next, on May 17, even though he was still without proofs, Clark sent a sample of the revised title page and in the same letter remarked that, in the event that he would be unable to publish very soon, he would be facing three or four "dead months" from a market point of view, since summer was not the time to sell books like the Kino volumes. At the end of the letter, evidently unable to contain himself any longer, he blasted out: "One thing is certain, I shall go no farther with this series, whether these volumes are a success or not. One such experience is enough, especially under existing conditions."

Bolton's next letter June 14 was another irritant. He informed Clark: "I shall need another set of page proofs. . . . Please yield to my simple request for proof on thicker and less shiny paper. My eyes have gone to pieces on this Kino, all on account of undesirable proof paper." To this letter he added several pages of observations — "explanations" as he called them. Some were "picky" but many had a measure of validity. He was working, however, for on June 27 Robertson could acknowledge receipt of the pages — "two weeks" had become three months.

Clark was absent from Cleveland at the moment. When he returned and took one look at the proofs, which had been extensively reedited by Bolton, he went right through the ceiling. This was hardly the way to handle page proofs, and he told Bolton so in no uncertain terms in a letter of July 23:

The foreman of the composing room has looked over the proofs and held them for my attention, because, as he truly says, it will be cheaper with a large part of this proof to throw out the standing type and to reset completely. In all my thirty years I have been in the publishing business I have never seen page proof come back in the shape in which this has come, especially after the large amount of editorial work and changes done on the galley proof. In one case before me, the addition of an extensive note throws out forty-nine pages; and this is no exception. If the matter were straight body matter and without foot-notes it would not be so bad, but with the double difficulty, the changes are going to be slow and very expensive. Before proceeding with this I must hear from you as to whether you will pay for the changes. I can not afford to do so.

He was so thoroughly provoked that he went on to wonder if the University of California Press might not like to have the whole publication as of that moment and pay Clark only for the costs to date. Next, Bolton had objected to the title; Clark reminded him that he had approved the same earlier in the year. The title page, said Clark, had already been set in electrotype and would be expensive to change.

On July 28 Bolton drafted an apologetic reply but still held his ground on the matter of the title page. He came back to it again in a September 14 letter. He liked the inclusion of "Pimería Alta" but objected to the use of the padre's two given names, Eusebio Francisco; he had no quarrel with the second but felt that Eusebio was forbiddingly off-beat; Padre Kino might be sufficient on the book's spine. Clark, more or less in desperation, finally capitulated, September 24. On one count he refused to go along with a recent Bolton request. Bolton had asked that the date of publication be given as 1918, even though the likelihood of the volumes appearing before the end of that calendar year was almost nil. Clark was emphatic; to put a 1918 date of publication would mean that he would be selling "last year's book" as soon as it hit the market.

In late October Bolton had a few more pages to send back. He observed that there were a few corrections but felt certain that resetting would not be necessary. At this point he let Clark know that he seriously disagreed with him over the amount of resetting already done — "having been a printer myself I understand these matters and can recognize unnecessary running over." Throughout his life Bolton was proud of his years as printer's devil on the Tomah *Journal* and referred thereto time and again.

Finally, in March 1919 the Kino volumes appeared — *Kino's Historical Memoir of Pimería Alta–A Contemporary Account of the Beginnings of California, Sonora, and Arizona, by Father Eusebio Francisco Kino, S.J., Pioneer, Explorer, Cartographer, and Ranchman, 1683–1711.*

It was a joint imprint of the Arthur H. Clark Company of Cleveland and the University of California Semi-Centennial Publications. The Kino translation was a few months short of eleven years from contract to appearance. Reviewers recognized and lauded what was becoming a Bolton pattern, namely, prefacing the documentary body of the book with a carefully constructed historical introduction which gave the running story therein contained.[4]

This might seem to be, but it was not really, the end of the Kino story. On May 1, 1919 Clark sent Bolton a long letter:

> Kino is finished and we have just completed the figuring of the costs thereon, which on account of the delay which ran us into war time prices, prove, as I expected, absolutely discouraging. Even though we advance the price 25%, it is simply impossible to break even on the publication and I do not feel that the publication will stand a selling price greater than 25% over what we had originally contemplated.
>
> Of the extra expenses, I feel that the following should be borne by you. In fact, most of them are covered by your agreements in your various letters.

Clark then itemized in detail costs totaling $953.60.[5]

> The above total takes no cognizance of the $150.00 already charged to you November 23, 1917, for holding the type, in addition to which we paid another $98.00 for the same expense. In addition, we are out interest, cash discounts, overhead, carrying charges, increased cost of advertising, circulars, higher selling expense, and many other items.
>
> I want to do what is right and fair in the matter. For this reason, before making the charge, I submit the above to you, asking what you think is right in the matter, in view of the excessive delay on your part in fulfilling your contract and the extraordinary delay in reading and returning the proofs to us. . . .
>
> I shall appreciate your giving this matter your earliest consideration and letting me hear from you promptly.

Bolton "considered" many of these items preposterous. His reply to Clark has survived in neither his nor the Arthur H. Clark Company file. There was an answer, however, for in 1924, Bolton told his lawyers that he had protested at the time. One thing is certain; he did not pay the bill. Bank drafts were made on Bolton by Clark, on August 20, 1919, and on May 1, 1920, but Bolton refused to sign both. By April 29, 1921, Clark seems to have decided that efforts to collect would be unavailing, for as of that date the Arthur H. Clark Company: Accounts Receivable show the sum of $1185.16 written off as uncollectable.[6]

A few weeks later, however, Clark evidently changed his mind, for as of July 1, 1921, his attorney sent Bolton another bill, this one for $1875.70. This stirred Bolton to action and on July 10 he replied: "This figure $1875.70 is a new one to me. Has there been another war since the statement totaled $953.60?" Bolton refused to honor the statement without more detail furnished. Once again the matter went unattended.

Time passed. Next, on April 18, 1924, Clark presented a new listing of debits — this time the sum, after royalties had been deducted, was set at $2183.56.[7] Bolton was informed that, unless his check for this amount was received within fifteen days, Clark's lawyer, Clarence A. Shuey of San Francisco, would be instructed to take the matter to court. Bolton at first was taken aback; next he was furious; then on May 14, 1924, he engaged the Berkeley firm of Clark, Nicols and Eltse to represent him.[8] Clark meantime had instructed his lawyer to proceed. The case went to the Superior Court, County of Alameda, in May,[9] and the hearing was set for November.

Not until a year later, on November 24, 1925, did the case come to trial. The intervening year was filled with postponements and continuances, suggestions of out-of-court settlements and rejections thereof by the two contenders. At the trial Bolton's attorney (the defense) pleaded that, since there had been no legal action within four years of the matter, namely, the date of the first statement of April 1919, the statute of limitations prevailed. Acting on this technicality the court ruled: "From the foregoing findings the court concludes that the defendant is entitled to judgment, that the plaintiff take nothing and that the defendant have and recover his costs." Arthur Clark's attorney appealed and filed for a new trial. This was set for April 29, 1926, but there was a continuance granted to May 19. Bolton's attorney, G. Clark, informed him that he felt that "they would take $750 and call it square"; Bolton evidently did not act upon this suggestion. On May 19 the two attorneys appeared; a long deposition from Arthur Clark was read; the defense challenged, since the original account books had not been produced; the court sustained the position, ordered the plaintiff to adduce such evidence, and continued the case to August 24, 1926, at 10:00 A.M. There were still other continuances, but a letter from Attorney Monell to Arthur Clark, February 9, 1929, is the last correspondence on file.

With no final evidence existing or available, perhaps, the final word on the whole incident must be the statement of Arthur H. Clark, Jr., in a letter of November 30, 1972:

> Here our file of correspondence ends [Monell to Clark, February 9, 1929]. If there was any further correspondence it is no longer here. . . . To the best of the knowledge of Paul Galleher and myself,

the matter died a natural death after 1929 or 1930. . . . I am certain that there was never any settlement, but merely a prolonged cease-fire.[10]

The battle with Arthur Clark is not the most pleasant episode of the Bolton story. Bolton was a stickler for perfection, but sometimes this trait tended to be highly aggravating to others. And so it was for publisher Glasgow and editor Johnson. The outcome of that story had a different twist, however; for Bolton it would be a painful experience in a different way. His very skill as a writer would become the case in point, his inability to meet deadlines somewhat secondary.

Bolton had missed the September 1, 1917, deadline set by Glasgow and Johnson for the delivery of the Spain in the Southwest manuscript. He had completed eight of eleven chapters, but then he got a bit of a break. The editors had decided to drop the Chambers volume from the series; this decision put Johnson in a position where he had to send off a please-do-me-a-favor letter on November 20 to ask Bolton to include a chapter on "Louisiana under Spain." Before this letter reached Bolton, the manuscript was on its way to New York, five and a half months beyond the original deadline. Then Bolton wrote November 26, calling attention to the several pages of "explanation" which he had included after the Preface.

In the first of these explanations he indicated his choice of the title for the volume, "The Spanish Borderlands."

> For the main title I prefer *The Spanish Borderlands.* . . . I took the phrase from one of your suggested subtitles. It is interesting, accurate, distinctive, and does not conflict with the title of my volume of documents.

Then he told Johnson that his package contained two versions of the story, a long and a short one: the short one, written on white paper, could stand on its own; the long version was developed on yellow pages which were added throughout. He suggested that the first five chapters of the long version might be extracted and published as a separate volume, which could follow Richman's in the series and might be called "The Northern Mystery"; the remainder of the manuscript could then stand and become "The Spanish Borderlands." It was an attempt to place two volumes instead of one in the series, but Bolton soon found that he was playing with someone just as foxy as himself and just as determined.

As mentioned, when Bolton sent off his manuscript, he had not received Johnson's letter of November 20; he had warned that there might be some overlapping between his final chapter and the book of Chambers. With the Johnson letter in hand, on November 28, he enthusiastically agreed to expand his final chapter and tell the whole of the Spain-in-Louisiana story. In this same letter he wondered if, perhaps, he might still add a chapter on "frontier life and institutions."

Apprised that the Bolton manuscript was in Johnson's hands, Glasgow sent a check for $375.00 — the contract had stipulated that half the author recompense would be paid on receipt of manuscript and the other half on publication.

There follows a hiatus in the Bolton-Johnson correspondence, at least as preserved, after this letter. The next letter from Johnson, January 20, 1918, would seem to indicate that there was at least one exchange. Somewhere and in some fashion Bolton had heard that his manuscript was not suitable for the series, that it was of interest primarily to the antiquarian because of its heavy overload of detail, but hardly attractive to the general reader. In the letter of January 20, Johnson reminded him that Bolton had not indicated "what you propose to do or just what you expect me to do with the manuscript — shall I return it to you for rewriting?" Johnson went on to note that the manuscript was too learned, too detailed, too scholarly — "just throw to the winds your scholarly instinct to be exhaustive and give me a graphic picture of types."

On February 2, 1918, Glasgow's office returned the manuscript to Bolton. That same day Johnson wrote a quite detailed critique of the effort, which added up to the verdict that it did not do the "popularized" job required for the series. He counseled Bolton to the effect that, if he would lock himself in a room, without manuscript, without notes, without sources, and then from his vast knowledge of the field proceed to tell the story, he would most probably produce precisely the book which was desired.

This rejection of the Borderlands manuscript came at the time when Clark was after him for the return of the Kino galleys. Further, he was quibbling with his co-editor, Hart, over maps in the Denoyer-Geppert series. He was indeed finding himself overextended, a situation which under ordinary circumstances he could have mastered. The real problem was psychological; his attempt to popularize, to "Parkmanize," the story of his Spaniards had been a very dismal failure. It was, to say the least, very deflating.

At this point in 1918, discouraged and somewhat depressed, he let the Borderlands manuscript sit. He just could not develop enthusiasm. By mid-1918 Johnson's patience was growing thin. On July 24 he inquired what progress was being made on the revision and rewriting. He waited six weeks and then, with no reply, he tried again on September 5. This brought a frank letter from Bolton; a telegram from Johnson September 15 was the next: "Dismayed to learn that you have not been working on your manuscript all these months - had understood that you would make the revision at once - delay is embarrassing to me - please wire earliest date you will send manuscript to 225 Fifth Avenue." The telegram evidently did not jolt Bolton, for Johnson came back two weeks later: "What am I to think of an author who won't reply to urgent telegram?" He went on to remind Bolton that he had asked to get into the series and ended with the hint that Bolton "act like a gentleman."

Four months later, on January 14, 1919, Johnson, now obviously and seriously vexed and disturbed, inquired:

> What are we going to do about your manuscript for the *Chronicles?* Am I to understand that you mean to finish it or that you wish us to look elsewhere for an author? . . . The months are slipping by and I have only your repeated promises, in which I must confess that I am rapidly losing faith.

Bolton was working. On March 28 he sent off the manuscript with the message: "Have completely rewritten it, and hope that you will think it improved." The package reached New York in early April. On April 16 Johnson wrote: "The manuscript has arrived at last safely." It got immediate attention, but, unfortunately for Bolton, not approval. This last bit of unpleasant information was passed on to him in a long letter from Johnson, April 23:

> This morning I received from Mr. Glasgow a letter which expresses my own opinion of your manuscript so completely that I wish to quote from it at some length.

> "The author has gathered a great quantity of valuable building material but he has not erected a building. He has made a certain orderly arrangement in piles of this material but nothing more. The work of the architect is not done. Or, to change the figure, the author has dug out of the ground a great quantity of valuable ore, of which he has sent you here a small load. He sent you last summer a larger load of the same ore and you returned it to him to be refined, but instead of refining it in the furnace of his mind he has simply shoveled away a part and what he has sent you now is less crude than the other.

> What is to be done? It appears as though Professor Bolton has not the artistic faculty sufficiently developed to write one of our books. And yet he is a scholar of distinction and it is apparent that he has a theme well adapted to a living narrative full of color and movement. It would be a considerable loss to us to eliminate his

name from the series. But we cannot print the book as he has written it, nor does it seem likely that we should be willing to print any revision of it that he would be capable of making.

I said above that the book is not capable of being revised by which I mean that the ordinary pruning and underbrushing which an editor gives to a manuscript would not make this manuscript suitable to the series. There is, however, another kind of revision, meaning a new projection by an author of imagination, based upon the materials which the first author has collected."

I need not tell you that it grieves me to have to make this report; but we may as well face the stern facts. Let me say at the outset that I do not entertain the slightest doubt of your good-will and purpose. I know that you have labored hard and long to give literary form to your material. You have done your utmost to meet my wishes. Yet, as Mr. Glasgow says, we must consider the series as a whole; and we would surely stultify ourselves if we published your manuscript in a series which is announced as an attempt make history readable as well as accurate. You asked to be taken into the series because you appreciated our purpose and approved of it. In your first letter, you expressed the laudable desire to do for Spanish America what Parkman did for New France. I welcomed your proposal because I knew that there was a splendid field of work which no other American scholar knew so much about as yourself. It is equally clear to me that no one else can write this volume except by using your materials. So there we are at an impasse.

Mr. Glasgow has intimated in his last paragraph that there may be a way out of our predicament. It involves, however, self-renunciation on your part and great responsibility on ours. We can find a writer of literary distinction who will re-write and re-shape your book, using your material, and we could publish the book under your name, with a preface in which you acknowledge the services of so-and-so as your assistant or revisor. In that case, we should need your first (longer) manuscript, so that the revisor might have a larger fund of material to draw upon.

If the thought is repellent to you at first, please take my word for it that this method is used by publishers far oftener than the public is aware. . . .

I sincerely hope that you will accept this solution of our difficulty. You wish the volume in the series and so do we. Whatever is done to your manuscript will not make the book less yours. The materials will all be yours; and no stuff will go into the volume which is not accurate and certified as such by you. . . . Please turn the proposal over in your mind, and let us have your decision as early as possible. One reason why I have been so insistent on having your revision was because I feared some such delay as this. . . .

Bolton received this letter and was crushed this time, not simply deflated. He carefully framed a reply; the handwritten draft of this letter reveals a tortured piece, with lines crossed out, words substituted, giving every evidence of something done with great thought. He was hurt and disheartened, but there was still the conviction that he should put his historical message into that series, where he knew that "his Spaniards" belonged.

The date of your letter, "April 23," was portentous. I wish that you had selected another day for your job.[11] I hardly need say that your report was hardly a cause for rejoicing on my part. If it is a matter of concern to you, please be assured that I bear you no ill will. My manuscript is not what you want, and no one can question your right to judge. If you want a good black horse and I offer you a good bay one, I have no right to be offended if you do not care to buy it. Perhaps, I am color blind, and my horse is more nearly drab in color. But you will pardon me, I am sure, if admitting color blindness I imagine in him a good point or two. I shall not attempt to demonstrate them to you. I like Mr. Glasgow's figure of the use of the shovel in preparing my manuscript. In reality I used a steel pen.

Your spirit is kindly, but I get little comfort on being told that I did my best and failed, or that my silly ambition was laudable, and it adds nothing to my happiness to be told that there are others as incompetent as I who yet are made to appear respectable. Under the circumstances I should be flattered to be told by you that I have some ability as an investigator, but in the present connection the compliment is somewhat [?].* I do get some satisfaction from your admission that no one else can write the volume except by using my material.

I may be an ass, but I trust that I am not an altogether unreasonable one. I got you into this trouble, and I am under obligation to do my best to help you out. I am humiliated beyond expression and may decide to desert the pen for the shovel. . . . I consent therefore, with humiliation, to your plan, but first I wish to know who the revisor is to be. There are some persons whom I would not permit to touch my manuscript under any circumstances. I should also like a pretty clear understanding of the form of obligation which I should be expected to make in the Preface, and I should wish to reserve the right to approve the result for historical accuracy.

Of one or two things I am still confident (perhaps you will kick the remaining props out in your next letter). I have not merely assembled materials, as Mr. Glasgow says. I have covered in one sweep and given meaning to a frontier extending from the Caribbean to the Pacific, which no one else has treated before; I have interpreted my materials in terms of motive and movement; I have brought into relation and given significance to a vast series of hitherto isolated episodes; I have laid a background for the English and American southwestward movement. I have revealed phases of international relations which no one else has discovered. I respect Mr. Glasgow's opinion of my art, but I have seen no reason to accept his judgment of my history.

---

*The carbon copy of this letter has not survived in the Bolton File. The remaining word or words in this sentence are not distinguishable in the handwritten draft.

On May 11 Johnson answered this letter with a note designed to smooth, he hoped, some of the possible hard feelings created by his previous one. He told Bolton that the "overhaul" would be done in their office. And, among other things, he assured him that he would have the last word and that his judgment as to facts would be final. It would be some months before Bolton learned the identity of the person revising the manuscript — Constance Lindsay Skinner.* In those intervening months Bolton had many less than kind things to say about "him" or "X" which were the designations by which he referred to the revisor.

The first revised chapter went off to Bolton on November 10 with a letter from Johnson asking him to "go over this chapter with microscopic care . . . and then please return it to me with suggestions and criticisms . . . to assist the revisor in his further writing." No one thought to hoist the alarm warnings, but the idea would have been a wise one, for many stormy months were ahead. Many an angry letter would be carried across the continent by U.S. Mail and sometimes, when the mails were not judged rapid enough, the telegraph wires would be turned white hot. At the moment he did not have much time to give close attention to the first chapter and noted, besides, that it would be difficult to criticize a single chapter. He did express disapproval of the proposed chapter listings which had accompanied this packet and took occasion to review quickly the sequence of the Borderlands story for the information and guidance of the revisor, indicating that the rewrite man seemed to need this badly.

A second installment of the revision was dispatched on January 5, 1920. Nothing happened. Johnson became impatient and on February 16 asked if Bolton was ready to report. Three more weeks passed. Then, on March 7, Johnson sent off the following:

> I must confess to some irritation and to great disappointment because you do not reply to my letters. We are waiting to learn your opinion of the revised manuscript. The publishers are naturally impatient to know whether you can use this revision — make it your own — or whether they must turn elsewhere for a contributor to the series. They cannot wait indefinitely. Why do you not answer my letters of January 5th and February 16th?
>
> With this letter I am sending the rest of the material for the book as completed by the revisor. . . . I am enclosing some extracts from letters of the revisor to indicate wherein his point of view differs from yours. . . . We wish you to take this material from the revisor, shape

---

*Constance Lindsay Skinner contributed two volumes to the Chronicles series herself, *Pioneers of the Old Southwest* and *Adventurers of Oregon;* she was later involved in the quite successful and popular "The Rivers of America" series, ultimately as editor.

the book in this pattern, and make the book your own. I may not reveal the name of the revisor but I can assure you that you may trust his literary as well as his sense of historical values. . . . I believe that you can make these chapters into a good book, worthy of publication in the series. . . .

May I suggest, then, that you work up the book on the basis of these chapters and finish it with great care, so that it can go directly to the printers? . . . And since I have done so much for you in getting the material into shape to serve as a pattern, I think that the manuscript which you return should be as perfectly edited as to relieve me of some editorial labor. We have, as I have said, spent much money already on the book; and I think that we have created an obligation on your part which you ought to meet. . . .

Johnson enclosed in this letter some of the notations which he received from the revisor. This document is of real interest, since it indicates some of the problems with which Bolton had to contend as he rewrote his manuscript; one or two statements hint at the tone:

The difficulty is that Dr. Bolton's point of view is that of the antiquarian rather than the historian. This point of view is indicated not only in the manuscript which he has submitted, but by the statement in his letter that he wants to show that Spain colonized the West Indies and Mexico and was sending explorers north and west. This is shown, as should be shown, in the books in the series by Richman and Shepherd dealing with territory other than the present United States. In the present book, *The Spanish Borderlands,* you are not intending to give an extensive account of Spanish colonization in the Americas. What American readers of American history will want to know is . . .[A rather lengthy paragraph about the relative importance of the Spanish-Huguenot story and that of the founding of Saint Augustine, the revisor opting for the former] . . . This book should not be written from the Spanish standpoint but the American, and it should not deal too much with North America outside the present United States. . . .

It is not hard to imagine what steam comments and attitudes of this stamp generated on the eastern shore of the Bay of San Francisco.

The Johnson letter and the comments from the revisor brought a reply from Bolton, who by this time was not simply mad, but "hopping mad."

My first peep is not reassuring. For instance I am not of the school of writers who speak traditionally of "the dark shadow of Spain," or suppose that "Spanish institutions in the New World crumpled like a house of cards at the touch of the Anglo-Saxon". . . . There is no excuse for another book written in the old spirit of ignorance or prejudice. . . . The revisor sees in Spaniards only "explorers." This impression must be corrected.

Johnson did not like the tone of this letter of March 17 and on March 25 fired back a broadside. Bolton came back (April 3):

> What I meant was that in judging your revision I should be disposed to accept your judgment on matters of style and selection of incidents, and should be disposed to be insistent on my own notions in matters of general historical interpretations. This is another way of saying that after your complete annihilation of any slight literary pride which I may have had, the only refuge of self-respect lay in daring to hope that I might venture some historical opinion with regard to your revision.

Having taken time to study the revision carefully, Bolton, in letters of May 5 and May 7, began to get down to specifics in his criticism and disagreements. In the first letter he observed:

> When I received the revised manuscript I saw no chapter devoted to Texas. As I read on I found Texas treated under the head of New Mexico. I am trying to restrain my feelings (and I have struggled at nearly every turn of the page), but surely you do not intend to follow the arrangement described above. . . .
> Some parts rewritten by the revisor seem to me to be very good. . . . Some of his work is rotten — to speak as freely as he has done in occasional notes which I find penciled on my manuscript. . . .

The second letter was an angry piece, and long. Bolton showed the revisor faulty in knowledge and as bad in interpretation; he pointed out several examples to substantiate such judgments. He was most perturbed by the overall tone "affecting the whole spirit of the book . . ."

Still incensed, a couple weeks later (May 19) he wrote to Glasgow and laid great stress on the completely unhistorical attempt on the part of the revisor to lump the Texas story with that of New Mexico. He did not appreciate the revisor judging which missions were important and which were less so, with the latter being eliminated. "I appreciate that he is a novice in the field and will try to be prudent." About this time, in May 1920, Glasgow took over the correspondence from the seaboard side of the continent; Johnson, because of ill health, had to pull back for a time.

Glasgow knew that Bolton was working, but by August 1920 the publisher was becoming anxious to have the manuscript back. A late September telegram nudged Bolton. One of mid-October reminded him that the manuscript, promised the week before, had not arrived. Finally it did show on Glasgow's desk. He went to work immediately. On October 25 he sent off a long letter to Bolton:

> I have just finished reading your manuscript, *The Spanish Bor-*
> *derlands,* line by line with great care. . . .
> I am certain that you have produced one of the most notable and
> impressive books of the Series; in fact, one of the best short books of
> history ever written. Most of this history is new to me, as it will be
> new to a great many readers, for I think that I have read more
> American history than the majority.
> I agree with all you have done since the manuscript was last sent
> to you to be finished, except as follows. . .

The suggestions were of relatively minor nature: several chapter titles
might be better this way; part of the proposed Introduction would fit more
properly in the Preface; some of the Texas Indian battles could profitably
be eliminated so as not to detract from reader interest; and like observations. It was in this letter that Bolton probably for the first time learned
that the revisor was Constance Lindsay Skinner. In a letter of October 31
Glasgow told him that in several places in his revision he had dropped
interesting persons or cut too thinly and that these sections had been
restored from the original manuscript — Vizcaíno, Fray Luis Cancer,
details concerning Portolá, and so on. Bolton did not quarrel with these
minor alterations. That same October 31 he was writing: "I can feel that
now I have 'come through' with my obligation to you."

Glasgow's printers worked rapidly, and the first batch of galleys went
off to Bolton, by first-class mail, on the morning of November 23. Bolton
picked them up at the post office Sunday morning and worked through
until 1:30 Monday morning, so as to have them in Monday's mail on their
return. The next batch Glasgow held until Bolton got to Boston. He had
been signed to give the lectures in the Lowell Institute Series of that year
(1920-21) and was delighted to have an opportunity to "bring his message" to the stronghold of New England. The Bolton file is slim for these
Boston weeks — he had no secretary and, hence, there were no carbon
copies; one has to guess from Glasgow's letters just what was passing
between the two men. One of these letters presupposes a hot one from
Bolton. Glasgow wrote on January 13:

> I have your maledictory this morning. . . . There is apparently a
> difference of opinion between us as to what is important in this book.
> You will say that you are the author of the book and that your deci-
> sion should govern. On the other hand, I call your attention to the
> fact that this book is one of fifty in the series which has been planned
> and carried out by others. Forty volumes of the series have been
> published and have proved successful beyond any works of history
> ever published in this country. This proves that the conception of
> the series is right, and that the Editors know their business.

Glasgow concluded this letter with the hope that he would see Bolton en route back to California, on the afternoon of Saturday, January 15.

Maybe Bolton did not receive this letter before leaving Boston; at any rate he did not keep the Saturday appointment. Monday morning, January 17, Glasgow was thoroughly provoked and fired off a letter both to Berkeley and to Boston, with a copy of Bolton's letter of November 29 enclosed. The theme was: no proofs — you promised these before you went back to California — Saturday afternoon, no you — what is the explanation? — you have failed in a fundamental agreement to return proofs promptly. And he went on, dressing Bolton down in unequivocal terms.

When Glasgow received no reply to this letter by January 21, he fumed: "You are the most thorny and perverse man with whom I have ever done business." He then proceeded to rehearse the background: nearly four years ago you undertook to write a volume — you could not satisfy the editor, so we employed an assistant for you — you used the assistant's work — "I am still hoping that you will rectify yourself and come across with the proofs and relieve the situation which threatens to be embarrassing for both of us; if you do not, you will find yourself facing a claim for damages which will astonish you."

Bolton received this blast and was mad enough to fire back a telegram the evening of January 23: "I resent your communication as unfounded in fact, unfair in spirit, and insulting in tone — I have dealt in perfect good faith from first to last." Glasgow got this cryptic message and returned a telegram of his own: "All right - but are you coming across with the proof or not - wire answer." Glasgow followed with a letter later that same morning: "I admit that my last letters were one-sided. . . . You have had the proofs in your possession eight weeks. I am anxious to have the work correct but I think that you might have done the corrections in two weeks." Before Bolton could have gotten this letter, he telegraphed January 25 that some of the proof had been sent. More followed quickly, and by February 1 the last batch was on its way.

Glasgow wrote on February 7 that all had been received but then went on at some length to disagree with changes demanded by Bolton. For example, Glasgow felt that Bolton had inflated the importance of the drive for Mexican independence, not convinced that Hidalgo had "rung another Liberty Bell." He chided Bolton for having talked of New England provincialism in interpreting American history during his recent Lowell Institute lectures and wondered if Bolton's outlook on the Mexican Revolution might not be an example of "Berkeley provincialism."

Bolton was not amused, but he at least began his reply of February 12 calmly: "I accept all your changes, but not in every case with approval, but with resignation, which is the mood into which I have fallen. I can't quarrel any longer, for I have something else to do." But then he wound up and let Glasgow have some of his own "medicine." Bolton told him that it was obvious that he had a lot of history reading to do and added that he owed it to himself to do some of it. Glasgow took his beating in good spirit and wrote back February 24: "Your letter of the 12th instant put me in the best of humor. It is always a pleasure to me to deal with a man who will fight back when he is attacked and who holds no malice."

The first of the page proofs went west on March 18. Thereafter they moved rapidly in both directions. On April 16 Glasgow informed Bolton that the last pages had reached him that morning and that the book was ready to be plated. "I think that you are to be congratulated on the excellence and accuracy of the book as a whole. It has been one of the most costly books in the series for me, but to offset that I think that it is one of the best."

Then, on July 28, 1921, Glasgow could write: "I am glad to be able to send you at last one copy of your Spanish Borderlands." The book was not technically published until a few days later, awaiting the British copyright. And so ends the story of *The Spanish Borderlands,* a story which had run over just short of five years.

The Spanish Borderlands experience was a painful, maddening, deflating, and humiliating one for Bolton. He had put much of himself and his dreams into the several versions before winning the approval of his editors. Yet in perspective it may have been a most salutary ordeal. No one, not even historians and scholars who may not be noted for their sparkling literary style, relishes being told, and bluntly, that he cannot write. Many of the remarks of Johnson and Glasgow cut deeply, but perhaps, they served to force Bolton to turn himself into an artist as well as scholar and "antiquarian." Miss Skinner vexed him often, but still he may have learned the "lighter touch" from her. Several of his later books, notably *Outpost of Empire* and *Rim of Christendom,* and finally the *Coronado* were awarded prizes for more than the excellent scholarship contained therein. The first two were "gold-medaled" by the Commonwealth Club of San Francisco as the finest book by a California author" in 1931 and 1936, respectively. The third received a George Bancroft Prize.

There is no evidence in the Bolton Papers, at least no correspondence, to show that his path ever crossed that of Miss Skinner. He acknowledged his debt to her in the crisp two sentences with which he concluded the Preface of the *Borderlands:*

My original manuscript for this book was written on a much larger scale than the Editor desired. In the work of reduction and rewriting, to fit the Series, I have had the able assistance of Miss Constance Lindsay Skinner.

How extensive that assistance was it is difficult to determine. The drafts of the volume are not complete in the Bolton Papers but there is enough to show that the final book was Bolton's; he did accept occasional paragraphs from Miss Skinner's re-write and did, in many instances, follow the episodes which she winnowed out of the earlier versions.[12] In any event, between them they produced a notable book.

It must have been some consolation to have such judgments of the finished product as those of the two Robertsons, both scholars of prominence. William Spence Robertson, in the *MVHR* (December 1922), wrote:

> . . . the author is exceptionally well fitted to describe the Spanish activities in the debatable land, for he lived for a score of years in Texas and California and studied these regions extensively in libraries and archives. . . . From the preface one gathers that this illuminating volume had to be abbreviated to bring it within the scope of the *Chronicles of America*. It is unfortunate that, as this reviewer has reason to believe, certain portions of the story were omitted altogether.

James Alexander Robertson reviewed the book for the *AHR* (April 1922):

> Professor Bolton told this story well and interestingly, and his narrative is full of action as befits the story of Spanish exploration and colonization in what is now the territory of our own country. Throughout he makes abundant use of the old chronicles and accounts, but to this he has added his own vast knowledge of the territory, gained both by intensive study and in part by personal visitation.

No one is likely to challenge seriously a claim that of all Bolton's writings none reached more readers or better fixed his name in circles historical than *The Spanish Borderlands*. It was not his greatest piece of scholarship, but what it did was something which no other of his books accomplished so well. It defined the area of his interest, gave that area a distinctive and fitting name, and inextricably linked Bolton therewith.

10

The Early 1920s

I N LATE 1918 Department Chairman Morse Stephens had come back to work after a serious illness and was beginning to hatch some highly interesting plans for Herbert Bolton. During the period when Bolton had just completed the Kino manuscript and was rewriting *The Spanish Borderlands,* Stephens approached him with the suggestion that a year in Europe might be of great benefit to him. The Mexican archives he knew well, but his contacts with the great Spanish depositories had been wholly indirect, through the reports of his "boys," the Native Sons Traveling Fellows, and his oldest helper, Eddie Dunn. They had furnished him, and the Bancroft Library, with thousands of pages of transcripts and copies from abroad. It could be said that Bolton knew the famous Archivo de Indias well, but somewhat like a blind man knows the world about him through the eyes of others. Stephens' plan was to remedy that curious situation. He felt that Rafael Altamira would be the key to the solution, and for some time back Stephens had been in contact with the Spaniard. Ever since Altamira had been on the West Coast in the summer of 1915, as one of the featured speakers in the historical extravaganza in connection with the P.P.I.E., both Stephens and Bolton had been in rather regular correspondence with the great Spanish historian. Stephens plotted an exchange between the two men. The war prevented the exchange in 1918. But now with the war ended, Stephens opened negotiations for the 1919–20 year. Bolton was overjoyed.

On the afternoon of April 16, 1919, however, several of the men from the university were returning to Berkeley from the funeral of Phoebe Apperson Hearst, who had been so generous in her benefactions to the University over the years. They had reached the East Bay side and were bouncing along in the great red train, from Adeline into Shattuck, when Morse Stephens was seized with a heart attack, slumped, and died in the arms of Dean William Morris Hart. The others, Bolton among them, stood by helplessly.

The death of Stephens was a shock to all who knew him. Even though his health in recent years had been anything but robust, he seemed to have recovered his old vigor. He left his mark not only on the university, where he had been since 1902, but on the Bay Area and the entire State of California as well. He had become the symbol of the university, both on campus and off.

His death catapulted Bolton overnight into a position of new responsibility, leadership in the Department of History. The regents at their meeting of August 12 confirmed him as chairman; in the interim he had at the president's request assumed all the burdens of the office.* Immediately, the dream of the year in Spain had to be pushed into the background, to wait for a more propitious time. Some of his other plans, too, had to be shelved for the moment.

One of the first things which Bolton and the department had to do in the late spring of 1919 was to think of the reorganization of the freshman-sophomore course program; the search for a Stephens replacement, truly important, had to yield to this more immediate problem. Everyone recognized that no one would be able to make "History 1" the learning experience which it had been for several generations of California students. Stephens had told, in his truly inimitable way, the story of the development of Europe to class after class and had created a sense of fascination for the past. This must be preserved at all costs, but the question was how. As end product of the departmental discussions a dual answer emerged: the underclassmen would be offered a choice: "History 4" would continue the tradition of the European survey; a new course, "History 8," would be added, this one an experiment with a somewhat similar overall American approach.

Ever since Bolton had come to Berkeley, he had watched Stephens at work and with the passing years had done some dreaming. If the European story could be told as a package in which nationalist lines were obliterated, why, he asked himself, could not the story of the Western Hemisphere family of nations be told in the same fashion? These nations had similar backgrounds, as colonial children of European mother-countries;

---

*Bolton continued as department head from 1919–40 with the exception of a two-year hiatus between 1922 and 1924. After the 1922–24 term of service of Louis J. Paetow, the pattern of the university calling for biennial election and non-immediate reelection was forgotten; each year the president would request that Bolton continue, and regularly Bolton would accept.

they had within the space of half a century broken with those mother-countries and embarked on their own independent sovereign existence. Perhaps, similarities in their national period had not been quite as striking, but underneath their respective Anglo and Latin exteriors were traits as much in common to make them Americans, as there were to make Englishmen and Germans, Frenchmen and Italians, Scandinavians and Poles — all — Europeans. Even differentness could be enlightening, and educational. The United States was the most successful of the American family of nations, but that fact did not necessarily give it the right to monopolize the field. Just as Bolton had been introducing a broader approach into his North-America-based courses on the colonial period and the West, why would not an equally broad approach fit a truer "American" history? The circumstances of 1919 gave him a chance to try.

"History 8" had its first trial run in 1919–20. Bolton had expected a couple dozen or maybe a couple hundred students; he was surprised, and gratified, when some eight hundred opted for the new course. His reputation as a fine teacher was well established on campus; word leaked to newcomers that now they would not have to wait until upperclassman years to see and hear him in action. A couple of teaching assistants have provided a description of their experiences of working with Bolton in the "History 8" class:

> During his prime he was incredible. I served as a T.A. in the famous History of the Americas course. He lectured on Mondays and Wednesdays at 11 A.M. in Wheeler Auditorium, to about 900–1000 students. These students then came to us in the third meeting of the week, in batches of 20–25. Bolton was very insistent that the sections be small enough so that lively discussion could take place. Also we were expected to give weekly short quizzes. The students were required to read outside books and report on them in a format which we all agreed upon in discussion with Bolton. So there you had it — the senior professor devoting himself religiously to teaching and the devoted TA's carrying out a well-programmed teaching arrangement. I suspect that some of the "student unrest" [in the 1960s] which had its roots in the casual attitude of senior professors would not have existed, had all the senior faculty been as available to students as Bolton always was and as concerned about teaching as he always showed himself to be.
>
> One of the "sights" on the UC campus which I witnessed over and over again was Bolton's walk from his office to Wheeler. Some of us always had to report to Bolton at about 10:45 A.M. that all was in readiness for his lecture. He was adamant that the huge wall maps always be in place well ahead of the lecture and that this be reported to him. Then he moved. He walked down the hall to the elevator

and crankily awaited its arrival. On his way to Wheeler he almost angrily repulsed any conversation or interruption of any sort to his concentration. He was a prima donna at that moment. He was getting ready to give all of his talents to that lecture, and nothing must divert his mind from that effort.

  I sat through two years of his History 8 [History of the Americas] lectures as T.A. I remember analyzing them at the time and finding them not without flaws. Sometimes he rambled (though his dislike of interruptions before going to Wheeler Aud, as contrasted with his expansiveness afterwards, certainly suggests that he did review and prepare each time); sometimes he was corny; sometimes he was repetitious. But he did come across with such enthusiasm that any blemishes were lost in the vivid sense of "being there" that he got over to undergraduates.[1]

  For that first year and the one or two following, Bolton, as he often admitted and as his graduate assistants of those days attest, had to work hard and rather constantly to bring his new course into sharp and manageable focus. For a while the chapter segments of the ultimate syllabus were often not ready very long before his assistants passed them out in class. These early helpers not infrequently had to meet him shortly after he reached his office on class mornings, had to hurriedly type the material, and then run it off; Bolton would have worked late the night before to have the draft in shape.

  "History 8" quickly was in contention, in Bolton's own reckoning, as his favorite course. He loved it and was at his showmanship best twice a week on the platform of spacious Wheeler Auditorium; the enrollment of hundreds in the early years grew to a thousand plus. Besides giving him a chance to tell the thrilling all-American story, this course also afforded him the opportunity to emphasize the close relationship between history and geography; he developed the series of huge maps for the classroom, which were later reduced photographically and included in the printed syllabus.

  "History 8" served another purpose over the years which greatly pleased Bolton. Its numbers enrolled convinced the budget-makers that the department needed a sizable share of graduate assistantships; Bolton had a half-dozen or more fellowships to award to promising graduate students for his History-of-the-Americas quiz-sections. Helpful in the 1920s, this fund became vital in the Depression decade ahead.

The demands of "History 8" were only a few of the things which complicated the life of the new department chairman. Quite as soon as he had engineered the reorganization of the lower-division history offerings, he had to begin the search for a Stephens replacement. He canvassed his friends around the country for suggestions. The university would have wished to attract an established scholar, a man approximating in some degree the stature of the deceased professor, but it soon became evident that any success at that level was out of the question, at least for the upcoming academic year. A young man, Bernard Fuller, was signed to a one-year contract for 1920–21. The quest continued through the fall and into the first half of 1920. Names proposed included: Guy Stanton Ford of Minnesota, a fellow graduate student with Bolton at the University of Wisconsin in the mid-1890s; Charles Downer Hazen; George Matthew Dutcher; William C. Lingelbach, another Bolton fellow graduate student, this time at the University of Pennsylvania; Payson Jackson Treat of Stanford; and a pair of "younger men" who in those days were building reputations, Carlton J. H. Hayes and Conyers Reed. Lingelbach was quite universally the department's top choice; he was willing to come west for the 1920 summer session, but California could not woo him away from Pennsylvania. One thing which came out of this search was the embarrassing fact that the University of California's going salary scale was not properly competitive; climate was attractive, but it was not enough. The result was that the department went into 1920–21 still shorthanded on the European side, at least for advanced work and graduate direction.

The administration thought of solving this situation by strongly hinting to William Morris that he postpone his scheduled sabbatical. Morris had already generously done this in 1919–20, following Stephens' death. Bolton would not hear of this second postponement and, jealously protective of his staff, carried on a vigorous fight with the president, and won.*

Ultimately, the department had to abandon its dream of bringing in an established scholar. Despite the strong letter of Bolton to the dean March 3, 1921, informing him that the California salaries were in instances lower than those commanded by recent graduates, the administration refused the funds to allow Bolton and his mates to become truly competitive. The result was that they had to let their budget dictate a

---

*General David Prescott Barrows, successor to Wheeler in the presidency, and Bolton had been and continued through the years to be warm friends, but on occasion during Barrows' tenure, 1919–23, the two strong men collided.

choice. That spring they signed young Franklin C. Palm, freshly doctored at Illinois; in the fall 1921 he joined the staff. This bit of business finally done, Bolton had one less distracting worry and time-consuming problem.

As the autumn weeks ran, he had to give time and thought to another project. Earlier in the year he had accepted the invitation to deliver the 1920–21 series of Lowell Institute lectures at Boston. He was most pleased to be able to take his message, "The Growth of Spanish Power in North America, 1492–1821," into what he had come to think of as "enemy territory," the land of the Cabots and the Lodges, the Adamses, George Bancroft, and the traditional Anglo-oriented interpretation of American beginnings.

Those December-January weeks proved a most pleasant experience. Newspaper coverage was good, but he probably made few firm converts to his newer version of "American" history. He met old friends at Harvard, such as Turner and Haskins, and later (April 28, 1921) wrote to the former thanking him for many delightful evenings. Even so, he was very content to return home; his dozen years on the West Coast had thinned his Wisconsin blood and turned him into a confirmed Californian and a mild-winter man.

Back in Berkeley, he had another document-series project. En route to Boston he had tried to see Edward Doheny in Los Angeles, hoping to re-enkindle the oil man's earlier expressed interest in a series on "Spain in America"; he wanted to suggest that, with affairs in Mexico now calmed, Doheny might think of beginning the $10,000 annual subsidy once promised for five consecutive years. Doheny evidently did not have "an hour to spare." Ever resourceful, early in this year 1921, Bolton wrote to several of the regents of the university, not precisely asking for funds but wondering if they might have any ideas about sources which might be tapped, individuals who could be interested in financing a project which would do honor to the university and the State of California. This time he was "selling" the idea of a series of "Great American Travels to the Pacific Coast," an extension of and companion to the monumental Thwaites series, *Great Western Travels*. He told how his Bancroft assistant, Joseph J. Hill, already had a number of travel diaries ready to go, how there were others in the Bancroft Collection, and slyly indicated that he himself had eight diaries for the Juan Bautista de Anza expeditions to California in Spanish days. The regents evidently had more pressing business and other interests for the university; nothing came of this "sales pitch," but it did show Bolton's untiring enthusiasm.

The 1921–22 year opened with the department fully staffed for the first time in late years. In addition to Palm, Chapman was back from his year as an exchange-professor at the National University of Chile; Morris, too, was back, bags bulging with materials for his study of the English medieval sheriff. Even so, Bolton still felt that he could hardly go off to Columbia as visiting professor for the second semester. He thanked William Dunning for the invitation. Besides departmental obligations, he foresaw that he would be busy with E. D. Adams of Stanford on a school history of California — *California's Story* would appear in 1922.[2]

Before that second semester ended Bolton was into a major on-campus battle; this time he was wearing the hat of the director of the Bancroft Library. For some time past there had been plans to expand the Doe Library's reading room and other facilities, in order to cope with the rapid increase in enrollment. The space used by the Bancroft Library and the offices of the Department of History was an area elected for preemption. The Bancroft was to go to the fourth floor and the historians to equally remote places. Bolton fought the proposed moves fiercely. On May 12 he sent an extra long memorandum to President Barrows. He argued eloquently, particularly against the Bancroft Library's being relegated "to the garret." It was nationally, even internationally famous; it was one of the university's most important possessions and one of its best show pieces; the use to which its collections were being put could be measured by the number of first-class studies beginning to appear on the book shelves of scholars and libraries. The space "in the garret" planned for the Bancroft was inaccessible, too cramped, too difficult to control; among other things the area could not be remodeled for effective use and service. The next day, fearing that Barrows might never look at so long a statement, Bolton boiled down his arguments to a pithy and pungent one-page statement. But this was one campus battle which he did not win; in the summer of 1922 the Bancroft Library went to the fourth floor. As a result Bolton's office was moved to the soon-to-be-familiar Library 426. Within a few years this office acquired its characteristic Boltonian decor: its book shelves lined and groaning with his own and the books of friends and admirers, with the theses and dissertations of his many students, its corners piled high, and about two-thirds of the floor space covered. Off its massive worktable, set before a cluttered equally large rolltop desk, came the California volumes, the new Kino and the Coronado biographies, and more of his books. There before the worktable many projects were planned, dissertations outlined, theses sketched. Also not a few major book or manuscript deals were concluded when Bolton acted as director of the Bancroft Library. Son Herbert recalls how "Dad kept his office unbearably hot — at least 80 degrees" and "it was always blue with smoke." Many graduate students could have validated this description of Library 426. There were times, too, when it threatened to get hotter still as one of Bolton's secretaries recalls:

The ashtray was always overflowing, and periodically Dr. Bolton would empty it into the wastebasket which stood under the table. Sometimes the cigarettes were not totally extinguished. There had been at one time, I believe, a serious fire in Dr. Bolton's study, but this was before I came to work for him. [The report is correct; the date was 1936; there are pieces for that year in the Bolton Papers with charred edges.] One day I was seated in my usual place on the far side of the great table, a place from which there was no escape unless Dr. Bolton gave me leave, when slowly smoke began to rise from the metal waste basket beside him. I watched for a moment that seemed like an hour and, seeing no reaction on his part, cried out "The waste basket is on fire." Dr. Bolton ignored my interruption and went calmly on talking or dictating. Just as I was becoming panic-stricken, he casually picked up the basket, circled the huge rolltop desk, and set the flaming container out on his little balcony. Never again, and there were several times when smoke began to curl up from the waste basket, did I ever say a word. Result: The basket usually went to the balcony to burn itself out before the point of total combustion. But whenever such an incident occurred, I wondered if this was to be the time someone seeing the smoke would alert the fire department.

Bancroft Library "in the garret" proved to be far from inaccessible. Bolton probably wished often that his dire prediction had been closer to the truth, in order that he might work uninterruptedly in Library 426. His only quiet hours, regularly, were those when he returned to his desk after dinner at home, or on weekends.

Along with all the moving Bolton taught in the summer session of 1922. He prepared for those hectic weeks by taking off right after the close of the semester. First, with friends, he did a turn through the New Mexico-Arizona Indian country — Háwikuh, Zuñi, Ácoma, some of the valley pueblos, and then the Hopi towns. Next there was a week in the Yosemite country, during which he gave three lectures on the history of that fascinating region and made some of his first contacts with the men of the National Park Service, a connection which in time would become very much a part of his scholarly life.

When the new semester (1922–23) began, he was delighted to be once again "just a teacher." In accord with the new patterns adopted by the reorganization of the university, he was relieved of the chairmanship after his two years of service. Louis J. Paetow was the department's choice as successor. Bolton's period of luxuriating, with only his Bancroft duties, his classes, and his research and writing, was too quickly interrupted by a hospital sojourn. His health was regularly good, robust even, but occasionally an infection or a virus caught up with him. In September 1922 it was an infected tooth which hospitalized him and kept him out of circulation for almost a month. The enforced inactivity did not afford him

Herbert Bolton with the tools of his trade — manuscript, pen, and cigarette. Photograph taken in Berkeley, California, in the late 1930s.

much working time, but it did give him a certain amount of thinking time. It may have contributed to some of the careful planning for the future which he outlined to Frederick Jackson Turner in a long letter of November 8. It gives a valuable insight into Bolton's historiography:

Let me thank you for your kind letter of recent date. My health is very much improved and I am back at work again in full swing. The trouble was a bad infection in my throat, caused by a tooth which was filled when it should have been extracted. It sent me to the hospital for two operations and kept me from my work for about a month. The trouble has not all disappeared yet, but all is going in the right direction so that in time I should be all sound again.

You caution me against the danger to creative production from too much teaching. I fully appreciate the force of what you say and am on my guard. Your kindly advice gives me a chance to say to you what I am glad to have you know.

For a long time I have been working in the sources, dealing with minute and less minute subjects. They have lain on the borders rather than within the field of most other students. In the process I have gained a new insight into the meaning of my own particular scraps of history, have found where they fit in, as it seems to me, and have conceived a new unity for the American story, one which gives vital significance to many things for which most students have found no place and which they have regarded as relatively unimportant. I have reached a point now where it seems to me that I ought to spend a little time in setting forth in synthetic fashion some of my general results, in order to bring together from my point of view the scattered materials, and help others to see their meaning in the great story of human development. After I have finished one or two tasks of this kind, I definitely plan to go back to monographic work and the editing and publication of documents, in order to place certain portions of the western story on a more solid foundation.

As I see it, the editing of documents, monographic writing, and synthesis must go on side by side, or with relatively short intervals in between, otherwise they are likely to become barren. Documents selected without a point of view or from a conventional point of view are likely to be badly selected. On the other hand, synthesis without fresh research and fresh materials very soon becomes pointless. These comments may help you to understand what I think I am doing and why I am doing it, and will let you know what I plan to turn to in the future.

I might add that the writers of textbooks from the conventional point of view are so slow in seeing the bearing of research in the field which has interested me, that it is almost incumbent upon me to do something to get the point of view and the results before teachers and elementary students. I believe that such synthetic work as I am trying to do will help my graduate students to see the meaning of their work. . . .

This was not the first time that Bolton had written to Turner giving some of the basic elements of his approach to history, something of an *apologia pro vita sua.* As early as June 4, 1914, he had written:

I am interested in your statement that the papers prepared by myself and my students astonish you by the definiteness of information regarding the Spanish advances. . . . Your remark gives me occa-

sion to say that I have always realized that my papers on local episodes of Southwestern history have been fearfully heavy with details
which will disappear in the writing of the general history. . . . But I
realized also that in a field so new and so foreign to most American
students it was important that not merely the general results should
be stated, but that the setting must be furnished, so that the generali-
zation might have some meaning. . . . As I see it, until the field is
covered by monographs of this kind, we shall have no basis for a
clear understanding of the work of the Spaniards in the American
West. This helps to explain the dreariness of most of what I have
written.

One of the syntheses which he was planning to write was a text for his
History of the Americas course. This early he was talking and beginning
to lay out the book which he never quite had the time to write. This book
was in and out of his thinking and correspondence very often in the next
years, and there are ample indications that the travelers for the large
national publishing houses were constantly urging such a book, each with
the hope of being able to land the manuscript for his company.

Eventually some historians would fault Bolton and many of his students for what they would term a narrow, purely regional, puerile, heavy-
in-detail approach to history, but later that fall (1922) Bolton received
one of those heartwarming bits of recognition which sometimes comes
to a scholar from an altogether unexpected source. Pasquet of France had
done a bibliographical article on American history writing for the *Revue
Historique* and had noted several of Bolton's works. Bolton had written
to thank him and received a letter in return with this statement:

I look upon you as being with Professor Alvord, Professor
Turner and some others, one of the men who have done the best work
in rescuing American history out of the rut of tradition. You have
conclusively proved that there is something else to be said on the topic
of American colonization besides Plymouth Rock, Pocahontas, and
other time honored stories.

Bolton might have wished that more of his American colleagues would
be getting the message which the Frenchman had been alert to recognize.

Bolton felt that he had to do a little campaigning in November. Paging
through George M. Wrong's volume in the "Chronicles of America"
series, *The Conquest of New France,* he was more than a bit shocked to
read that Vérendrye or some members of his party were the "discoverers"
of the Rocky Mountains in the 1740s. He could not resist sending off a
long letter to the good professor at the University of Toronto, more or less
pleasantly quarreling with both his history and his geography. He pointed

out that the Spaniards as far back as Coronado had known the New Mexican ranges belonging to the Rocky Mountain cordillera, and also that several years prior to the time that the Vérendryes had seen the northern Rockies, the French Mallet brothers, out of the Illinois country, had gone along the Front Range in Colorado before showing in Santa Fe in 1739. Bolton rather enjoyed "needling" colleagues for such historical slips, and he did so now and then.

CAMPUS IN-FIGHTING

During the second semester (1922–23) he had another on-campus fight on his hands — at least Chairman Paetow turned a communication over to him for an answer. The Department of History was under fire for laying too much emphasis, so it was said, on the history of Spanish America. This was one of the reasons advanced for the deferral of Chapman's promotion to the rank of full professor, which had been urged by the department. Besides, the Executive Committee of the University of California had voted to cut the regular two-semester courses of Chapman and Priestley to a single semester. Bolton was furious and wrote to President Barrows April 6, commenting rather pointedly that no one of the members of the Executive Committee was competent to make that reduction-of-hours decision. On the Chapman case he fired off a long and heated memorandum to Dean Leuschner. He made the observation that the charge of overemphasis on Western and Spanish-American history practically said that the department should not do what it was best equipped to do in terms of manpower, research materials available, and student patronage. He suggested that the committee's next advice might be that Kroeber switch from his studies of the California Indians to concentrate on those of Florida, so that John Swanton of the Smithsonian Institution might devote his attention to the West Coast tribes;[3] or, perhaps, the University of California should not study mining but leave that to the University of Nebraska. He was in rare form and multiplied such absurd examples and then ended by wondering if perhaps the achievements of the Department of History in the area of publication by its staff and students, to say nothing of its number of graduate students, may have made departments less productive a shade jealous. As mentioned before, Bolton could be tough in the in-fighting, when history or its students were threatened or dealt with unfairly.

This sort of sniping occurred periodically through the early 1920s. On a later occasion there was another sly thrust which Bolton parried with a letter to Dean Leuschner (October 31, 1924); the complaint again was overemphasis on the Spanish-American side. Chapman, he contended, was the only real Latin Americanist in the department. Priestley, granting that he had become an authority on Mexico, had interests which ranged more widely; Bolton reminded Leuschner that Priestley was doing a great deal of research and offering courses on French colonialism. He himself, he affirmed, was not and never had been a Latin Americanist in the true sense; his prime interests were the American West and the American Southwest, the Spanish Borderlands, and both of these areas should be labeled United States history, granting that this U.S. history might have a definite Spanish flavor. In time the critics of the Department of History gave up and allowed Bolton to build as he and his colleagues thought best.

During the early months of 1923 Bolton, not distracted by the affairs and business of the department, was able to devote much time to his other job, that of director of the Bancroft Library. He planned, budgeted, schemed, and began to do some early begging. He was in contact with George Watson Cole, librarian of the Huntington, inquiring about his future plans and suggesting various ways in which the two great California research libraries could cooperate. Huntington's recent acquisition of a number of Kino letters intrigued Bolton and possibly made him a bit jealous, but he limited his correspondence to exchanges with Cole. He started to develop, without the later formal organization, the Friends of the Bancroft Library. The manuscript-copy holdings were growing; to his own thousands of pages, copies gathered by his "boys," especially the Native Sons Fellows, were constantly being added. And it took time to organize the library in the new quarters "in the garret."

THE BERKELEY FIRE OF 1923

When the new semester (1923-24) opened, Bolton was still an administratively unencumbered professor, and he was looking forward to a great year. The summer had been dry, as usual. As the autumn weeks went by and the warmer Indian summer days came, all California, again, and as usual, lived in dread of the fire hazard. In the early afternoon of September 17 a high tension wire in the Berkeley hills, northeast of the campus, broke, and a grass fire was ignited. The breeze was stiff, and before the flames were controlled, they had eaten down the hill, almost to the Bay, destroying everything in their path. The Bolton home at 1526 Scenic was in the path of the fire. Except for a few pieces of silverware, Mrs. Bolton and the girls, at home at the time, were able to save nothing;

the home which all the Boltons had come to love was a complete loss.*
Fortunately, no one in the community was injured, but the total loss was
horrendous. Only a shift in the wind saved the campus and the south
side from being engulfed. Despite the family loss of around $25,000, Bol-
ton was better off than many of his colleagues, as he explained in a letter
to former student Roy Gittinger, who sent a worried note of commisera-
tion, as did many of his friends:

> Yes we were in the path of the flames, and they cleaned us up
> nicely. With the exception of a little silverware we saved nothing
> from the home. Fortunately my manuscripts and other work materials
> were over at the University, so I am not crippled in that respect,
> although I have lost several thousand books.

It was much the same message in answer to many other letters. He did
mention to a very concerned Charles Hackett October 8 that the insurance
came close to covering the estimated loss ($15,500 against $25,000); he
also informed Hackett that the family was reasonably comfortable in a
rented house on the south side of campus, at 2925 Garber, "up near the
Claremont Hotel."† In the next several years the Boltons moved several
times, until in 1926 they settled for a longer period on Cedar Street (2661)
— it was not easy to find adequate housing for a family of eight in those
post-fire years, until reconstruction caught up with housing needs.‡
Finally, however, in 1933, after a full decade of living in seven successive

---

*In later years, and from bits of reported conversations by Bolton and others,
more information on "things lost" came to light. The private library, the beginnings
of whose accumulation went back to Bolton's student days, was mentioned to Gittinger, but there is really no check on what it contained. The Bolton daughters feel
that much of the matching correspondence of Frederick to Herbert through the
years was destroyed, the complement to the Herbert-to-Frederick file which has
given so many insights to Bolton's earlier years. Lost, too, was the reportedly rich
file of letters to Mrs. Bolton, written from Mexico after 1910 during Herbert's
archival forays across the border, and giving some of his personal experiences with
the Mexican Revolution and the revolutionaries.

†Many of the professors were less well insured than Bolton. The university
organized a Relief Commission to assist all the victims. Bolton received a check for
$726.00 from this fund.

‡Frances Bolton had already left home; hence, space was not required for her.
The Boltons lived in the Garber Street residence into 1925; then followed a chain
of short stays in rented quarters on Bayview Place, Greenwood Terrace, Indian
Rock, Santa Barbara, and Le Roy. By the time they found a home at 2661 Cedar the
family had dwindled, by marriages; they were on Cedar until 1933, when they moved
into their fine home on Buena Vista Drive.

rented houses, Gertrude and Herbert Bolton moved into their own home on Buena Vista Way in the Berkeley hills. By this time most of the children had left home, but Bolton wanted room so that the children could feel free to visit with their families. Also the Depression gave a welcome assist by driving down construction costs. With architect Edwin Lewis Snyder, he planned a lovely Spanish-type home. It was large and roofed with heavy red Moroccan tile. There was a spacious living room, with beamed ceiling, a large fireplace, and a great window which looked out to the Golden Gate. The entry hall was floored with polished red bricks, and a stout wrought-iron railing guarded the winding stairway to the second floor, which had numerous bedrooms and baths. Here, too, on Buena Vista, Bolton purchased an adjacent fifteen-foot strip of land for Gertrude's dreamed-of greenhouse and flower garden. They spent just short of twenty years in this, their last home.

As the year 1924 opened, the future gave promise. Although the Berkeley fire had been upsetting, all else seemed to be moving smoothly. Since the decade opened he had put two new books on his shelf: *The Colonization of North America* and *The Spanish Borderlands*. The Bancroft Library "in the garret" was winning more recognition and patronage, and its director attracting more and more eager graduate students. Bolton had launched a new approach to American history, and it was being tested in classrooms around the country. What he did not foresee in those early January days was the "crisis" which would hit him in mid-1924 and put him through another run of tortured summer weeks.

11

The Question of
the Texas Presidency

D URING THE SUMMER of 1923 several letters had reached the
Berkeley campus which opened what was to develop into an interesting episode in Bolton's life.[1] Robert E. Vinson of Texas had
resigned as president at the end of the school year 1922–23 to accept a
like position at Western Reserve University, Cleveland. Two of Bolton's
friends, Eugene Barker and Charles Hackett, were on the search committee for a successor to Vinson; they wrote to Chapman and Paetow,
soliciting an opinion on Bolton as a possible man for the Texas post.
Chapman wrote back July 3:

> Professor Bolton has established wide contacts with the people
> of this State. He is in constant demand as a speaker and lecturer. . . .
> Widely known as he is here in California, I am sure that he would be
> even more appreciated in Texas, which has always been the head and
> center of his historical interests.

Nothing came of this for the moment, but that exchange with Barker
seems to have put Bolton's name very definitely "in the hat." Chapman,
great friend that he was, evidently could not keep the news of the feeler
to himself. Bolton may also have heard from other sources that the Texans
were searching for a new president. In a letter of November 11 to Barker
he wrote:

> You may have wondered why I have been so mum about the
> presidency question down there. It has not been for any lack of
> appreciation of your efforts in my behalf and of the compliment
> which your committee paid me. I have preferred to let the matter
> take its course. You probably can understand this. I was quite con-
> tent to let Porter dig up anything that he could find here and abide
> by the consequences. I shall watch developments with interest,
> because I have never ceased to feel close to the University of Texas.

[156]

Nothing else happened until March 22, 1924, when Bolton received a cryptic telegram from Hackett: "Is rumored here that the presidency will be offered either you or Ford of Minnesota or Works of Cornell - in conversations with Sutton - remember it is believed that he would like to have the job for himself." Dean William Seneca Sutton had been serving as acting president, but he was not the faculty's first choice as Vinson's successor permanently.

With the passing years Bolton seemed fated periodically to be "haunted" by the University of Texas — always in pleasant and very complimentary fashion, but still very disturbingly. Fourteen years before, when at Stanford, he had been pushed into a corner by friends and powers at Austin in the weeks following the death of George P. Garrison. To go to Texas as chairman or not, this had been the question which gave him several tortured weeks that summer of 1910. And the decision to be made had been further complicated by the offer from Morse Stephens of California. In many respects Bolton was in for a replay of the summer of 1910, with some of the circumstances changed.

The operation of the University of Texas for some years past, almost from the very beginning to be exact, had been seriously, almost disastrously, bedeviled by Texas politics. The memory of the disgraceful interference by Governor James F. Ferguson, in 1917, was still much too vivid and painful a memory. As the months following Vinson's departure slipped by, the faculty became much concerned; they wanted to be sure that their new president would be an academic man. The Faculty of the College feared a possible power play by the faculties of the professional schools, and all feared the possible appointment of a nonuniversity man. Back in November 1923 Hackett had complained to Bolton that the men of the law faculty had managed, through pressure on the regents, to get themselves advanced ahead of the academics. Among the latter there was little trust in the regents.

This lack of confidence in the regents seemed fully justified in May 1924, when word leaked out that the board had offered the presidency to Governor Pat M. Neff, soon to conclude his term of office in the capitol.[2] Neff, incidentally, had named most of the current regents to the university's governing body. The fact that Neff, immediately on being apprised of the regents' action, sent that body a long telegram declining, made little difference, even though this was very soon known. The other fact — that the regents had actually made Neff their first choice — was enough to touch off an explosion of resentment within the university faculty, and around the state. The situation was not calmed by the statement appearing in the Austin *Statesman* of May 17 "To the People of Texas" by Regents Sam P. Cochran and Frank C. Jones who had dissented from the majority in the executive session of May 15. These two men had tendered their resignations and explained their action: "We believe it to be contrary to the best interests of the University and the State, and wrong in principle, to select as President of that institution the Governor of the State who holds the appointive power with respect to the Board of Regents. . . ."

When Neff declined their nomination, showing more good sense than many Texans credited him with having, the regents went into executive session late on that afternoon of May 16 and unanimously selected Guy Stanton Ford, dean of the Graduate School, University of Minnesota. Regent Chairman Lutcher Stark sent off the official telegram. Although the regents refused to confide in the Austin press, the *Statesman* picked up the information on this action from the Associated Press, which in turn had learned of the development from Minneapolis. The next day the *Statesman* announced that Ford had returned a negative reply, with thanks. Then speculation ran rampant around Austin. The refusal of Ford, it was figured, put Bolton at the top of the list. For the moment, however, interested parties did not know whether Bolton had been contacted by the regents.

On Sunday May 18 Barker wrote Bolton; then on Tuesday he sent a telegram asking him to take no action until that Sunday's letter arrived. In said letter Barker told him that Ford had been named and had declined, and that at the moment Ford had a telegram from Stark, asking him to reconsider "at least to the extent of coming to Texas for the next meeting of the Board, May 28." Barker, convinced that Ford would not yield, told how he and Porter* had gone to see Joe Wooten (one of the regents) that Sunday morning:

> Porter and I didn't spare the somber colors in our description of conditions in the Faculty. We insisted that what the Faculty must have, and soon, is assurance that a competent and respectable (respect inspiring) man be chosen. He agreed. We then nominated that man — yourself.

Barker went on to sketch the situation and the character and temper of the regents; next he spoke of the very real threat of a possible political appointment; he felt that he could assure Bolton enthusiastic support from the ex-students and from most of the faculty. He concluded with a fervent plea that Bolton come, if invited.

---

*Milton Blockett Porter, professor of pure mathematics, had been a colleague of Bolton's during his Austin days.

The presidency affair was developing into a comic opera. Regent Wooten had been more than willing to listen. Since word of the Neff selection leaked out, he and Chairman Stark had become the prime targets of criticism, especially from the ex-students. Wooten had not improved his image by his statement to the press, on Friday May 16, defending the original selection of Neff. He had described the governor as an

> exponent of law and order, the true and tried friend of education, and a firm believer in the Christian religion. A real scholar, a brilliant lawyer, a wise statesman, and, above all, a Christian gentleman. The University in honoring him would be doing honor to itself.

Wooten was in so deep that he was ready to grab at the possible lifeline which Barker and Porter were throwing him.

The outspoken and pugnacious Will C. Hogg, chief spokesman for at least a sizable group of the ex-students, particularly from the Houston area, had begun the anti-Neff, anti-regents campaign on Friday with a telegram to *the governor,* hot enough to melt the wires:

> While nothing but pity for you and sympathy for the University is in my heart, you can do yourself great credit and render a stupendous service to the University by declining to accept the office, for assuredly quite a majority of the people of Texas will resent to the utmost the method of selection, regardless of any real or fancied qualifications for that particular service which you possess.

This telegram was probably sent before it was known that Neff had formally declined, on Thursday afternoon, but it does indicate how rapidly word of his selection got out of Austin.

Hogg, by no means placated by Neff's having declined, had next demanded that Stark resign as chairman of the drive then in progress for the university's proposed Memorial Stadium. Further, he suggested that both Stark and Wooten voluntarily withdraw from the board of regents — both were ex-students and it was contended that their vote for Neff had been tantamount to treason. This aspect of the fight warmed considerably in the next days.

Meanwhile, Barker and his confederates were busy. On Friday May 23 he telegraphed Bolton: "Need information - did information arrive [meaning some word from the regents] - if so are you coming." The information needed was personal data to supplement the Barker-Porter dossier on Bolton given to Wooten to show that, even though Bolton had never been in an executive position in a university, he still had ample

administrative experience and university know-how. Bolton's friends by
that date were fully confident that the regents at their next meeting,
Wednesday May 28, would name him.

They were not wrong. Early the afternoon of May 28, informed now
that Ford would not reconsider or even come to Austin for a conference,
the regents named Bolton and authorized their chairman, H. J. Lutcher
Stark, to dispatch the following telegram:

> Board of Regents in session today unanimously elected you
> President - the salary is ten thousand a year plus a residence - can
> promise hearty support of Regents, faculty, students, ex-students
> and general public. If possible your acceptance today would be
> appreciated as your favorable answer would harmonize all parties -
> please refrain from publicity for present - wire reply.

Also sent at 2:30 P.M. on that same Wednesday was a more personal
message from Stark: "Have just sent you official telegram regarding presidency of the University of Texas - Nita and I urge you to wire acceptance - please don't consider we are rushing you too much - kindest
regards."

This Wednesday action of the regents was a better kept secret than
theirs of May 15. On the morning of May 29 Bolton had a telegram from
Hackett, which had been sent off the evening before. The *Statesman* of
May 28 had simply been able to note that the regents in their meeting had
addressed themselves to the problems of the budget; no other information was available. Hackett, too, was in the dark, when he assured Bolton: "Faculty sentiment that if offered the presidency you could release a
bad situation and that you could accept with reservations that would not
compromise you - the Faculty would be with you as a unit." There was no
doubt that Bolton had many friends at Texas outside the Department of
History; some had known him as colleagues or students in an earlier day;
some possibly knew that Texas had tried to persuade him to come back
from Stanford a dozen or more years before, following Garrison's death.

After a night of thought, on Thursday morning, May 29, Bolton sent
Stark a long telegram:

> My election to the presidency of the University of Texas does
> me great honor - the position is worthy of the best talent in the land
> and offers an inspiring opportunity for constructive service in a noble
> state - before accepting I would wish to confer on some matters -
> otherwise, in order not to keep you waiting, I must decline now -
> there are questions of policy to discuss - the salary does not seem
> commensurate with the responsibility and dignity of the position

unless adequate expense funds granted - I can come at your convenience any time within three weeks.

Stark evidently was expecting such a reply by Bolton, since early Thursday afternoon he wired back:

> For your information next Regents meeting June twelfth - would be glad to have you meet the Board here at that time - in fact members of the Board anxious to have you here - annual meeting of ex-students May thirty-first - they are anxiously awaiting your acceptance - kindest regards.

Then later still, now with Bolton's telegram in hand, Stark sent a long message which he hoped would quiet Bolton's expressed anxieties:

> Your wire May 29 - previous salary seventy-five hundred plus home - Board thought ten thousand plus two thousand expense fund plus a secretary would be all they could spare out of our limited legislative appropriation for this year - preparing our biennium request to the legislature on June 12 as per my wire and any increase in salary could be easily adjusted I am sure - come at any time for meeting with executive committee but Board cannot be called until June 12th - awaiting your decision as to time of visit before making your message public - ex-students meeting Saturday - regards.

To this Bolton replied the next day: "Shall come to meet Regents on June twelfth."

Stark was relieved to have this assurance that Bolton at least would come for the June 12 meeting. With an unprecedented number of ex-students converging on Austin for their meeting the next day, with all the recent publicity occasioned by the election-of-Neff incident and with rumors rife that Stark and Wooten were in for at least an unmerciful verbal beating at that meeting, Stark felt that he now held a "hidden ace." The news of the May 28 action by the regents was officially announced to the ex-students at noon on Saturday, May 31.

The news spread like wildfire. The Saturday afternoon *Statesman* bannered the story with multiple headlines:

> BOLTON MAY LEAD VARSITY
> California Educator Tentatively Accepts
> Salary Question is Only Point of Issue

The universal reaction was one of joyous relief. The regents probably took their first deep breath of the past several weeks. The faculty was reassured and the ex-students were jubilant. The threat of a political appointment seemed to be stayed.

That same Saturday afternoon Barker wrote: "Well, it's certainly on the lap of the gods. . . . I have felt pretty certain that you were elected the other day and that you would attend the next meeting, June 12, and accept. . . . I'll be gone, but talk to Porter before you confer with the Board." Barker was heading for a summer commitment at the University of Chicago. In this letter Barker shared with Bolton much of the content of the dossier which he and Porter had passed on to the regents some days before. This quite lengthy run-down detailed Bolton's virtues, his capabilities, and his many quasi-administrative positions and experiences. (Barker explained that this was necessary since lack of formal executive involvement had been considered as one of his weak spots by some of the regents.) The promotion piece had ended with a short paragraph to the effect that Bolton "is a Democrat, a Christian, and, we believe, a church member. Certainly he is in hearty accord with the church as a great uplifting social force." In his own hand on the typed copy sent to Bolton, Barker jotted the following, more or less as an apology: "There may be some question of the propriety of this; it ought to have nothing to do with the matter, but it has with this board, and on careful reflection I put it in." Bolton, to be sure, was forgiving; he was probably more than a little amused as well. He would not have quarreled with the "Christian" part, but the "church member" was something else. In a letter to Frederick February 1, 1902 while he was still at the University of Texas, Bolton had spelled out his views on the subject of church-going. He had asked Frederick:

> Do you people attend church? We do not, but people here all do. They are very religious. Have daily chapel, and many professors teach Sunday School classes. I haven't the time. I am needed at home to help take care of the children.

Sentiment in Texas had not changed and neither had Bolton's. His religion was his own; organized religion would never be a part of his life. Neither was his political affiliation quite that of a "Democrat," at least not in the Texas sense.

The reaction in Texas was almost universally enthusiastic, save among the hard-core Baptists who were dubious. Barker told Bolton not to worry about this. Hackett reported: "The ex-students are behind you; the Faculty looks to you as their 'Deliverer'; the students are with you; the public opinion of the state is with you. It is openly and commonly talked that you can come in with the best terms any President has been able to get." He closed, pleading with Bolton to accept.

Faced with a major decision, Bolton shared the news with Frederick. At the end of a June 2 letter Herbert wrote: "You will be interested in the enclosed copy of a telegram which I received from Texas. I have not made a decision one way or the other, but I have consented to go down to confer with the Board on June 12. If you have any good advice send it along." To this Frederick came back immediately on June 6:

> I read in the Sunday paper of your election to the Presidency of the University of Texas. This morning your note confirmed the newspaper item. Sincere congratulations to them and to you.
>
> My advice is to accept unless you find some unusual conditions which I do not anticipate. You need not give up scholarly work. Harper of Chicago showed how to combine the two. Stipulate that clerical help must be adequate, that there be a real executive secretary and a dean of faculties. You must be free to formulate policies and free from details. . . .
>
> You can make Texas an outstanding center of research in Southwest history and can more easily control the situation than in California where there are apparent mean jealousies. In Texas as president you can have real power to deal with such situations.
>
> Of course there will be annoyances anywhere, but I believe that conditions of your selection are so auspicious as to make acceptance the only rational thing. They like you, they want you, and unanimously ask you. Such a combination makes it an opportunity. It is a great state with wonderful possibilities. . . . You can do a unique work there and it will be the crowning period of your life. I hope that you will accept and believe you will. . . .

By the time Herbert received this letter from Frederick, his own thinking had crystalized in another direction.

As the early June days ran, Hackett was insistent. There was another telegram on Wednesday June 4: "Jeanie [Mrs. Hackett] and I hope that you will stay with us during visit to Austin - better still we hope that you will bring Mrs. Bolton - Executive Committee of Faculty Club desires to give smoker in your honor June twelve - advise time of arrival and Barker and I will meet train."

The rest of that first week of June added up to truly difficult days for the "president-elect." There were so many factors involved in an ultimate decision, all of which had to be considered and weighed carefully and sensibly. Bolton sincerely loved Texas and had the fondest of memories of the University where he had discovered the historical orientation which was proving to be his life's work. He had staunch friends there, besides. He was fully aware, however, that politics had made a mess of what could have and should have developed into a great school. He had little stomach for that brand of politics — university politics could be fun; dealing with professionals could be something very distasteful, and he was not sure that he wanted to take on that duty, with his eyes open. Further, he was realistic enough to recognize, despite all statements to the contrary from varied sources, that acceptance would mean the end of his scholarly life, at least for the years in office and possibly forever. At this point he was just beginning to taste the excitement of his "California period," and he had in Sidney Ehrman a benevolent patron to back his ambitions. Another consideration was Mrs. Bolton's feelings; she was not strong, and the demands made upon her as the wife of the president might well be too much for her to accept. Besides, while she liked the Texans, she distinctly disliked the Texas climate, which she had found extremely difficult years before. Pros and cons were heavy on both sides; by Sunday morning, June 8, he had reached a decision: He would not accept.

That day he sent off telegrams to Stark and to Barker, both with substantially the same message. The Barker message is a bit fuller:

> I have decided to remain in California - therefore my intended conference will not be necessary - my decision is not due to any fear that we could not arrange mutually satisfactory terms but to reluctance to leave scholarship for administration - it would cost me the struggle of my life for I recognize the splendid opportunity for service in a state and a university and with friends that I love - the confidence shown me by faculty and the alumni overwhelms me - consult Stark before giving out.

The telegram to Stark he closed: "Your confidence I prize above expression." Stark was unprepared for such news. He came back with a long telegram on Monday, June 9:

> Answering your telegram - see no reason why you should be compelled to give up scholarship in doing administrative work - you would be surrendering the arduousness of teaching - let me again urge you to withhold your decision until you have had a conference with Board and made a personal investigation of the situation - am withholding your telegram from public until I receive your answer - Nita joins me in urging this course and would deem it a great favor if you come for conference.

Bolton did reply, and that same day:

> Having made my decision I think that I had better not go to Austin - I fear I should find friendships and opportunities so alluring that my judgment would be overruled by my inclinations - I am profoundly sorry to deny your personal request.

Stark was determined to pull out all the stops. Mid-morning of June 10 he wired a Berkeley friend, Roberta Lavendar:

> Thanks for your message - have been in wild communication with Dr. Bolton and am bringing all possible pressure to get him to come to Austin for conference - urge that you see him and prevail upon him not to announce his declination for the present - wire reply as am leaving for Austin tonight at seven A.M.

At the same time Stark sent still another wire to Bolton:

> Have discussed privately with influential alumni all over state - everyone urges that you come to Austin at least for a conference with the Alumni and Board - by leaving today you could meet with Board on night of twelfth - your refusal has cast a gloom over the situation.

All of these pressures did break down Bolton's resolve to avoid the temptations of a visit to Austin. He wired Stark that he would come but noted that he would not be able to arrive until the morning of June 13.

It is easy to envision Herbert Bolton in the parlor car, as the train rolled through "his" Borderlands, busily jotting down points for his speech to the regents and to the alumni.[3] He was not reconsidering his decision of Sunday June 8. His reason for making the trip at all, he gave later (June 14) to a reporter of the Austin *Statesman*:

> I did not come to Texas University to discuss the presidency of the University. I had twice declined that post, and I only came at the personal and urgent invitation of Chairman Stark of the Board of Regents. I came in the hope that I might be of service to Texas University by telling the regents and ex-students what I think to be the great needs of Texas University. . . . The University of Texas is a university of destiny.

The Austin days were something of a personal triumph for Bolton. They began on that Friday the thirteenth in somewhat comic fashion. Stark drove down to San Antonio to meet Bolton's train, presumably arriving at six o'clock in the morning. He was working with erroneous information; Bolton's train was in at three-thirty, and knowing the country he had taken a bus to Austin. The chairman of the board returned empty-handed. Bolton, meanwhile, had been resting quietly in Barker's office, in Garrison Hall. When the rather frantic searchers finally discovered him, they quickly whisked him over to the meeting of the regents, late in the morning.

He spent two hours with the board, speaking his piece with force and candor: immediate cessation of outside and political interference in the running of the university; complete academic freedom for the faculty; generous subsidies for graduate work; the "unshacking" of the campus, meaning the rapid elimination of the many too many supposedly temporary wooden classroom buildings, threatening to become a permanent eyesore, to say nothing of a fire hazard; a more realistic salary and expense account for the university's president. He was convincing and, according to him, the regents promised action, albeit unenthusiastically and grudgingly. He left that conference feeling that he had struck a blow for progress; at least the regents who had invited him to be their president had heard what might have been his conditions for acceptance.

As he emerged from the meeting with the regents, there occurred the one untoward incident of the Austin days. Hackett was waiting impatiently to drive him off to a luncheon at the Austin Country Club, where he was scheduled to talk to a faculty group; he was already long overdue. A reporter from the *Statesman* pressed for a statement. Bolton, tired and anxious to be off to his next appointment, did not particularly appreciate the badgering tactics of the young man. He gave a statement, a terse three word one, a firm and unmistakable "Go to hell!" Hackett acted quickly, cornered the reporter, promised an interview the next morning — at which time, incidentally, Bolton was at his gracious best.

At the luncheon with the faculty group he reported some of the points he had made to the regents, and they cheered his candor and audacity. Later that Friday afternoon he was finally deposited at the new Stephen F. Austin Hotel, only recently opened, and had some welcome moments of quiet, a chance to refresh himself a bit before the smoker which the ex-students had scheduled for that evening.

It was at this smoker that Will C. Hogg pledged the quarter of a million dollars to underwrite the plans which Bolton had sketched for the university's immediate future, particularly the establishment of graduate fellowships. The ex-students were thrilled to be told that their University of Texas could, and very soon should, be in competition with the dozen top universities of the nation. Bolton interestingly and realistically located his first ten, all on or above the "Baltimore-Berkeley line" and left the South a completely open field for the first bold comer, and he predicted Texas in that role. It was a busy evening. Stark later complained that he could not get near enough for a few quiet words. Even Will Hogg, who had to leave early in order to go off to Europe the next day, had no better luck. By the time Bolton got back to the hotel, there was not too much of the night left for sleep.

The *Statesman* of June 14, which carefully charted his movement of that and the previous day, reported that he checked out of the Austin at ten o'clock in the morning. At this point Hackett had set up the interview with the man from the press who had approached Bolton the previous afternoon. After a tour with Hackett to see how Austin had developed in recent years, Hackett drove him to San Antonio where he boarded the Sunset Limited for home.

During the Austin stay a new dimension had been added to the picture. Bolton was definitely impressed by the treatment he had received and heartened by the promises which he had wrung from the regents and also by the Will Hogg pledge of a quarter of a million dollars to put graduate work on a sound footing. Hackett and friends had insisted that he reconsider. Bolton knew that he did not want the Texas presidency as a permanent thing, but another alternative had come up for consideration — the possibility of his coming to Texas for one year. In this way the faculty would be encouraged by the dissipation of the threat of a political appointment; the promises of the ex-students which had been made largely to him could be fulfilled; new patterns and policies might be set. It was felt that the regents after a year could hardly dare bring in anyone but a man whose background was academic and nonpolitical.

A long letter from Hackett, written Sunday night, June 15, told Bolton that this alternative maneuver would be acceptable to his friends and even to two of the regents who had been queried on the matter. Porter wrote the story of the last days to Barker, in Chicago. On June 18 Barker pleaded with Bolton to come at least for the proposed year, in order to get things rolling in the right direction: "Go ahead and accept. Get to Texas as soon as you can. Explain to Stark privately that it is for a year, but say nothing about it publicly."

The Austin schemers continued active. The evening of June 17 Hackett reported:

> Porter and I believe everything satisfactorily arranged with Regents, faculty, and ex-students - don't announce decision until receipt on Friday of letters from me, Porter and Lomax - Hogg endowment absolutely fails if Splawn elected - additional aid from him if you accept - certainty of Splawn's election if you decline - the call for you to save us is far more apparent than when you were here.

Another Hackett telegram of the next day was even more explicit, and considerably more anguished:

> The morning papers carry interviews by local Regents that you are considering the presidency on year's leave of absence - Wooten expressed hope to me this morning that you would accept - I know positively that the day before you arrived the Regents voted authority

to Stark to offer presidency to Splawn without calling another meeting in case you decline - you alone can save the University by accepting at least for a year - we could hardly understand how you could refuse to give just one year to saving and developing the University - pay no attention to a few disgruntled Neff Baptists - Baker, Mathews, and University churches have endorsed you - if you take the presidency until February you will surely guarantee University's future and will save it from one who will surely bring it and us to stagnation.

The regents' back-up man was Walter Splawn, a Texan. His academic credentials were respectable enough — a graduate of Baylor, and master's from Yale, and a doctorate from Chicago. He had chaired the Department of Economics at Texas from 1918 to the time of his appointment by Governor Neff to the Texas Railroad Commission. At the moment he was on the ballot for an elective term to the same commission. To Hackett and others in the university family, Splawn was a rank *politico;* they very definitely did not want him as their president.

Bolton possibly did wait until he had the letters from Texas of which Hackett had written. At any rate, on Friday June 20 he drafted the following telegram to Stark:

I regret to tell you again that I have decided to remain here with my research and writing - it pains me greatly to disappoint you after your fine courtesy - I realize the superb opportunity there and my best wishes go with you in your efforts to build a university of the first class - I shall let you publish my decision.

This telegram, sent to Stark at Orange, Texas, followed him to New York. From New York's Plaza Hotel the chairman made another attempt to shake Bolton's determination:

Just arrived in New York receiving your telegram and Hackett's letter - would you be willing to try Hackett's suggestion with understanding that you could resign at any time you should find the situation not to your liking - you could consider the matter permanently settled - wire collect.

Bolton, evidently considering the matter closed, does not seem to have replied to this last. On Thursday, June 26, Stark returned to the attack: "Please let me have a reply to my message - four members of Board are here now - all anxious to hear." To this Bolton wired back: "I must repeat my decision to remain here - the one year plan does not seem desirable - the call to Texas is strong but I have obligations and opportunities here also - best personal wishes."

Without knowing of Bolton's telegram to Stark and hoping that he was still "considering," Hackett tried with another fervent plea (June 26):

> Wish could depict gloom of faculty through fear you decline - other man already elected - if you decline education perishes - in a campaign for political office he received yesterday official endorsement of Ku Klux Klan - Hogg hates both politics and Klan - no fellowships - you could in six months save situation and in year lay foundations of imperishable monument - you are called to save education - how can you remain indifferent while it perishes.

Bolton must have had to say no to Stark or someone else still another time, for, when on July 5 he sketched the telegram to be sent to Regent H. A. Wroe, he penciled on the draft "fifth declination." His message read: "I regret to inform you that I have decided to remain here - I have wired Chairman Stark this decision since he left for New York - best regards."

This was the end. Later that same Saturday, acting on orders from Stark, still in New York, Regents Joseph S. Wooten and H. A. Wroe tendered the presidency of the University of Texas to Walter Splawn, who immediately accepted. The next day Hackett sent the front page of the *Statesman* without comment. The news was bannered in the top headline.

Splawn held the post for what has been described as an undistinguished triennium. The 1924 affair did have ultimate good results, for in 1927 the University of Texas inherited an excellent president in the person of Dean Harry Yandell Benedict.

Bolton disappointed many. Later in the month (July 26), writing to an Austin friend, Mrs. Caswell Ellis, about another matter, he added a long paragraph at the end of the letter to explain his action. It is a summary of the reasons for his decision to decline the Texas presidency:

> It is not fair to say that I "turned the University of Texas down." To make the decision which I had to make was a most painful task and I could not escape the pain whichever way I decided. Texas, the University, and friends there have a tremendous appeal. So also have the University of California and my work here. I have been thirteen years here. I feared for Mrs. Bolton's health in that position and in that climate. I am right in the midst of work which no one but myself will ever do. I had to decide between two great opportunities, or obligations, whichever you may call them. With great anguish I decided to stay here. I probably shall have regrets every day as long as I live, but probably would have been the same if I had turned it around.

Word got around the country and some of Bolton's colleagues in the profession commented in letters. His brief reply to Professor St. George Souissat, University of Pennsylvania, became almost a "rubber-stamp" answer. On August 15 he wrote Souissat:

> It was, as you say, very difficult for me to say no to the Texans, but I feared for Mrs. Bolton's health in that climate and that position; on the other hand I could not bring myself to admit that the job on which I have been working for twenty years is not worth sticking to. In other words, I hated to succumb to opportunism.

12

Benefactors, Books, and Baggage

EVEN BEFORE THE TEXAS INTERLUDE the friendship between Herbert Bolton and Sidney Ehrman was ripening. This relationship, based on their mutual interest in California history, most assuredly influenced Bolton's decision to stay in California, for Bolton at long last had found an "angel," a man as interested as himself in making the known and the still unknown materials for the history of California available to students and researchers. Sidney M. Ehrman, a successful San Francisco attorney, had long been fascinated by the story of his California. In Bolton he found a man who could help him fulfill a dream. Precisely how, or when, they became acquainted is not clear; however, it was an ideal pairing: Bolton had the documents, pages and pages of them and most of these very little known, relatively difficult of access to the ordinary writer; Ehrman had the funds and what was highly significant, the public-spirited urge, which was so admirably characteristic of the San Francisco Jewish community of the day. One of the first tips about what was going on showed in a Bolton letter of February 3, 1923, in which he reported to Ehrman that the translation of Palóu's *Noticias* was progressing rapidly — Nellie Vandegrift Sanchez was his coworker.* A few months later (May 9) Bolton informed President Barrows that he had found a man willing to subsidize the publication of "five volumes of American history" — it was his kind of American history, to be sure. He added that these would be the Palóu materials on early California. Bolton's "California period" was just beginning. Following the Palóu volumes in remarkably rapid succession would come the Crespi, the Anza, the Font, and the Knopf imprint of the *Outpost of Empire*.

Ehrman's relationship might have had something about it of the Renaissance prince patron of learning and scholarship, but he made every

---

*Nellie Vandegrift Sanchez will be recognized as the author of *Spanish Arcadia* on California history and has other works to her credit. Less well known is the fact that she was sister-in-law of Robert Louis Stevenson.

effort to keep it from being upsetting or embarrassingly patronizing. There were frequent invitations to Professor and Mrs. Bolton to take dinner at his San Francisco home or to spend a summer week or two at the Ehrman lodge at Lake Tahoe. The Boltons were at Tahoe for five relaxing and pleasant days in the summer of 1925. When everything had been added up, which is not quite possible, the contribution of Ehrman over the years to Bolton's projects would probably reach close to $50,000.

For some time back Bolton had been planning to publish the important document of Arredondo on Georgia-Florida. He had ranged Florida in his line-up of the Spanish Borderlands a few years before and was anxious to show that the area, in truth, did belong. He had put his graduate student Mary Ross to work and their mutual project was well under way about the time that the connection with Ehrman began to develop. Bolton did not want to leave the job only partially completed and told Ehrman that he wished to finish it before giving full attention to the California enterprise. Anxious to see his own project begun, Ehrman generously suggested that a subsidy for the Arredondo might be the answer and promised the same. As a result *Arredondo's Historical Proof of Spain's Title to Georgia: A Contribution to the History of One of the Spanish Borderlands* and its companion volume *The Debatable Land: A Sketch of the Anglo-Spanish Contest for the Georgia Country* were published by the University of California Press in 1925. Not only did Ehrman* pay publication costs, he made it possible for Bolton to send his two Georgia volumes to a number of his friends, "compliments of the author" (the pattern set with the Arredondo Ehrman continued through the years). Turner, as always, was one of those favored, and he wrote Bolton a congratulatory note. Bolton answered August 9 and, among other things, commented in a sentence or two on his concept of the Borderlands:

> Some persons might get the impression that in this book I have roamed a long way from my proper habitat. But you, of course, will know that just as your American frontier ran north and south as a unit, so my Spanish frontier ran east and west, from ocean to ocean, and was a unit.

---

*While speaking of Sidney Ehrman, it might also be noted that Bolton at this time, and through the years, proved a rather adept beggar and was able to interest other men of means in his work, the Department of History, and the Bancroft Library. For instance, there was Juan C. Cebrián who furnished funds to make possible the preparation of a guide to the Spanish-American holdings of the Bancroft and the university library, a valuable bibliographical tool. Cebrián did not stop there; in later years he was most helpful in arranging for Bolton to add to the Bancroft collection of manuscript copies from the archives of Cebrián's native Spain, and later still Don Juan supplemented the university research grants to Bolton, so that he might have a full-time assistant to further his work.

Once again, in writing to his old master, Bolton set down his concept of and approach to history. He was doer rather than theorist: hence, these chance bits are valuable, and many of them were shared with Turner.

The introduction to the Arredondo volume was issued under separate cover as *The Debatable Land*. Editors turned to authorities on the colonial Southeast for an evaluation of the effort. In the *MVHR* (March 1926), James Alexander Robertson expressed pleasure at seeing "his" Border- land recognized; he commended Bolton highly, among other things, for the maps developed for this volume. Excellent maps were being consis- tently noted as a regular feature of Bolton's studies. Verner W. Crane was the choice of the *AHR* editor; after praising many features of the book (October 1925), he closed: "This vivid narrative . . . sustains the reputation of Professor Bolton and his school for sound and enterprising scholarship." For a number of years Bolton himself knew that he was training a "school of historians," but now it was a fact gaining recognition in the profession.

The "California series" came next (1926–31) — Palóu, Crespi, Anza, Font, *Outpost of Empire*. Reviewers found what the profession had come to expect, in any Bolton product, excellence, and they said so in glowing terms.

THE CALIFORNIA PERIOD

The first books published in the "California period" were the four volumes of *Historical Memoirs of New California, By Fray Francisco Palóu, O.F.M.*, coming out in 1926. Besides smaller gifts to assist in the preparation of the manuscript, Sidney Ehrman bore the full cost of the printing to the extent of $6000. These volumes were a notable contribu- tion to sources available on the early history of California and were uni- versally hailed as such by reviewers. Also assisting Bolton with the Palóu translation were Lydia Lothrop, successor to Nellie Vandegrift Sanchez, and Mary M. Blake, in Mexico City, as copier and verifier. The volumes were published by the University of California Press.

With the Palóu Bolton tried something which worked so successfully that he tried it several times later. When he edited this lengthy "Noticias de la Nueva California," he prefaced the translation with a long, orginial historical introduction. Feeling that many individuals might not be able to afford the larger set, he asked the press to issue the historical introduc- tion as a separate small volume. *Palóu and His Writings* proved a distinct success.

The next volume published in the "California period" was *Fray Juan Crespi, Missionary Explorer on the Pacific Coast, 1769–1774*, issued in

1927. Bolton was already looking forward to telling the full story of the Portolá party en route to found Alta California.

In early June of the same year the Crespi was published, Sidney Ehrman was once again in contact with Bolton, this time by letter. He wrote: "Will you accept the enclosed honorarium [there is no clue to what the amount of the check was] as a very slight evidence of my appreciation for your splendid work? It has been a genuine pleasure for me to have humbly assisted in presenting it." Bolton was abashed and hesitated to accept. In a letter dated June 5 Bolton indicated that he would accept but only that he might proceed immediately with work on the Anza volumes and thus be able to put aside another task which had seemed more proper, but much less attractive and tantalizing:

> As you know for several years I have had lying on my desk the first draft of a college textbook covering the ground of my course in the History of the Americas. Half a dozen publishers have been on my wings begging permission to publish the book and promising fabulous royalties. The originality of my book, the crying demand for a book on which to base an introductory course in Western Hemisphere history, and the evident needs of my family, have made it Quixotic, if not sinful, not to set aside temporarily those things which you and I love to do, and which are certain to have permanent value for scholarship. It would take me a year, or perhaps more, to complete the other book. I hate to think of setting aside Anza. . . .

The Ehrman assistance was evidently substantial enough to cause him to set aside the Americas draft and to turn all his writer's energy to Anza, for that is what he did. The editing of the California documents or others was always the "dessert" in Bolton's scholarship.*

With the Anza story Bolton had a first real chance to put into practice a technique which was to be one of the very distinctive and characteristic marks of his later writing, which he would use on the Kino, the Coronado, and the Escalante. He would try to combine field work with manuscript study. In a word he followed his heroes on the trail, with document or diary in hand. He retraced their expeditions and movements step by step, summer after summer, during semester breaks and Christmas holidays, or whenever he could find the time and had the funds to indulge this passion for exactness. Some of the trips were relatively short — ten days or so — such as that of Christmastide 1926 when he went to Sonora, Mexico, to trail Juan Bautista de Anza along his route to California, out of that Mexican province which had been his home base. Again in 1927–28

---

*Bolton talked often of the textbook on the history of the Americas, but never did get around to finishing what he always called "Mama's book," that one which might have paid "fabulous royalties."

Herbert Bolton in 1920, digging at site of Carmel Mission, California.

he was in the field with Frank C. Lockwood of the University of Arizona, tracing the path Anza had followed with Fray Francisco Garcés in 1774, the "short cut." Like Anza, Bolton and his party went from Tubac to Caborca, thence along the treacherous and trying "Camino del Diablo" to Sonoita and Yuma. After doing that Devil's Highway stretch, even with modern helps, Bolton had no difficulty in seeing why the shrewd Anza chose the longer way — from Tubac down the Santa Cruz valley to the Gila and down the Gila to the Colorado junction — when in the next year, 1775, he was commissioned to deliver his company of pioneer settlers to the Bay of San Francisco.

Herbert Bolton, shown here with a guide, traveled at times as collaborator-at-large for the National Park Service. Such travel enhanced his writing as well as his teaching.

Returning from his Sonora-Arizona excursion Bolton made a careful accounting of his expenses to the university comptroller, since this trip, like many other California-related expeditions, was to be paid for from the Ehrman Fund — the total came to $777.58. Next, in the way of finishing up, he wrote to Lockwood and asked him to please make peace with the Mexican consul at Tucson, against another day when they might again need this official's goodwill and kindly services; after traveling the Devil's Highway, they had crossed the border at a point other than their original port of entry at Nogales.

Bolton had hoped that the Anza volumes would be ready before the end of the decade. They had top priority on his work schedule in 1928 and into 1929, apart from his administrative responsibilities and classes. Although several of the five volumes were ready, it was 1930 before the last of them came off the press. Sidney Ehrman turned over to the regents of the university the munificent sum of $12,000 to defray printing and publication costs. The five-volume set, *Anza's California Expeditions,* was a triumph. The next year the companion volume, *Font's Complete Diary: A Chronicle of the Founding of San Francisco,* completed the California series. In 1931 the introduction to the Anza volumes would appear under the Knopf imprint as *Outpost of Empire: The Story of the Founding of San Francisco.* Bolton and Sidney Ehrman had other plans for the future, but the "California period" was at an end.

HELP FROM MORE ANGELS

As director for the Bancroft, Bolton was more or less regularly confronted with some tempting piece or pieces which he should have liked to be able to acquire for the Bancroft collection. What the Bancroft needed was a Sidney Ehrman — someone financially interested in seeing it become a great depository of bits and chunks of California history. Such was the situation in 1927 when the Bancroft was offered a sizable file of early California newspapers. But the library was next to penniless. Bolton went to work. Some time before he had had contact with Paul Bancroft, one of Hubert Howe Bancroft's sons. Paul Bancroft had expressed some interest in further developing his father's collection. Bolton remembered this and decided to see just how interested he might be. He was gratified when Bancroft sent a check for the $1000 which Bolton had hinted would put the newspaper file in the Bancroft collection. Bolton thanked him: "It will add another item to the remarkable collection which your father collected with such wisdom and judgment." On March 5, 1927, with the air of a successful bargainer, Bolton informed Bancroft that he had been able to get the newspapers for $850 and asked what was to be done with the remaining $150. To his deep satisfaction Bancroft came back to suggest that the "profit" should go into the acquisitions fund.

Emboldened by his success with Paul Bancroft, Bolton decided to try his luck with another potential "angel." Some time before he had talked with Templeton Crocker, of another old California family. He had hopes of involving Crocker in a project complementary to that which Sidney Ehrman was backing. Ehrman's love was Spanish California; Bolton hoped that Crocker might become interested in making the major documents of American California available to scholars and students, at least for the earlier period. Accordingly, June 6, he wrote Crocker: "I realize that you have many temptations of this kind. But I think of no work more likely to give you satisfaction, because it falls in with the great interest you have always taken in early California history." The specific prize which he was dangling before Crocker was a proposed two-volume edition of the Sutter Papers, which his student Clarence DuFour had well under way toward readiness for publication. Bolton sent off his come-on letter and sat back to see what might happen.

Ten days later on June 15 Crocker came back with a short note, in which he first congratulated Bolton on the edition of Palóu and then continued:

> Regarding the publication of the work connected with the American Pioneers, I regret that I do not feel able to undertake the matter myself at this moment. If you will let me know approximately, what

the cost would be for the work connected with the Sutter Papers, I will see if I cannot get some of my friends' interest sufficiently aroused to project it.

Bolton answered immediately (June 16), telling him that it would be difficult to estimate definite costs; however, he set $3000 as the likely bill for the printing of "two fine volumes"; in addition, he noted, he would have to supplement DuFour's income, and this would run around $2000. He noted that the Native Sons had already authorized assignment to DuFour of a fellowship stipend for 1927–28 of $1500. Therefore, he set $5000 as the tab for the Sutter proposal. Part of the money subsequently was given.

When his patron Sidney M. Ehrman gave $12,000 to publish the Anza volumes, the history-minded San Francisco attorney could have very justifiably concluded that he had paid adequate tribute to Clio. But 1931 brought a still more generous gift. Son Sidney (Tod) had inherited some of his father's love and esteem for history. The occasional visits of Bolton to the Ehrman home and to the Ehrman summer place at Lake Tahoe helped to stimulate this interest. Tod Ehrman had enrolled at the University of California, majored in history, gone on to graduate work, and taken a master's degree — European history was his field of interest. Study in England was his next step. While there he became suddenly ill and died quickly, baffling the best medical minds his father could assemble. Deeply grieved, Sidney Ehrman cast about for a way to keep his son's memory alive in the Department of History which he had loved. In March 1931 he established and endowed the Sidney Hellman Ehrman Chair of European History. James Westfall Thompson would be the first appointee, in January 1933.

EUROPE AT LAST

The makings for still another worthwhile project for some as yet unknown benefactors came about unexpectedly in the early summer of 1930. Bolton had made his annual report to the Grand Parlor of the Native Sons, telling of the work of Charles Nowell and George Tays, traveling fellows of 1929–30, and nominating Helen Carr and Vernon Tate as candidates for 1930–31. At this point, it seems, that either the history chairman or the committee told him not to worry about a 1931–32 appointment. Because of the Depression Bolton naturally concluded that this was to be the end of the NSGW fellowships and saw this source of aid to his graduate students being terminated. He was both relieved and surprised when he was informed that he was to be the 1931–32 traveling fellow of the Native Sons of the Golden West. They had decided that the master himself should be a belated beneficiary of their generosity. Not only was he the chosen recipient, he was to be granted the dual stipend, $3000. A dream he had long cherished could now be realized. He recognized, however, that he would hardly be able to spend an entire year off campus; among other considerations the NSGW grant would certainly not be adequate to allow him to fulfill his obligations to his family without his university salary. He explained his predicament but agreed that he would be able to spend a long summer abroad, from mid-May to mid-August. The Native Sons saw the problem and willingly sanctioned such an arrangement. He immediately began long-range planning to make the best of those 1931 summer months. In due time he began to request letters of introduction which might facilitate entrée into archives and libraries which he planned to visit in Spain, Italy, and Holland. He asked for a letter from his friend Archbishop Edward Hanna of San Francisco — he and His Excellency, the archbishop, had often exchanged letters and on occasion Bolton was Hanna's guest at dinner. That letter would open doors in Rome. Vitally interested as he was in the Jesuits of New Spain and already putting together his biography of their Padre Kino, he wanted to be sure that Jesuit doors, too, would be open. He asked Father Edward J. Whelan, president of the Jesuit University of San Francisco, for a similar passport.

As he contemplated the months ahead, he had another reassuring prospect. Helen Carr, who had worked with him and for the department during several previous years, was currently in Spain as a Native Sons fellow. She wrote that she had materials spotted for him in the Archivo de Indias, especially Kino pieces and others in which she felt that he would be particularly interested. This sort of help would stretch his summer weeks, which were already, as he recognized, far too few for all he wished to accomplish.*

Bolton left Berkeley on May 13, 1931.[1] He sailed from New York on May 19, aboard the S. S. *Europa*. He debarked at Cherbourg and hurried quickly through France to Seville and the Archivo General de las Indias. He spent thrilling days there and at other Spanish archives, all of which

---

*Departmental secretaries played a large part in Bolton's life at California. First there was May Corcoran; next came the very efficient Marjorie Clark and Mrs. Wallace. Later in the 1920s Helen Carr held the position until she became an NSGW fellow and then Bolton's research assistant; she was succeeded by the first of the Fessenden sisters, Ellen, and then by Josephine ("Jodee" to the generations of the 1930s). Maxine Chappell then was first departmental secretary and next, during the retirement years, Bolton's assistant. In later years Bolton was assisted by Virginia Thickens and Margaret Mollins. One and all were integral to his academic life on campus.

he knew so well, but secondhand. He went on to Barcelona, whence he took a quick side trip to see Majorca, Fray Junípero Serra's island. Days in Rome were interesting. The next stop was the Kino country, rugged Tyrol; he visited Segno, his Black Robe's birthplace, and talked with a number of the Kino (Chini) family still living thereabouts. He crossed into Bavaria where Kino had spent his young years as a Jesuit in training, along with other non-Spanish Jesuits who would later show in the Spanish Borderlands. Bolton tarried a few days in Belgium en route to Holland and the central Jesuit archive at Valkenburg. In those days what the Jesuits had been able to salvage of their pre-1773 records was housed in safe and neutral Holland — this archive has more recently been transferred to Rome. At Valkenburg Bolton found not only a very warm reception, but more importantly many things of great use to his studies of the Black Robes of colonial Mexico. He took some copies and earmarked many more, to be copied as soon as he could amass the necessary funds. As he wrote to Mrs. Bolton and those at home, he considered the too few days at Valkenburg one of the highlights of his trip. Time, however, was running out. London was his last stop. In early August he sailed for New York, on the S. S. *Samaria*. He was back in Berkeley for the opening of the new semester.

As quickly as he could, he began to canvass his good friends, telling them of all the new materials he had seen in Europe and slyly underlining Bancroft's lack of funds for the acquisition thereof. The ploy worked — Allen Chickering, Mrs. Fred Bixby, and Mrs. Edwina Bryant put several hundred dollars at his disposal for Bancroft copies. He also had another sort of begging to do, and again was successful. On returning he found to his dismay that the university budget committee had allotted only half of the $1800 which he had requested for a research assistant. He turned to Juan Cebrián, who had helped him before, and explained his predicament. Cebrián not only made up the difference for that year but was also equally generous in the following; the good man was truly appreciative of what Bolton was doing to bring notice of his fellow Spaniards' exploits in colonial North America to the American public.* The confidence shown in Bolton by Cebrián and the Native Sons was indicative of the reputation which he had acquired by 1931, not only in his own state, but nationally and internationally as well.

---

*Bolton's first assistant was Helen Carr, back from Spain, and, when she went onto part-time basis in the second semester, he enlisted Theodore Treutlein. The latter worked for him full-time the next year and, thanks to his wide language competence, proved most helpful. Bolton could handle the Spanish of his new materials, and also the German, but in Latin and Italian he was not comfortable.

13

At the Top
of His Field

B Y THE MIDDLE 1920s Herbert Bolton was universally recognized as *the* authority on the story of the Spaniards in North America. Students from all over the country were heading to Berkeley, in order to study under his direction. About this time he was receiving his first international recognition. Others within his profession consulted him on Borderlands problems and projects. An excellent case in point shows in a long letter of September 10, 1925, to France V. Scholes. Illinois-born and Harvard-educated, Scholes found himself, for reasons of health, in the Southwest and one year in the Department of History at the University of New Mexico. He wanted to work in the history of his adopted state and had recurred to the "master" for suggestions, stating a preference for the colonial period. Bolton took great pains and time to encourage what to him was a highly laudable ambition. He cited George P. Winship and others who had covered the Coronado period; he called attention to John Lloyd Mecham who had written of the Rodríguez-Chamuscado and the Espejo-Beltrán expeditions; he mentioned that George Hammond was even then in process of "founding" New Mexico with Juan de Oñate; he noted that Charles Wilson Hackett had told the story which almost "ended" New Mexico in his study of the Pueblo Revolt, and he further told Scholes that work was under way, at Berkeley, on the reconquest. There remained, he pointed out, two major gaps in coverage, the period between Oñate and the Revolt, and the eighteenth-century era after Vargas (this last he observed would be full of Indians and have a bit of French seasoning). Scholes, as is well known, opted for the "middle period" of the seventeenth century and became the authority and a ranking name in the Borderlands field.* There were later exchanges between the two, and Bolton liked to refer to Scholes as one of his "adopted boys."

---

*A number of Scholes' students arranged to have the January 1971 number of *The Americas* (XXVII, no. 3) dedicated to him and therein placed seven excellent studies inspired by him. There is a certain amount of biographical data, but, unfortunately, no formal bibliography of his many writings.

The isolated incident of the Scholes matter points to the unique reputation that Bolton was acquiring as "*the* man to go to." Many of the students who had started out in his History of the Americas class at Berkeley had already long established themselves in the field. Bolton's approach to history had been published in skeletal form, at least, in 1928 in *History of the Americas: A Syllabus*. It had been well enough received that publisher Ginn & Company suggested a revised edition which appeared in 1935. When the syllabus was first published Bolton got many letters of thanks and congratulations from his colleagues across the country. Some of them, such as Isaac J. Cox, formerly at Cincinnati and then at Northwestern, had introduced the Americas approach into their classrooms.

In the early 1930s it can be said that Bolton reached the top of his profession. At home, university authorities in May of 1931 named him to the Sather Chair. For a long time the Sather Professorship had been the department's only endowed chair, given years before by Jane Sather to honor her father, Peder Sather — this along with the famous Sather Gate and the Campanile. The first Sather Professor had been Morse Stephens. University authorities had allowed the chair to remain vacant after Stephens' death, but now, in 1931, they seemed to feel that Bolton had grown to adequate stature. The Sather Professorship paid $9000. That same year Bolton's national colleagues voted him the highest honor they could bestow on a member of their own profession. They named him vice-president of the American Historical Association, which meant automatic succession to the top spot the next year.*

In late summer 1932 he began planning his presidential address. He decided to talk on "The Other Jesuits in North America." This, he felt, would give him the opportunity to note the fact that Francis Parkman in *The Jesuits in North America* had been too sweeping with that title, leaving out the Spanish story altogether. When he applied to the university for travel funds (October 7), he was evidently still determined on that same topic, for he listed "The Jesuits of New Spain" as the subject of his proposed presidential address. Sometime thereafter came the shift. A couple of years later he confessed to Peter Guilday (September 8, 1934):

> When I prepared my presidential address for the Toronto meeting it was at first my plan to write a paper on "The Other Jesuits in

---

*Actually, 1931 was the third year Bolton had been considered for the vice-presidency: the first time was in 1921 when Bolton had assured the committee that he would gladly defer to Woodrow Wilson — former professor, president of Princeton, as well as former President of the United States; the second nomination had gone in 1928 to Ephraim Douglas Adams, Bolton's long-time friend and his department chairman at Stanford.

North America" — I had sketched out the first part of the address but later decided that "The Epic of Greater America" would be more suitable for an international meeting.

Evidently he came to feel that it would be more gracious to pay tribute to the host nation by putting Canada into proper focus among the twenty-odd Americas. There may also have been the thought that the Toronto rostrum offered a banner opportunity to give wide exposure to his cherished "approach" to American history.

Toward the end of November he was informed that the University of Toronto planned to confer on him a Doctor of Laws degree, at the time of the AHA meeting in December. This would be his third honorary degree. The first had been an LL.D. degree presented by St. Mary's College of California (Moraga), when in June 1929 Bolton had been invited to be commencement speaker; the second had come in October 1930 from Saint Ignatius College (University of San Francisco). This third degree was conferred at a special convocation of the University of Toronto, which immediately preceded the "presidential session" of the AHA. There would be five other similar honorary degrees in his lifetime.

Chester Martin read the long citation presenting Bolton to University Chancellor H. J. Cody:

> At the request of the Senate of the University of Toronto I present to you that he may receive at your hands the degree of Doctor of Laws, honoris causa, this distinguished and well-learned man, Herbert Eugene Bolton. . . . On this first occasion on which the American Historical Association has met outside the boundaries of the Great Republic, and within the gates of this University, the University of Toronto desires to confer its highest honour upon the head of the Association. . . .
>
> The University desires not only to honour the American Historical Association through its president, but also honour that President (and honour itself) because of his personal achievements and leadership in the field of historical study. Herbert Eugene Bolton, who now holds the office of president of this Association, is one of the outstanding historians of our day. . . . President Bolton is by common consent an inspiring teacher who communicates to his pupils a genuine enthusiasm for historical research and historical writing. He believes in youth, and in their sanity of mind and body, in their wider outlook, in the opportunities they will have and make, and this faith is justified by results. His ardour, his almost boyish energy, and his personal friendliness make friends and disciples of his students, and yet he does not submerge their independence by his wealth of knowledge. But more than this, Professor Bolton has really been the founder of a historical school that has devoted its special attention to the influence of Spain in America. The Spanish colonial

empire, which even more than a century and a half ago was
richer and more imposing than that of France and England, has
found its interpretation in this school of historical scholarship, in the
United States, of which Doctor Bolton has been the acknowledged
and inspiring leader. Latin America, in southern and central America, and in the Southwestern United States, has been his special field
of investigation. He has really blazed a new trail of historical investigation. . . . And now Professor Bolton is carrying his studies into a
still higher realm. He is seeking to make a synthesis of these various
influences which have contributed to the making of this continent. If
the purpose of Hispanic American history has been to enlarge the
horizon of American history, so as to include the whole continent, it
is obvious that the place of Canada in this picture has yet to be considered. This is one of the particular features of interest that Professor Bolton's work suggests to us. His work in enlarging the bounds
of "American" history can have its repercussion in these northern
regions of the continent. . . .

To this long encomium, parts of which interestingly would serve as an
introduction to his own address, Bolton responded with sincere thanks.

With these formalities concluded, the university convocation
adjourned and the meeting of the American Historical Association was
declared in session. Bolton expected to be next, but there was a part of
the program about which he had no knowledge.

A group of Bolton's former students had their own tribute for the master, "a handsome work in two volumes, *New Spain and the Anglo-American West,* a collection of source materials with introductory essays and
annotations." His "boys" and Mary Ross had been planning this Festschrift for many months. George P. Hammond and Charles W. Hackett
were the editors, and Mary Ross had carefully compiled the long list of
Bolton's writings for inclusion therein. This tribute meant more to Bolton
than the Toronto degree, the AHA presidency, and most other things
which had happened to him. After his return to Berkeley he expressed his
gratitude to the contributors:

I feel most apologetic for not telling you before how deeply I
appreciated your part in the presentation volumes prepared by my
students for the Toronto meeting of the American Historical Association. The idea was most generous of them, and a tribute which I
prize more highly than I can express.

As you well know, there is no phase of my work that I value so
much as my association with my students. It is with them that I find
my most satisfactory fellowship. Young men and women are open
minded and forward looking. I am an optimist because I believe
young men and women worth teaching. A pessimist in the teaching
profession must be essentially dishonest, pretending to do something
he does not believe in.

Then the important moment in the professional life of the historian named to the AHA presidency had come. Bolton rose and quipped pleasantly:

> This afternoon, in the business meeting, when I announced there would be no speech making, everybody cheered. I am sorry, both for your sake and my own, that I am not permitted to make the same announcement now. Unfortunately, the preparation of a presidential address is part of the price one must pay for the great honor of being president of the American Historical Association. It would not be so bad if there were only one sufferer.

Bolton's address, "The Epic of Greater America," was in reality his History of the Americas course condensed to an appropriate length for a presidential address. The secretary of the AHA summarized it in his report of the meeting (*AHR*, XXXVIII, 435):

> The theme of the presidential address of Herbert E. Bolton, of the University of California, was especially appropriate in a meeting on Canadian soil, where uppermost in thought were the historical relations of two great countries of North America, for it was a masterly synthesis of the development of the Western Hemisphere. Dr. Bolton presented a point of view which should correct our perspectives in considering the history of the Americas, South as well as North.

The whole meeting left Bolton with many memories, mostly joyous, but there was a moment of sadness. At the business session, over which he presided, two of his former professors, dead in 1932, were briefly memorialized. Ulrich B. Phillips paid tribute to Frederick Jackson Turner, who had helped make Bolton a historian; Frederic L. Paxson did the same for John Bach McMaster, who had guided Bolton's doctoral dissertation at the University of Pennsylvania.

The weeks after the return from Toronto Bolton felt a certain sense of malaise. A hint of what may have been troubling him comes from a letter of January 31 to Walter H. Sage, University of British Columbia, in which he remarked that he had heard "very few echoes" from his Toronto address. To friend Eugene Barker he confided the next day: "I have heard very few echoes from my speech and the silence is somewhat ominous." Evidently he expected the enthusiasm of the AHA members (423 had been present) to match his own for the "Americas approach."

Actually this address to the American Historical Association in time became the basis of a major controversy revolving around Bolton's "Americas approach." Later critics would use it as evidence of what they termed the "Bolton thesis." In 1939 when "The Epic of Greater America" was reprinted in *Wider Horizons of American History,** Arthur Preston Whitaker took the opportunity to voice some of his reactions and those of others in the profession in the *Mississippi Valley Historical Review* (December 1939):

> As the reviewer re-read the essays in the volume, the features of Professor Bolton's work which stood out most clearly were, first, his insistence upon the need for the study of American history in a continental or "hemispheric" sense of the term, and, second, his gallant effort to right the wrongs which Latin America has long suffered at the hands of historians in this and other countries.
>
> While most of what Professor Bolton has said in these essays will doubtless command general agreement among historians, there are some features of his scheme of American history which seem to require revision or a shift of emphasis. For instance, his assertion of the "essential unity of the Western Hemisphere" and "fundamental Western Hemisphere solidarity" in the period since independence may be a fine ideal for the future but it is hardly an accurate description of the past. Again, he is sometimes carried away by his enthusiasm for the Latin American cause; and in the Latin American field his main·interest lies in Spanish America rather than Brazil, and in Mexico and the borderlands rather than Spanish South America. This is illuminated by the fact that three of the four essays relate to Mexico and the borderlands. It is also illustrated by his statement that "till the end of the eighteenth century . . . Mexico City was the metropolis of the entire Western Hemisphere" — a statement that would not be accepted at Bahía or Rio de Janeiro or Lima any more than at Boston or Philadelphia or Quebec.

After these and similar observations Whitaker concluded in considerably more tempered vein:

> Whether or not one agrees with Professor Bolton on these questions and others the specialists might raise, there can be no doubt that the sum total of his achievement as represented by these essays is one of high order and richly entitles him to the enviable position that he holds among American historians. His frequently demonstrated talent for grasping the larger significance of local history has set a high standard for scholars engaged in that kind of work.

---

*Also included in *Wider Horizons of American History,* published by Appleton-Century, were three other of Bolton's most notable essays: "The Mission as a Frontier Institution in the Spanish-American Colonies"; "Defensive Expansion and the Significance of the Borderlands," the main address of a conference on Western history at the University of Colorado, Boulder, in 1929; and "The Black Robes of New Spain," an address given at the 1934 meeting of the American Catholic Historical Association.

This "unity of the Americas" idea was one point with which many in the profession disagreed. After December 1932 he himself betimes regretted one or other sweeping statement made in his AHA presidential address, when he was caught up in the enthusiasm of trying to sell his Americas approach to his colleagues. In 1940 this "unity of the Americas" idea became the topic for one of the sessions at the December meeting of the American Historical Association. Later still, Lewis Hanke gathered the papers of that meeting into one of the volumes of the Borzoi Books on Latin America — *Do the Americas Have a Common History?*[1] The book was introduced by a somewhat tendentious discussion by the editor and published in 1964. Once more the myth of the "Bolton thesis" was resurrected. Bolton hardly thought of his American approach as a thesis. It was not something which he set out to prove; it was primarily a way of looking at all-American history from a broader perspective than that of restrictive nationalism which so often ended in warped vision and distorted interpretation.

Through the middle years of the twentieth century there were several studies published on the writing of American history and the men who wrote it. Harry Elmer Barnes was broader in his coverage than simply the writing of American history, but he had the following observation to make:

> E. G. Bourne and Herbert Eugene Bolton brought a new perspective into the study of colonial history by joining Prescott's interests with exact scholarship and emphasizing the importance of Spanish colonization for the early history of North America.[2]

In 1952 came *American History and American Historians* by H. Hale Bellot:

> The Southwestern and California school, of which the leader is Professor H. E. Bolton, working in the area in which the social foundations are Spanish, finds itself driven to make of American history more than the history of the United States.[3]

Michael Kraus, in his chapter "Frontier and Sectional Historians," devoted considerable space to Bolton and his school, ranking him right after Turner in order of importance:

> The way of the frontier has not always been from East to West; in the very earliest days of our history it was from South to North. In the study of New Spain's contributions to American history no one has done more important work than Herbert Eugene Bolton. Beginning with the exploration of Mexican archives, he enlarged the field of investigation to include materials of the homeland in Spain to

round out his story of the Spanish Borderlands in North America. Going beyond his preceptors, McMaster and Turner, Bolton proclaimed the epic of greater America in which the essential unity of American history, North and South, has been stressed; his has been literally a history of the Americas, not merely the story of the expansion of thirteen colonies into a nation. His researches in anthropology, cartography, and history took him all over lands once part of Spain's empire in North America.

In a textbook, *The Colonization of North America, 1492–1783* . . . written with Thomas M. Marshall, Bolton gave the key to his point of view. More emphasis was placed on non-English colonies and on those English colonies which were not among the original thirteen. . . . Bolton stimulated many students to follow the paths he trod himself, and the historian who would gain more than an Anglo-American viewpoint on our history, must read the works of this teacher and his disciples.[4]

Harvey Wish commented in his book on the American historian:

> In the Far West, Herbert E. Bolton . . . trained Western historians to transcend the Anglo-American synthesis of Turner with an Anglo-French and Anglo-Spanish viewpoint based on archives in Paris, Madrid, and Mexico City, as well as collections within the United States. The interaction of the Americas as a unit absorbed his attention and became one of his most popular academic lectures. In this spirit he wrote several volumes on the significance of the Spanish Borderlands in the light of frontier conditions, the colonization of North America, and the advance of the Spanish conquistadors like Coronado or missionaries like Father Kino, ever stressing the role of geography, topography, and anthropology.[5]

Midway through the decade of the 1960s the conceptualists were riding the wave of popularity in the interpretation of American history and speaking condescendingly of most everything which had been done up until that point. One member of that persuasion, in 1965, evaluated Bolton in the following paragraph:

> At the University of California, whose specialists in Latin American history made it a leading center of study, Herbert E. Bolton developed after 1911 the dominant school in the United States. He attracted many students into research on Spanish soldiers and missionaries in the borderlands, where Spanish settlement impinged on that of other empires. Those studies gave Bolton the idea that all of the Americas have a unitary history shaped by common experience. Every year he preached this pan-Americanism to a thousand students in his course on the History of the Americas, and his numerous disciples took up the refrain. Bolton lacked the analytical ability to make his concept fruitful; he gave a specious appearance of significance to a program of fragmentary research.[6]

Interestingly, the writer shows his "fragmentary" knowledge of Bolton and his work. Acquaintance with the second Festschrift of Bolton's students, *Greater America,* reveals that the master's interest and direction went far beyond "research on Spanish soldiers and missionaries in the borderlands." Indeed, Bolton's "pan-Americanism" was less an attempt to prove "unitary history shaped by common experience" than to broaden the American student's understanding and appreciation by exposure to an American past less than predominantly Anglo in its data and embrace. Bolton has survived such misinterpretation and misunderstanding.

In spite of the controversy which subsequently developed over Bolton's American Historical Association address, few could disprove his singular position as the authority in the area of Spain in North America. This was the position he had earned for himself by the early 1930s. By this time his reputation had exceeded even national boundaries. Twice in his lifetime he was recipient of international recognition — first from King Alfonzo XIII of Spain in 1926 who named him Knight Commander of the Order of Isabela la Católica for his twenty-odd years of teaching and writing about the Spaniards and their enterprise in the Americas, and second from the King of Italy, who in December 1931 made him Knight Commander of the Crown of Italy.

14

His Favorite
Black Robe

B OLTON HAD FIRST BECOME acquainted with Padre Eusebio Francisco Kino in 1907, and, of all places, in the Archivo General de la
Nación, Mexico City. There he had uncovered one of the padre's
very intimate writings, almost a diary, which told of long years on New
Spain's northwestern frontier of Pimería Alta. When Bolton blew off the
dust of decades and opened the *legajo* to read its title page, he at once recognized the significance of his find. All the experts said that this manuscript,
"Favores Celestiales," was long since lost, and some of them doubted that
it ever existed. But here it was. And, as Bolton read, out of the pages
emerged a man so remarkable that he had to have been one of the greatest frontiersmen of Spain's northward advance.[1] A dozen years later
Arthur Clark had published Bolton's translation of this manuscript, but
even then Bolton knew that he was not through with Kino; he would not
be finished until he had told the padre's fuller story in a full-length biography. He had already begun to gather Kino materials and remained
always on the watch for more. During the 1920s he had been busy with
other Borderlands stories, but Kino was always on his mind and the subject of numerous field trips which he sandwiched into his schedule frequently. By 1931 he had his desk cleared of most immediate business and
could concentrate on the man who had become "his favorite Black Robe."

As already detailed, Kino was very much a central figure in his European summer of 1931; likewise, he was the subject of numerous shorter
trips into northern Mexico, Sonora, and Baja California. In December
1929 while in Mexico City on other business* he had had the opportunity

---

*Bolton was sent to Mexico City at university expense in December 1929 for
the purpose of assessing a collection of books and manuscripts offered to the University of California for purchase and for inclusion in the Bancroft Library. The asking
price for the Monday Collection was $50,000; Bolton suggested its value to the

[190]

to survey the western slope of the Sierra Madre Mountains. From Mexico City he had taken a train to Culiacán, where he rented a car, and then worked his way up the "camino real" for five days, to Hermosillo, Sonora. This gave him the opportunity to follow the path of the Black Robes northward across their "four rivers" up to the Río Sonora to the lower reaches of Pimería Alta, or Kino country.

In the early 1930s as Bolton seriously set to work on the Kino biography he had at least two other opportunities to trace the steps of his favorite Black Robe. The first was a May–June 1932 trip — another "Kino reconnaissance." With son Herbert along as companion and driver, Bolton saw Mazatlán and Guaymas, Gulf ports familiar to the Black Robe, the peninsula where he had his first missionary experience, and then points in Sonora. The auto mileage for the junket totaled 2,390 miles, and there were other miles by water and by train.[2]

Bolton requested funds for the second trip from the Social Science Research Council (February 9, 1933) — this time intending to cover the northern reaches of the eastern slope of the Sierra Madres where the Jesuits had toiled. His request to the council was too late, but with a university research grant a year later, Bolton and his son were again off to Sonora and northern Mexico. Between March 22 and May 7, 1934, the two drove 5,904 miles; they took two difficult jumps by local air service, and traveled a couple more stretches by horse and burro. After covering the eastern slope they crossed over to the country around Cananea, went down through the historic Valle de Sonora, and came back into the United States at Nogales. Bolton was in and out of Parral several times and arranged to have a thousand or so pages of manuscripts from that rich archive copied for his own and his students' use. It was only after these trips of filling in the gaps in his acquaintance with the "West Coast Corridor" and eastern slope of the Sierra Madre Mountains that Bolton felt he could speak about Kino and the other Jesuits fully confident of having come as close as possible to experiencing something of their adventures.

As fascinating and gigantic as Kino was, Bolton constantly saw him as part of a team — that whole Jesuit band which had missioned both slopes of the western Sierra Madre Mountains northward into Arizona and had set up a complementary advancing line across the Gulf on the barren peninsula of California. They all fitted into that segment of the Borderlands story. He wanted to know more about them and to write

---

Bancroft would be closer to $5000, since the library already had in its possession a good two-thirds of the printed materials offered. This was his recommendation to President Campbell (February 6, 1930) and some months later to Nathan Van Patten, Stanford librarian, when that institution received the same offer.

about them all; in a very manageable way they showed how the mission was a frontier institution par excellence of the Spanish empire in America.

The whole Jesuit story, in turn, was only part of the larger work Bolton had been preparing for years — the story of the Spaniards in North America. He told new University of California president Robert Gordon Sproul* of his long-range plan in a letter March 31, 1931:

> For many years I have been preparing to write a synthesis and interpretation of the history of Spanish North America. It will embrace the old administrative unit called New Spain, including the Isthmus, Central America, and the northern Borderlands, from discovery to the end of the Spanish rule about 1822. I hope to do for New Spain something like Parkman did for New France. But my account will be not nearly so long as his because I am more concerned with interpretation and synthesis than with narrative detail. Moreover, like every sound interpretation, it must rest on thorough research. Anything else would be guess work.

During his inter-semester vacation in December 1930 and into January 1931 Bolton had taken a quick turn through Central America. He had long ago learned that the history of the Spaniards in North America had really begun when Balboa and the rest first settled on the narrow strip of the Isthmus of Panama in 1509. Even if the little republics were not as closely tied with the history of the Pacific Slope as was Mexico, these provinces did figure in the story. He was anxious to add this chunk of geography to his fund of on-the-ground experience. He planned to use it immediately in his classes and, ultimately, to give greater authenticity to this overall story of Spain in America which he wanted one day to write.

The second semester 1933–34 he was on leave, once again, working on his "Spaniards in North America" project. The university had given him $500, under History Grant No. 401, which was going to be sort of a magic number in his academic bookkeeping of the 1930s. The Social Sci-

---

*Robert Gordon Sproul succeeded Campbell as president of the University of California in 1930. He was pulled out of the comptroller's office to succeed him. Bolton heartily approved of this decision. Through the next years he and Sproul became fast friends, the two men having great respect for one another. Bolton felt secure with an understanding and sympathetic leader at the top; Sproul was very much aware of the strength of Bolton on campus and of his prestige in national academic circles. In general Bolton was fortunate in the university presidents under whom he served at Berkeley. Wheeler appreciated him quickly; he and Barrows were sound friends, even though there were disagreements; Sproul was warm and supportive; only with Campbell did he feel something of a strain, but in this he was far from singular.

ence Research Council was equally generous, so that he might have a research assistant. Theodore Treutlein, who was finishing his doctoral dissertation, continued through the year in that capacity.

Summer 1934 Bolton took a break from his work on the Kino biography to play with these broader aspects of the Black Robe story in the north. By September he decided that he was ready to put together the Jesuit chapter of his projected larger work on the Spaniards in North America. He further decided that he would like to try it on a live audience and thought that a session of the American Catholic Historical Association, which regularly met concurrently with the AHA, might be an ideal sounding board. Accordingly, he wrote Peter Guilday, executive director of the American Catholic Historical Association, and offered the paper. Guilday replied with enthusiasm. His paper, presented in December 1934, was entitled "The Black Robes of New Spain."[3]

A hint of what Bolton was trying to do in his Jesuit studies comes in a report to Graduate Dean Charles B. Lipman, in November 1934. Lipman had asked for a detailed report from the various grantees around the university who were operating, in whole or in part, with funds from Project 11 of the University of California's Institute of Social Sciences. Some of Bolton's moneys came from that source; therefore, he complied, and with considerable detail, on November 22. Among other points is the following:

> My aim in connection with Project Number 11 is to assemble the necessary documentary materials, do the necessary field work, and carry out the monographic studies on which to base a synthesis of the history of Jesuit activities in Sinaloa and Sonora, with reference to their relations to the native populations, their methods, and their contribution to the foundations of present day society in the regions where they operated. . . .

He explained that much of his own work of the past several years, especially that on Kino, had been a very specific part of the general project and went on to note that the work of several of his students was closely related to the main intent of Project Number 11 — W. Eugene Shiels, Jerome V. Jacobsen, Theodore Treutlein, Peter M. Dunne. He accounted for the use of the funds provided to date and concluded with the request for a 1935 appropriation of $1750. This was detailed as follows: $1000 for the continued services of Dr. Marion Reynolds, as Latin translator, $500 to support further field work in the summer of 1935, and $250 for the acquisition of pertinent archival materials — actually, the budgeteers cut this figure, but he was allocated $1300 for 1935–36.

By May 1935 the Kino biography was ready, but Bolton still had no publisher. He had more or less lived with the hope that Alfred Knopf would pick it up and issue it as a companion to *Outpost of Empire,* which he considered it to be. However, this latter volume had not lived up to sales expectations, and when approached Knopf released Bolton from the contract option of having a first look at "his next two books." This left Bolton free to shop around. The House of Macmillan had expressed interest. Bolton, accordingly, made a deal with them. He strongly demurred, however, when Macmillan wished to tie the projected "History of the Americas" text with acceptance of the Kino volume. Harold S. Latham, Macmillan vice president, finally yielded, and negotiations were concluded to Bolton's satisfaction. Macmillan was not interested in the several volumes of Kino documents which Bolton also proposed, and this was a disappointment to him. Even so, the Kino manuscript went off to Macmillan in mid-1935, and Bolton then began to plan his immediate future around a readiness to see it through as expeditiously as possible. This time his favorite Black Robe was not going to be the sort of stepchild which the padre had been, when the volumes of "Favores Celestiales" were appearing for the first time off the presses of Arthur H. Clark. Bolton had learned the hard lesson about not allowing himself to get overextended. He did other things in the next months, but commitments were largely in function of the forthcoming Kino volume.

For example, he had time to play detective in late May 1935. An unnamed individual had approached the San Francisco bookman John Howell with an Anza manuscript for sale. The wily dealer, more than a little suspicious, asked to hold the manuscript for a day or two. Immediately he contacted Bolton, who compared the piece with a photostat in his possession, taken only a few years before in Mexico. Bolton wrote Howell that some patriotic person might be found to buy the manuscript and return it to the Archivo General de la Nación (Mexico) from which it had quite certainly been removed — had he been writing today he would have had to say "allegedly stolen."

September found Bolton saying no-thank-you to a very tempting invitation from Secretary of State Cordell Hull, to serve as one of the official United States delegates to the organizational meeting of the Pan American Institute of Geography and History (PAIGH). When Bolton reported the invitation and his refusal to Sproul, September 19, he did not miss the opportunity to note that four of his "boys," along with Carl O. Sauer of the university's Department of Geography, were named as delegates —

Arthur S. Aiton and Irving A. Leonard of Michigan, Charles W. Hackett of Texas, and J. Fred Rippy of Chicago. He never tired bragging about the achievements of his students. To be sure, there was a strain of personal pride therein, but also a great deal of deep-down sincerity and much satisfaction for the achievers themselves.

Even though the first months of 1936 found him busy with galleys and page proofs for the Kino, there was one invitation in June from the twentieth-century Jesuits which he could not turn down. The invitation was to speak at the inauguration of the Jesuit Historical Institute of Loyola University in Chicago. Two of his former students, Fathers Jerome V. Jacobsen and W. Eugene Shiels, were on the faculty and had convinced the Loyola president, Samuel Knox Wilson, himself a historian, of the desirability of setting up a group of scholars to dig more deeply into American Jesuit history. All concerned were unanimous in their choice of Bolton to keynote the new venture. On June 11 he put his message into "The Jesuits in America: An Opportunity for Historians."[4]

The institute which Bolton helped to inaugurate that day knew a number of productive years, and its quarterly, *Mid-America*, under Jacobsen's editorship, especially served as an outlet for many excellent short studies on Jesuit history by Bolton's "boys" and other scholars. J. Manuel Espinosa, on the institute staff for several years, contributed a volume to the monograph series. *Crusaders of the Rio Grande* was fundamentally the doctor's dissertation on Don Diego de Vargas and the reconquest of New Mexico which he had done under Bolton's direction. Bolton could rightly feel that he had some share of paternity in the Loyola Institute; his enthusiasm for Black Robe history had proved contagious, and here was another example of his ability to inspire his students. Bolton also should be given some credit for another historical institute which came into being in the 1930s. This was Charles Hackett's Institute of Latin American Studies at the University of Texas — Hackett was Bolton-trained, came to Texas after completing his work at the University of California, picked up the Spaniards-in-the-Southwest interest which had lapsed somewhat since Bolton's departure from Austin in 1909, and carried it forward with enthusiasm, drive, and fine imagination.

In July, when the university mail service put on his desk in Library 426 six copies of *Rim of Christendom: A Biography of Eusebio Francisco Kino, Pacific Coast Pioneer,* Bolton probably experienced one of the great thrills of his long productive life. Without quibble, it was his most original piece of scholarship; this carefully reconstructed life of his favorite Black Robe was from start to finish Bolton's work; he had, so to speak, "to start from scratch." No one before him had done even a basic sketch to point the way.

Earlier in the year, while squabbling a bit with the Macmillan people over matter of illustrations and some other points, he had told one of the editors that this work had been the product of years of work, the outlay of around $5000, and the amassing of some seven thousand pages of manuscript copies, most of which he had collected himself — and all this did not mention the weeks and months of travel in Mexico and abroad.[5]

After the appearance of the volume the editor of the university's *California Monthly* asked him to tell something of the making of the Kino.[6] He did so, with relish, in a delightful article entitled "Archives and Trails," cleverly hinting by the very title his approach to history writing. He told of how he had first "discovered" Kino and then had come to appreciate the importance of his padre, "the outstanding figure of his quarter-century on the Arizona-Sonora-California border — one of the giant personalities, indeed, in the whole missionary story of North America . . . a link between West Coast Mexico and the United States' Southwest." He had "named the book 'Rim of Christendom' because Kino spent his life on the very outer edge of the North American frontier, endeavoring every day and every hour to push farther out the periphery of European civilization." The search for materials had taken him "to all foreign countries with which Kino had relations" — "to Italy where he was born; to Germany where he was educated; to Spain in whose colonies he labored; to Mexico City, head of the Jesuit province to which he belonged; to Rome, capital of the Order in all the world; to France, where Kino's maps were eagerly studied and brazenly pirated by geographers and cartographers; to Holland whither some of his writings have recently wandered." He thoroughly enjoyed telling how the famous letters of Kino to the Duchess of Aveiro, great benefactor of missionary effort in her day, had turned up. They were in private hands, and then had come into the possession of the great London book dealer, Maggs. When they were offered to Bolton for the Bancroft at $21,000, he and the Bancroft were caught penniless. He appealed to Max Farrand of the Huntington Library, and the purchase by that library was made for $18,750. He concluded his story: "So Kino's letters to the Duchess sold for $235 a page. Larger sums than this have been paid for letters to a lady, but probably never for letters written by a Jesuit."

Only half of the adventure, he confided to his interviewer, was in the archives; the other half, on the trail, was just as exciting.

> The writing of "Rim of Christendom" was an adventure on the trail as well as in the archives. I wanted to see Kino's world as Kino saw it, understand the words of his diaries and letters, know the scene of his labors, visualize the conditions under which he worked, relive the experiences which he recorded. So I literally followed his foot-

steps from the cradle to the grave. . . . This exploration and trail following has helped to make vivid every chapter in the great pioneer's life. Without it his diaries would be mere words, and his travel routes mere black lines on a flat map.

He told some of his experiences in the field, and showing through them all is his own exuberance. From this forthright account one can come to only one conclusion: writing the life of Kino was fun.

The reviews were favorable. He was pleased with the comments of Arthur Scott Aiton in the *Mississippi Valley Historical Review.* Aiton, since 1923, had become one of the ranking authorities on New Spain.[7] He would have expected an enthusiastic review from his friend and two-time companion on the Kino trail, Frank C. Lockwood, but the fact that this appeared in *The Saturday Review* indicated to Bolton that his book was considered to be of interest to a reading public far wider than that of the professorial world. John Bartlett Brebner, himself a colonialist of no mean stature, highlighted in the *American Historical Review* the "trail aspect" of Bolton's research:

> Professor Bolton and his subject are kindred spirits. Father Kino was much happier on the trail beyond the frontier of Mexico than as a sedentary priest. Professor Bolton, emerging from Bancroft Library to trace Kino's expeditions in actuality, has instilled into his story vividness and authenticity often lacking in the history of exploration. He has been no less ardent in discovering and assembling from the archives of Europe and the Americas a surprising quantity of Kino's writings. He masks his broad yet exact scholarship under an entertaining, even colloquial, narrative style.[8]

Almost a year later, on June 10, 1937, he was asked to be present at the annual awards dinner of the Commonwealth Club of San Francisco. That evening he was awarded his second gold medal; his *Rim of Christendom* had been judged by the Literature Medal Jury as the outstanding work by a Californian in 1936.

15

Still Going Strong

THE KINO BIOGRAPHY was Bolton's last major book published for the next dozen years, in fact, until long after his retirement. *Cross, Sword and Gold Pan,* a collection of ten sketches on the history of California and the Southwest, had also appeared in 1936, but was a reprint of work done five years earlier.* With the exception of the publication in book form of four essays in 1939, all of which had been written prior to 1936, Bolton limited his writing to article-length pieces and periodic work on a biography of Coronado, still several years into the future. This left him more time during the next decade for traveling and speaking, trailing, departmental staff business, and his continuing efforts in behalf of the Bancroft Library. Falling within this last category was perhaps one of the more exciting experiences of his later professional life, indirectly something like his finding the long-lost Kino manuscript in the Mexican archives years before. This discovery, too, came quite by accident.

It was a dreary February morning in 1937, as damp winter mornings can be in Berkeley. Bolton, already hard at work in Library 426, received a phone call.[1] A man's voice came across the wire, telling Bolton that one of his students had informed him that a University of California professor named Herbert Bolton was the man to consult in his present predicament. Beryle Shinn informed him that the previous summer, while tramping around in the Marin County hills, he had picked up a small metal plate, ideal he felt to cover a developing hole in the floorboard of his car. Just recently, Shinn continued, when he had time to put the piece of metal to

---

*Phil Townsend Hanna, editor of the pictorial *Touring Topics* (predecessor to the more recent *Westways*) solicited the popular series of historical vignettes which were published throughout 1931. The series began with Coronado discovering Zuni, in the January number, and ended, in December, with the momentous event of 1848 at Sutter's Mill.

[198]

use, the floorboard hole getting bigger and bigger, he had noticed that it had marks, orderly marks, possibly some sort of tattooing, on one side. He had brushed it vigorously but was unable to make sense out of any of the marks, save possibly one series which might spell D-R-A-K-E. This much information aroused Bolton's curiosity, and he asked Shinn to bring the metal piece over to Berkeley, to his office. Bolton confessed, in his paper read to the California Historical Society the evening of April 6:[2]

> I surmised its identity even before seeing it, from a very general description which he gave me over the phone. My mind leaped to the conjecture at once, because for years I had been telling my students to keep an eye out for Drake's plate and the silver sixpence bearing the image of Queen Elizabeth.

The next day Shinn appeared at Bolton's office. Bolton, meanwhile, had done some quick research to refresh his memory on the details of Drake's visit to California and of his several weeks pause on the coast while the *Golden Hind* was being careened and readied for the long run back to Mother England across the Pacific. Learning from Chaplain Fletcher's account of the brass plate, inscribed and "fixed to a faire great poste," precisely what he should look for, Bolton thought he could see enough of the heavily obscured lettering come to life that he immediately felt that the "tablet" was authentic and just as quickly termed Shinn's discovery "one of the most sensational in all California history." Years later a Bolton student of that age recalled with obvious relish the professor's reaction the next day, when he met his large History 8-B class in Wheeler Auditorium:

> I'll never forget the day when he came into the large lecture hall and announced that "a great discovery was made — the brass plate of Sir Francis Drake's ship has been found." The class sort of got excited too, and when Professor Bolton announced that more arti-facts were sure to be found at the ocean and "we should all go over there," the class followed him outside the lecture hall as if going on a crusade. Of course, as soon as we left the lecture hall and re-grouped near Sather Gate, it dawned on all of us that we were not going at all, because very few students had cars. But it was the initial excitement that was important, the excitement of Professor Bolton, and espe-cially his ability to excite students for further research.[3]

Bolton personally may have been convinced of the authenticity of the plate, but he knew that his word would not be enough. The wording of the inscription conformed to what the Drake materials said was inscribed on the plate which was affixed to a tree or to a post. But he was no expert beyond that point; the whole thing might be a very clever forgery. If the plate were authentic, however, he wanted this fact established and, further, he wanted it for the University of California. One rather reassuring fact relative to authenticity was that Shinn quite obviously was not trying to peddle it; he seemed to have no mercenary motives. Bolton immediately sought to enlist the interest and assistance of Allen L. Chickering, president of the California Historical Society. Chickering enthusiastically rose to the challenge to raise funds to have the plate examined by professionals and also to reward Shinn.

On the evening of April 6, at a meeting of the society, very fittingly held in San Francisco's Sir Francis Drake Hotel, a formal announcement of the discovery was made. Actually word was already out. Bolton read a paper which gathered the historical data concerning Drake's foray into the Pacific — his exploits as the *Golden Hind* sailed northward from Tierra del Fuego up the western side of the two American continents, catching the Spaniards off guard, and then the thirty-six-day pause in a protected inlet along the California coast, before undertaking the long circuitous voyage home. Next, as a historian, he analyzed the inscription in relation to the general description of what the plaque contained, as found in the contemporary accounts. The wording was the following:

BEE IT KNOWN VNTO ALL MEN BY THESE PRESENTS
IVNE. 17 . 1579
BY THE GRACE OF GOD AND IN THE NAME OF HERR
MAIESTY OVEEN ELIZABETH OF ENGLAND AND HERR
SUCCESSORS FOREVER I TAKE POSSESSION OF THIS
KINGDOME WHOSE KING AND PEOPLE FREELY RESIGNE
THEIR RIGHT AND TITLE IN THE WHOLE LAND VNTO HERR
MAIESTIES KEEPEING NOW NAMED BY ME AND TO BEE
KNOWNE VNTO ALL MEN AS NOVA ALBION.

G FRANCIS DRAKE

Then having set the state of the question, Bolton offered a series of observations which constituted his opinion of the plate. Close to two months had elapsed between Bolton's first conversation with Shinn and this public statement; hence, even the skeptic would have to admit that he had had time to do a certain amount of study and research. He detailed his conclusions:

> Either the plate is a clever fraud, perpetrated by someone who carefully studied Fletcher's words, or it is genuine, as I fully believe. . . .
> The plate is crudely made, fashioned as best it could be under the circumstances. This is one of the best testimonials to its genuineness. . . .

The plate was found about a mile and a half west-northwest of San Quentin, near Cunningham Cement Works and Greenbrae. The places named are on the north shore of Corte Madera Creek and Inlet, which open on the east into the main San Francisco Bay. . . .

The evidence furnished by the plate itself and the circumstance of its discovery leave little room to doubt its authenticity. The lettering and the spelling of the inscription are in keeping with the period and with the Drake documents. The piece of brass on which the notice of possession was so crudely printed bears a marked resemblance to the plentiful brass-work of sixteenth century ships. . . .

Finally, since Drake's Bay has so long been regarded as the site of Drake's landing, a bogus tablet presumably would have been planted near that place, or, if the hoax were recent, perhaps near Bodega Bay, not near San Francisco Bay which has long been rejected as the site of Drake's landing place. . . .

The exact location where the plate was found may or may not have any bearing on the question of the identity of the harbor in which Drake beached his ship. . . . It is conceivable that investigation may prove that the plate was discovered on the very site where Drake nailed it to the "firme poste," and at that beach at the foot of the hill was the very spot where he careened and repaired the *Golden Hinde.*

The following week the piece of brass was "physically delivered to the University of California, together with a sum of money for the purpose, among others, of being used for such test or tests as to the genuineness of the Plate as might seem desirable." These were to be extensive and intensive, and the results would not be publishd until 1938.

The last sentence or observation in Bolton's paper to the historical society, concerning the possible location of Drake's stopping place, he felt to have more rhetorical than real historical validity. Almost immediately after the public announcement of the discovery, a certain William Caldeira came forward with the story of how he had found this plate on a ranch bordering on Drake's Bay some years before, how he had washed it off and seen the word "Drake," but how after keeping it for a few weeks had considered it useless and had thrown it from his car as he went along the road between San Quentin and Kentfield. This tale had nothing to do with the authenticity of the plate, only with the possible location where it had first been "nailed to the firme poste." Bolton did not reject the Caldeira story, as is evident in a reply which he sent, May 20, 1937, to an inquiry from Captain Oswald T. Luck, Royal Navy, at Bromley, Kent, England:

I am writing to say that we now know that it has been picked up at least twice within the last three years, the first time about a mile from the northern end of Drake's Bay in approximately latitude 38° 2½'. The second time it was found farther south on the north shore of San Francisco Bay just west of San Quentin Penitentiary not far from latitude 37° 57'.

Manifestly neither of the places mentioned is exactly on the site of the "firme poste" to which the plate was nailed by Drake, but the former location is very near the site which was determined by Professor Davidson. . . .

The Drake Plate business took a great deal of Bolton's time through the spring months of 1937. He quipped about it on several occasions in his correspondence. To Irving A. Leonard (April 2), while thanking him for the reprint of an article, he went on: "But [I] have not had time to read it for the reason that Drake left a brass plate in California which has turned up to plague me." And to Lingelbach (April 25):

> You would be surprised if I were to tell you how much time I have had to spend over the little piece of brass which Drake nailed to a "firme poste" and after three hundred and fifty eight years chanced to come my way. It is not highly important, but has been intensely interesting to the general public, and I have had to play my part, hoping that the incident may be worth one or more millions to the University.

Although there was, off and on, discussion of the plate, a year or so later Bolton's judgment seemed to be proved sound, when the report from the Electro-Chemical Laboratories of Columbia University was submitted. Drs. Colin G. Fink and E. P. Polushkin summarized their findings:[4]

1) There is no doubt whatsoever that the dark coating on the surface of the plate is a natural patina formed slowly over a period of many years.
2) Numerous surface defects and imperfections usually associated with old brass were found on the plate.
3) Particles of mineralized plant tissue are firmly imbedded in the surface of the plate. This is likewise very positive proof of the age of the plate.
4) Cross sections of the brass plate show (a) an excessive amount of impurities; and (b) chemical inhomogeneity; as well as (c) variation in grain size. All these characteristics indicate brass of old origin.
5) Among the impurities found in the brass of the plate there is magnesium, which is present far in excess of the amount occurring in modern brass.
6) There are numerous indications that the plate was not made by rolling but was made by hammering, as was the common practice in Drake's time.

CONCLUSION
On the basis of the above six distinct findings, as well as other data herewith recorded, it is our opinion that the brass plate examined by us is the genuine Drake Plate referred to in the book, *The World Encompassed by Sir Francis Drake,* published in 1628.

It had all taken time but, if pressed, Bolton would admit that it had been great fun. Not often, he would have quipped, do historians stumble onto this peculiar kind of "document." To the end he felt that evidence, historical and scientific, proved the authenticity of the plate.

He knew that there were skeptics. President Sproul shared with him the confidential letter (1938) of Professor Earle R. Caley of the Frick Chemical Laboratory, Princeton University, which severely criticized the Fink-Polushkin report, this on metallurgical grounds. More active and vocal was R. B. Haseldon, Curator of Manuscripts of the Henry R. Huntington Library, who carried on quite an exchange of correspondence and opinion with experts in matters sixteenth century. Bolton was not impressed, entered into no long argumentations, but instead soon became engrossed in other projects which had suffered during the brass-plate days. The University of California, rather universally inclined to go along with its Sather Professor, proudly displayed the historic treasure in the Bancroft Library in handsome fashion.

Now and again after the late 1930s there were skeptics who stirred doubts, one or other within the University of California family itself. Even before Samuel Eliot Morison in the second volume of *The European Discovery of America: The Southern Voyages, A.D. 1492–1616*, p. 680 (1974), labeled the artifact "as successful a hoax as the Piltdown Man or the Kensington Rune Stone," the director of the Bancroft Library, James D. Harte, had initiated a reexamination of the "Drake Plate." The Morison challenge hastened the process. New approaches and highly sophisticated testing techniques, not available in the 1930s, were called into service by the Bancroft investigation team. In late July 1977 the Bancroft Library issued a report, *The Plate of Brass Reexamined,* in which these later findings and opinions were presented. The cautious conclusion was that "the evidence it assembles has turned out to be essentially negative." Director Harte, however, did not consider this study a "definitive or conclusive word on the subject" and suggested that "doubtless at later dates other inquiries and further commentary will be forthcoming from different sources to probe again into the nature and origin of the artifact that has attracted so much attention since its discovery."

THE BANCROFT'S BEGGAR

Bolton's comment to Lingelbach about "hoping that the incident [the Drake Plate affair] may be worth one or more millions to the University" was something of a tip-off to one of his activities of those middle 1930s. They were rather successful "begging years." The Depression had slowed, but not completely checked, the flow of funds from benefactors for the purchase of materials for the Bancroft. A $200 gift from James K. Moffitt in 1933 had made possible the acquisition of photostat copies of the lengthy and important Jesuit *anuas* (yearly reports from Mexico to Rome) of 1614 and 1615. In this way, Bolton was able little by little to bring copies to the Bancroft of the archival treasures he had found in Europe during the summer of 1931. In September of the same year J. F. Shuman and friends had gathered moneys to purchase the very valuable E. P. Jones Papers, a body of excellent source materials on early San Francisco, American period. Now in 1936 Bolton was again in touch with these same benefactors.

In March the Warren Gregory Fund, established for the acquisition of Californiana, was augmented by its second $5000. The year before the English house of Maggs Brothers of London, knowing the Bancroft interest in Jesuitica, contacted Bolton and offered a sizable collection of Jesuit pieces for $10,000. Bolton was most definitely interested, but funds were lacking. He did manage to drive down the asking price to $7000. He wrote to Sproul, but the university was still experiencing hard times as a result of the Depression, and that price was out of range. Bolton again contacted friend James K. Moffitt, but having just recently received help from him, did not set his hopes too high. He wrote J. F. Shuman, too, who also had proved himself a friend of the Bancroft Library. Shuman alone could not stand the expense, but he did rally a number of his friends; together they raised the necessary sum. In September 1936 Bolton sent Shuman and a long list of individuals fervent thank-you's for adding this collection to the Bancroft's manuscript holdings. Between Bolton's own copies and acquisitions such as this, the Bancroft was developing an outstanding collection of materials for the story of the Jesuits and their work in Spanish North America.

The next year Maggs Brothers was dangling before them another prime piece of Jesuitica. During the troubles of the Spanish Civil War someone spirited out of Spain and sold to the English dealer the original manuscript, 711 folios in all, of Padre Miguel Venegas, S.J., from which his confrere Andrés Burriel had published, in 1757, a three-volume *Noticia de California*.[5] Maggs, successful in the past in using Jake Zeitlin as the American agent, sent him the manuscript. The Los Angeles bookman lost no time in notifying Bolton personally. A comparison between this original "Empresas apostolicas . . . en la conquista de California" and the Burriel version, which the Bancroft held, showed that this editor had taken many liberties with the Venegas text, which was historically a much superior piece of writing and reporting. Bolton needed no convincing; he immediately felt that the Venegas manuscript, which was the first careful history of Baja California, belonged in California, and specifically in the Bancroft Library. Again, however, the asking price was simply out of reach. Bolton was not going to give up easily. He assured Zeitlin of his deep interest and asked to be allowed to hold the manuscript for a while, in the hope of finding a benefactor who would purchase it for the university. Next, he made a request that he be permitted to photostat the manuscript. Maggs Brothers, evidently feeling, based on the report from Zeitlin, that they would ultimately unload the treasure on the university, consented.

At this juncture Bolton approached his friend Archbishop Edward Hanna, told him what an important piece of Catholic Californiana the Venegas was, and asked for help. Hanna succumbed to the "sales talk" and, at least, furnished the several hundred dollars necessary for the photo-stating. Bolton had his photostats and permission to use the Venegas material for his own research, but the fact that the original manuscript was available plagued his librarian's soul. It was one thing to be satisfied with copies of archival materials, themselves unattainable; it was quite another to actually have a valued and attainable original. Bolton held onto it. Then early in January 1938 Zeitlin wrote Bolton that Maggs wanted either the manuscript or their asking price of $7500; he did hint that the English house might come down to $6500. Bolton decided to make an all-out try to find a donor or donors. He explained his predicament to Shu-man; he wrote eloquently to Señorita Maria Antonia Fields; he talked to others. He did get $100 from Frederic Paxson Howard of Carmel and the promise from this gentleman that he would try to interest others. By February, with activity reported "up north," Zeitlin informed Bolton that he was authorized to drop the asking price to $6000 but with the warning that the English dealers would accept nothing less. Shuman had again risen to the occasion; he assured Bolton that he was confident that he could raise half the sum and suggested strongly that Bolton tap President Sproul for the other half. This game, and such it had almost become, went on into the next year. Shuman then told Bolton that he had $2500. Bolton went to Sproul once more, in March 1939. To make a long story short, the Bancroft Library did obtain the Venegas manuscript later in that year.

DEPARTMENTAL BUSINESS

Bolton's life in those later 1930s was not all "brass and manuscripts." As was so characteristic of his entire career, there were always many projects being carried on simultaneously. As the 1936–37 year opened, there was a glimmer of hope portending the easing of the Depression; departmental salary cuts had been restored.* But alongside this bright

---

*In 1933–34 Bolton had cut his own salary to $7896, and others in like proportion.

cloud was one definitely of more somber hue. The Department of History was mourning the sudden death of a most promising young professor, Louis J. (Pat) O'Brien. His passing pointed up a problem facing the department. The recent growth of the student load, especially at the graduate level, seemed to call not simply for an O'Brien replacement, but also for new additions to the staff. With the hardest of hard times seemingly passed, the Department of History began to pressure the administration. O'Brien had been a European man; obviously, he had to be replaced. The department also felt that it immediately needed at least one more Americanist, and then with the day of Bolton's mandatory retirement coming in the not too distant future, in 1940, it was time to start thinking of his replacement. For now, however, Howard M. Smyth (A.M., Stanford; Ph.D., Harvard) would be the new European man. In a letter of December 3 to Sproul, and with a strong supporting memorandum from Frederic Logan Paxson, who had joined the departmental staff in 1932 as recipient of the Margaret Byrne Professorship of American History, Bolton brought up the matter of a new American-history man. Suggested for immediate consideration were two prominent younger men, both rising in stature, Avery O. Craven and Merle Curti. Paxson wished to bring Craven to Berkeley and add Curti to the Department at UCLA. Neither of these men was interested in a change.

Right after the first of the year in 1937 Bolton began to press Sproul (January 3) to be authorized to add Lawrence Kinnaird as the man to share his own teaching and research burden and in 1940 become his successor. Kinnaird was added to the departmental staff in August, 1937, coming in from the university's branch at Davis. With him on campus, Bolton could face the future with fewer worries. During study years Kinnaird had been his teaching assistant; next for several years more he had been research assistant with the task of readying for publication the sizable Pinart collection of materials on the Spaniards in Louisiana. He knew the Borderlands and was developing a large interest in the history of California. With a few years of "seasoning in the big leagues" Bolton was confident that Kinnaird could carry on the "Bolton tradition" with great credit.

SOME NEW INVOLVEMENTS

Still another interest of Bolton's in the late 1930s which claimed more and more of his time in ensuing years was work with the National Park Service (NPS). Building upon a relationship that had begun to develop in 1933 when Thomas C. Vint, chief architect of the NPS, had asked him to serve on the advisory committee of the newly formed Historic American Building Survey (HABS),* the NPS had named him in 1936 to their advisory board. University duties and distance had prevented his faithful attendance at the meetings of the board, regularly held in those early years on the eastern seaboard. In June 1937, however, the NPS, wishing to profit by his expertise, asked him to go south and report on the reconstruction under way at Mission La Purísima, next on the Camino Real after Santa Barbara. Again, in early September, he was in Saint Louis, to look over the site of the projected Jefferson National Expansion Memorial on the historic riverfront and to talk with civic leaders and NPS officials. Bolton heartily approved the idea of memorializing the figures and the events of the westward sweep of Americans — Anglo-Americans — into the lands acquired by the Louisiana Purchase. He was, however, very pointed in his insistence that the Anglos were not the first on the ground in much of the Purchase territory.

In early 1938 he devoted considerable time to a job which interested him greatly. He had been asked by Editor-in-Chief James Truslow Adams and Managing Editor R. V. Coleman both to serve on the advisory council for and to contribute several sketches to the *Dictionary of American History,* which was published in 1940, in five volumes, by Scribners. Recognizing a chance to get some of his history into this reference work, he set to work with verve and vigor. On March 3 he sent Coleman "a batch of articles which you may or may not wish to use for the *Dictionary,* some of them possibly already assigned to others. . . ." Included in the batch were half a dozen articles which he had specifically been asked to prepare, primarily segments of the California story. He included several others, such as the note on Escalante's expedition which he felt should be in the work, and also one or so others, like the piece on Los Adaes, which the editors did not pick up, feeling that these had not sufficient national pertinence. Besides his own sketches he sent several done by his students to fill up what he considered to be notable oversights in the planning. The editors were grateful for Robert Denhardt's piece on the horse and Adele Ogden's short history of the sea otter trade; someone else had been assigned the Bear Flag Revolt, so John Hussey's effort went for naught.

In April he went over to Santa Fe for the meeting of the Advisory Board on the National Parks, Historic Sites, Buildings and Monuments.

---

*Originally the HABS was a function of the relief program of the Central Welfare Agency (CWA), but when that agency was phased out the HABS, having proved its very real national worth, was picked up by the NPS, the American Institute of Architects, and the Library of Congress, and given permanence.

In August he was back in the field, once more on the Escalante trail. Torrential rains prevented him from fulfilling his plans. With the new semester scheduled to open on August 22, he could not tarry until the weather might clear, so that physically impassable roads might become simply normally impassable.

SOUTH AMERICA FIRSTHAND

The Seventh Pan American Conference was scheduled to meet in Lima in December 1938. As the autumn weeks rolled by, Bolton's desire to attend this inter-American gathering grew stronger and stronger. For much of his academic life he had read of, and taught and written about those "other Americas" of the southern continent. After many years he had the opportunity to make a quick turn through the so-called Middle Americas. Mexico, of course, he knew well, the northern half better, perhaps, than most of his United States fellows. But, as the old saying went, "he was born thirty years too soon"; most of his academic life was lived before the days of generous travel grants and the time-saving speed of air travel. He even antedated the age of generous sabbaticals, and even when the occasional leaves came, the heavy demands of raising and educating a large family left him without the accumulated savings which might have made far-ranging travel possible. He hated to be an armchair historian in respect to areas of the Western Hemisphere with whose history he was so familiar.

Earlier in the year he had inquired of Leo S. Rowe of the Pan American Union how one became a delegate to those all-American gatherings. Rowe may never have received that letter; in all events no reply was forthcoming. As time ran, Bolton's hopes dwindled. He confided to Irving Leonard, at the moment working with the Rockefeller Foundation, that he would probably have to be content with attending the early December meeting of the Advisory Board of the National Park Service and the late December meeting of the American Historical Association, in Chicago. But then, on November 14, he decided, once again, to test the old advice "nothing ventured, nothing gained" and wrote to President Sproul. He wondered if the university, so much involved in Latin American studies, should not be represented at Lima. He quietly reminded Sproul that, even though his "wondering" was late, he could still be on hand for the December 9 opening of the conference, were he to fly South.

Sproul was sympathetic. Then, rather perfectly timed, came word from the Rockefeller Foundation of a grant of $1000; Bolton knew well that he had Irving Leonard to thank. To add to this Sproul authorized

$700 from the President's Emergency Fund and noted that he could add another $300 for travel and research. Bolton would go as a representative of the University of California, and after the conclusion of the conference at Lima, he could do a goodwill tour through South America. Nothing could have excited him more.

Time was short. He sent off a hurried note to Mexican friend Vito Alessio Robles, asking him to send to Lima fifty, or better a hundred, copies of the Spanish translation of his "Epic of Greater America." (This Mexican scholar had arranged for the translation of the Toronto address, and it had appeared the year before under the title of "La Epopeya de la Máxima América," as Numero 30 in the series of publications of the PAIGH.) He felt that this would be a fine goodwill piece to indicate to the Latinos what the University of California was trying to do. Next, he hurried off cancellations of December commitments, got his passport and other papers in order, and started the various shots required. He was cutting corners, timewise, to such an extent that he would have to take his last typhoid shot in the Canal Zone. First semester finals would begin almost immediately after his departure; hence, there was little problem with his classes, and Kinnaird was happy to cover for him. Kinnaird also had to cover at the other end of the period, when his anticipated six weeks lengthened into two months absence; he would not return to Berkeley until early February.[6]

Friday morning, December 3, the Pan American plane was in the air well before sunup. It can safely be affirmed that no one of the fourteen passengers aboard or even the all-Mexican crew looked down on the ground below and saw as much as the professor. He knew much of the land firsthand. He could envision Anza and Kino and Mange and the rest of his friends of long ago along the watercourses, such as they are, in the canyons, climbing the hills, moving across the cactus-studded wastelands. He reveled in this new dimension given to his trailing of the pioneers. In flight from Hermosillo to Los Mochis he was reminded of the trip a few years before with son Herbert. There was a landing at familiar Mazatlán and another at Guadalajara. In a long day he covered 1650 miles. It had taken Anza weeks, and Serra too, on hard journeys from San Gabriel to the viceregal capital.

When he took off from Cristóbal (Canal Zone) mid-morning of December 7, he was heading, if not into the unknown, at least into the unexperienced. Historically, however, he was perfectly at home as he looked down to see sixteenth-century acquaintances plodding along — Balboa, Andagoya, the Pizarros, Almagro, Benalcázar. When they passed Paita (Peru) on Thursday, Bolton had some other thoughts; Drake had raided the town en route to California; Bolton wondered where on the *Golden Hind* was attached that piece of brass which would be inscribed, left behind, be found, and cause such a stir in California of 1937.

The conference in Lima opened on Friday evening, December 9 — "a formal pageant," with speech by President Óscar Raimundo Benavides of Peru. Bolton's next days were full. At a huge reception tendered the Americans by the United States colony of businessmen, Bolton met Cordell Hull for the first time. He had many pleasant experiences during the week, but one, he felt, was worth recording. He had visited the Convento Grande de San Francisco Solano, and he reported in letters home it was truly *grande*. At the door he was met by a little friar who, on hearing his name, beamed and told him that he had read some of his books. The Fray Portero went off to bring the Father Guardian to show the distinguished visitor around. He found the Franciscans of Lima as hospitable and charming as their brethren of California and Mexico.

The affairs of the conference were due to end on Friday, December 23, but already Bolton was anxious to begin his "grand tour." Thursday afternoon he took off for Arequipa, which was of special interest to Bolton since from its colonial foundries had come many of the mission bells for California. That city, too, brought back memories of the Almagros, father and *mozo*, of Pedro Valdivia and his lady, Inés Suárez, for all had used Arequipa as a staging point from which they set out for Chile and its disappointments and hardships.

Saturday was Christmas Eve. Bolton went over the Andes and up to Lake Titicaca. He was back to Arequipa that night and spent Christmas there, which in South America is much more a religious feast day than a holiday after the United States pattern. The next several days he was in the heart of Inca land, at the ancient imperial capital city of Cuzco, at Macchu-Picchu, and New Year's Day at quaint little Pisac. There was a full, but much too short, day in La Paz (Bolivia). Then he had to recross the Andes and head for Chile; he had been named one of the United States delegates to the Conference on Cultural Cooperation of the United Nations, meeting in Santiago. Busy days there followed. The day before he left Santiago, he wrote: "The University [of Chile] called a special session, and in a public function made me an honorary member of the faculty, a distinction conferred on only two persons hitherto. It is their highest form of honorary degree."

On January 11 he made his ninth crossing of the Andes and flew on to Buenos Aires, where his old, old friend Eddie Dunn was his delighted host. There was a quick side trip to Montevideo. He next visited Asunción (Paraguay), Iguassú Falls, São Paulo, and Rio de Janeiro. From Rio he went to Recife (Pernambuco), which he found "unusually attractive," and drove over to Olinda. Having put down at Port-of-Spain, Trinidad, he swung quickly over to Caracas (Venezuela), so as to complete the full litany of the South American nations.

The run over the Caribbean called forth many more historical memories — it was there that "his" history and "his" Spaniards opened their great American adventure. It had been a wonderful experience, but, even so, he was happy to put down in Miami, February 1 — he confessed that for several hours past he had been pushing hard with his feet, in order to hurry the plane along. When he deplaned in San Francisco on February 3, his anticipated six-week tour had lengthened into two very full months.

February 1939, and March too, found Bolton involved in his own "Operation Catch-up," and to complicate matters he felt that he should accept a number of requests that he talk to one or other group around the Bay Area. As he explained to his correspondents, he considered that he owed this to the university which so generously had helped to subsidize his trip. Ranging farther afield, he went south to be the Pan American Day speaker at UCLA and in May to Bakersfield to give an address at the dedication of the Garcés Memorial there. As the summer rolled along, he found himself periodically involved in meetings which had been scheduled at Treasure Island or in the City during the 1939 Fair. At one of these, the meeting of the National Education Association, on August 22, he spoke on a theme already of deep interest to him and made more compelling as a result of his recent experience — "Cultural Cooperation with Latin America." In the next years Bolton would be asked to play and replay that theme song and would be more and more thankful for those two months in South America. No longer would he be talking from documents and books; he had been on the ground, or a bit above it, but still close enough to see.

16

Seventy and Out,
But Not For Long

THE ACADEMIC YEAR 1939–40, presumed to be the last of Bolton's tenure, found him cutting back and readying for the turnover. His History 8 he passed on to Kinnaird, and he tried to plant the seed with the administration that Kinnaird might very well use some help — Engel Sluiter was the name he had begun to drop. Bolton did hold onto his History 181 and his seminar. This cut-back in load was just as well, for he had a busy year ahead, and no small amount of his time would be spent off campus.

In October he was once again in contact with the NPS. He had gone to a meeting in Santa Fe to address the meeting of the American Planning and Civic Association, his subject: "Escalante Way — An Opportunity for the National Park Service." Afterwards he took off on a field trip with several of the NPS men and George P. Hammond, to check out portions of the young friar's trail of 1776. At this time the NPS had in mind a possible Escalante National Monument and was happy to have Bolton along since he had already done much visiting along that trail. On this occasion the experts of NPS Region Three were interested in finding a 1776 marking, supposedly seen in 1884 by H. L. Baldwin of Salt Lake City, while working for the United States Geodetic Survey in southern Utah. Unfortunately, Baldwin could not accompany the party, and from his verbal instructions as to the location, the group could not find the rock. The expedition did give Bolton a chance to cover another segment of the Escalante trail.

A rather interesting account of this expedition gives in addition to an excellent description of it, some valuable information concerning Bolton's health as he neared retirement. It is a letter of Jesse Nusbaum, senior archaeologist in the National Park Service, addressed to Preston T. Hutchins, agent for the Mutual Life Insurance Company of New York,

[212]

at Oakland, and dated December 13, 1939. How or why Hutchins had been referred to Nusbaum is not clear, but here are his very enlightening observations:

> Reference is made to your letter of November 24, requesting any information I might care to submit in regard to the status of health of Dr. Herbert E. Bolton, dean of the department of history, University of California, and any ideas as to why life insurance should or should not be issued on his life as he approaches his 70th birthday.
>
> In October of this year it was my privilege, following the superintendents' conference of the National Park Service and associated meetings with the American Planning and Civic Association, to act as guide and informant for the field tour following thereafter, beginning at Santa Fe and traversing nearly 1200 miles of secondary and tertiary roads in the more remote and inaccessible parts of New Mexico, Utah, and Arizona, and ending at Grand Canyon.
>
> Dr. Bolton rode with me in my car throughout the tour and upon its completion we returned by car to a very remote section of the Navajo Indian Reservation near Kaibito Springs in northern Arizona searching for two days by foot and by car for a purported Escalante inscription of 1776. Following that, Dr. Bolton, the writer, and others traced the Escalante trail from the end of automobile transportation to Chu-skeese on the south rim of Navajo Canyon, north of Kaibito, across this canyon and down the Colorado River, crossing Navajo Canyon over slick rock formation. This is the most difficult trip I have ever taken with saddle and pack animals in 35 years of exploration in remote parts of the Southwest. The stock was without water for as much as 28 hours and Dr. Bolton and other members of the party were without food, and with extremely limited quantities of water, for 20 hours. He was the one person throughout the trip who never complained once of the hardships. . . .
>
> Whenever practicable on the trip, Dr. Bolton slept with his light and glasses on so that he could pick up a manuscript and study during the night should he awaken. He is an indefatigable worker.

The prospect of retiring for Bolton meant anything but slowing down. It was more a shifting of emphasis, time for many of the activities and projects which had been pushed aside in the past and for the new needs and new opportunities which were constantly cropping up.

In the years of the late 1930s he became involved in another bit of business having to do with the Borderlands. Envisioning 1940, folk of New Mexico were laying elaborate plans to commemorate the fourth centennial of the Coronado expedition into their state and the Southwest. A national commission was established with Clinton P. Anderson as its director. Both New Mexico and Arizona set up their state commissions. The National Park Service was also very much involved, since so many

national sites and monuments over which it had care were in the Southwest. Through 1939 the NPS issued a series of monthly releases, prepared by experts, entitled "Our Own Spanish-American Citizens and
the Southwest Which They Colonized," hoping through wide publicity
to focus national attention on the area and its history. The next year this
series was followed by another of the same general character, to which
Bolton was asked to contribute an article — "The Significance of the
Coronado Cuatro-Centennial." The Coronado Cuatro-Centennial plans
went far beyond the to-be-expected pageants and fiestas. The University
of New Mexico projected a series of scholarly volumes, to be published
by its press and to tell the story of Coronado, his predecessors and his
successors in the Southwest, with George P. Hammond, in those years
professor of history and dean of the graduate school of the university, as
the editor.*

Hammond, who knew that Bolton was planning a new biography of
Coronado, suggested to President James F. Zimmerman of his university
and also president of the Coronado Cuatro-Centennial Commission, that
he write Bolton to ask that he consider publishing this work in the Cuatro-
Centennial Series. On December 11, 1939, Bolton so promised. With this
pressure the study of Coronado rose to the top of Bolton's list of projects
for the next years, edging ahead of Escalante, Garcés, Mange, Salvatierra
— all of whose stories he planned to tell during the retirement years just
ahead. The full story will be told in the next chapter.

LOOKING TOWARD RETIREMENT

As the 1940s opened, he still "owed" the university a last semester —
or, better, the university still owed him a last semester. Consistently one
of the areas of concern foremost in his mind was the staff of the Department of History. In early January, 1940, he sent several long memoranda
to President Sproul. He asked that George Guttridge be advanced to full
professor; that associate professor rank be given Lawrence Kinnaird; that
Woodbridge Bingham and Howard Smyth be raised to assistant professors. Again he proposed that a young man be added to the staff to carry
some of the American load, and another to relieve Franklin Palm in later
European history courses — for the first spot he favored Engel Sluiter,
for the second John F. Ramsey, at the University of Alabama. He called

---

*Hammond had been and continued as the very successful editor, as well as
the spirit behind the Quivira Society series.

attention to the fact that he himself and Thompson* were due to retire and warned that these two professorships would have to be filled, or at least the titles reassigned — the Sather and the Ehrman Professorships. And since Eugene MacCormac was only one more year away from mandatory retirement, in 1941, a replacement to pick up the antebellum period of United States history should soon be a top priority need.

There was considerable discussion in the department that spring concerning the Ehrman chair reassignment. The English historian William Edward Lunt had been eliminated; then William L. Langer of Harvard and Charles K. Webster of London moved up for consideration; Bolton strongly favored the idea of bestowing the honor on one of the staff and his choice was Robert J. Kerner — Kerner† ultimately was named Sather Professor and the Ehrman chair went to Raymond J. Sontag of Princeton. While the Sather chair was still under discussion Bolton had ideas: he felt that Priestley and Morris deserved consideration, if the honor was to go to someone already in the department; if it were to be conferred on an outsider he suggested J. Fred Rippy of Chicago and Arthur S. Aiton of Michigan, both his "boys" and with established reputations in the Latin American field. He had still another idea which he passed on to Sproul (April 25). Lesley B. Simpson, Department of Spanish, who had done outstanding research and writing on the colonial institution of the *encomienda* and, further, had become a recognized interpreter of Mexico, was proposed as a possibility; it would mean his shifting to history from Spanish, but that should offer no insurmountable problem. Two names were proposed as eventual replacement for MacCormac — Avery O. Craven, who had been in the department's thinking previously, and a new name, that of John D. Hicks of Wisconsin. Hicks was the ultimate choice and would join the department in 1942.

Bolton's academic days were running out — July 20 would be his seventieth birthday and by university statute that meant that by the time the new academic year opened he would be *emeritus*. He was, however, closing out his career in a blaze of glory. On April 28 the San Francisco Native Sons of the Golden West honored him; the Grand Parlor did so more formally, with a long resolution of recognition and thanks, "in regular session assembled at Bakersfield, California, May 20–23, 1940."

---

*James Westfall Thompson was the first holder of the Sidney Hellman Ehrman Chair of European History in 1933. He had replaced Louis J. Paetow, who died in 1928, in the department.

†Kerner came to California from the University of Missouri in 1928.

On April 30, as he finished his last lecture to his History 8-B class, the students presented him with a gold wristwatch in token of esteem and appreciation. On May 2 he wrote, curiously enough, to the present writer: "I have given my last lecture in History 8-B and have my last seminar meeting tonight." On June 12 he traveled back to his Pennsylvania alma mater to receive his fourth honorary Doctor of Letters.

A letter from President Sproul received August 2 as the fall semester was beginning — the first semester in twenty-nine years without Professor Bolton as a member of the staff — summarized in a few words Bolton's contribution to the teaching staff at the University of California:

> In the turmoil of starting a new academic year, which is always accompanied by the feeling of great difficulties to be overcome, I am reminded that there may be a special reason for concern this year, in that we are starting our program without the active aid of Herbert E. Bolton, Sather Professor of History and Director of the Bancroft Library.
> We have been fortunate in having you on the faculty of this University. The reputation which the institution has won as a teaching center and a leader in research, is mainly the accumulation of the reputations won by the scholars on its staff, and to that reputation your contribution has been outstanding.

The friendship between these two men would continue through the next years.

In November Bolton had two reasons to travel to Washington, D.C., the first, a meeting of the Advisory Board of the National Park Service. He had anticipated for some time the day when he could be a more regular participant in the affairs of the board. Coming close on the heels of the NPS meeting was a major planning conference organized by the Office of the Coordinator of Inter-American Affairs, Department of State. The conferees were Latin Americanists from every stamp, and Bolton had been asked to address one of the sessions of the group on November 8. Friend Ben Cherrington wanted him to repeat the substance, at least, of his NEA address on cultural cooperation which he had given shortly after his return from South America. Many of those in attendance at the conference were former students of Bolton's and did not need his fervent message and plea for understanding since he had taught them that lesson many years before. But the experience was important to Bolton, for he felt the invitation indicative of the fact that at long last his "Americas vision" was catching on and becoming an integral part of national policy.

Besides these business trips and a few weeks on the trails of both Coronado and Escalante, Bolton spent still more of the first months of his retirement on the road, speaking to hundreds of students in colleges and universities across the country. January 1941 he spent two weeks, traveling and lecturing on both sides of the Rockies, in Colorado, Wyoming, and Utah. From Utah he wrote home: "This talkie-talkie business is pretty silly, and I don't know how long I would be able to stand myself — or people stand me!" But he was back on the road in March, this time with stops in Reno, Virginia City, and Carson City. His next letter home was from Chicago. He traveled south all the way to St. Augustine, Florida, before heading back to California via Washington and numerous stops in Ohio.

The evening of May 6 found him back on a very familiar platform, the stage of Wheeler Auditorium, as he delivered the Fourth Bernard Moses Memorial Lecture. He pulled together some ideas from his developing Coronado story, entitling the lecture "El Dorado: The Coronado Expedition in Perspective."

By the end of May he was pleasantly busy with rather familiar business. On May 14 he received a letter from Edward A. Dickson, member of the University of California Board of Regents, naming him editor-in-chief of the projected ten-volume Centennial History of California. The idea had been in the air for several months in anticipation of the centennial year in 1950. The regents intended the job to be handled by the university, with all its various branches cooperating, and the press doing the ultimate publishing. They were willing to allocate a sizable appropriation to get the work started but predicated ultimate completion with an even more sizable appropriation from the state legislature. Bolton, they felt, was the logical man to head the project, his reputation and knowledge and his current *emeritus* status. He lost no time in putting a plan for implementing the series onto Sproul's desk — how to proceed, the immediate financial needs, a cooperating office at UCLA, suggested authors for the ten volumes, with a division of subject matter into decade stories, at least in the later years. In these early stages, John W. Caughey, UCLA, was his coeditor in the Southland, with a small office force. In Berkeley Bolton was able to get the appointment of Maxine Chappell as his secretary and assistant and turned over to her capable direction many of the day-to-day details of the project, installing her across the corridor in Library 427.

Bolton's schedule for the fall of 1941 included more travel and more speaking engagements. Then in mid-November while in Pullman, Washington, directing a several-day Institute on Latin American Relations, he received the shocking news that Chapman had been stricken with a massive heart attack and had died almost immediately. Completing the Institute at Pullman, Bolton hurried back to speak on "Some Bases for Hemisphere Understanding" in a University of San Francisco lecture series, and then crossed the Bay to a saddened Department of History. The University had been hit twice within days: Chapman was dead and Priestley had suffered what seemed to be a debilitating stroke. Within a few weeks Lawrence Kinnaird was summoned to Washington and soon would be on an extended mission to Chile for the Department of State. Bolton's comment to a correspondent that "our corps of Latin Americanists began to disintegrate" was very true.

These developments would affect Bolton's immediate future. At the end of the first week of December he was in Riverside, presiding as chairman, in place of Priestley, over the symposium of the Riverside Institute of World Affairs. He was thus in the Southland on that fateful Sunday, December 7, when the Japanese attacked Pearl Harbor. By the time he returned to Berkeley he was a citizen of a nation at war. Even before that Sproul had asked him to take temporary charge of the affairs of Bancroft Library:

> In accordance with our telephone conversation, I should be much pleased if you would take over the direction of the Bancroft Library during the illness of Professor Priestley. For the present, I shall ask you to act without formal appointment but if, as unfortunately seems probable, Priestley's illness is of long duration, I shall take steps to make a more formal appointment.

RECALL TO ACADEMIC DUTY

By January 1942 besides his official appointment as editor-in-chief of the Centennial History of California — this was to pay $6000 a year for the next several years, a most welcome addition to the somewhat less than adequate pension from the university — there was the formal appointment as Director of the Bancroft Library. He had also been asked to accept a position as lecturer in history, to fill in for Kinnaird until his return from Chile. The chairmanship of the department excepted, he had returned as of January 1942, to the same positions he had held before July 31, 1940. Retirement had lasted exactly three semesters, but Bolton was not complaining. On January 30 the *Daily Californian* carried a feature interview, "Return of the Sather Professor," and it was obvious that Bolton was happy to be back.

The unanticipated recall to "academic duty," while it was most delightful, did complicate Bolton's life for a time, since, as a free agent, he had made certain commitments which had to be honored. Involvement as editor-in-chief of the California Centennial History took a good deal of time as he sought to lay out the project and then to plot its financing for the six years ahead. He submitted his budget to the comptroller of the university later in September, calling for an outlay of $157,000, which included staff salaries, honoraria to authors ($1000 for each volume), and the probable printing costs for the twenty-three volumes projected.

There developed in the latter half of 1942 a definite rift between Regent Dickson and Bolton over the way the story of California was to be told. Bolton held for the topical approach, without completely sacrificing chronology; Dickson wanted something more strictly chronological, almost a year-to-year chronicle. Bolton had been ready to submit his ideas to the regents at their October meeting in San Francisco, but shortly before, learning through a conference with Dickson what the latter wanted, he decided to hold back and informed Sproul that he was not yet prepared to report. He followed this strategic retreat with a letter to Dickson (October 26), in which, among other strong statements, was the following: "If this plan [for the topical approach] is approved, I shall continue enthusiastically to carry it forward, but if it is required that the one you propose be followed, I shall request President Sproul to appoint someone in my place as editor." After this ultimatum he called a *junta de guerra* in Los Angeles and sat down with several of the men committed to contribute to the series to lay out further battle plans, if needed — John W. Caughey, Owen C. Coy, Robert G. Cleland, William H. Ellison, and Lindley Bynum backed his position.

In the spring of 1943, however, the centennial history project was faced with another serious problem which brought it to an end — at least as far as a joint project with the state of California. No small amount of time and money were expended in lobbying at a distance for State House Resolution No. 137. This was the bid for an appropriation of $200,000 which would have put California behind the project; up to this time the entire funding had been from the university. In May came the disappointing word that the bill had failed to pass. Then began the salvage operation, since too much preliminary work had gone into the cause to allow the idea to die. By late June Bolton had an alternate proposal on Sproul's desk only slightly more modest than the original. He had had a conference with Samuel T. Farquhar, director of the university press, and had done some figuring. The idea of a dozen volumes, to be called the "Chronicles of California" seemed feasible. However, it was not until November that Sproul gave the go-ahead signal, so that Bolton could contact his prospective authors and ask for firm commitments.

Besides teaching, which Bolton had missed the most during his short retirement and the assignment on the centennial history project, there was involvement with James F. King in preparing a set of Latin American history maps for classroom use with Denoyer-Geppert as publisher, and

Herbert E. Bolton
OSARIO
1-JUNE-42
RITZ
MEXICO

A caricature of Herbert Bolton done during the 1942 summer
excursion to Mexico City with the National Park Service to discuss
a Coronado International Monument.

more work with and for the NPS during the early 1940s. In May of 1942
he was asked to go to Mexico as a member of the United States delegation to discuss with the Mexicans the possible establishment of a Coronado International Monument.

The idea of establishing on the Arizona-Sonora border a Coronado
International Monument was well over a year old. Both governments
had expressed interest, and preliminary discussions had been carried on
at the diplomatic level in preparation for a meeting of representatives of
the two nations to settle many of the details. The National Park Service
had been charged with the responsibility for the United States. Hillory A.
Tolson, Chief of Operations, NPS, then set the meeting for late May in
order to have Bolton, "the Coronado expert," in the delegation.

By May 27 the Mexican trip had taken on some of the aspects of a holiday excursion, with the wives of the NPS men also in the party — Mrs. Tolson, Mrs. M. R. Tillotson, Mrs. Aubrey Neasham; Mrs. Bolton had been invited but declined. They were also joined by Sam Weems, assistant superintendent of Blue Ridge Parkway, and his wife. Most had arranged to go on to Mexico City by train, but Weems had his car and wanted to drive. Bolton eagerly jumped at the invitation to go with him and his wife, anxious to see once again sections of Mexico along the Pan American Highway which he had not visited since the days of his archive adventures many years before. His sincere love for Mexico never waned, and he thoroughly enjoyed the trip, long and tiring though it was; the Weemses were delighted to have such a knowledgeable tour guide.

In Mexico City the United States delegation headquartered at the Ritz. They were in Mexico from May 31 to June 11. The conversations with the Mexicans were cordial. That delegation was headed by Carlos Villas Pérez, chief of the Office of National Parks of Mexico, and included men from the forestry service, as well as Rafael Fernández MacGregor, commissioner on the international boundary. In general the Mexicans were as enthusiastic about the idea as were the Americans, although they felt that they might encounter considerably more problems in obtaining the lands in the designated area. In this their apprehensions were proved correct, for the Cananea Cattle Company, which controlled much of the land on the Sonora side of the proposed park, blocked the move to turn prime grazing territory into public domain. Villas Pérez, who immediately after the meeting went up to Sonora to run a preliminary survey, was unable to clear this private-interest hurdle and soon lost his enthusiasm, or he may have been instructed to abandon the project. In all events, the United States subsequently decided to drop the "international" aspect of the scheme and to create its own Coronado National Monument in southern Arizona.

A SECOND RETIREMENT

On March 1, 1944, his recall to duty at the university was terminated and he was "re-retired." The late spring request of Paxson for material to be included in the chairman's report to the president for the 1943–44 year gave Bolton the opportunity to review his work of the past several years:

> Having been retired July 20, 1940, from my position as Sather Professor of History, I was appointed lecturer in History in January, 1942. Thereafter I taught five consecutive regular terms in addition

to the Summer Session of 1942. On March 1, 1944, I was again
retired.

In each of the five semesters I taught a lower-division course
(8A-B: History of the Americas), an upper-division course (189A-
189B: History of the Pacific Coast and the Southwest), and a seminar (281A-281B). In the year I was in retirement (1941) six students in History finished their work for the Ph.D under my direction.
Since I returned to teaching five of my students received the Ph.D
and a larger number the M.A.

He continued, detailing other university activities. He had been chairman
of the Committee on the Hispanic American Regional Group Major;
chairman of the Committee on Latin American Visitors to the university;
editor of volumes on California history, sponsored by the university
press; in 1943 member of a national committee to aid the National Library
of Peru.* As to work outside the university he noted that he was a member of a four-man committee, appointed by the Catholic Church, to gather
evidence for the possible canonization process of Fray Junípero Serra.
He paid well deserved tribute to his assistant, confessing that much of
this was made possible by "the very efficient help of Miss Maxine Chappell, who deserves a large part of the credit for whatever I have accomplished." Concluding, he added: "Before closing I wish to tell you how
greatly I have appreciated the opportunity to return to teaching, which
has always been my favorite sport."

Those twenty-six months, from January 1942 to March 1944, had
been a kind of tonic, so to speak, which gave him renewed vigor. The
only reason he was ready to face a new retirement period was that he
could be freer to do a number of things which had accumulated of late.
He by no means intended to go off to a life of leisure. The same day he
sent his report to Paxson (April 18), he forwarded a request to Sproul
for "the continuation of Miss Chappell's appointment as my secretary
for the academic year July 1, 1944 to June 30, 1945." He gave extended
reasons for this petition and concluded: "Although I have been retired
I am engaged in University work which will keep me just as busy as ever,
and I hope will be as productive for some time into the future as it has
been in the past." In due time this request was granted, as was also that
for a renewal of the grant of $250, for 1944–45, from the university's
Institute of Social Sciences.

----

*The Andean nation lost its centuries-old accumulation of manuscript and book
treasures in a fire. Bolton was chairman of a special committee to search out North
American scholars who had worked in the Lima archive and had collected copies
of documents in an effort to replace the lost materials.

Retired or not, Bolton's personal schedule had changed very little over the years as was brought out in a plea in August to the university's committee on wartime gasoline rationing. He was asking in a very persuasive tone for renewal of his "B" card:

> I come to the University by streetcar seven days a week at 9 a.m., and go home for dinner by streetcar also. I return to the University every night at 8 p.m., and go home at 11 or 12 p.m. At that time the streetcar service is irregular and I frequently have to walk or wait an indefinite time for a car. In any case, I have to walk a quarter of a mile up a steep hill after leaving the streetcar, which is contrary to my physician's orders, since I am uninsurable on the ground of what they call heart trouble. Though I am not teaching this semester my whole time is devoted to University work. . . .

At least some of his time was devoted to university work, but his last years would be filled to overflowing with many other involvements as well.

17

Retirement So-Called

I
T WAS REALLY WITH 1945 that what might euphuistically be called his
retirement began. Although Bolton's university appointment as lecturer in history had ended the year before, there was still much work
which demanded his attention daily. Among other things, the last two of
his one hundred and four doctors were completing their dissertations.
The Coronado biography due George Hammond now many months past
was still unfinished; the "Chronicles of California" series had to be completed; in addition Bolton was looking forward to time for other projects
long postponed; the National Park Service, now that he was a free agent,
was minded to put him to work more often in his status as collaborator-
at-large, and that is where the story of these years really begins.

In the spring of 1945 the NPS asked him to go on a tour of the Colorado River basin in connection with a survey it was making. The government was being pressured to build a series of dams and reservoirs along
the course of the river, for power and irrigation — the drive for water was
already on in the surrounding states. The NPS, fearing that such a program might end some of its prime recreational facilities in the Southwest
and, more importantly, eliminate some of the important historic sites and
trails, determined to carry out a careful survey to present to the national
legislators who soon would be faced with a decision.

M. R. Tillotson, chief of Region Three of the NPS (the Southwest),
explained the NPS intent in asking Bolton for his collaboration:

> It is our intention to publish a report of the survey. The Report
> should include:
> 1. General statements on the history, archeology and geology
> of the Colorado River Basin. . . . It is desirable to have a map or
> chart of the basin showing the location of important historic sites
> and early routes of travel and exploration, such as Escalante's route,
> the Old Spanish Trail, and Frémont's route.
> 2. . . . We would like to have these subjects presented in the
> report by well-known authorities and would deeply appreciate it if
> you would consent to prepare the historical statement . . .

This was a ready-made vacation for Bolton, and he jumped at the chance to be back in his beloved Southwest, especially with government assistance and at government expense. The travel part of the assignment was fun; the preparation of the report, something a bit less than that. He did finish it, however, that fall.

THE CORONADO STORY

Bolton's acquaintance with the NPS covered a span of more than fifteen years. Often some area proposed for exploration was of mutual interest, making it doubly advantageous for Bolton when he was invited to go along with an NPS team. Such had been the case with the trails of both Escalante and Coronado. Bolton often worked closely with NPS director Newton B. Drury and Tillotson. He had been invited, for example, to be a part of the NPS team that would inspect the Big Bend country of Texas in April and May, 1944. Bolton wrote to suggest that since the party would be so close, the NPS might be interested in doing a bit more Coronado work in the Panhandle, before moving south to the Big Bend assignment. Both Drury and Tillotson approved the suggestion, and Tillotson picked up Bolton at Flagstaff. From there they drove into the *barranca* country between Amarillo and Lubbock. Writing to Mrs. Bolton and family from Lubbock (April 27), he announced with an air of triumph: "I have settled the canyon question – not tentatively (as I told them) but permanently." He was now finally and firmly convinced that Coronado's "great barranca" simply had to be Palo Duro Canyon, and nothing else. From late April and into May they were in the field inspecting the Big Bend country. The State of Texas had deeded to the United States several hundred thousand acres in the area with the idea that a national monument might be laid out there. Bolton's presence and assistance had been greatly appreciated by the NPS team. In a letter of May 20, Hillory Tolson thanked him:

> All the members of the Big Bend group are delighted that you could be with us; that you were enabled to "pin down" the Coronado Trail in the Palo Duro region; that you contributed so much in furnishing us with some of the historical background of the Big Bend region.

Tillotson (June 6) was even more detailed in his letter of thanks:

> Also I derived the greatest personal pleasure and satisfaction from being with you while you were identifying the exact Coronado route. The more I think of it and the more I have been able to study

the limited source materials available to me, the more I am convinced that you are correct in your thought that the Palo Duro and
its tributaries satisfy the description much more accurately than
Yellowhouse.

It was particularly helpful to have you with us on the Big Bend
trip. Your account of the Ugalde campaign and other historical
events connected with the Big Bend region in general gave me a
much deeper appreciation than ever of the history of that section of
the country. I know that Mr. Maxwell, Mr. Dodge, and I now have
a much better idea as to some of the lines along which our interpretive program for Big Bend National Park should be developed;
thanks to you.

Although Bolton had been planning to write the biography of Coronado for many years, his more serious work of tracing the exact route
of the conquistador had begun after George Hammond had asked him
in 1939 to submit his biography for publication in New Mexico's Coronado Cuatro-Centennial Series. Thereafter, the telling of this story had
become the central concern of his writing efforts.

Unlike the Kino biography Bolton was, with Coronado, building on
the work of earlier scholars. Besides taking advantage of newly uncovered
source materials, however, what distinguished his Coronado work from
theirs, to some extent, was this determination to pin down the exact route
his conquistador had taken. After 1939 this was the object of much of
his work in the field.

On January 12, 1940, Bolton with a half-dozen companions had
headed south from Tucson to pick up the four-hundred-year-old trail of
Don Francisco Vásquez de Coronado. In the party, besides Bolton were
three of his "boys," George Hammond of the University of New Mexico,
Russell Ewing of the University of Arizona, Aubrey Neasham, Region
Three historian of the NPS; W. Ward Yeager, NPS forester, and Harold
Walter, an Albuquerque photographer and friend of Hammond completed the team. They had decided to follow the steps of Coronado literally; hence, they hurried south to Compostela. Late morning of January
20, in spirit they waved good-bye to Viceroy Antonio de Mendoza and
headed for Cíbola. Along the route they strayed off the so-called highway
rather often in order to touch as many points mentioned in the Coronado
records as possible. At Hermosillo, after laying over for two days' worth
of repairs to their station wagon, they cut inland, worked their way
through the gorge of the Río Sonora and into the Valle de Sonora, on to
Cananea, and thence to the international boundary at Naco, arriving there
the afternoon of February 1.

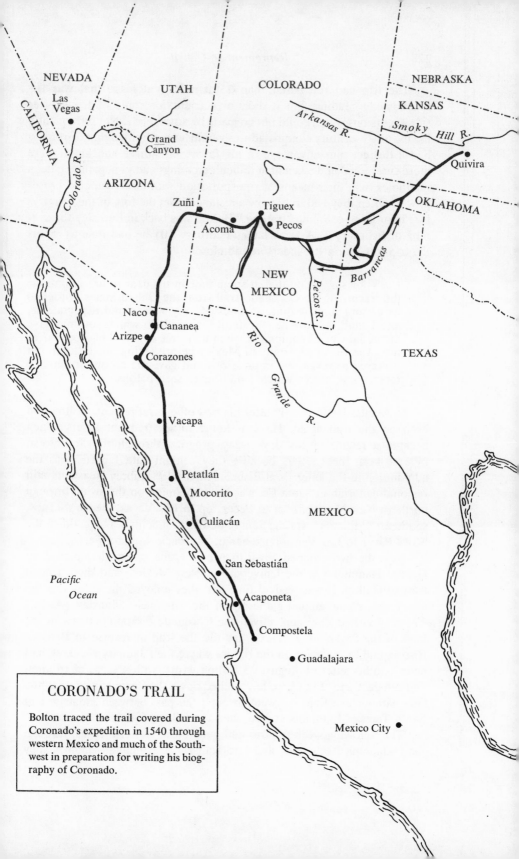

NEVADA

UTAH

COLORADO

NEBRASKA

Las
Vegas

KANSAS

CALIFORNIA

Arkansas R.

Smoky Hill R.

Colorado R.

Grand
Canyon

Quivira

ARIZONA

Zuñi

Tiguex

OKLAHOMA

Ácoma

Pecos

NEW
MEXICO

Barrancas

Pecos R.

Naco

Cananea

TEXAS

Arizpe

Corazones

Rio Grande R.

Vacapa

Petatlán

Mocorito

Culiacán

MEXICO

San Sebastián

Pacific
Ocean

Acaponeta

Compostela

Guadalajara

Mexico City

CORONADO'S TRAIL

Bolton traced the trail covered during
Coronado's expedition in 1540 through
western Mexico and much of the Southwest in preparation for writing his biography of Coronado.

The trip had run better than 2500 miles — at least, that was the speedometer reading, but it did not account for some of the shorter side excursions which could not be made by automobile. Not infrequently the twentieth-century conquistadores would have admitted that Coronado had a distinct plus advantage in his favor: his horses and mules were more surefooted and efficient at difficult crossings and in negotiating deep mudholes than their means of transportation with all its vaunted horse-power. Often they had to borrow assistance from the folk of the country-side in order to continue "trailing." Bolton was back in Berkeley the eve-ning of February 3. A week later (February 10) he had time to report the trip to Clinton P. Anderson and closed:

> Your suggestion that at some time in the near future I continue the tracing of the Coronado trail from the United States border to its eastern limit is quite in line with my wishes and expectations, and I shall be extremely grateful for any help which you may give me in the way of equipment when that time comes. I had been over most the Coronado route in Mexico before taking this last trip but it served to revive my impressions and gave me an opportunity to reach some places which I had never seen before.

In August 1940, shortly after his first official retirement, Bolton had been on the trail again. He sent home rather frequent letters which became a record of his day-to-day progress through the Southwest. "Please keep these letters because they contain data I need" was the admonition in the letter from Bisbee, August 19. Aubrey Neasham, still regional historian at Santa Fe, was his companion on the swing through northern New Mexico, over to Pecos, up to Las Vegas, thence to Taos, southeast to Picurís, over the Sangre de Cristo mountain range, down the Mora River to Las Vegas once again, and back to Santa Fe.

Next the two dropped down to Albuquerque, where they picked up George Hammond at the University of New Mexico, and then headed west to Gallup. It was festival time and they enjoyed the color and the excitement of the annual gathering of the tribesmen. Saturday (August 17) they visited Zuñi and relived the Coronado disappointments in the land of the Seven Cities. Next they did the trail in reverse to Benson, Bisbee, and to the point on the border where their January checking had ended. In his letter of August 23 Bolton wrote, with a sense of triumph and satisfaction: "I think we have nailed down the Coronado route to the Gila without question. He went through the pass between Pinaleno and Santa Teresa Mountains and reached the Gila at Calva."

The following week the trio had gone on to western Texas, through the Oklahoma Panhandle, and into Kansas. In panhandle country they again concluded that Palo Duro and Tule Canyons were the "barrancas" in Coronado's records for that country. Back in Berkeley, Bolton set to work to complete his manuscript, promising it to Hammond for the next year.

Unfortunately 1941 was only the first year in a long wait for George Hammond. In the fall of that year, Bolton told Hammond that Don Francisco was haunting him day and night and that he was "going into his fourth color — yellow, green, pink, and now pure white." He often wrote successive drafts of a book manuscript on various colors of paper. He went on to express more than mild concern that the recently published study of A. Grove Day, *Coronado's Quest*, and ironically issued by the University of California Press, might make his own projected work on the conquistador less than necessary. He confessed that he had simply paged through the book, so as to avoid being influenced by it.

Two years later, while still working on the manuscript, Bolton came upon some very valuable and hitherto unknown Coronado materials — the records of Don Francisco's *residencia* and of the similar trials of several of his key lieutenants.* The discovery had been made through George Hammond. Bolton immediately recognized that these documents were likely to contain much new data on his conquistador hero. There was one big problem, however: these records were in the original steno-graphic script of the court reporters. In his younger days and with keener eyesight he would have reveled in the challenge, but by 1943 he was less inclined to wade into extensive paleographic labor and, besides, he was getting very impatient to finish his story. He had some funds from the Institute of Social Science Grant No. 581; these he supplemented with money of his own and some from other sources; then he went to an old friend, Professor Agapito Rey of Indiana University, one of the most skilled Spanish paleographers in the country, to request assistance.† With an easily readable Spanish transcript he would be perfectly willing to do his own translating. Rey agreed, and the first packet of transcripts went west to Bolton late in the year.

----

*The *residencia* was the Crown's review of the actions of an official at the close of his appointment or term of office. Charges and complaints against the officer were presented to a *juez de residencia* and a judgment passed by the latter, or in instances by the Crown itself. Out of the records of these proceedings many details often come to light.

†Historians of the Borderlands are indebted to Agapito Rey for the many excellent translations of important Spanish sources; he very often worked with George Hammond.

Early in January, 1944, shortly before his second retirement, Bolton had given a progress report in a letter to long-suffering George Hammond on the long overdue Coronado:

> You no doubt are wondering how far up the road Coronado has come by this time, and all I can say is that I am giving it all the time I have, which is considerable, and that progress is being made. I had practically finished the book on the basis of the old materials when I began to get consignments of new stuff from Dr. Rey, and am now devoting myself to that. As you know, it will enable us to give a lot more detail and to some extent to set aside some of the old conclusions. But it takes time. . . .

On September 19, 1945, he told Hammond: "To come at once to the point, the Coronado book is not ready to send to the printer." He promised to try for the end of October but would make no firm promise. It was becoming something of a ghost haunting him rather continually. Besides field work with the NPS in the Colorado River basin and elsewhere, part of the reason for this further delay in 1945 was his summer commitment to a Latin American lecture-teaching tour. Bolton, motivated by a desire to do more to aid his country during World War II, had written to former student William L. Schurz with the Division of Cultural Relations, Department of State, suggesting that there might be a need for a lecturer or teacher with his knowledge of Latin America and his contacts. Response was favorable, and Herschel Brickell arranged for a lecture-teaching tour during the summer months of 1945.

Bolton missed yet another tentative deadline, set for October 1945, but through the early months of 1946, was seriously intent on finishing the Coronado biography. He turned down several other rather tempting lecture invitations. Maybe some of this determination to stay home and finish the Coronado book this time was tied in with the fact that George P. Hammond would soon be on the Berkeley campus permanently, as director of the Bancroft Library. When Hammond was still in Albuquerque, it was less embarrassing to write periodically to say that "Coronado is taking shape, and that I hope before long to have it ready for your inspection" — this was a February 26, 1946, message. To have to face him day after day might be somewhat less than comfortable. Of course, Bolton was in large measure responsible for setting up this situation, since he had campaigned strongly and, according to stories, on one occasion very vehemently, for Hammond's appointment to the Bancroft post. At any rate, Bolton stayed close to his desk, at least for the first half of 1946, with his conquistador hero.

Finally in 1947, the Coronado manuscript was ready, and Bolton bundled it up and sent it, not to George Hammond, but to a New York publisher. Since 1939, the presumption had been that his Coronado biography would be the first volume in the Coronado Cuatro-Centennial Series which the University of New Mexico Press was issuing one by one as the manuscripts accumulated. Further, the press had even talked to him of using not only the Coronado, but also his projected Escalante study in the series. There seems to have been no formal contract drawn, but Bolton's not infrequent exchanges with George Hammond, editor of the series, are ample evidence that both parties were proceeding on the basis of, at very least, a gentleman's agreement. Then came the temptation.

Whittlesey House, a division of McGraw-Hill Book Company, had announced a Southwestern Fellowship Award for the best manuscript with a Southwestern theme. This prize was to be $1000 and publication. Joseph Henry Jackson, for long years book-reviewer for the San Francisco *Chronicle,* aware of Bolton's developing Coronado biography, called his attention to the contest and also tipped off the publisher that here was a book which would be an honor to Whittlesey House's list. Accordingly, on July 24 a telegram went out from Editor William E. Larned, informing Bolton that the prize competition would close on September 8 and suggesting that he make no commitment until receipt of the airmail letter which was following. With confidence in Jackson's judgment, Larned offered Bolton an immediate advance of $2500 against future royalties and gave him fair hope that the Coronado might well win the nod of the Whittlesey House Prize jury.

Publication by a national house, with its large distribution network, and particularly the advance and the possible prize money were alluring, something almost like manna from heaven in the parched desert of retirement income. Bolton had never been much of a financial manager nor one to think of the future, save in terms of new research projects, new books, or ways to amass transcripts of archival materials. At a festive family gathering one of his daughters once wrote two very true lines into a little poem on "Dad": "But money to him was only a game / He brought up his family on honor and fame." The oft-talked-of book to implement and complement the History of the Americas course *might* have brought substantial royalties, but he never got around to putting it together. So many other projects were much more appealing and exciting — Palóu, Anza, Kino, Coronado, Escalante, and in his dreams for the future, Mange, Garcés, Salvatierra, the still untranslated Venegas history of California. His many writings won him great scholarly esteem but never made him a wealthy man. His rationale was that the Coronado book might change that pattern, when he most needed such a break — unless there was some supplement, as during the days of his return to teaching or his connection with the California Centennial project, his retirement income was somewhat less than $4000 a year, just about two-fifths of his salary as Sather Professor. So without word to the University of New Mexico or the Coronado Cuatro-Centennial Commission, the manuscript went off to McGraw-Hill, on August 28.

Word traveled quickly. Hammond, on the ground at Berkeley and deeply respecting his old master, was embarrassed but did not quite know how to proceed in what was a truly awkward situation. Fred E. Harvey, director of the University of New Mexico Press, had no such scruples. In early September he wrote to Bolton and to McGraw-Hill to express surprise, chagrin, and vexation. Larned of Whittlesey House, recognizing immediately that he had picked up a "hot potato" and fearing possible involvement in a lawsuit, asked Bolton (September 12) for an explanation. Bolton contended that without a formal contract New Mexico had no strict right or enforceable claim. There were exchanges from three directions; the situation was, to say the very least, highly explosive. Then a compromise was effected. The University of New Mexico Press picked up the McGraw-Hill contract, with the same terms as to the advance and subsequent royalties, so that it might print, publish, and issue *Coronado on the Turquoise Trail* as Volume One of its Coronado Cuatro-Centennial Series; McGraw-Hill agreed to take the New Mexico printings, to give the volume the Whittlesey House joint imprint, and to assume the task of national distribution. This edition came out as *Coronado, Knight of Pueblos and Plains*.

Although Larned warned Bolton, in January 1948, that the study might be judged too scholarly by the prize committee, in April he could happily report that the Coronado manuscript had won the Whittlesey House Southwestern Fellowship Award. This prize was conferred, with much fanfare and publicity, at the Texas Institute of Letters Awards Luncheon in Dallas, on November 12, 1948.

Bolton had come a long way in the thirty years since Allen Johnson and Robert Glasgow were telling him that he lacked the ability to tell a story with artistry of words. There is little question that the book, when it appeared in 1949, did benefit by having a national house as its sponsor. *Time* and *The Saturday Review* took note of *Coronado*, as did the historical journals. Robert Glass Cleland, in the *AHR* (July 1950), voiced a judgment which the profession would have seconded with a heavy majority:

> Herbert E. Bolton's place in American scholarship is too well known to require comment. To the history and understanding of the Spanish Southwest he rendered as great a service as Frederick

Jackson Turner rendered to the history of the West. . . . His publications have become almost classics of the kind. *Coronado* . . . is another product of the tireless research in archives, libraries, and on the trail. . . . The book has the Bolton hallmark. It is comprehensive, authoritative, written with meticulous attention to detail.

The maneuvering of Whittlesey House, too, was undoubtedly responsible for the Coronado's being chosen as the History Club's* selection for January 1950. On its own merit alone, however, in May 1950 the book won the George Bancroft Prize as an outstanding book in American history.[1]

Even with the completion of the Coronado biography well after Bolton's retirement, about the only evidence on the surface, at least, that Bolton was not a full-time employee of the University of California showed at payroll time. With the California Centennial imminent, President Sproul had asked him to serve as coordinator of the university's efforts as well as those of UCLA and the other branches; this task entailed some planning and much correspondence. In the late spring of 1947 he was again nudging his authors in the "Chronicles of California" series, so that he might make a June progress report to the press.† There was a trip to Philadelphia in late April, when he read a paper before the American Philosophical Society. "The West Coast Corridor" was a short preview (he had been allowed just twenty minutes) of the book which he was projecting, and in order to prepare it he was asking for a grant from the society.[1] It was in this short study that he sketched the concept of the Spanish northward advance into the Borderlands along three well-defined corridors. The society voted him a generous subsidy to continue this work, for which his own and the researches of a number of his students of the 1930s had piled up the raw materials. It was this grant which helped to bring Virginia E. Thickens into his research-assistant family. He would need her help, for in the fall of 1947 he foresaw the loss of his secretary and assistant for the past nine years — Maxine Chappell was to marry and move out of the state.

Finally, during the late 1940s Bolton was busy once again soliciting funds for other proposed writing projects. Included in his plans was the study of Escalante which he had been working on for almost twenty-five years. Soon there would be others as interested as Bolton in having this friar's story in writing, and they would provide the reason for the completion of still another Bolton biography.

---

*The History Club was a book club begun in the 1940s.

†The "Chronicles of California" series never materialized as a strict series, but some scattered volumes prepared for the series subsequently were published.

18

Franciscan Company and End of the Trail

D URING A LARGE PART of his scholarly life Bolton kept rather constant company with the friars and the padres in his Borderlands. In the early days he had worked "with" the Franciscans as he uncovered the story of colonial Texas. Then Kino had introduced him to the Jesuits, and he became fascinated not only by his "favorite Black Robe," but also reveled in following Kino's brethren up the "west coast corridor" and in learning, in large measure from the padres, how the mission became one of Spain's premier frontier institutions. When Bolton moved to California, the friars were again prime objects of his research and writing; even when Anza was his hero, the Franciscans were prominent in the story, particularly one Fray Francisco Garcés, whose fuller story he wanted some day to tell. For a couple years after completing his Coronado biography he was again consorting with the friars — Fray Junípero Serra and a younger contemporary of the California Padre Presidente but in another Borderland, one Fray Silvestre Vélez de Escalante. Then in late 1949 very live Franciscans intruded into his life. For a time he was, so to speak, in a "Franciscan period."

The first of the friars with whom he became involved in the late 1940s was an old acquaintance of his "California period," Fray Junípero Serra. There was in those years a strong upsurge of enthusiasm in pressing for the canonization of Serra as a saint of the Catholic church. This is a highly complicated and technical process which consists of a certain series of canonically established steps. The initial stage is one of serious investigation into the life and character of the person under consideration, and here is where Bolton fitted in. With the possible exception of Father Maynard Geiger, O.F.M., who had already begun his extensive and intensive researches into the career of his confrere, no American was likely to be better acquainted with Serra's American years than Bolton. His assistance had been enlisted by Franciscan superiors and by the bishop of the diocese of Monterey-Fresno, Philip G. Scher, under whose canonical jurisdiction the preliminary investigations took place. Bolton was happy to cooperate, although he often joked about his role, "a damned Protestant," in so solemn a Catholic proceeding. He certainly had documentary evidence which might serve as answers to such probing questions as: how objective Palóu was as a biographer; what examples might be adduced of Serra's "heroic virtue"; what the background was of his not infrequent altercations with civil authorities, and how saintly Serra's conduct in such disputes was; what his attitude was toward the Indians, toward fellow Spaniards in California, toward the friars who were his religious subjects and coworkers.

In 1949, for his contributions to the Serra cause Bolton was given papal recognition by the conferral on him of knighthood in the Equestrian Order of Saint Sylvester. Next, on December 12 he became the fifth scholar to receive the Serra Award, conferred by the Academy of American Franciscan History. When informed earlier in the year by Father Roderick Wheeler, O.F.M., that he was the 1949 nominee, he thanked the Friar Vice-Director of the Academy but confessed frankly that he would hardly be able to cross the continent to receive the honor, at least not at his own expense. Father Wheeler had not thought to make it clear that Bolton would be the Academy's guest "from portal to portal." Among other things in that first letter of May 28 Bolton gave a rather interesting rundown of recent activities:

> With teaching, which I am forced to do for a meager living; contributing my bit to the Serra Cause; the completion of a book on Coronado, and the proof-reading just ahead of me; work on two historical films for the California Centennial Celebration (Paramount), speech making for these same festivities. . . . I have been kept busy night and day, and only my toughness has enabled me to survive. . . .

A number of his friends in the Washington area were invited to the ceremonies and many attended to share the evening with him. The morning celebration was religious, centering around the Solemn Mass in honor of Nuestra Señora de Guadalupe, patroness of the Americas. The academic session, following a festive dinner, was held in the auditorium of McMahon Hall, on the campus of the Catholic University.

It was the bicentennial year of the arrival of Serra in America. Serra was the theme of the three speakers: Juan Hervas, bishop of Majorca, contributed a paper on Serra and Spain, which was read by His Excellency the Spanish ambassador; next the ambassador of Honduras and historian, Rafael Heliodoro Valle, spoke, then Maynard Geiger, who was already

beginning the study which would produce the very scholarly biography of
Serra a dozen or more years later.

Father Roderick Wheeler had the task of presenting Bolton, and
friar director of the academy Alexander Wyse then read the citation of
the award:

> Noting with admiration the unique place among historians of
> America enjoyed by Herbert Eugene Bolton by reason of his
> researches and writings extending over half a century and recalling
> with particular gratitude his contributions to the history of the
> Franciscan Missions of California and the Southwest and desirous
> of paying tribute in the most significant manner in its power to his
> assistance in the process of Beatification of Fray Junípero Serra,
> Founder of the California Missions.
>
> By vote of its Academic Council and with the approval of the
> Minister General and the General Definitorium of the Order of
> Friars Minor, the Academy of American Franciscan History is proud
> to bestow the highest honor within its reach upon that distinguished
> gentleman and scholar . . . in recognition of his lifelong devotion to
> the history of the Franciscan Missions of California and the South-
> west and in tribute to his invaluable contribution to the Diocesan
> Historical Commission in the cause of Fray Junípero Serra.

Foreseeing that the session would be lengthy, Father Roderick had
enjoined the honoree to make his remarks brief. For Bolton, they were!
His brief talk was later published in *The Americas,* under the title "The
Confession of a Wayward Professor."[2] He "confessed": "I wrote it on the
train, and my rhetoric may reflect some of the bumps in the roadbed. . . .
I ought to warn you that what I have to say comes from the mouth of a
Mayflower descendant and the grandson of a Methodist minister." He
followed with a short sketch of the origins and development of his his-
torical interests, especially that as regards the missions of New Spain.

These twentieth-century friars were one of the last groups in a long
list of grateful people who had sought across the years to formally thank
Bolton for his services as scholar and historian. In the last dozen years
he had been honored by Marquette University of Wisconsin (1937, Doctor of Humane Letters), the University of New Mexico (1937, Doctor of
Laws), University of Pennsylvania, his second university alma mater
(1940), the University of California (1942), and the University of Wisconsin, his first university alma mater (1945).

THE ESCALANTE TRANSLATION

Bolton spent much of his time in 1949 and early 1950 in the company
once again of another Franciscan with whom he had been acquainted for
many years. Escalante was one of several projects which he still had in

Herbert Bolton, left, was recipient of eight honorary degrees such as the one given here by the University of California in May 1942. To the right of Bolton are President Robert Gordon Sproul and Ralph T. Fisher.

mind to tackle, and even before a formal request for completion of the translation — which would come in mid-1949 — Bolton was prospecting far and wide for research funds for various projects including the Escalante. He appealed to Professor Raymond T. Birge, university grants chairman (March 11); "The West Coast Corridor" was his proposed study; he requested $1500, two-thirds of which was to go for secretarial assistance, maps, and so forth with the remainder earmarked for acquisition of manuscript copies which were necessary but available in neither his own nor the Bancroft collections. A like appeal went to Waldo Leland (March 21), petitioning an ACLS (American Council of Learned Societies) grant. An August 6 request to Kernan Robson was more detailed and less modest. He outlined his intended projects: (1) the editing and publication of the Venegas manuscript on Baja California, (2) a biography of Gasper de Portolá, (3) the history of California under Spain and Mexico, (4) the attempts in the late eighteenth century to connect' Spain's two northern outposts — Santa Fe and Monterey — which meant the Escalante and the Garcés sagas. As mentioned, the request was hardly modest, in that he asked for $12,500 and suggested that a like grant for the second year would be ideal. He wanted $4000 each for two assistants, $2000 for field work and supplementary manuscript materials, and $2500 for himself in order that he might be relieved of the necessity of teaching at San Francisco State College.*

Midway through 1949 Professor Joel E. Ricks, of Utah State University and president of the Utah State Historical Society, approached him about his Escalante study. The Utah people were anxious to see in print the story of the young friar and his companions who, in 1776, while attempting to open a path of communications between Santa Fe and Monterey, had trailed through a sizable section of their state. They knew that Bolton's interest in the friar and his expedition went back almost a quarter of a century, when in 1926 he and some of his University of Utah summer students had begun to trace out sections of the Escalante trail. Further, it was common knowledge that in the intervening years he had on several expeditions covered the rest of the trail, and in some stretches more than once. Bolton's reaction to the Ricks overture was favorable; the latter wrote back that Leland H. Creer, one of Bolton's doctors, would be in Berkeley in August and that Creer would talk over terms and other matters.

In the summer of 1926, when he was invited to teach at the University of Utah, Bolton had accepted with enthusiasm; he foresaw summer weekends giving him a chance to get onto the Escalante trail, as the eighteenth-century friar and companions sought to open a path from Santa Fe to the West Coast. He was not disappointed. Before he returned to Berkeley he had retraced the trail in Utah from northeast to southwest and, after the summer session, had seen the land from Montrose, Colorado, to the Utah border. In the fall of the next year he was able to follow the party eastbound through the so-called Dixie Strip, out of Saint George, Utah. A Bolton letter of July 9, 1927, to W. T. Atkins, one of his companions

---

*Beginning in the fall of 1947 and continuing through the 1948–49 year as well, Bolton lectured at San Francisco State College (then located at Buchanan and Hermann), on Tuesdays and Thursdays, teaching History 8 (History of the Americas) and History 189 (The Pacific Coast and California). He was able thereby to supplement his annual income by $2500.

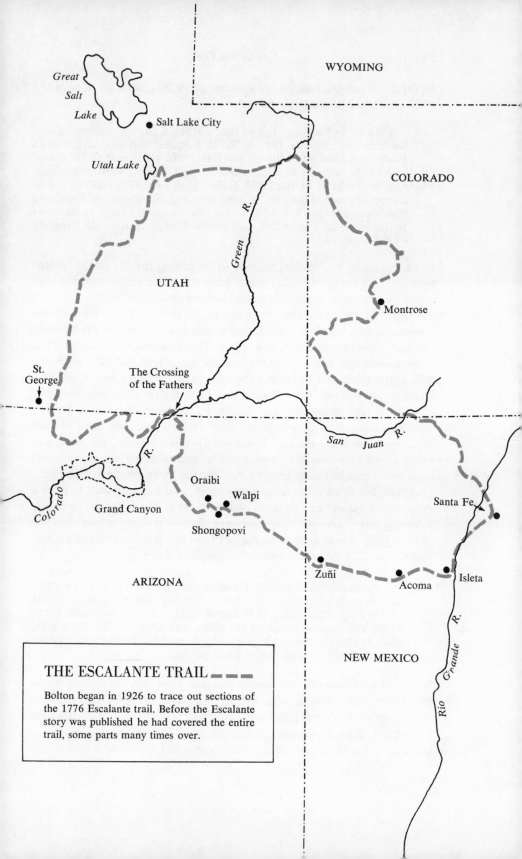

Great
Salt
Lake

● Salt Lake City

Utah Lake

WYOMING

COLORADO

UTAH

Green R.

● Montrose

St.
George ●

The Crossing
of the Fathers

San Juan R.

Santa Fe ●

Colorado R.

Oraibi
● Walpi
● ●
Shongopovi

Grand Canyon

ARIZONA

Zuñi
●

Acoma
●

● Isleta

NEW MEXICO

Rio Grande R.

THE ESCALANTE TRAIL — —

Bolton began in 1926 to trace out sections of
the 1776 Escalante trail. Before the Escalante
story was published he had covered the entire
trail, some parts many times over.

on the Escalante trail during the summer of 1926, gives some idea of the 1927 trek through the Dixie Strip:

> We picked up the trail at Black Rock Canyon, followed Escalante up the mesa at Temple Road, pursued him east to Cooper's Pockets, northwest to the Canna Reservoir, northwest to Fredonia, east to the edge of Buckskin Gulch, past Navajo Well and northeast to the head of Buckskin Gulch in the neighborhood of Paria. There we reached the limit of automobiling, as we watched Escalante disappear over Buckskin Mountain. At this point I hope to take him up on horseback next fall, and follow him at least to the crossing of the Colorado.

Even this early, Bolton had seemed to be getting the Escalante volume very close to completion, but there were still some sections of the trail which he wished to traverse. The end loomed in sight.

Again in July 1941, before going to Stanford to teach the summer session, he had been able to sandwich in a little Escalante exploration. He had already contacted Newton B. Drury, director, National Park Service, with the idea and expressed the hope that the NPS might be sufficiently interested to finance the expedition and give him Jesse Nusbaum as companion. The NPS still had plans for the Escalante trail, and clearances had come through. Nusbaum, evidently foreseeing Drury's favorable reply, had already begun preparations, as a long letter of June 19, 1941, indicates. He had contacted Norman Neville, the excursion boatman of Medicine Hat, and made a deal whereby the party could have two boats but only have to pay for the extra boatman. He had a photographer lined up to accompany them, and had arranged to have a government car at Lee's Ferry to pick them up at the end of the river run. Between July 1 and July 8 of that year, Bolton realized a long-standing hope — to be able to float down the San Juan and into the Colorado River. Later (July 15) he told Gregory Crampton of the trip:

> We finally got away on Tuesday and spent the next seven and a half days floating down the river, running rapids, getting soaked, drying out, hitch-hiking to Rainbow Bridge, racing mountain sheep which ran parallel to us on the cliffs, and generally having a good time. It was real sport. Incidentally, I reached the Escalante crossing, and it all opened out as plain as day.

Such had been some of the experiences that went into the making of the Escalante story. Now almost exactly twenty-three years later, Bolton was committed to a publisher and could pull the manuscript off the shelf for the last time. In October Ricks informed Bolton that the Board of Control of the Utah State Historical Society had approved a motion "to offer you $2500 for your translation of the Father Escalante Diary, edited by you with necessary illustrations." Ricks regretted that the board could not authorize funds for further exploration, which Bolton had suggested. He indicated that the *Utah State Historical Quarterly* would hope to publish the work early in the next year (1950). This was agreeable to Bolton. His translation was complete at least in rough; he would only have to develop the historical introduction, ready the Bernardo Miera y Pacheco contemporary map, and add his own "trail map." He got down to business, but in what might be termed "later Bolton" fashion, slowly. There were distractions and then the trip to the East in middle December.

In January 1950 Bolton took pains to reassure Ricks that he was at work and that there was progress with the Escalante book. It did not get his whole time during the next months. In March he was Charter Day speaker on the university's San Francisco campus and through the heart of April he was on the East Coast, attending first a meeting of the Advisory Board of the National Park Service at Washington and then a session of the American Philosophical Society in Philadelphia. He turned down an invitation to teach the summer session at Oklahoma A & M in order to work on the Escalante translation. In the spring it was rumored that Bolton was intending to give the Escalante study to the University of New Mexico Press, as a companion volume to the Coronado. Knowing something of what had happened in the case of that latter manuscript, Ricks wrote to Bolton, who set his mind at rest with firm assurance that Escalante was committed to Utah and nowhere else. This was in May.

The weeks went by and Ricks still had no manuscript. He was in Berkeley in the summer and sought, diplomatically, to hasten production. That fall Russell Mortensen became editor of the *Utah Historical Quarterly,* and Ricks was only too happy to turn his "problem author" over to the younger man; well into the next year, however, Ricks continued to nudge Bolton from time to time. Mortensen, in October 1950, sent Bolton a masterfully diplomatic letter: he pleaded his need to set the *UHQ* publication schedules and noted that the *Quarterly* was being "bombarded" with queries as to when the readers might expect the long-ago-announced volume. Mortensen had, evidently, made the right approach, for Bolton answered almost immediately and promised at least the translation of the diary within the next few weeks. It was in Mortensen's hands by early December. Getting the historical introduction would take more time and more letters.

In these exchanges an interesting bit of information surfaced. Mortensen wanted a frontispiece and a dust jacket for the book, had a highly skilled young artist (Keith Eddington) ready to put Escalante atop one of Utah's canyon walls, but he, and Eddington, wanted to know how to garb the friar and his Franciscan companion, Anastacio Domínguez, in the illustration. Bolton was reasonably certain that the color should be gray, and for the skullcap also, but to make doubly sure he called on Father Maynard Geiger for confirmation. Geiger came back: "Make the habit grey!" The Franciscans in the colonial Americas were not always the "Brown Robes."

Finally, Bolton delivered the introduction. In late April 1951 Mortensen wrote that the manuscript was ready to go to press and voiced the hope that the "insertions" of which Bolton had spoken as likely to come were all in his hands. It was time, too, to talk seriously about the title; several had been suggested in their correspondence, "Pageant in the Wilderness," "Long Way Around," "Inter-Mountain Trek." The press work moved rapidly and by May 10 Mortensen wrote that it was ready to go into "page production." In July he arrived at the door of Bolton's office, Library Annex 456,* and personally presented the author with six copies of *Pageant in the Wilderness: The Story of the Escalante Expedition to the Interior Basin, Including the Diary and Itinerary of Father Escalante.*†

LATER BOLTON FASHION

The translation of the Escalante diary was Bolton's last book, completed only weeks before his eighty-first birthday. Although still active in the years since 1945, there had been a definite slackening in pace. He was perhaps growing more reflective as notes in some of his files would suggest. The summer of 1947, for example, he had given a course at Mills College (Oakland), "The Opening of the Southwest and the Pacific Slope." Classes did not begin, however, until July 5. The day before, on the holiday, he sought the quiet of his office. He could be relaxed, for he had already sketched the outline for the lecture of the next day. Besides, he was in a loafing mood. In recent weeks and months he had, with the aid of Maxine Chappell, been doing a certain amount of housecleaning in Library 426, putting some order into its packed shelves

---

*In January 1950 the Bancroft Library was again moved, this time to the annex of the Doe Library. This meant a move for Bolton, too, from Library 426 to Library Annex 456.

†The actual time of publication was 1951, but having been previously allocated as one of the issues of Volume XVIII of the *Utah Historical Quarterly* it carried the 1950 date.

and cluttered corners and bulging files. Maybe he wanted to test the efficiency of the operation; again, maybe he was just caught in a wave of nostalgia. At any rate, in the file for July 4, 1947, there is a fascinating page with his familiar but very legible scrawl — it started out as a clean sheet, not the reverse side of a page for one of his books or articles which he used so often for the first draft of his correspondence or even his class thoughts. That Fourth of July day he wrote:

> I begin with a confession. I have just taken down from the top shelf in front of me, the first on the left of a long row of letter files in my office. This is evidence that for the moment I have nothing more of interest than the dead past of my life. The dead past of others has been my plaything for most of my adult life — my own I have always shunned or put aside for current things ...

He had hit on an interesting year, 1931. It was the year that he had finally wrapped up Anza and its summer had seen him in Europe. He relived many exciting memories as he turned over piece by piece. Padre Mariano Cuevas, the Mexican Jesuit historian, had visited him — "a man of distinction and extensive experience who is not always highly critical." He had written to Monroe Deutsch recommending that Jodee Fessenden be retained as departmental secretary and that her monthly pay be raised from $85 to $95. He had been closing his deal with Alfred Knopf for publication of his introduction to the Anza series as *Outpost of Empire*. A January letter from Dexter Perkins told him that he had been named vice president of the American Historical Association. A March memo to Sproul outlined his plans of research and writing for the immediate future and closed with a fervent plea for a research assistant and secretary. He had thanked Sidney Ehrman for establishing the Ehrman Chair of European History. Later in the file he came upon the department's many recommendations for the first appointee to the equally new Margaret Byrne Chair of American History — he was probably grateful that it had gone to his colleague and successor to himself as chairman, Frederic L. Paxson; he may have smiled when he read how he had wondered, to Sproul, if Morison "could be blasted out of New England." There was a letter of congratulations to Thomas Bailey, whom Stanford had recently brought onto its staff — Bailey had more than lived up to the rosy expectations which Bolton had for him. There was his appeal to the Del Amo Foundation for additional funds for his upcoming European trip. Sproul's letter naming him Sather Professor was a precious memory. And there were those letters of introduction which had opened doors for him in Europe — from Governor Ralph, from Archbishop Hanna, from Father Whelan, S.J., and from President

Sproul, officially stamped with the university golden seal. He possibly reminded himself that he should bring down to the university the dozen or more letters to "Mama and All," sent from various points in Europe but still in Mrs. Bolton's keeping. The year had ended with notification that he had been made Cross Commendatore of the Order of the Crown of Italy. Nineteen hundred and thirty-one had been a memorable year. There may have been other occasions in the later 1940s when he allowed himself this sort of backtracking. Certainly there were other moments of reflection, for scattered through his papers of 1947 and especially 1948 are a number of pages headed "Dicho." He seems to have jotted down, in a free moment or when the spirit moved, what might be termed an aging scholar's *bon mot* of academic wisdom; some of these, while of general interest, are valuable as thoughts of a man hewn from a lifetime of experience as author, teacher, and scholar; they are undated.

Dicho: Most writers of book reviews appraise a volume for what it is not, thinking thus to advertise their own learning.

Perhaps what surfaces here is the basis for Bolton's life-long, no-book-review policy. When asked to write a review, he would usually quip: "I am so busy trying to prepare food for the critics that I have to refrain from writing many book reviews myself." This policy also gave him a logical way to avoid having to say less than complimentary things about the work or the research or the conclusions of someone whom he respected, but with whom he felt compelled to disagree or to censure. He often regretted the devastating review he had written of the Ralph Emerson Twitchell work on New Mexico as a quite young man, in 1912. He rarely made exceptions in this policy. One exception had been the long piece he did on Eugene Barker's *Stephen F. Austin*. In this instance he seemed genuinely thrilled to be able to say so many good things about the work and the person of its author.

Other statements are indicative of his attitude toward various aspects of his profession.

Dicho: Advice for writing a book — wear leather breeches and sit on them.
Dicho: It is interesting to speculate on what would have happened, if something else had happened, but it is phantasy, not history, although the two are sometimes mistaken for one another.
Dicho: No professor ever reads a book written by a colleague. In fact nobody ever reads a professor's book except a student who has to pass the course.

Dicho: A textbook is the pulp of an orange that has been sucked — all the juice has been taken out.

Dicho: Definitive monograph — the silliest phrase in academic cant. Einstein cast a thousand definitive monographs onto the scrap heap. Set forth what you know today. It may help someone to learn more tomorrow.

A 1947 dicho on the seminar, which, when matched with a comment in a 1950 letter to an Irvin H. Lande, Chicago, sums up Bolton's concept of this agency of graduate training:

Dicho: The seminar — The urge for self-expression — We lecture at you — You read books — They appear to you as something done — But you want to do something yourself.

Every trickle, every rivulet in a watershed contributes to the mainstream, and to the ocean. Follow it, it joins others. Learn to navigate the branches and you will soon find yourself sailing on the high sea.

Now add to that the formula which he outlined for Lande:

The important thing in a seminar is to choose a very broad field of inquiry, let each student choose some phase of it in which he is interested and tell him to "go to it" in his own way, and from time to time report on what he has found, the more unorthodox and unheard of the better. In this way each student will have something that is his own and worth defending. In this way the range of inquiry broadens, so-called "authorities" become relatively unimportant, and the student learns to think for himself, and broadens the range of historical knowledge.

AS SEEN BY HIS STUDENTS

Bolton was anything but the autocrat of the seminar table. Some colleagues and fellow historians felt that he was too permissive. After several years, however, the recollections of those who actually sat through his classes supported the validity of Bolton's philosophy on seminars. In general the attribute they stressed, and which is also echoed repeatedly in these statements, was his enthusiasm as a teacher.

In his graduate seminar he was even more successful in communicating his consuming interest in history. Bolton never thought of his seminar as a place of instruction in the mechanics of historical research. He frankly said that he left that sort of teaching to his colleagues. . . . In any seminar the subject matter might spread over several centuries and over the whole Boltonian range from Alaska to the West Indies, and from the Great Basin to Patagonia. As Bolton students we were supposed to be more or less prepared to understand. In fact, a virtue of Bolton's wide-ranging seminar was that his Latin American specialists received broad exposure to the history of the West and his Western Americanists got a grounding in the history of Latin America. The quality, of course, varied. Some of the offerings [of the students] were inadequately researched, poorly organized, or badly written. Bolton, nevertheless, almost always steered the comment to some element in the performance that was eligible for praise, even if it were only the map or other exhibit material accompanying the report. . . . He interpreted his role as mentor to mean that first of all he gave encouragment. It bespoke more confidence in human performance and less pleasure in fault-finding than most of us have. . . .[3]

From the generation of the 1920s were gathered the following "memories":

My [first] seminar report was not a good one, but he made no comment. I resolved that the next would be a *good* one and wrote an animated account. . . . The next day he stopped me in the hall and said enthusiastically: "That was a corking good report last evening." I mention this as his way of never discouraging a student by adverse criticism, but seizing any opportunity to voice encouragement when he could honestly do so. . . .[4]

As a teacher, I think, Bolton's method was to sweep the candidate along on his enthusiasm and bolster the process by himself setting an example of authentic scholarship. This approach, unless I miss the mark, was half conscious and half his innate nature.

The Depression generation found Bolton much as described by their seniors:

Certainly I have never known anyone who was capable of transmitting enthusiasm for scholarly research and writing as he was. After a twenty-minute talk in his office, I went out feeling that I wanted to write a book before I went to bed that night. . . . He said more than once that if a student had a viable research interest, the best thing a graduate teacher could do would be to stay out of his way.

The only research topics which he refused to countenance were those which lay close to his own work of the moment. He once told me that he never wanted it to be said that he had used the work of his graduate students as a basis for his own work.

I can't recall how many times I wandered into his office in almost total discouragement with my research work and emerged half an hour later with unbounded confidence and enthusiasm. He was without doubt the most stimulating teacher I ever knew.

The first characteristic of Bolton the teacher which I shall always remember was that he respected his students. He never frightened me as some professors who would petrify my brain. . . . He did expect his students to explore the field thoroughly and to blaze new trails. His questions in both oral and written examinations were so designed that they would enable students to show what they knew, rather than to expose their ignorance. He rejoiced with his students as their research opened up new fields of knowledge.

One of the things which impressed me most about Dr. Bolton was his dedication to students, any students. He always encouraged them, and was never openly critical or inclined to embarrass them for poor performance. He explained this approach to me once: "If you encourage rather than browbeat them, they will do their best. If their best is no good, they will disappear and no one will hold you responsible. . . ." He took great pride in his students and did not feel that they should try to do only what he did. Above all he encouraged them to write and publish. "Publish," he said, "and your administration and colleagues will leave you alone; you can stay or move as you wish."

Bolton had a friendly awareness of the worth of the individual, and everyone who came into his presence was made to feel this. . . .
Professor Bolton had immense enthusiasm for the work in which he was engaged, but he had a marvelous ability to allow others to share in his enthusiasm without making them share his particular viewpoints.

The enthusiasm to which many of Bolton's students responded was interpreted by others as less than positive at times. Some felt that it was rooted in his vanity, and was not, therefore, enthusiasm at all. What one student saw as a man's being caught up and carried on by love for his

work and a desire to share the excitement of discovery, another saw as
boastfulness, vanity. One of the contributors to the Bolton memories,
talking from the last half of the decade of the 1930s wrote:

> Some people of my generation thought Bolton was insufferably
> vain. Certainly he was not above intercepting you in the hall and
> pulling you into the office to serve as a captive audience while he
> read something he had recently written. I had (and have) the
> impression that this was more enthusiasm for the topic than for his
> own part in developing it. Perhaps a bit like Columbus and the
> Indies. If Bolton was vain, it was a childlike vanity based on
> delight at discovering a fascinating world. He really was so deeply
> steeped in what he was discovering that he and the topic were inter-
> mingled. This was brought home to me once when I visited him
> during his last illness. He came and went in his perception of the
> world around him in those last days. One particular day (when he
> didn't know me from Adam, except that I was familiar) he was in
> eighteenth-century Texas, talking about familiar figures and events
> as if he were recalling incidents of his own life.

Another student, this one in the earlier 1920s, mentioned the same
point of vanity and commented: "Some students thought he was vain
and boastful because he so obviously enjoyed telling of his explorations
and discoveries, but to me there was no vanity in the man, just a happy
acceptance of what he was and did." And on the same subject here are
the words of one of his students of the second decade of the century:

> I often asked myself whether I found in Bolton a man without
> faults. To some he may have seemed a bit conceited because he
> talked so often about himself and his research and his books. But I
> did not consider this egotism. I attributed it to his intense enthusi-
> asm, which was not limited to his own work but extended to that of
> others in the field. He was, in fact, rather humble. Sometimes he
> expressed doubts that his books would continue to interest readers.
> Sometimes he would remark that his achievements would be sur-
> passed by some of the "boys" he had trained. "Some of my boys,"
> he said, "are going up like rockets; they will rise to greater heights
> than I have risen." Perhaps it may be said that he was generous to
> a fault. All of his students he described as "able men." But I am
> sure that he knew that some were abler than others.

In 1945 the post-1932 generation of Bolton's doctors honored him in
a special way. These doctors, not wishing to be outdone by their elders,
planned a second *Festschrift* for the master, something to match the
earlier *New Spain and the Anglo-American West*. The initial idea was
to have it ready for presentation sometime in late 1940, on the occasion

of his retirement. But, as so often happens in such cooperative ventures, the essays promised were slow in coming in, with the result that 1940 came and went before the disappointed editors were able to complete the volume. Next United States involvement in World War II entered the picture, with calls to service, heavy demands on most everyone's leisure time, and shortages of many varieties; completion was further slowed. Adele Ogden, with Engel Sluiter assisting, worked tirelessly. Finally, in late 1945, with the volume definitely coming off the press, a gala presentation party could safely be planned. The evening of December 28 was chosen; the Colonial Room of San Francisco's St. Francis Hotel was reserved; invitations went out. That evening several hundred Boltonians, friends, and admirers gathered. Sidney M. Ehrman, by this time one of regents of the university, was the chairman; President Sproul, Chairman of History Paxson, and Edward Lynch of the Native Sons paid their tributes; Adele Ogden made the presentation. Bolton, to be sure, responded.

Greater America: Essays in Honor of Herbert Eugene Bolton was a handsome, and a large, volume.[5] Twenty-six of his post-1932 doctors contributed. The range of topics was as wide and broad as the hemisphere itself, at least the Hispanic and American-West parts thereof; the spread was indicative of the master's "American" interests. Included were twelve original maps, by as many of the writers, to show another facet of Bolton's inspiration, the importance of "geographic visualization."

The editors not only promoted the essays and brought the Bolton bibliography up to date, completing the earlier listings by Mary Ross in the first *Festschrift,* but they also conceived the wonderful idea of gathering the long list of his graduate students and requesting a record of their scholarly output. This very valuable section of the volume fills 125 pages – one would expect production from the doctors, but not a few of his several hundred masters, most of them secondary teachers, also had publication to report. The essays themselves "taught" Bolton nothing; he had pained through them all at seminar or dissertation stage and remembered them well, but it was most heartening to see what his "boys" and "girls" had done through the years "on their own," how his teaching, encouragement, and example had fructified. In quiet moments he could run through the long, long list of graduate students and recall many an evening at the Round Table. He would have been the first to admit that the teacher's life has bounteous rewards, rarely measurable in dollars and cents.

After thirty-five years of graduate teaching, had Bolton pushed pins into a map, he would have noted a Ph.D. in Michigan, Chicago, Ohio State, Illinois, and Northwestern in the prestigious Big Ten group; down

through Mid-Continent and the South there would have been pins at
Loyola-Chicago, Saint Louis, Washington-Saint Louis, Vanderbilt, Ala-
bama, Duke, Florida, Oklahoma, Oklahoma State, Texas, and Texas
A & M; in the Rocky Mountain West they would have shown at Utah,
Utah State, Brigham Young, Colorado, and Denver, and in the North-
west at Idaho, Oregon State, and Gonzaga, with representation at New
Mexico and Arizona in the Southwest. Most every major school in
California had its Bolton man, California-Berkeley, California-Davis,
UCLA, Southern California, Pomona, Occidental, Redlands, San Francisco State, San Diego State, Fresno State. Other graduates were with the
National Archives and the National Park Service. He boasted of them
and the books which they produced, which filled a sizable section of the
floor-to-ceiling shelves which, as already mentioned, lined his office. One
thing is certain: Bolton enjoyed his work with his students. One humorous
incident tells rather a lot of him and his relationship to his students. He
had received a royalty check which he pegged up outside his office door
with the note: "Encouragement to Young Historians." The check was for
thirty-five cents.

In a little less than a year after the appearance of *Pageant in the
Wilderness* Bolton's working days were over.[6] In those months he toyed
with several of his pet projects. Toyed does seem to be the right word,
for the old conquistador was running out of steam. For once in his life
he was becoming more of a talker than a doer. Portolá and especially
Garcés still intrigued him, but he got little accomplished. His files contain
a *borrador* (outline sketch) of a pageant for an upcoming celebration of
Alameda County, for which his counsel had been sought. There are a
few more bits for the Garcés story which he planned to do. But even his
usual correspondence dwindled.

In 1951 and early 1952 he was under more of an emotional strain
than he let on. Charles Hackett, who was ill with cancer, fell into a state
of melancholia and shot himself; this shook Bolton and saddened him
greatly. Then his daughter Laura, in a state of emotional depression, too,
took her own life. Next, daughter Helen died unexpectedly, following
post-surgical complications. All of these tragedies took their toll.

Then one June afternoon in 1952 Bolton was working at his desk.
When he tried to get up to go home, he found that his legs would not
obey. He had had a stroke. Friends rushed him to Herrick Hospital
(Berkeley). There was a short period of temporary recovery, and he
began to move around slowly, with difficulty, but a second stroke con-

fined him to bed at home for the next months until a series of smaller strokes finally broke down that rugged constitution. On the morning of January 30, 1953, he died. He had not suffered greatly, but memory of the recent past had deserted him; he lived in the pasts of the many about whom he had written, in his Texas of the eighteenth century, with his Black Robes of Pimería Alta, or with the friars and soldiers of early California. His colleagues and university friends often called, but rarely did they find him the old Bolton, even slowed down.

The family asked a colleague in the Department of Speech, who was also a minister, Professor Fred Stripp, to conduct the obsequies. He was buried in Sunset View Cemetery, Berkeley. He was mourned by his widow, four daughters (Frances, Eugenie, Gertrude, Jane), son Herbert, a number of grandchildren, and hundreds of his academic "boys" and "girls."

A FINAL TRIBUTE

After his death in 1953 colleagues noted Bolton's passing in various of the professional journals. Some of the notices were matter of fact, as that in the *AHR* (April 1953), but others were warm tributes to Herbert Eugene Bolton, historian, teacher, man. Understandably, editors asked one of Bolton's "boys" to recall the master; in one or other instance the editor reserved the privilege for himself. In general, these writers did not think it necessary to spend time proving their deceased mentor a top-rank historian, since he had very convincingly done that himself. There was a measure of repetition, but, even so, each writer did have some things to recall which were distinctive or which he put in a distinctive way.

One of Bolton's last doctors, William J. Griffith, wrote the obituary notice for the *MVHR* (June 1953): ". . . . a stimulating teacher, especially of graduate students. Although continuously absorbed with his own projects, he always had limitless time to encourage nascent students to believe in the importance of their own research. . . ."

The Franciscan historians asked George P. Hammond, one of his students of the 1920s, companion on the trail, and in 1946 his successor as director of the Bancroft Library, to write the "In Memoriam" for their quarterly, *The Americas* (April 1953). Hammond told Bolton's background and then commented:

> Men working under pressure as Bolton often was end up with frayed nerves, ulcers, or the like. But not so with Bolton. The world outside his study might be in turmoil, but within the walls of his office all was peaceful and quiet as he wrote his Coronado story,

Escalante's wanderings, or tackled a knotty problem. Coupled with this characteristic, he had an incomparable personal magnetism, and unquenchable zest for living, extreme devotion to his work, a keen and unflagging affection for his students, and a clear and discerning mind. He had unbounded faith in the goodness of humanity and never was known to say an unkind word or to criticize another. Cynicism found no part in his nature. To the end he was positive and forward looking, absorbed in his next book. . . .

Lawrence Kinnaird, as he wrote a Bolton sketch for the California Historical Society *Quarterly* (June 1953), recognized the problem he faced in assessing the role and place of a man whom he admired greatly and loved dearly. From his tribute:

> Men of superb achievements do not have to die in order that their contemporaries may realize their stature. . . . Few university men have the competence and physical stamina to be successful administrators, teachers, and authors simultaneously. He did it by putting in twice the working-hours of the average man. . . . Even if you had never seen the man, you would know from his methods of research alone that he was possessed of a powerful physique and a trained endurance. Careful study of archives was followed by work in the field. . . . It is doubtful whether any other historian has ever equaled his record for field work. . . .

The notice in the *Hispanic American Historical Review* (May 1953) was a joint effort of the California Latin Americanists, James F. King and Engel Sluiter, pooling their thoughts with Kinnaird and Hammond:

> The death of Herbert Eugene Bolton at his home in Berkeley on January 30 ended a career with few parallels in American historical scholarship. Though granted a dozen years beyond the biblical three score and ten, this kindly *conquistador* crammed into his busy life achievement that will always remain a marvel to the less gifted. . . .
>
> More important than these useful physical attributes [endless vitality, capacity for work, a rugged constitution] were certain gifts of the spirit, with which Professor Bolton was liberally endowed. He possessed a buoyancy, a zest, an enthusiasm which supported his own and his associates' enterprises. . . . He enjoyed, understood, and consistently brought out the best in people, whether living associates, or those other companions whom he discovered in the documents. Confident of his own powers, he was generous in recognizing and praising the accomplishments of others. . . .
>
> Many of these personal qualities carried over into Bolton's work as a teacher. But perhaps his greatest gift in the field was his rare ability to infuse his own enthusiasm into his students. . . . A practical

psychologist, Bolton chose to arouse interest and to stimulate work by example and by kindly guidance rather than to dampening budding enthusiasm by negative criticism. Although his personality will long live vividly in the memories of a host of former students and admirers, Bolton's final claim to fame must rest upon his scholarship. . . .

One of the editors who reserved for himself the privilege of memorializing Bolton was Father Jerome V. Jacobsen of *Mid-America* (April 1953). "Jakie," as Bolton always called him, was one of the twentieth-century Black Robes whom Bolton helped to get acquainted with Jesuit brethren of an earlier age (Bolton had half a dozen such among his doctors). Jacobsen wanted to pay honor, but he especially wanted to say thank-you, in his own name, that of the Jesuits, and of Catholics in general, for the fairness and understanding which Bolton so regularly showed in dealing with the work of "religious men in robes, black, brown, and gray."

> In his tender years [Bolton] learned a religious tolerance that became him so abundantly. As he told it, he and his schoolmates had been warned not to go near the Catholic church, because a man in black with horns might catch them. One day young Herbert decided to run past this fearsome place and its iron fence. In his dismay he found himself completely out of breath hanging on the iron pickets with half the distance yet to run. What was worse, in the yard was the man in black but without horns, and reading a book. The man smiled and said "hello" and went on reading. In days to come Herbert stopped at the fence to pass the time of day chatting with the man in black. . . . Prejudice had been wrung from Bolton forever. . . .
>
> At times when gratitude was expressed to Bolton for what he had done by his interest in the early men of the cross, his reply was as characteristic as it was generous: "Thank me? I have more thanks to give to the early padres for what they wrote. Suppose they had not come to the Americas, and suppose they had not written their observations and their histories — where would we pagans be?"
>
> Much could be said of the underlying principles which revealed themselves in Bolton's force of character. . . . While these characteristics were rather patent to many of Bolton's colleagues, a few were aware of an unusual quality — a natural reverence. He had reverence for the documents and for the persons of the past who spoke from the old manuscript pages. He had reverence for the people of whom he wrote, whose good deeds he praised and whose faults and foibles he told with human understanding. Though ever the impartial witness to truth, his pen seemed heavier when evil had to be recorded. Bolton approached each day's work with reverence and by his example instilled in the minds of students a respect for their fellow men and for the institutions of the present and the past.

Another editor who wanted to have his say was John Walton Caughey of the *Pacific Historical Review* (May 1953):

> There are, I think, more significant compliments to be paid him, but the first superlative that comes to mind concerns the way in which he devoted himself to the study and writing and teaching of history. It was his recreation as well as his vocation. . . . The first most tangible testament of his achievement as an historian is the corpus of his writings — forty volumes or more in book form and numerous shorter pieces contributed to journals. . . .
>
> As a contributor to knowledge, Bolton was not only assiduous in ferreting out the documents on which history must rest; he also was a devotee of testing this information in the field. . . . In the affairs of the mind he was an even more significant explorer. He is credited with the effective discovery of the Spanish borderlands as a field of historical research. . . .
>
> To my recollection the characteristic of his teaching that stood out above all others was his ability to instill enthusiasm. In large degree it seemed merely a matter of contagion. The pursuit of knowledge was to him full of zest, both at the stage of uncovering the individual facts and at the next stage of assessing and interpreting them. This faculty of taking a vital interest in every episode with which he dealt was much in evidence in his lectures. It animated his conversation. It also set the pitch for his seminars, which served primarily as a trial ground for the theses and dissertations on which his students were at work. . . .
>
> Not all his ideas convinced everybody. For example, there are still historians who recoil from the concept of the history of the Americas. . . .
>
> Another idea, less publicly stressed, was that it is usually more satisfying and significant to study the processes of building up than tearing down. Thus he preferred heroes to villains, and in his research dwelt on men of positive achievement. Another concept to which he gave more than lip service was that history and the neighboring disciplines constitute a team. He took pride in his own contributions to ethnology and geography. . . . These are some of the qualities that gave Bolton force in our profession.

Each piece quoted here in its own way has seemed valuable in memorializing Bolton as historian and teacher. Cumulatively they help to round out the image of the dedicated scholar, recognized as a giant in his time, tireless in his pursuit of evidence, in library, archive, field; equally dedicated teacher, kindly and considerate, admirable and inspiring, eager to pass on the lessons and the thrills of his experience of the past.

19

An Evaluation

ERBERT EUGENE BOLTON has been dead since 1953. Already it seems safe to assert, however, that he stands tall among American historians of the twentieth century and is very surely to continue so. The reasons for his claim to such prominence are many, sound and solid, compelling and convincing. He was and is one of the "greats."

He was the first major American historian to put the United States story, especially in its colonial years, into a continental setting, broadening the traditional "original thirteen colonies" orientation. In so doing he expanded most interestingly the cast of characters by introducing the men of New Spain's *Provincias Internas* and showing that they properly belonged in the American, even the United States, story. Francis Parkman had added the French to the cast. Early in the twentieth century Edward G. Bourne, with his *Spain in America* contribution to the original "The American Nation: A History'" series, had begun to introduce the Spaniards in a role other than that of the "heavies." James Alexander Robertson paid attention to the Spaniards in the Floridas. Bolton followed closely, chronologically, developing "his own field." He had one or other historian predecessor in writing of the Spaniards in the Southwest, such as Hubert Howe Bancroft and Charles Lummis, but otherwise most of those writing about the area had been anthropologists, ethnologists, archaeologists. After the work of Bolton and his students the area of the history of the West was extended considerably and the story ceased to be an almost unrelieved Anglo-American epic.

Enthused by the new dimension which he had given to American history, Bolton next, in his classes at least, sought to give that history a hemispheric sweep. The History-of-the-Americas concept was born. If one could talk of European history, why not also, he argued, of all-American history? Despite the contentions of his critics who thought to see in this a unity-of-all-the-Americas thesis, Bolton never claimed to

[255]

have a thesis to be proved. He did seem to come close at spots in his "Epic of Greater America" address at Toronto in 1932. In reality, however, the Americas device was a technique, an approach which sought by highlighting similarities and dissimilarities to heighten appreciation and understanding of the human experience in the Western Hemisphere.

He used that word thesis only once, in writing, and this in connection with an idea which he shared with Verner W. Crane in 1919:

> I have a thesis up my sleeve . . . where it may remain, to the effect that the great struggle for the continent of North America was not between France and England after all, but between England and Spain, and extended all the way from the Caribbean to the Pacific Ocean. . . .

Throughout his teaching-writing life he sought only to open for students and colleagues "wider horizons of American history."

Developing a new field as he was, Bolton throughout his scholarly life never ceased to be a woodlander, who knows that he must first have trees before there is a forest about which to rhapsodize. He felt that it was the job of some historians, pioneers particularly, to furnish the facts by dint of consistent and careful probings into the archives. He devoted himself to this aspect of his craft. He was not unaware of the value and need for interpretive history. When he had enough data, enough trees so to speak, he showed his skill in this kind of history writing — recall his "mission as a frontier institution" and his "defensive role of the borderlands," each a fertile seed piece. But primarily he went on to the end looking for more and new facts to enlighten his favorite pasts. He did not feel that being able to tell an historically sound and fulsome story was in anywise demeaning — he was working from unimpeachable documentation, not relying on intuition or charismatic vision.

Bolton, certainly, was not the first American historian to use foreign archives. He was, however, very much a pioneer in acquainting colleagues and students with the hitherto overlooked riches of the Mexican archives and in showing how much American history, even in its less broad sense of United States history, was hidden in the dusty *legajos*. He and his students turned more American attention to the even richer depositories of Spain. In days before easy transportation and generous travel grants made on-the-ground consultation possible, he stocked his own and the files of the Bancroft Library with document copies, so that sound research could be done at home.

Bolton was in a very real sense an inter-disciplinary man well ahead of the current emphasis. He had learned from Frederick Jackson Turner the valuable lesson of rallying varied data in order to make the past more understandable and meaningful. His heroes of the Borderlands made him a first-rate field geographer and their Indians, friendly and otherwise, an equally notable ethnologist and anthropologist.

Field work was his most enjoyed recreation and, by his own frequent confession, his prime hobby. His on-campus sometime friendly "critic," Carl Ortwin Sauer, paid him a fine compliment when in reviewing the Anza volumes in the April 1931 number of *The Geographical Review* he wrote:

> Today he is not only the dominant figure in Hispanic-American history but also one uniquely significant in the field of historical geography by the ever growing mass of sources and syntheses which he has published on the northern frontier of New Spain. . . . He speaks therefore directly to the geographer in a manner that the more conventional historian does not.

Few historians of exploration and pioneering have been able to write with greater authenticity from actual acquaintance with the area in which their subjects lived or flourished. The men of the National Park Service were often his companions on the trail, but he more than repaid their cooperation with the vast fund of document and book knowledge which he put at their disposal. He never felt comfortable in writing of one of his Borderlands heroes until he had relived the geographical aspects of their experiences. Bolton was not himself a great cartographer but, with expert assistance, he could translate his knowledge and observations into highly authoritative complements to the stories for which he furnished the words. His recognition of the importance of geography also translated itself into the very large classroom maps which were an integral part of his lectures.

His contribution to the field of American Indian ethnology had its beginnings early in his Texas researches as he saw how much new material about the tribesmen of the Southwest could be gleaned from his Spanish sources. At the same time the men of the Bureau of American Ethnology recognized him as a valuable resource person and enlisted his cooperation. Although his monograph on the Texas tribes got lost in the course of pursuing other interests and was never completed, more than a hundred articles on the Texas Indians, as already noted, are scattered through the two volumes of *The Handbook of American Indians North of Mexico*.

As a young man Bolton had studied economics. There was a time, early, when he wondered if this might be his future academic field. Later he regularly put this background to work in his writings and his classes. He did the same with the awareness of social factors in history which he had learned from Turner and from McMaster. As he became increasingly involved with Spain in colonial America, he was often grateful for the grounding which Haskins, Cheyney, and Munro had given him in the Middle Ages, not to mention his own acquired medieval expertise during the years at Texas when he was this young university's "medievalist in residence." He studied, taught, wrote, counseled from a richly varied background.

He may not have been a brilliant lecturer, but he was a great teacher. There was a certain contagious enthusiasm for history which he passed on to his young hearers, as so many of the students of Bolton attest. In the seminar, at that great round table which he had inherited from Morse Stephens, he was at his teaching best. In the one-on-one less formal meeting he was at his human best.

Few, if any, American historians have left as numerous an academic progeny as Herbert Bolton — more than one hundred doctors and several times that many masters. Years ago discerning observers saw developing at Berkeley what came to be called the "Bolton School," and hailed it so. By the mid-1970s the first generation was dwindling, but the line had gone into a second, a third, and even a fourth generation. There is a pride and a warm fraternity among Boltonians, as they enthusiastically continue many of the master's interests, seek to emulate his prodigious productivity and to keep alive his keen human understanding, that thing which his Spaniards call *simpatía,* which was one of his most marked characteristics as a man. There is a strain of Bolton academic blood in a surprising number of later twentieth-century Latin Americanists and Western historians. Few men, through students trained, have had quite as great an impact on the field of greater American history, continental and hemispheric.

Bolton was an important American historian, father of the Borderlands, member of the Turner-Bolton-Webb frontier trinity, and Latin Americanist, at least in the broad sense. Perhaps his most lasting contribution was as the pioneer in opening to research and study a sizable area of North America, to his time largely overlooked but since his day known as the Spanish Borderlands. So important was he in this work that it has been suggested that the Southwest might well be called the "Boltonlands."

A Bibliographical Essay

The major source for this study has been the collection of Herbert E. Bolton materials in the Bancroft Library, University of California at Berkeley. These Bolton Papers are divided into three sections:

Part One: Thousands of pages of Bolton transcripts, typescripts, photostats, and other copies of manuscripts from foreign archives collected through the years by Bolton.

Part Two: The Bolton Correspondence, 157 boxes in all. These are divided into Correspondence: OUT, 24 boxes; and Correspondence: IN, 133 boxes. The OUT category is made up of carbon copies of letters sent and handwritten drafts of others. (From Stanford days forward Bolton had secretarial assistance and thus could keep a record of his letters sent.) These letters are filed chronologically. The IN category is made up of various letters to Bolton and other kinds of material sent to him; these are filed alphabetically under the name of the sender or the originating department, institution, or agency.

Part Three: Forty-four large cartons of still unordered miscellanea — segments of book/article drafts, printed book reviews, etc.

A note in connection with the Correspondence: OUT, generally carbon copies. No one will pretend that this file is absolutely complete; however, spot checks have been made into files of several of Bolton's regular correspondents to test relative completeness (the Eugene Campbell Barker Papers at the University of Texas, Frederick Jackson Turner collection at Huntington Library, and the Bolton folder in the Bureau of American Ethnology Archive at the Smithsonian Institution, Washington, D.C.); few pieces, and none of consequence, were uncovered which are not in the Berkeley file.

The Bancroft Library has a quite invaluable collection of Herbert-to-Frederick Bolton letters, sent between the years 1885 and 1947. Most of these are handwritten; these letters are frequent through the earlier years and provide a uniquely intimate record of Herbert growing up, developing, dreaming, planning, coping with the problems of the present and trying to foresee and provide against those of the future. Four boxes contain 560 pieces.

This writer has also been able to draw on the memories, both written and verbal, of many Bolton students. He also had the same assistance from five of the Bolton children (Frances Bolton Appleton, Eugenie Bolton Johnson, Gertrude Bolton Coleman, Jane Bolton Adams, and Herbert, Jr.). The Boltons have relatively few letters and mementos of their father not turned over to the Bancroft Library.

Over the years there have been a number of articles on Bolton, many of these appearing in the months following his death in 1953. These have been variously used in the preceding. A partial listing:

BANNON, JOHN FRANCIS. "Herbert Eugene Bolton: His *Guide* in the Making," *Southwestern Historical Quarterly*, LXXIII (July, 1969), 35–55.

————. "Herbert Eugene Bolton — Western Historian," *Western Historical Quarterly*, II (July, 1971), 261–82.

CAREW, HAROLD D. "Bolton of Bancroft," *Touring Topics*, XX (November, 1928), 28–30, 40.

CARROLL, JOHN ALEXANDER. "Dedication to Herbert Eugene Bolton," *Arizona and the West*. I (Summer, 1959), 102–4.

CAUGHEY, JOHN WALTON. "Herbert Eugene Bolton," *Pacific Historical Review*, IX (April, 1953), 108–12.

————. "Herbert Eugene Bolton," in *Turner, Bolton, Webb — Three Historians of the West* (Seattle: University of Washington Press, 1965), pp. 41–74.

CHAPPELL, MAXINE. "Herbert E. Bolton," in *A Record of the Fiftieth Anniversary Celebration, May 5th and 6th, 1945,* commemorating the founding and initiation of Sigma Deuteron Charge of Theta Delta Chi Fraternity, May 15, 1895 (Privately printed), pp. 14–16.

DUNN, WILLIAM EDWARD. "Portrait of a Teacher: Herbert E. Bolton," *The Alcalde* [University of Texas], XLII (November, 1953), 54–56.

EMERY, EDWIN. "Bolton of California," *California Monthly* [University of California] XLVII (September, 1941), 12–13, 39–43.

ESCUDERO, CARLOS R. "Historian in Action — An Historical Adventure Story," *California Monthly*. XLVII (September, 1941), 14–16, 43–44.

FRIEND, LLERENA B. "Herbert Eugene Bolton and the Texas State Library," *Texas Libraries*, XXXV (Summer, 1973), 48–64.

GILBERT, HOPE ELIZABETH. "He Followed the Trails of the Desert Padres," *Desert Magazine*, XIII (July, 1950), 27–31.

GRIFFITH, WILLIAM J. "Herbert Eugene Bolton," *Mississippi Valley Historical Review*, XLVI (January, 1953), 185–86.

HAMMOND, GEORGE PETER. "In Memoriam: Herbert Eugene Bolton," *The Americas*, IX (April, 1953), 391–98.

HAMMOND, G. P.; KINNAIRD, L.; KING, J. F.; and SLUITER, E. "Herbert Eugene Bolton," *Hispanic American Historical Review*, XXXIII (May, 1953), 184–86.

HANKE, LEWIS, ed. *Do the Americas Have a Common History? A Critique of the Bolton Theory.* New York: Knopf, 1964.

HEALEY, MIRIAM. "Great Historical Sketches: Herbert Eugene Bolton," *The Pacific Historian* [University of the Pacific], XIII (Summer, 1969), 76–78.

HUNT, ROCKWELL D. "Herbert Eugene Bolton; An Appreciation," *Bancroftiana*, No. 8 (May, 1953), 1–2.

IVES, RONALD L. "Herbert Eugene Bolton, 1870–1953," *Records,* American Catholic Historical Society, Philadelphia, LVIII (March 1954).

JACOBSEN, JEROME V. "Herbert E. Bolton," *Mid-America,* XXIV (April 1953), 75–80.

KINNAIRD, LAWRENCE. "Our Distinguished Faculty: Professor Herbert E. Bolton," *California Monthly,* LXI (February 1951), 16, 30–31.

————. "Bolton of California," California Historical Society *Quarterly,* XXXII (June 1953), 97–103.

LOCKWOOD, FRANK C. "Adventurous Scholarship," *The Catholic World*, vol. 188, no. 824 (November 1932), 185–94.

MAGNAGHI, RUSSELL M. "Herbert E. Bolton and Sources for American Indian Studies," *Western Historical Quarterly,* VI (January 1975), 33–46.

POWELL, LAWRENCE CLARK. "California Classics Reread: *Anza's California Expeditions,*" *Westways,* LXI (October 1969), 24–27, 43.

RIPPY, J. FRED. "Herbert Eugene Bolton: A Recollection," *Southwest Review* XXXIX (Spring 1954), 166–71.

TREUTLEIN, THEODORE E. "Necrologias: Herbert Eugene Bolton (1870–1953)." *Revista de Historia de América,* 37–38 (January-December, 1954), 299–302.

————. "Deceased: Herbert Eugene Bolton," *American Historical Review,* LVIII (April, 1953), 791–92.

In 1964 the author edited a collection of Bolton's studies, several of them previously unpublished, under title *Bolton and the Spanish Borderlands* (Norman: University of Oklahoma Press, 1964); this has biographical notes by way of introduction.

Supplementary
Material

Chapter Notes

CHAPTER 1

1. This chapter relies heavily on information which Frederick E. Bolton, Herbert's brother and senior by four years, prepared at the request of his nieces in mid-1953 following their father's death (January). Bolton's daughters began almost immediately to gather materials for a life of their father. The first piece, of May 1953, was entitled "Uncle Fred's Recollections of Our Dad and His Comments Relating to Family History"; it exists now in the form of a thirteen-page manuscript. The second piece, thirty-three handwritten pages with a covering letter to the late Eugenie Bolton Johnson, October 29, 1953, sought to answer questions which she posed about her father's early years. Sometime after writing these two sketches, the editors of *Arizona and the West* asked Frederick to do an article on the young Herbert Bolton. This was published in said journal (IV, 65–73); it is a bit more formal, less delightfully folksy and adds little to the two pieces noted above, which are in the Herbert E. Bolton Correspondence, Bancroft Library.

   The Bolton daughters have put other varied family materials at the disposal of the biographer; principal among these are two pieces titled "Aunt Edwinna Bolton Nafus to Frances Bolton Appleton, May 3, 1953" and "Grace Bolton to Jane Bolton Adams and All of Herbert's Children, October 2, 1953." The Bolton daughters also made available the notes which Edwinna Bolton Nafus had made from the family Bible, which gave much information on ancestral and immediate family antecedents.

2. This remarkable collection of letters from Herbert to Frederick, over 560, dates from 1885 into late 1947. They are frequent, sometimes very frequent, into the second decade of the twentieth century. Then, as the two brothers became more absorbed in their respective jobs and works, the letters become less frequent. In this and the next chapter there is heavy reliance on this collection. It is in The Bancroft Library, University of California-Berkeley, having been given to that repository by Frederick Bolton after his brother's death — listed as "The Frederick E.

Bolton Papers." At this point it is in order to set down the footnoting policy for these letters which is followed throughout the book; most often the date of the letter will be given in the text; this collection is organized chronologically and, even when the date is not noted, the original can be turned up easily.

Scattered through the "Herbert E. Bolton Correspondence: IN" there are well over one hundred Frederick-to-Herbert letters, but these more regularly are from twentieth-century years. The Bolton daughters feel that their father had, like Frederick, preserved Frederick's earlier letters in what they called "The Spider Closet," but that these were destroyed in the 1923 Berkeley fire which burned the Bolton residence to the ground, along with several hundred more homes in the north-of-campus area.

3. This information is gathered from the notes of Frederick Bolton sent to the Bolton daughters, May 1953.

4. Nine Herbert-to-Frederick letters tell of the months as schoolmaster at York.

5. The main source of information dries up during the period when Herbert and Frederick are in State Normal School at the same time. After the summer of 1890, however, the flow of letters begins again. Never again does written correspondence cease for an extended time because the brothers are together. Hereafter, they are together only for short periods.

6. Frederick Bolton to Eugenie Bolton Johnson, October 29, 1953.

7. Thirty Herbert-to-Frederick letters report this second year at Normal.

8. Five letters, on the stationery of "The Butler House," Boone's principal hostelry, tell of this summer of 1891.

9. Seventy-four Herbert-to-Frederick letters are available for 1891–93.

CHAPTER 2

1. Data on background of University of Wisconsin has been drawn from Merle Curti and Vernon Carstensen, *The University of Wisconsin, 1848–1925*, 2 vols. (Madison: University of Wisconsin Press, 1949), Vol. I *passim*.

2. Running through this first University of Wisconsin period (1893–95) are fifty-two Herbert-to-Frederick letters.

3. See Ray Allen Billington, *Frederick Jackson Turner: Historian, Scholar, Teacher* (New York: Oxford, 1973).

4. The second University of Wisconsin period, the year of graduate study, produced thirty Herbert-to-Frederick letters and several Gertrude-to-Olive letters which Frederick also preserved in his collection.

5. Much of the information concerning the relationship between Bolton and Turner is contained in a questionnaire of 1928 when Bolton was asked to contribute to a Turner *Festschrift* in honor of his former professor's retirement at Harvard University.

6. The Herbert-to-Frederick letters are still the main source of information on these formative years. During the years at Pennsylvania (1897–99) Herbert was a faithful, sometimes prolific, letter writer; there are sixty-six letters for this period.

7. Herbert kept Frederick posted on his job-hunting woes, in thirteen letters, to bring the total for the pieces in the 1893–99 period to just short of two hundred.

CHAPTER 3

1. Frederick Bolton, "Random Memories of an Admiring Brother," in *Arizona and the West,* IV (Spring, 1961), 72–73.

2. There are thirty-seven Herbert-to-Frederick letters for the 1900–01 year at Normal.

3. Much of the story of these pages is drawn from the two dozen letters, September 1901 through July 1902.

4. *Recollections of a Texas Educator,* p. 37. Richard F. Fleming, University Writings Collection, the University of Texas at Austin, in a letter of August 29, 1969, was good enough to call attention to this Hubbard story. "Mama Hubbard," María Monsanto de Hubbard, was the widow of a man whom she had married when he was United States consul in Puerto Rico and had subsequently died in a similar post at El Paso, Texas.

5. This salary data has been gathered from the Minutes of the University of Texas Board of Trustees Meetings, in the Office of the President, the University of Texas at Austin.

6. For the rest of 1902 there are ten Herbert-to-Frederick letters. During the next several years, with Herbert more and more absorbed, the correspondence thins to twelve for 1903, eight for 1904, and twelve for 1905.

7. Titles of these pieces will be found in Appendix A.

8. The original publisher was the small Austin company, Gammel-Statesman.

9. With few Herbert-to-Frederick letters in 1904 and since Herbert's own file does not begin for another two years, the more intimate information for this period is thin. The flow of letters picks up again in the spring of 1905.

CHAPTER 4

1. The Jameson letters noted and quoted in this and the following chapters are in Bolton Correspondence: IN, The Bancroft Library. The earlier ones are among the first preserved in Bolton's own file, which dates from 1906. If he had a personal file prior to that date, it has not survived; the presumption is that he may have kept it at his home, which was completely destroyed in the Berkeley fire of September 1923. The IN file contains letters, etc. sent to him; these are filed alphabetically by sender.

His OUT file, which from this point forward will be drawn on heavily, is made up of carbon copies of his letters — these are filed chronologically; the OUT file also begins in 1906.

2. This and the 1905 letters are in the H. E. Bolton file, Smithsonian Institution, National Anthropological Archives, 4942.

3. The Herbert-to-Frederick letters bulk only to thirty-three for his last years at Texas; although few in number, they are often rich in content.

4. Herbert-to-Frederick, June 7, 1907, details the modern plans to exploit the mine. Some of the later developments connected with the company can be found in several letters in Bolton Correspondence: IN, under entry "Los Almagres Mining Company." J. Frank Dobie in his *Coronado's Children* tells the story of the mine; Bolton himself has a reference to the mine and the Miranda report which gave him the key to its location in his *Texas in the Middle Eighteenth Century*, p. 83.

5. This information is drawn substantially from John Francis Bannon, "Herbert Eugene Bolton: His *Guide* in the Making," in *Southwestern Historical Quarterly*, LXXIII (July 1969), 35–55. The sources are clearly enough indicated in the text to warrant, in most cases, non-repetition in these notes. The Jameson letters are in Bolton Correspondence: IN, and the Bolton letters and copies of the monthly reports in Bolton Correspondence: OUT.

6. HEB to Houston, August 11, 1907.

7. HEB to Houston, October 12, 1907. In a later March 1909 letter to President Houston Bolton gave a full report on this project and the uses to which the funds were put.

8. Elliott Coues, ed., *The Expeditions of Zebulon Montgomery Pike to the Headwaters of the Mississippi River*, 3 vols. (New York, 1895).

9. Bolton's own full discussion of this Pike find is in his article in the *American Historical Review*, XIII (July 1908), 798–827.

10. Father Zephyrin Engelhardt's major work on the California missions was yet to come, *The Missions and Missionaries of California*, 4 vols. (San Francisco, 1908–1915) but he was already publishing short studies on many of the missions. Later, when Bolton was established at Berkeley and turning much of his attention to the California story, he and the friar-historian became fast friends; there is a sizable file of correspondence between them in the Bolton Papers.

CHAPTER 5

1. The story of the Stanford "feeler" and sequel comes from the letters of Adams to Bolton and those of Bolton to Adams, in the Bolton Correspondence: IN and OUT, The Bancroft Library.

2. Herbert-to-Frederick, September 6, 1908.

3. Irving B. Richman (1861–1938) was a lawyer whose consuming hobby was the study and writing of history. He is best remembered for his little volume in "The Chronicles of America" series, *The Spanish Conquerors,* and the book for which he used these documents in question, *California under Spain and Mexico.*

CHAPTER 6

1. For Stanford background see Orrin Leslie Elliott, *Stanford University: the First Twenty-Five Years* (Stanford: Stanford University Press, 1937), and Edith M. Mirrieless, *Stanford, The Story of a University* (New York: Putnam, 1959).

2. The story of these weeks is drawn from materials in the Bolton Correspondence: IN and OUT, with an occasional assist from the Herbert-to-Frederick letters. The Henry Morse Stephens file is sizable. The Stephens Papers, University of California-Berkeley, yielded nothing new.

3. Bolton to Eugene C. Barker; the "Texas under Spain" project was one which never made it to the printed page.

4. *Re* this addendum by Bolton, it should be noted that it must have been done either around the time of the negotiations or, quite certainly, while Bolton was still at Stanford, since it is typed and has the peculiarity of other typed letters of this period, namely, done on a machine which made both comma and period impressions above the line.

5. See *supra,* Chapter 4.

CHAPTER 7

1. Frances Hartwell Janes to Rosaline Cady Bolton, November 3, 1911. This letter and several more to their grandmother Bolton are still in possession of the Bolton daughters.

2. On the history of the University of California two excellent works were issued for the Centennial Year: Verne A. Stadtman, comp. and ed., *The Centennial Record of the University of California* (Berkeley: University of California Printing Department, 1967), and Albert C. Pickerell and May Dornin, *The University of California: A Pictorial History* (Berkeley: The Regents of the University, 1968).

3. A short biographical sketch of Wheeler is contained in Stadtman, *The Centennial Record,* p. 15.

4. Much information can be gleaned *passim* from Stadtman, *The Centennial Record* and Pickerell-Dornin, *The University of California;* also from various University bulletins and particularly from the file of the *University of California Register.*

5. Short biographical sketches of Stephens can be found in various places, but see the obituary notice in the *American Historical Review* and the more extended appreciation in the *California Monthly*.

6. For the story of the Bancroft Collection see John W. Caughey, *Hubert Howe Bancroft* (Berkeley: University of California Press, 1946; reprinted by Russell and Russell, 1970).

7. This memorandum to Wheeler can be found in *Bolton and the Spanish Borderlands*, edited by John Francis Bannon (Norman: University of Oklahoma Press, 1964), pp. 23–31.

8. As the Bolton brothers became more and more engrossed in their work, the exchange of letters became more irregular. For 1912 there are only half a dozen letters from Herbert to Frederick.

9. The author is indebted to many Boltonians who shared with him much of the personal information on Herbert Bolton, both oral and written, in this chapter and those that follow. They are acknowledged individually in Chapter 8, note 7, where they are quoted extensively. He is also grateful to Eugenie Bolton Johnson and the three surviving Bolton daughters and their brother Herbert, Jr., for sharing so many family memories. Jane Bolton Adams recorded on tape an hour's worth of "Recollections of My Parents." One August afternoon in 1972 the four daughters gathered and talked with the author. Herbert, Jr., once thought of writing an essay about his father as "My Most Unforgettable Character"; he gathered much information in the form of notes which he put at the disposal of the author.

CHAPTER 8

1. *The Pacific Ocean in History,* edited by Henry Morse Stephens and Herbert Eugene Bolton (New York: Macmillan, 1917).

2. Dunn, "Portrait of a Teacher: Herbert E. Bolton," *The Alcalde,* Vol. 42, no. 2 (November 1953), 54–56.

3. Bolton to Dunn, November 20, 1914.

4. The present writer has had the opportunity to hear several of these students talk of this seminar of 1946. The outline of topics is included in *Bolton and the Spanish Borderlands,* edited by John Francis Bannon, pp. 67–85.

5. A short biographical sketch of Chapman is found in John Francis Bannon, "A Dedication to the Memory of Charles Edward Chapman, 1880–1941," in *Arizona and the West,* XII (Winter 1971, 321–24).

6. Data on Bolton's graduate students can be found in *Greater America: Essays in Honor of Herbert Eugene Bolton* (Berkeley: University of California Press, 1945).

7. By arbitrary decision, borrowings from these letters received have been used here and in later chapters without specific credit to individual writers — some of the contributors wished not to be identified; therefore this practice has been followed throughout. Thanks to the following for sharing memories: Maxine Chappell Bethel, Philip C. Brooks, Ellen Fessenden Dickie, George P. Hammond, John H. Kemble, James F. King, Lawrence Kinnaird, John Tate Lanning, Irving A. Leonard, Max L. Moorhead, Charles E. Nowell, Adele Ogden, Helen Carr Tittle, Theodore E. Treutlein, Donald Worcester, Ione Stussey Wright. Other Boltonians have shared memories orally.

8. For an account of the Native Sons of the Golden West fellowship program see the article by George P. Hammond, "The Native Sons of the Golden West," in *Homenaje a Don José María de la Peña y Cámara,* edited by E. J. Burrus and G. P. Hammond (Madrid: Jose Porrua Turanzas, 1969).

9. The *HAHR* began publication in 1918.

10. The first number of *Hispania* appeared in February 1918.

CHAPTER 9

1. There is a sizable Arthur H. Clark file in Bolton Correspondence: IN, pulled together under the publisher's name. Bolton's letters to Clark are in Bolton Correspondence: OUT, and arranged chronologically.

2. The letter is undated, save for the year, but presumably was written in June or July, 1913.

3. The many letters of Allen Johnson and Robert Glasgow cited in this chapter are found in the Bolton Correspondence: IN, under their last names.

4. Frederick W. Hodge in *AHR* (January 1921) and Isaac Joslin Cox in *MVHR* (December 1919).

5. The statement of Clark, May 9, 1919:

Cost of resetting and making entirely new plates for the title page	7.95
Changes from copy and editorial work on the proofs in excess of 5%, on Volume 1	209.00
Changes from copy and editorial work on the proofs in excess of 5%, on Volume 2	162.00
Increase in cost of binding from 20¢ to 32¢ per volume	120.00
Increase in cost of press work	135.00
Increase in cost of making the folding map over original quotation	10.06

Increase in cost of making plates over original
    quotation   8.15
Increase in cost of paper   287.00
Increase in cost of brass binding dies   4.60
Increase — freight   9.84

    $ 953.60

Beside each of these items on Clark's statement Bolton wrote a firm "NO."

6. This writer is grateful to Arthur H. Clark, Jr., who generously took the time to check the company's files and furnished bits of very helpful information for the post-1921 sections of this chapter.

7. The Clark statement of April 18, 1924 was the following:

1917
Nov. 23   Rental of type tied up over six months on account of not returning proof, as authorized in 3 of your letters $150.00

1919
May 7   Copyright entry blanks, 3 sets Kino, notary fee, transportation, etc. as per contract   16.50

1919
Aug. 6   Cost of pulling special proofs as per yours 8/15/17, 574 pp.   89.00

Cost of resetting headings and paragraphs increased cost of composition, as per yours Oct. 22, 1917   274.00

Rental of type, additional   235.00

Cost of special proofs, as per yours 6/17/18   49.00

Cost of resetting and making entirely new plates for title page, old title being okd by you   7.95

Making new frontispiece, as per yours 11/14/18   19.36

Changes from copy and editorial work on proofs in excess of 5 per cent on vol. 1, as per contract and your letters agreeing to pay same   209.00

Changes from copy and editorial work on proofs in excess of 5 per cent on vol. 2, as per contract and your letters agreeing to pay same   162.00

Increase in cost of binding from 20¢ to 32¢ per volume   120.00

Increase in cost of presswork   135.00

Increase in cost of making the folded map over original quotation   10.06

Increase in cost of making plate   8.15

	Increase in cost of paper	287.00
	Increase in binding dies	4.60
	Increase in cost of freight	9.84
1924		
Apr. 18	Interest at 7% after various royalty credits have been deducted	651.60
		2438.06
	Less royalty credits	254.50
		$2183.56

8. The lawyers' letters are filed in Bolton Correspondence: IN, under title of firm — Clark, Nichols, and Eltse.

9. *Arthur H. Clark* v. *Herbert E. Bolton*, Superior Court, Department 3, County of Alameda, No. 77765.

10. Arthur H. Clark, Jr., to John Francis Bannon, November 30, 1972.

11. Reference, no doubt, is to the expression of the time, "Twenty-three, Skidoo."

12. There is a third part of the Bolton Papers not yet fully organized or ordered. Scattered through several of the forty-odd cartons are bits of the *Borderlands* manuscripts and drafts.

CHAPTER 10

1. See Note 7, Chapter 8.

2. Herbert Eugene Bolton and Ephraim Douglass Adams, *California's Story* (Boston: Allyn and Bacon, 1922).

3. Swanton was the great authority on the Indians of the Old Southwest.

CHAPTER 11

1. Materials for this story are found, mainly, in the Bolton Correspondence. This writer has also seen the files of the two Austin dailies of the day, the *Statesman* and the *American;* he has chosen to use the former. The Barker Papers, in the Barker Texas History Center, University of Texas, were consulted, but yielded little more additional data.

2. The minutes of the meetings of the Board of Regents proved disappointing as a possible source of added information. The minutes for the meeting in which Bolton was chosen president were dictated to the secretary at a later date and so noted under May 28. The minutes for the meeting of May 15 are no more revealing.

3. In the Bolton Papers is a small sheaf of telegram blanks, covered with notes for this speech.

CHAPTER 12

1. The running account of this European trip is drawn from a series of letters written to Mrs. Bolton, which are still in the possession of the Bolton daughters and which were made available to this writer. In this and in other instances of extended travel Bolton would very often write home, frequently daily, and tell what he had done. These letters kept the family informed of his doings and also served as a quasi-diary record for his own future use.

CHAPTER 13

1. *Do the Americas Have a Common History? A Critique of the Bolton Theory,* edited by Lewis Hanke (New York: Alfred A. Knopf, 1964).

2. Harry Elmer Barnes, *A History of Historical Writing* (Norman, University of Oklahoma Press, 1938), p. 261.

3. H. Hale Bellot, *American History and American Historians* (Norman, University of Oklahoma Press, 1952), p. 36.

4. Michael Kraus, *The Writing of American History* (Norman, University of Oklahoma Press, 1953), pp. 286–287.

5. Harvey Wish, *The American Historian* (New York: Oxford, 1960), p. 205.

6. John Higham, *History, the Development of Historical Studies in the United States* (Englewood Cliffs, N. J.: Prentice-Hall, 1965), p. 41.

CHAPTER 14

1. Bolton told of the discovery in his article, "Father Kino's Lost History: Its Discovery and Its Value," Bibliographical Society of America *Papers,* VI (1911), 9–34.

2. Much of the information on these and other field trips is a result of the strict accounting demanded by the comptroller of the University of California. The Bolton Papers even contain the gasoline receipts neatly packaged.

3. Published first in *Catholic Historical Review,* XXI (October 1935), 257–82; reprinted in *Wider Horizons of American History* and in Bannon, *Bolton and the Spanish Borderlands.*

4. Published in *Mid-America,* XVIII (October 1936), 223–33.

5. HEB to Hale, February 24, 1936.

6. "Archives and Trails," *California Monthly,* XXXVII (October 1936), 19, 40–42.

7. Aiton in *MVHR,* XXIII (December 1936), 395–97.

8. Brebner in *AHR,* XLII (April 1937), 555–56.

CHAPTER 15

1. The California Historical Society devoted a Special Publication, No. 13 to the story of the Drake Plate, *Drake's Plate of Brass: Evidence of His Visit to California in 1579* (San Francisco: California Historical Society, 1937).

2. Bolton's paper appears in this Special Publication, No. 13, pp. 1–18.

3. Letter, Thomas G. Fogarty to the author, December 30, 1970.

4. The full report is found in another Special Publication of the Society: Colin G. Fink and E. P. Polushkin, *Drake's Plate of Brass Vindicated* (San Francisco: California Historical Society, 1938).

5. The extended title is: *Noticia de la California y de su conquista temporal y espiritual hasta el tiempo presente, sacada de la Historia manuscrita, formada en México año de 1739, por el Padre Miguel Venegas, de la Compañía de Jesús; y de otras Noticias y Relaciones antiguas y modernas.*

6. The information on the trip to South America is drawn from the quasi-journal for this trip found in the Bolton Correspondence: OUT, December 1938 to February 1939. The journal is composed of eighteen letters which he wrote to his wife and family, and which he later gathered for future reference.

CHAPTER 17

1. First published in the *Proceedings* of the American Philosophical Society, Vol. 91, no. 5 (December 1947), 426–29. Reprinted in *Bolton and the Spanish Borderlands* by John Francis Bannon, pp. 123–32.

CHAPTER 18

1. Maynard Geiger, *The Life and Times of Fray Junípero Serra, O.F.M.* (2 vols., Washington, D.C.: Academy of American Franciscan History, 1959).

2. *The Americas,* VI (January 1950), 359–62.

3. Ten years after Bolton's death the then young Western History Association, at its 1963 meeting in Salt Lake City, had a session on its program, "Three Historians of the American Frontier: Turner, Bolton, Webb." John Caughey was asked to prepare the paper on Bolton. All three papers were first published in *The American West* (Winter 1964); somewhat

expanded they appeared in book form as *Turner, Bolton, and Webb,* by W. T. Jacobs, J. W. Caughey, and J. B. Frantz (Seattle: University of Washington Press, 1965).

4. To this point in the present chapter opinions of Bolton have been a matter of printed record. This quote and those immediately following for the next several pages were culled mostly from exchanges with Boltonians who responded to the author's appeal for "memories of HEB." See also Chapter 8, note 7.

5. This volume was published by the University of California in 1945.

6. Materials in the Bolton Papers for 1952 are few and, of course, non-existent after mid-June. Data for the next several paragraphs come primarily from the recollections of the Bolton family and from Bolton's University friends and colleagues.

APPENDIX A

Bolton's
Published Works

THE BASIC WORK on the Bolton bibliography through 1932 was done by Mary Ross in her contribution "Writings and Cartography of Herbert Eugene Bolton," to *New Spain and the Anglo-America West: Historical Contributions Presented to Herbert Eugene Bolton* (2 vols., Los Angeles, 1932). The editors of *Greater America: Essays in Honor of Herbert Eugene Bolton* (Berkeley, University of California Press, 1945) carried the listings into the 1940's. Only a few major titles remained to be listed herein.

1900
"Our Nation's First Boundaries," *The Western Teacher*, IX, no. 2 (October 1900), 64–67.

1902
" 'De los Mapas,' " Texas State Historical Association, *Quarterly*, VI (July, 1902), 69–70.
"Some Materials for Southwestern History in the Archivo General de México," Texas State Historical Association, *Quarterly*, VI (October, 1902), 103–12; VII (January, 1904), 196–213.

1903
"Tienda de Cuervo's Ynspección of Laredo, 1757," Texas State Historical Association, *Quarterly*, VI (January, 1903), 187–203.
Trans., documents on the Philippine Islands, in Emma Helen Blair and James Alexander Robertson, eds., *The Philippine Islands, 1493–1803* (55 vols.; Cleveland, Clark, 1903–1909): "Affairs in the Philipinas Islands, by Fray Domingo de Salazar" [1583], V, 210–55; "Two Letters to Felipe II" [Gerónimo de Guzmán, and Jhoan de Vascones, 1585], VI, 76–80.

1904
With Eugene Campbell Barker, *With the Makers of Texas: A Source Reader in Texas History* (New York, American Book Company, 1904).

Trans., documents on the Philippine Islands, in Emma Helen Blair and James Alexander Robertson, eds., *The Philippine Islands, 1493–1803* (55 vols.; Cleveland, Clark, 1903–1909): "Trade between Nueva España and the Far East" [1617], XVIII, 57–64; "Events in the Filipinas Islands, from the Month of June, 1617, until the Present Date in 1618," XVIII, 65–92; "Description of the Philippinas Islands" [1618], XVIII, 93–106; "Relation of the Events in the Filipinas Islands and in Neighboring Provinces and Realms, from July, 1618, to the Present Date in 1619," XVIII, 204–34; "Letter from Francisco de Otaço, S.J., to Father Alonso de Escovar" [1620], XIX, 35–39; "Relation of Events in the Philipinas Islands and Neighboring Provinces and Kingdoms, from July, 1619, to July, 1620," XIX, 42–70.

1905

"Practical Suggestions Concerning the Organization of Historical Materials in High School Work," *Texas School Journal* (March 1905), 1–7.

"The Spanish Abandonment and Re-occupation of East Texas, 1773–1779," Texas State Historical Association, *Quarterly,* IX (October 1905), 67–137.

1906

"The Founding of Mission Rosario: A Chapter in the History of the Gulf Coast," Texas State Historical Association, *Quarterly,* X (October, 1906), 113–39.

"Massanet or Manzanet," Texas State Historical Association, *Quarterly,* X (July, 1906), 101.

"The Old Stone Fort at Nacogdoches," Texas State Historical Association, *Quarterly,* IX (April, 1906), 283–85.

1907

"Spanish Mission Records at San Antonio," Texas State Historical Association, *Quarterly,* X (April, 1907), 297–307.

1908

"Material for Southwestern History in the Central Archives of Mexico," *American Historical Review,* XIII (April, 1908), 510–27. Translated into Spanish by José Romero in the *Boletín de la Sociedad mexicana de geografía y estadística,* III (Mexico, 1909), Nos. 5 and 7.

"The Native Tribes about the East Texas Missions," Texas State Historical Association, *Quarterly,* XI (April, 1908), 249–76.

"Notes on Clark's 'The Beginnings of Texas,'" Texas State Historical Association, *Quarterly,* XII (October, 1908), 148–58.

Ed., "Papers of Zebulon M. Pike, 1806–1807," *American Historical Review,* XIII (July, 1908), 798–827.

1909

"Portolá's Letters Found," *San Francisco Call* (San Francisco, Calif.), October 17, 1909.

1910

"Records of the Mission of Nuestra Señora del Refugio," Texas State Historical Association, *Quarterly,* XIV (October, 1910), 164–66.

More than one hundred articles on Indian tribes of Texas and Louisiana, in Frederick Webb Hodge, ed., *Handbook of American Indians North of Mexico* (2 pts.; Washington, D.C., Government Printing Office, 1907–1910), Smithsonian Institution, Bureau of American Ethnology, Bulletin 30.

1911

Trans. and ed., "Expedition to San Francisco Bay in 1770: Diary of Pedro Fages," Academy of Pacific Coast History, *Publications,* II (July, 1911), 141–59.

"Father Kino's Lost History, Its Discovery and Its Value," Bibliographical Society of America, *Papers,* VI (1911), 9–34.

"The Jumano Indians in Texas, 1650–1771," Texas State Historical Association, *Quarterly,* XV (July, 1911), 66–84.

1912

"The Obligation of Nevada toward the Writing of Her Own History," Nevada Historical Society, *Third Biennial Report . . . , 1911–1912* (1913), pp. 62–79.

"The Spanish Occupation of Texas, 1519–1690," *Southwestern Historical Quarterly,* XVI (July, 1912), 1–26.

1913

Guide to Materials for the History of the United States in the Principal Archives of Mexico (Washington, D.C., Carnegie Institution of Washington, 1913). Carnegie Institution of Washington, Publication No. 163, Papers of the Department of Historical Research.

"The Admission of California," *University of California Chronicle,* XV (October, 1913), 554–66.

"New Light on Manuel Lisa and the Spanish Fur Trade," *Southwestern Historical Quarterly,* XVII (July, 1913), 61-66.

"Spanish Activities on the Lower Trinity River, 1746–1771," *Southwestern Historical Quarterly,* XVI (April, 1913), 339–77.

1914

Athanase de Mézières and the Louisiana-Texas Frontier, 1768–1780, (2 vols., Cleveland, Clark, 1914).

"The Founding of the Missions on the San Gabriel River, 1745–1749," *Southwestern Historical Quarterly,* XVII (April, 1914), 323–78.

"Mexico, Diplomatic Relations with" [the United States, 1821–1914], in Andrew Cunningham McLaughlin and Albert Bushnell Hart, eds., *Cyclopedia of American Government* (3 vols., New York, Appleton, 1914), II 422–25.

1915

Texas in the Middle Eighteenth Century: Studies in Spanish Colonial History and Administration (Berkeley, University of California Press, 1915), University of California, Publications in History, Vol. III.

"The Location of La Salle's Colony on the Gulf of Mexico," *Mississippi Valley Historical Review*, II (September, 1915), 165–82. Also in the *Southwestern Historical Quarterly*, XXVII (January, 1924), 171–89.

1916

Spanish Exploration in the Southwest, 1542–1706 (New York, Scribner's, 1916).

"The Beginnings of Mission Nuestra Señora del Refugio," *Southwestern Historical Quarterly*, XIX (April, 1916), 400–404.

"The Writing of California History," *Grizzly Bear*, XIX (May, 1916), 4.

1917

Trans. and ed., "Explorers' Visits to San Diego Bay Told of in Diaries" [Cabrillo and Vizcaíno], *San Diego Union* (San Diego, Calif.), January 1, 1917.

"The Early Explorations of Father Garcés on the Pacific Slope," in Henry Morse Stephens and Herbert Eugene Bolton, eds., *The Pacific Ocean in History* (New York, Macmillan, 1917), pp. 317–30.

"French Intrusions into New Mexico, 1749–1752," in Henry Morse Stephens and Herbert Eugene Bolton, eds., *The Pacific Ocean in History* (New York, Macmillan, 1917), pp. 389–407.

"The Mission as a Frontier Institution in the Spanish-American Colonies," *American Historical Review*, XXIII (October, 1917), 42–61.

"The Spanish Missions of California: Their Relation to the General Colonial Policy," *Oakland Tribune* (Oakland, Calif.), April 22, 1917.

1918

"Cabrillo and Vizcaíno Visit Catalina Island, 1542–1602," *The Islander* (Avalon, Santa Catalina Island, Calif.), July 16, 1918.

Ed., "General James Wilkinson as Advisor to Emperor Iturbide," *Hispanic American Historical Review*, I (May, 1918), 163–80.

1919

Kino's Historical Memoir of Pimería Alta: A Contemporary Account of the Beginnings of California, Sonora, and Arizona, by Father Eusebio Francisco Kino, S.J., Pioneer Missionary Explorer, Cartographer, and Ranchman, 1683–1711 (2 vols., Cleveland, Clark, 1919); also in University of California, Semicentennial Publications, 1868–1918 (1919).

Trans. and ed., "Father Escobar's Relation of the Oñate Expedition to California," *Catholic Historical Review*, V (April, 1919), 19–41.

Ed., "The Iturbide Revolution in the Californias," *Hispanic American Historical Review,* II (May, 1919), 188–242.

1920

With Thomas Maitland Marshall, *The Colonization of North America, 1492–1783* (New York, Macmillan, 1920).
"The Old Spanish Fort on Red River," *Daily Oklahoman* (Oklahoma City), April 11, 1920.

1921

The Spanish Borderlands: A Chronicle of Old Florida and the Southwest (New Haven, Yale University Press, 1921). The Chronicles of America Series, Vol. XXIII.

1922

With Ephraim Douglass Adams, *California's Story* (Boston, Allyn and Bacon, 1922).

1924

"An Introductory Course in American History," *Historical Outlook,* XV (January, 1924), 17–20.

1925

Arredondo's Historical Proof of Spain's Title to Georgia: A Contribution to the History of One of the Spanish Borderlands (Berkeley, University of California Press, 1925).
With Mary Ross, *The Debatable Land: A Sketch of the Anglo-Spanish Contest for the Georgia Country* (Berkeley, University of California Press, 1925).
"The Mormons in the Opening of the West," *Deseret News* (Salt Lake City, Utah), October 24, 31, November 14, 25, 1925. Also in the *Utah Genealogical and Historical Magazine,* XVI (January, 1926), 40–72.
"Spanish Resistance to the Carolina Traders in Western Georgia, 1680–1704," *Georgia Historical Quarterly,* IX (June, 1925), 115–30.

1926

Historical Memoirs of New California, by Fray Francisco Palóu, O.F.M. (4 vols., Berkeley, University of California Press, 1926).
Palóu and His Writings (Berkeley, University of California Press, 1926).
"José Francisco Ortega," *Grizzly Bear,* XXXVIII (January, 1926), 1.

1927

Fray Juan Crespi, Missionary Explorer on the Pacific Coast, 1769–1774 (Berkeley, University of California Press, 1927).

A Pacific Coast Pioneer (Berkeley, University of California Press, 1927).
"Juan Crespi, a California Xenophon," *Touring Topics,* XIX (July, 1927), 23, 48.

1928

History of the Americas: A Syllabus with Maps (Boston, Ginn, 1928; new edition, 1935).
"Escalante in Dixie and the Arizona Strip," *New Mexico Historical Review,* III (January, 1928), 41–72.
Articles in the *Dictionary of American Biography* (20 vols.; New York, Scribner's, 1928–1936), on Juan Rodríguez Cabrillo, García López de Cárdenas, Francisco Vázquez Coronado, Juan Crespi, Eusebio Francisco Kino, Athanase de Mézières y Clugny, and Francisco Palóu.

1930

Anza's California Expeditions (5 vols.; Berkeley, University of California Press, 1930).
"Defensive Spanish Expansion and the Significance of the Borderlands," in James Field Willard and Colin Brummitt Goodykoontz, eds., *The Trans-Mississippi West: Papers Read at a Conference Held at the University of Colorado, June 18–June 21, 1929* (Boulder, University of Colorado, 1930), 1–42.

1931

Font's Complete Diary: A Chronicle of the Founding of San Francisco (Berkeley, University of California Press, 1931).
Outpost of Empire: The Story of the Founding of San Francisco (New York, Knopf, 1931).
"Anza Crosses the Sand Dunes," *Touring Topics,* XXIII (May, 1931), 7.
"The Capitulation at Cahuenga," *Touring Topics,* XXIII (November, 1931), 7.
"Coming of the Cattle," *Touring Topics,* XXIII (March, 1931), 7.
"Coronado Discovers Zuñi," *Touring Topics,* XXIII (January, 1931), 8.
"The Founding of San Diego Mission," *Touring Topics,* XXIII (April, 1931), 7.
"Fremont Crosses the Sierra," *Touring Topics,* XXIII (October, 1931), 7.
"Gold Discovered at Sutter's Mill," *Touring Topics,* XXIII (December, 1931), 9.
"In the South San Joaquin Ahead of Garcés," California Historical Society, *Quarterly,* X (September, 1931), 211–19. First printed in the *Bakersfield Californian* (Bakersfield, Calif.), May 19–22, 1931. Also reprinted by the Kern County Historical Society, Bakersfield, California, May, 1935.
"Jedediah Smith Reaches San Gabriel," *Touring Topics,* XXIII (June, 1931), 7.
"Oñate in New Mexico," *Touring Topics,* XXIII (February, 1931), 8.
"Trapper Days in Taos," *Touring Topics,* XXIII (July, 1931), 7.

1932

The Padre on Horseback: A Sketch of Eusebio Francisco Kino, S.J., Apostle to the Pimas (San Francisco, Sonora Press, 1932). Translation, *El incansable jinete: Bosquejo de la vida del p. Eusebio Francisco Kino, S.J., apóstol de los Pimas* (Mexico, Buena prensa, 1940). Reprinted by the Loyola University Press, Chicago, in 1963, with an introduction by John Francis Bannon.

1933

"The Epic of Greater America," *American Historical Review*, XXXVIII (April, 1933), 448–74. Translated by Carmen Alessio Robles, *La epopeya de la máxima América* (Mexico, Bosque, 1937), Instituto panamericano de geografía e historia, Publicación Número 30.

1934

"Pack Train and Carreta," *California Monthly*, XXXIII (November, 1934), 4, 6.

1935

"The Black Robes of New Spain," *Catholic Historical Review*, XXI (October, 1935), 257–82.

1936

Cross, Sword and Gold Pan (Los Angeles, Primavera Press, 1936).
Rim of Christendom: A Biography of Eusebio Francisco Kino, Pacific Coast Pioneer (New York, Macmillan, 1936).
"Archives and Trails," *California Monthly*, XXXVII (October, 1936), 19, 40–42.
"The Jesuits in America: An Opportunity for Historians," *Mid-America* XVIII (October, 1936), 223–33.

1937

"Francis Drake's Plate of Brass," in *Drake's Plate of Brass: Evidence of His Visit to California in 1579* (San Francisco, California Historical Society, 1937), 1–16. California Historical Society, Special Publication, No. 13.

1939

Wider Horizons of American History (New York, Appleton-Century, 1939).
"Escalante Way — An Opportunity for the National Park Service," in Harlean James, ed., *American Planning and Civic Annual* (Washington, D.C., American Planning and Civic Association, 1939), 266–73.

1940

"Cultural Coöperation with Latin America," National Education Association, *Journal*, XXIX (January, 1940), 1–4. This article, sometimes under slightly different titles, was translated and published in Latin American newspapers and magazines, and appeared also in other United States periodicals, including the following: *Hispanic American Historical Review,* XX (February, 1940), 3–11; *International Quarterly,* Vol. IV, No. 4 (autumn, 1940), 21–24, 59; and *Southwest Review,* XXV (January, 1940), 115–25.

Articles in the *Dictionary of American History* (6 vols.; New York, Scribner's 1940), on "Alta California," "California, Russians in," "California, Spanish Exploration of," "California Missions," "California under Mexico," and "California under Spain."

1949

Coronado, Knight of Pueblos and Plains (New York, Whittlesey House, 1949).

Coronado on the Turquoise Trail, Knight of Pueblos and Plains (Albuquerque, University of New Mexico Press, 1949). Volume I, Coronado Cuatro Centennial Publications, edited by George P. Hammond.

1950

"The Confessions of a Wayward Professor," *The Americas,* VI (January 1950), 359–62.

Pageant in the Wilderness: The Story of the Escalante Expedition to the Interior Basin, Including the Diary and Itinerary of Father Escalante (Salt Lake City, Utah State Historical Society, 1950).

Bolton's
Academic Progeny

1909 (Texas)

Masters

BROWN, Elise Denison
BUCKLEY, Eleanor Claire
NEU, Charles Louis Ternay

1910 (Stanford)

Master

DUNN, William Edward

1912 (California)

Masters

LEONARD, Beulah [Hershiser]
NIHART, Vera Howard [Brooke]
WATKINS, Lucy Rebecca
WHARTON, Rebecca Gaskin

1913

Masters

DuFOUR, Clarence John
ELLISON, William Henry
GROVER, Elsie Jeanette
HALL, Laura Mabel [Kingsbury]
PAISLEY, Minnie McDonald
SMITH, Una Deming

1914

Doctor

MARSHALL, Thomas Maitland

Masters

BARTH, Florence Edith
COAN, Charles Florus
GOODYKOONTZ, Colin Brummitt
LOVE, Clara Maud
MARTIN, Mabelle Blanche [Eppard]
MARTIN, Thomas Powderly
SCULL, Carolyn Beatrice
STANTON, Florence Belle
THOMAS, Helen Harland [Blattner]
TUTTLE, Maria Anna [Wendels]

1915

Doctor

CHAPMAN, Charles Edward

Masters

BOUDINOT, May Fidelia
CARRILLO, Esperanza
CORNISH, Beatrice Quijada
HOWDEN, George

[283]

1916

Doctors

DAVIDSON, Gordon Charles
GITTINGER, Roy
GOODWIN, Cardinal Leonidas
PRIESTLEY, Herbert Ingram

Masters

ALBRIGHT, George Leslie
BRIGGS, Marie Elizabeth [Bradford]
HILL, Joseph Abner
RAMAGE, Helen
SELLERS, Martha [Dobbin]
STONE, Edna Harriet

1917

Doctor

HACKETT, Charles Wilson

Masters

BIGLAND, Fanny Woodhull
    [Gaddis]
BROWN, Marion Agnes
CARROLL, Mary Pius
CLEVENGER, Zula Allena [Smith]
COBB, Jesse Ludowick
COLLINS, Hazel Minnie
DUNN, Maude Eunice [Wilson]
GORHAM, Mildred Ide
HAWKINS, Edity Jane [Lamb]
MECHAM, John Lloyd
POCKSTALLER, Theodore
REDFIELD, Marion Lowrie [Haskell]
STEWART, Mildred Minnie

1918

Doctors

COY, Owen Cochran
NEFF, Andrew Love

Masters

AITON, Arthur Scott
BINKLEY, William Campbell
HAMLIN, Alfred Street

JONES, Ethel Mae
KUYKENDALL, Ralph Simpson
LEWIS, Anna
McFARLAND, Bertha [Blount]

1919

Doctors

ELLISON, William Henry
POCKSTALLER, Theodore

Masters

AMICK, Myrtle Elizabeth
ELLISON, Joseph Waldo
HICKOK, Laura Laurensen [Byrne]
LOTHROP, Marian Lydia
OTTO, Mildred Talitha [Lanphere]
ROSS, Mary
UNDERWOOD, Marion L.

1920

Doctors

BINKLEY, William Campbell
COAN, Charles Florus
RIPPY, James Fred

Masters

BJORK, David Knuth
DICKSON, Edith May [Montgomery]
JOHNSON, Roxana Galletly
VANDEGRIFT, Rolland A.

1921

Masters

HAMMOND, George Peter
HILL, Lawrence Francis
JOHNSON, James Guyton
McBRIDE, Sister Margaret Mary
MARSH, Roy Elmer
POWELL, Anna Irion
SOLOVSKY, Ruth Mary [McGinty]
WHEATON, Donald Whitney

1922

Doctor

MECHAM, John Lloyd

Masters

BOONE, Lalla Rookh
CARNES, Sister Loyola
COUCH, Esther Tanner
CRUDEN, Davina Ruth
DORNIN, May
HATCH, Flora Faith
HEALEY, Ettie Miriam
LEONARD, Charles Berdan
MOTT, Orra Anna Nathalie
NASATIR, Abraham Phineas
ORD, Ellen Frances
PHELPS, Mildred Chick [Pyle]
SNOW, William James
TOOR, Frances

1923

Doctors

AITON, Arthur Scott
BJORK, David Knuth
ELLISON, Joseph Waldo
HILL, Lawrence Francis
SNOW, William James
WERNER, Gustave Adolph
WHEATON, Donald Whitney

Masters

ALLEN, Henry Easton
BLUE, George Vernon
CALDWELL, Ruth Elizabeth
LEE, Harriet Evadna [Rogers]
LESLEY, Lewis Burt
MALIC, Elmer Eyre
MATHEWS, Mabel Laura
MILLER, Maxine Miner [Waterman]
O'NEIL, Marion
O'NEILL, Kate Navin
REYNOLDS, Rose Andrée [Turner]
REYNOLDS, Thomas Harrison

TREMAYNE, Frank Gilbert
WHITNEY, Mildred Haven [Vernon]
WYATT, Fay Savage

1924

Doctors

HAFEN, LeRoy R.
HAMMOND, George Peter
JOHNSON, James Guyton

Masters

BARRETT, Lynn Murray
BOYCE, Marjorie Gray
CLARK, Effie Elfreda [Marten]
FLACK, Lena Elvina
HANSON, George Emmanuel
HELWIG, Adelaide Berta
LEWIS, Donna Mae
PETERSEN, Emily Jane [Ulsh]
POTTER, Olive Mae
RHODES, Elizabeth Roulette
ROSEBROCK, Adeline Marie
THOMAS, Aldred Barnaby

1925

Doctors

CARNES, Sister Loyola
CORNISH, Beatrice Quijada
RYDJORD, John

Masters

ARCHER, Kate Worthington
BRADY, Lena Margaret [Reed]
BRADY, Ralph Hamilton
BRANNEN, Laura Adeline
  [Halverson]
DOPPLEMAIER, Susie [Sutton]
FRANCIS, Jessie Hughes [Davies]
FRANCIS, Kathryn Lee [Langston]
GAY, Mabel Theressa
GRAY, Vallene Gifford
HICKOX, Frances Catherine
HOPPER, Violet Hannah [Baker]

1925 *Masters* (continued)

HOUSTON, Mary Ruth
LANNING, John Tate
McLAUGHLIN, Roberta Evelyn
 [Holmes]
McNALLY, Mary Cecilia
MOUNGOVAN, Julia Belle
 [Longfellow]
OGDEN, Adele
POPHAM, Clara Ethel [Kyle]
RAMER, Leo James
ROMNEY, Thomas Cottam
STEWART, Pearl Pauline [Stamps]
STORRS, Joseph Bertrand
VERKAMP, Narcissa Louise
 [Parrish]
WHEELER, Mayo Elizabeth

1926

Doctors

CREER, Leland Hargrave
LOTHROP, Marian Lydia
NASATIR, Abraham Phineas

Masters

BREED, Noel Jerub
CAUGHEY, John Walton
DERR, Lucile Elizabeth
HALL, Gladys Harriet
LOUNDAGIN, Agnes Bird [Scobey]
McGILL, Edith Louise
OAKLEY, Dorothy Ida [Yerxa]
POTTER, Elizabeth Gray
RANCK, Mabel Aley
REYNOLDS, Albert Wade
RICKARD, Ruth Louise
RINN, Ida Louise
ROWLAND, Donald Winslow
SCHULHOF, Martha
SISSON, Virgil David
STANGER, Francis Merriman
SWANSON, Dorothea Louise
WAUGH, Evelyn Marguerite

1927

Doctors

BREED, Noel Jerub
DuFOUR, Clarence John
LEADER, Herman Alexander
LEONARD, Charles Berdan

Masters

AGEE, Flora Laurette [DeNier]
BENNETT, Bessie Price
BERETON, George Harold
BYRD, John William
CODY, Cora Edith
CRABBS, Isabel Margaret [Parker]
DREWES, Rudolph Herman
FELDHAMMER, Josephine
GOODWELL, Ruth Emma
JOHNSON, Isabel Mae [King]
KAHL, George Gary
KEAN, Anne Eugenia [Hughes]
KINNAIRD, Lawrence
KLEIN, Edith Mabelle
LARSON, Letitia Mary [Wilson]
MITCHELL, Richard Gerald
POWERS, Grace Sarah
ROWAN, Alfred John
STOCKWELL, Wilhelmina Godward
WHITE, Chester Lee
WYTHE, Lois

1928

Doctors

CAUGHEY, John Walton
HOOLEY, Osborne Edward
KINNAIRD, Lawrence
LANNING, John Tate
LEONARD, Irving Albert
NEU, Charles Ternay
REYNOLDS, Albert Wade
THOMAS, Alfred Barnaby

Masters

BALDWIN, Mary Agnes [Oyster]
BELL, Hazel Ada

BONNETTO, Florence Edith [Busch]
BURTON, Marian Lee [McGlashan]
CARPENTER, Lana Louise [Bates]
CHENEY, Doris Maxine
CROSSET, Lena
CULLINAN, Nicholas Cecil
DUNLAP, Florence McClure
FARISS, Jessie
JERNIGAN, Eva Ida
McQUAIG, Grace Elizabeth
  [Flachenecker]
ROSS, Ivy Belle
RYAN, Ella Ward
SMITH, Marian Elizabeth
WILEY, Alma Pearl

1929

Doctors

BROSNAN, Cornelius James
ROMNEY, Thomas Cottam
WYLLYS, Rufus Kay

Masters

ADAMS, Dorothy Quincy
CHAFFEE, Everett Barker
FAWCETT, Helen
GOLDING, Mary Frances
GUEST, Anna Lee
LATIMER, Frances Ludwick
POWELL, Etta Olive
RICE, Wilma Lucie [Edsen]
STAFFORD, Mary Magdalene
  [Cortez]
STEWART, Charles Lockwood
WERNER, Marion Beatrice

1930

Doctors

ROWLAND, Donald Winslow
STANGER, Francis Merriman
STOCKWELL, Wilhelmina Godward

Masters

BLUM, Eva Lereta [Dill]
CHILDERS, Laurence Murrell
BROOKS, Philip Coolidge
HOHENTHAL, Helen Alma
HOSEA, Minnie Loyola
LAWRENCE, Eleanor Frances
O'CONNELL, Agnes Catherine
TATE, Vernon Dale
TITTLE, Helen Salisbury [Carr]
TREUTLEIN, Theodore Edward

1931

Doctors

HELWIG, Adelaide Berta
McPHERSON, Hattie Mae

Masters

ANSBERRY, Merle
AUCUTT, Lucille
BEWLEY, Lucille Katherine
  [Johnson]
BURKHARDT, George Stedman
CARLSON, Toma Elizabeth [Akers]
CHAFFEE, Eugene Bernard
CRAIG, Lois Maxine
EWING, Russell Charles
FERGUSON, Ruby Alta
GENTRY, Mildred Lois
GIBSON, James Biggars
HALE, Lewis P.
HALLIDAY, Ruth [Staff]
LINDSSEY, Martha Janice
McDONALD, William Ernest
MALLOY, William Doyle
MELGARD, Helen Winifred
MEYER, Edith Catharine
PARKER, Alice Christine [Krauter]
ROGERS, Walter Harold
SAWYER, Byrd Farita Wall
THOMPSON, Margaret [Ballard]
TRUNK, Eleanor Harriett [Rabin]
WALTER, Virginia Melba
WATTENBURGER, Ralph Thomas

1931 *Masters* (continued)

WINTER, Carl George
WRIGHT, Agnes Elodie
YERXA, Gertrude Olive
ZIMMERMAN, Carla Alice [Russell]

1932

Doctors

NOWELL, Charles Edward
PARKER, Robert J.
SMITH, Wallace Paul Victor
TAYS, George

Masters

AITKEN, William Teenyson
CARRIKER, Marie King
CASSEL, Herbert Wilbur
CLEAVELAND, Alice Mae
COLLYER, Gilbert Abram
DYKE, Dorothy Jeannette
FORCE, Edwin Truesdell
FORCE, Mary Elizabeth [Harris]
HOWATT, Edward Dalton
McMULLEN, Leon Russell
MILLS, Hazel Emery
RICE, Hallie Evelyn
SAMPLE, Ina Powers
SCHETTER, Adrienne Estelle
THOMPSON, Margaret Alice

1933

Doctors

BROOKS, Philip Coolidge
LESLEY, Lewis Burt
SALANDRA, Dominic
SHIELS, William Eugene
TEESDALE, William Homer

Masters

BOWLES, Emily Marie
CROW, Esther Frances [King]
CRYSTAL, Helen Dermody
ELLSWORTH, Rodney Sydes
FERGUSON, Xenophon

GILBERT, Hope Elizabeth
GUTHRIE, Chester Lyle
HARROD, Thomas Martin
LAWRENCE, William David
SHUBERT, Helen Victoria
SLUITER, Engel
SPAETH, Reuben Louis

1934

Doctors

DUNNE, Peter Masten
ESPINOSA, Jose Manuel
EWING, Russell Charles
GARRETT, Julia Kathryn
JACOBSEN, Jerome Vincent
McCUMBER, Harold Oliver
TATE, Vernon Dale
TREUTLEIN, Theodore Edward

Masters

AVINA, Rose [Hollenbaugh]
BEAL, Samuel Merrill
CORREIA, Delia Richards
DAVIDSON, Donald Curtis
DORNBERGER, Suzette
KEMBLE, John Haskell
MELOM, Halvor Gordon
PLANER, Edward Thomas
SEVERNS, Alma Leone

1935

Doctors

FRANCIS, Jesse Hughes [Davies]
HALE, Lewis P.
HUNTER, Milton Reed
NEASHAM, Vernon Aubrey

Masters

ALBERTSON, Hope Frances
   [Kennedy]
AMES, George Walcott
CLAYTON, Lloydine Della [Martin]
HUSSEY, John Adam
KING, James Ferguson

LUTHER, Esther [Barnes]
MAHAKIAN, Charles
WEBB, Warren Franklin

1936

Doctors

FORCE, Edwin Truesdell
NELSON, Al B.
PUTNAM, John Franklin
STEWART, Charles Lockwood

Masters

BARIEAU, Sally Lambeth
CRAMPTON, Gregory Charles
CUNNINGHAM, James Stewart
DeROJAS, Lauro Antonio
FOSTER, Winifred Emily
FOX, John Samuel
HUGHES, Lloyd Harris
NUNN, Ruth Eloise
PARK, Shirley Harriet [Hannah]
RUTHERFORD, Amy Oakley
SHIELDS, Robert Hale

1937

Doctors

DAVIDSON, Donald Curtis
GUTHRIE, Chester Lyle
KEMBLE, John Haskell
SLUITER, Engel

Masters

DENHARDT, Robert Moorman
EARLY, H. Eugene
EMERT, Martine
GROSS, Harold William
LAMB, Ursula [Schaefer]
OSOFFSKY, Lettie
WALKER, Charles Watson
WRIGHT, Ione Stussey

1938

Doctors

HAINES, Francis D.
JAKEMAN, Max Wells
OGDEN, Adele

Masters

BAIRD, William Harrell
DOWNING, Margaret Mary
HAWKEN, Edward Jay
NG, Pearl
PYLE, John William

1939

Doctors

BANNON, John Francis
BOONE, Lalla Rookh
GIBSON, George Davis
KING, James Ferguson
McSHANE, Sister Catherine

Masters

BLYTHIN, Margaret Allewelt
LINDSELL, Harold
McCAFFERY, Walter Joseph
SOUTH, Arethusa Aurelia

1940

Doctors

BORAH, Woodrow Wilson
DOWNEY, Sister Mary
FOX, John Samuel
JOHNSON, Harry Prescott
O'NEIL, Marion
TICHENOR, Sister Helen
WRIGHT, Ione Stussey

Masters

ANDERSON, Geraldean Aikman
GILBERT, Benjamin Franklin
MURPHY, Edmund Robert
PADEN, William Guy
WORCESTER, Donald Emmet

1941

Doctors

CRAMPTON, Gregory Charles
WILEY, Francis

1942

Doctors

DAVIS, William Lyle
GRIFFITH, William Joyce
HUSSEY, John Adam
MOORHEAD, Max Leon
O'CALLAGHAN, Mary

Master

THICKENS, Virginia Emily

1943

Masters

COBB, Gwendolin Ballantine
JOHNSON, John James

1944

Doctors

DOWNEY, Thomas Edward
EMERT, Martine

Index